D0848940

The Algerian War and the French Army, 1954–62

The Algerian War and the French Army, 1954–62

Experiences, Images, Testimonies

Edited by

Martin S. Alexander, Martin Evans, J. F. V. Keiger

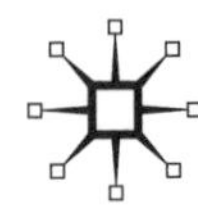

First published 2002 by
PALGRAVE MACMILLAN
Houndmills, Basingstoke, Hampshire RG21 6XS and
175 Fifth Avenue, New York, N.Y. 10010
Companies and representatives throughout the world

PALGRAVE MACMILLAN is the global academic imprint of the Palgrave Macmillan division of St. Martin's Press, LLC and of Palgrave Macmillan Ltd. Macmillan® is a registered trademark in the United States, United Kingdom and other countries. Palgrave is a registered trademark in the European Union and other countries.

ISBN 0–333–77456–6 hardback

This book is printed on paper suitable for recycling and made from fully managed and sustained forest sources.

A catalogue record for this book is available from the British Library.

Library of Congress Cataloging-in-Publication Data
The Algerian war and the French army : experiences, images, testimonies / edited by Martin S. Alexander, Martin Evans, J.F.V. Keiger.
p. cm.
Based in part on papers presented at a conference held at Salford University, 1996.
Includes bibliographical references and index.
ISBN 0–333–77456–6
1. Algeria–History–Revolution, 1954–1962–Congresses. 2. France. Armée–History–20th century–Congresses. I. Alexander, Martin S., 1955. II. Evans, Martin, 1964– III. Keiger, John F. V.

DT295 .A5576 2002
965'.046–dc21 2002023879

10 9 8 7 6 5 4 3 2 1
11 10 09 08 07 06 05 04 03 02

Printed and bound in Great Britain by
Antony Rowe Ltd, Chippenham and Eastbourne

Contents

Preface

The idea for this collection of essays originated with a conference on the Algerian War organized at Salford University back in 1996. The conference was organized by the European Studies Research Institute at Salford in collaboration with the Centre for European Studies Research at Portsmouth University and received generous financial support from the British Academy. However, the present volume contains new essays, excludes others and is a quite different being to its progenitor. What was most original in the conference was the witness sessions of army personnel with key roles in the war alongside opponents of that war. Many of the ex-soldiers were testifying for the first time about their activities, their motivation and their memories of the war. They openly admitted that, given the continued sensitivity about the war even a generation later, they would not have spoken at an equivalent conference in France. Some of the witnesses whose testimony is recorded here have since died – Georges Mattéi and Major Paul Léger – and it is appropriate that we record our thanks as historians to two individuals who experienced in very different ways the horrors of the 'war with no name'.

Thanks are also due to other individuals who helped in the transformation of this work from conference to collection of essays. Heather Lally and Louise Graham organized the logistics of the conference with military efficiency; Drs Ahmed Aghrout and Redha Bougherira have provided unrelenting assistance of a technical and academic nature from conference to collection. Paul Leahy skilfully translated difficult French texts scattered with arcane military terminology. Alexander Zervoudakis not only secured the participation of the ex-army witnesses, he worked tirelessly to ensure accurate translations of their testimonies and arranged for the provision of detailed biographical information so that the officers' Algerian War service may be situated correctly within their army careers as a whole. Martin Evans, in turn, negotiated the participation of MM Mandouze, Mattéi, Sigg and Sirkidji and helped establish their biographical résumés. Finally, throughout their work the editors have been indebted to the enthusiasm and assistance of the former Director of the European Studies Research Institute at the University of Salford, Professor Geoffrey T. Harris.

Notes on the Contributors

Nacéra Aggoun wrote her doctoral thesis for the Université de Paris VIII (Saint-Denis) on 'La guerre d'Algérie dans la vallée du Chélif (Miliana-Orléansville), 1945–1958'. She is a member of the Institut Maghreb-Europe in Paris, where she has taught research methods (notably on using oral sources) for the DEA Maghreb programme and a seminar on the Algerian War's social history.

Martin S. Alexander is Professor of International Relations at the University of Wales, Aberystwyth. He held the Chair of Contemporary History and Politics at the University of Salford, 1994–2000. Among his works are *The Republic in Danger. General Maurice Gamelin and the politics of French defence, 1933–1940* (Cambridge University Press, 1993) and, as editor, *French History since Napoleon* (Arnold, 1999).

Michael Brett is Reader in the History of North Africa at the School of Oriental and African Studies, London. He is editor and translator of Charles-Robert Ageron's *Modern Algeria: A History from 1830 to the Present* (Christopher Hurst, 1991). He has written many articles on modern North Africa.

Philip Dine is Senior Lecturer at Loughborough University. He is the author of *Images of the Algerian War: French Fiction and Film, 1954–1992* (Clarendon Press, 1994), and *French Rugby Football: a Cultural History* (Berg, 2001).

Martin Evans is Reader in Contemporary European History at the University of Portsmouth and Director of the Centre for European Studies Research (CESR). He is the author of *The Memory of Resistance: French Opposition to the Algerian War* (Berg, 1997), and co-editor (with Ken Lunn) of *War and Memory in the Twentieth Century* (Berg, 1997).

Jacques Frémeaux is a graduate of the Ecole Normale Supérieure and is Professor of Contemporary History at the Université de Paris IV (Sorbonne). He had published *La France et l'Islam depuis 1789* (Presses Universitaires de France, 1991), and *Le monde arabe et la sécurité de la France depuis 1958* (Presses Universitaires de France, 1995).

Jean-Charles Jauffret is Professor at the Institut d'Etudes Politiques at Aix-en-Provence, where he directs the DEA programme in Military History,

Defence and Security. He has published extensively on the French army and the Third Republic, and is a co-author of the published guide to the Archives of the Algerian War at the Service Historique de l'Armée de Terre at Vincennes. His books include *Soldats en Algérie, 1954–1962. Expériences contrastées des hommes du contingent* (Editions Autrement, 2000).

John F. V. Keiger is Professor of International History at the University of Salford and a graduate of the Institut d'Etudes Politiques, Aix-en-Provence. He is the author of *France and the Origins of the First World War* (Macmillan – now Palgrave Macmillan, 1983), *Raymond Poincaré* (Cambridge University Press, 1997) and *France and the World since 1870* (Arnold, 2001).

Mohammed Khane wrote his doctoral thesis on *Le Monde* and its treatment of the Algerian War. He has taught French civilization at the University of Bradford and at the Hong Kong Baptist University.

Eckard Michels is Lecturer in German Studies at Birkbeck College, University of London. He pursued his postgraduate studies under the direction of Professor Klaus-Jürgen Müller at the University of Hamburg, and has published *Deutsche in der Fremdenlegion, 1870–1965. Mythen und Realitäten* (Ferdinand Schöningh, 1999).

Hugh Roberts is a Senior Fellow of the Development Studies Institute, London School of Economics and Political Science, and previously lectured in politics and history at the University of East Anglia, the Institute of Development Studies, University of Sussex, and the School of Oriental Studies in the University of London. He has been a Visiting Professor in Middle Eastern and North African politics at the University of California, Berkeley. A specialist on Algeria, he is the founder and secretary of the Society for Algerian Studies. His book on Algerian politics, *Commanding Disorder*, was published by I. B. Tauris, 2001.

Brigitte Rollet has lectured in the School of Languages and Area Studies at the University of Portsmouth and is a specialist on French film, discourse and culture. She now teaches at the British Institute in Paris.

Martin Shipway is Lecturer in French Studies at Birkbeck College, London. He is the author of *The Road to War: France and Vietnam, 1944–47* (Berghahn, 1996) as well as articles in the *Journal of Imperial and Commonwealth History* on French colonial policy in Indochina and on the Madagascar insurrection of 1947. He is now working on a general comparative study of decolonization, to be published by Blackwell.

Bernard W. Sigg is a psychoanalyst, honorary consultant in psychiatry and a vice-president of the ARAC (Association Républicaine des Anciens Combattants). His books include *Le Silence et la Honte. Névroses de la guerre d'Algérie* (Messidor, 1989), *Les murs de la psychanalyse* (Messidor, 1990) and *Algérie, années 90: politique du meurtre* (Lysimaque, 1998).

Alexander J. Zervoudakis wrote his PhD on French intelligence and the Indochina War at King's College, London (Department of War Studies). He has published 'Nihil mirare, nihil contemptare, omnia intelligere: Franco-Vietnamese intelligence in Indochina, 1950–1954', in M. S. Alexander (ed.), *Knowing Your Friends. Intelligence inside Alliances and Coalitions from 1914 to the Cold War* (Frank Cass, 1998), and articles on French airpower and air intelligence in Indochina in the *Revue Historique des Armées.*

1

The 'War without a Name', the French Army and the Algerians: Recovering Experiences, Images and Testimonies

Martin S. Alexander, Martin Evans and J. F. V. Keiger

Memories, methodologies, myths

> I recognised the lump in my throat, that impotent and furious disgust: it was what I used to feel on catching sight of a member of the SS. French army uniforms today caused me to shudder just as I did at the sight of swastikas. I observed those young boys smiling in their camouflage uniform... Yes, I was living in a city under occupation, and I loathed the occupying forces with more distress than I did those of the 1940s [because of all the links I had with them].[1]

Jules Roy, *pied-noir* writer and veteran of the Second World War and Indochina, could have been speaking of Algeria when he claimed that: 'It was hardly worth going to war against the Nazis only to become the Nazis of Indochina.'[2]

> They had the taste for liberty, the sense of justice and the instinct for generosity. They wanted to create a multiracial, free, fraternal and prosperous society, to set an example for a world divided between rich and poor peoples. One word symbolised their ambition: 'integration'! Opposite under the striking red and green banner of Islam, the enemy preached racial hatred and religious fanaticism, the arbitrary terrorism of a one-party dictatorship... To win the hearts of the population, they turned themselves into medical orderlies, administrators, water irrigation project managers, overseers of the rural economy... To protect them, they also became policemen, judges and executioners.[3]

The authors of the first two views were the anti-war intellectuals, Simone de Beauvoir and Jules Roy, who were revolted at the way, as they saw it, the French soldiers were acting in Algiers like Nazis. The author of the third was Jean Pouget, a French military veteran of the wars in Indochina and Algeria, still lionizing the army's work 18 years after the end of the latter conflict. These quotations exemplify the Manichean perspective that has framed the great bulk of writing on the Algerian War and the French army. It is a perspective that eschews complexity and divides the conflict into one between heroes and villains, black and white, good and evil. The war's messy realities become simplified into two polarized narratives where on one reading the French army are sadistic torturers waging a 'dirty war' and, on the other the National Liberation Front (FLN) are fanatical terrorists inflicting savagery upon defenceless civilians.

This edited collection rejects reductionist interpretations. Harnessing military and anti-war veterans' testimonies to the latest archive-based scholarship, it sets out to dissolve myths and misleadingly simplistic images. It embraces the complexity of events between 1954 and 1962, recognizing that the war underwent several phases and changed character more than once in these years. It does so in order to draw out the enormous diversity of experience, image and memory.

The war cannot be talked about in the singular; it must be talked about in the plural. The Algerian conflict was not just about war as military operations: it was also about battles over ideas, beliefs, loyalties, perceptions, traditions. In this collection, rethinking the war does not equate with rehabilitating any faction, interest group or myth; nor does it aim to rehabilitate the role of the French army in Algeria. Instead the aim was to go beyond polemic and recrimination and to seek greater understanding of the war's varied nuances. The more the war's complexities are researched, the more imaginative the questions asked of the experiences of the 'Algerian generation', the greater appear the ambiguities of that experience. It was sometimes terrifying, sometimes exhilarating, sometimes downright boring. Some French soldiers took part in major sweeps (*opérations de ratissage*) in which units systematically combed the land in search of the enemy, and knew real fear; many more experienced the cafard and the ennui of long nights on quiet guard duties or manning undisturbed posts in the freezing chill of the desert. Thousands of Algerians were active members of the ALN, playing dangerous games of hide-and-seek in the streets and markets of Algiers, Oran, Constantine and Bône, or waging guerrilla war from hideouts in the ravines and caves of the Collo hills, the Kabylie and Aurès mountains. But some two million spent the war as internal refugees under armed guard, uprooted by the French military administration to resettlement camps (*centres de regroupement*) hundreds of kilometres from their homes.[4]

Distinctive collective memories have developed on both sides of the Mediterranean since the war's end in 1962. Attempts to establish scholarly approaches ran up, for many years, against taboo subjects, such as the French army's use of torture, and state-sponsored myths that acquired the status of public articles of faith, 'invented traditions'.[5] In one case these illuminated the dawn of the Republic of Algeria; in the other, they revealed a France in the twilight of her imperial power, adjusting painfully to 'mere' hexagonal status as she rediscovered her identity as a European power.

Within the newly independent Algeria the war was glorified as a struggle for national liberation. The heroes were the ordinary people who had united behind the FLN. It was proclaimed as the war of 'one and a half million martyrs', the number officially claimed by the FLN to have been killed by the French between 1954 and 1962. Through the war Algeria had recovered national sovereignty and an Arabo-Islamic identity. These were the precise meanings given to the war after independence, and they became the founding images of new Algeria.[6] Teaching in schools and universities in Algeria after 1962 was closely monitored by the government.[7] The emphasis was placed on the outbreak of the nationalist action on 1 November 1954 and the role of the FLN. The contribution of all rival organizations (e.g. the MNA – Mouvement Nationaliste Algérien – and the PCA – Parti Communiste Algérien) was largely ignored. The Algerian people were constantly reminded that those who fought – those now in power – were the custodians of a historical memory. The dominant image propagated by the regime was that the Algerian people had united as one behind the revolution.[8] Thus the experience of pro-French Moslems which fractured this image of national consensus was suppressed.[9] Those who had not participated in securing national liberation could not challenge this. The myth of unity in the effort to throw off French shackles conferred legitimacy on the post-independence regime and at one and the same time denied legitimacy both to any potential rivals for power and potential alternative narratives of the course of the liberation struggle.

On the French side other legacies – but at least as many ambiguities – persisted after the end of the war in 1962. Until June 1999 the events in Algeria between 1954 and 1962 were not officially recognized as a war. They were described as counter-insurgency operations or as a law-and-order problem. French governmental and military discourse labelled the ALN units and individuals as 'outlaws', 'brigands', 'rebels', 'terrorists', but systematically and deliberately denied them the status of warriors or combatants.[10] This non-recognition was a symptom of the way that, at an official level, the Algerian War became taboo. One French conscript was told, on being demobilized: 'You've seen a lot of things in Algeria. Don't talk about them in France, because that would only fuel the propaganda of the Communists and of bad Frenchmen, of the François Mauriac type.'[11]

Those newspapers such as *Le Monde* and weekly journals critical of French atrocities in Algeria, *Témoignage Chrétien, France-Observateur* and *L'Express*, similarly attracted opprobrium from right-wingers devoted to Algérie Française, such as Jacques Soustelle, former Governor-General of Algeria, who described such publications as 'The big names in anti-French propaganda'.[12] However, as Mohammed Khane's chapter here demonstrates,

Le Monde's position during the war was much less clearly oppositional, and its reputation as such was a self-congratulatory *post hoc* invention.[13]

The 1980s saw attempts to view the war in a more detached manner. During the 30th anniversary commemoration in November 1984 an international conference took place in Algiers to assess the significance of 1954–62. Particular emphasis was placed on the international context.[14] At the end of the 1980s the Centre National de la Recherche Scientifique (CNRS) in France made a concerted effort to open out the Algerian War as a permissible and legitimate field of research. In this respect the Institut d'Histoire du Temps Présent (IHTP) and Jean-Pierre Rioux were prime movers. They organized three conferences: the War and Christian Opinion; the War and Intellectuals; and the War and the French.[15] One aim was to encourage historians to go beyond public myths and polemic and to conduct comprehensive academic research. Another was to create a new climate of honesty and openness – no issue was to be taboo. Previously, most books were the work of participants. These, through their memoirs, sought to justify their actions and positions during the war. Rioux called for a more detached approach. In 1992 this was followed up by a large-scale conference on the memory and teaching of the war.[16]

In 1999 the trial of Maurice Papon for his role in Jewish deportations from the Gironde in 1942–4 prompted other revelations about his responsibilities as Prefect of Police for the Seine (a post he assumed in March 1958) in the massacre of Algerians by Parisian police on 17 October 1961.[17] At the time the world was shown images by photo-journalists of the shocking violence perpetrated on the streets of Paris.[18] But there was little subsequent reportage, no historical investigation for thirty years and never a judicial inquiry – even though this bloodletting was later termed by a French lawyer 'the Krystallnacht of the Paris police'.[19] In a debate in the National Assembly in 2000, the French Communist Party (PCF) demanded a parliamentary commission of inquiry. Lionel Jospin, French prime minister at the time of the Papon trial, rejected this call. Instead he announced that access to the archives of the Algerian War would be widened.[20] For Jospin, it was the role of historians to subject the past to forensic scrutiny, a view confirmed by a Circular issued from the prime minister's office in April 2001. This instructed six ministries to ease access to official records relating to the Algerian War, Jospin adding the gloss that this be 'for historical research, in particular by people from the scholarly or university communities'.[21] Dominant official memories in France during the 1960s and 1970s could finally be modified, even rejected outright. The government had, in effect, given the green light to historians to challenge the previous 'authorized' history, a history synonymous with an uncritical narrative for the official view of France, the French cause and French wartime governments. Inevitably this earlier, 'received version' of France's conduct in Algeria had generated an officially sanctioned version of events in 1954–62 replete with anachronisms, omissions, decontextualization and 'state lies' (in the phrase of Jean-Luc Einaudi, the first to write a full-scale book about the 17 October 1961 atrocities).[22] 'The national community', declared Jospin in November 2000, 'is not weakened by the act of remembering but, on the contrary, is reinforced.'[23] The Papon episode signalled a shift in France from facing up to the 'Vichy syndrome' to facing up to the nation's colonial equivalent.[24] Indicative of the warmer climate for historical research into the war was the international conference held on 23–25 November 2000, under the auspices of French President Jacques Chirac, *La Guerre d'Algérie au miroir des décolonisations françaises*, a tribute to the life's work of Charles-Robert Ageron, doyen of historians of decolonization.

However, this new openness is selective. During a rash of claims and counter-claims aired in *Le Monde* in late 2000, General Marcel Bigeard, a paratroop veteran of Dien Bien Phu who was intimately involved in counter-insurgency in Algeria in 1956–7, continued to deny the use of torture. Simultaneously, General Jacques Massu, who directed the Battle of Algiers, and subsequently General Paul Aussaresses, who in 1956–7 was on the intelligence staff of Massu's 10th Parachute Division, admitted in print that 'institutionalized torture' became routine.[25] However, despite such revelations, a systematic, scholarly inquiry into these events and what Massu called a 'generalized use of torture' throughout French military operations remains blocked because the archives on the Battle of Algiers – the key episode in the torture controversy – are to remain closed until 2017.[26]

Fresh research, particularly since the early-1990s, has stimulated new reflections and different understandings about the 1954–62 period. An example of this is the controversy as to the numbers killed. There is still no consensus on the total number of dead in all sorts of categories. First, as regards the French army's dead a figure of 17,456 was given currency by Alistair Horne in 1977 and was reproduced by John Talbott in 1980.[27] By 1998 this figure had been revised upwards to 23,196 (of which about 15,000 in combat or assassinations). To take a specific and celebrated unit, the Foreign Legion lost 1,964 dead – many of whom though wearing French uniform had neither French nationality nor were likely to have set foot in France.[28] Additionally, losses on the French side should include those Muslims killed in French service: Algerian servicemen in the French army, native police, self-defence units, and the *harkis* (volunteer auxiliary infantry). Recent figures suggest that 3,267 police and self-defence personnel and 1,345 regular Muslim servicemen were killed. As for the *harkis* the work of Maurice Faivre has succeeded in quantifying quite accurately the numbers serving at particular dates, but has made little progress in determining precisely the number killed either in active service before 19 March 1962 or in the subsequent bloodletting of the purges in the first months of independence.[29]

If death tolls have not readily found acceptance on the French side, how much more controversy surrounds the losses among Algerians. The issue is complicated by ambiguity over who had combatant status. The Algerian Ministry of War Veterans gives the figure of 152,863 FLN killed.[30] The death toll among Algerians as a whole will never be known accurately. These deaths, however, have been a crucial political and ideological weapon in the service of a founding national myth of sacrifice and Muslim unity in struggle – and death. This explains the figure of a 'million martyrs' once touted by Algeria's post-independence regime. Moreover, a lot of death was inflicted by Muslim on Muslim. One estimate, drawing on French figures, puts the number of Algerian civilian deaths at the hands of the FLN at 16,000.[31]

Always a contentious issue, the battle over the death toll had led the French authorities to allege that the number the Algerians claimed were killed was vastly inflated for propaganda purposes. Asking how many were killed, and by whom, raises fundamental questions about the precise nature of the Algerian War. Historians face the task of setting the record straight about who killed whom. It is well enough known that *harkis* were killed in their thousands by the FLN during the French withdrawal in the summer of 1962. Much less familiar is that *pied-noirs* demonstrators were shot dead in a fusillade fired by French soldiers in the Rue d'Isly massacre of 26 March 1962, or that the operations between the OAS and the French forces of order caused 563 deaths in February 1962 alone.[32] Many on the Algerian side lost their lives in FLN/MNA fratricide, notoriously at the 1957 Melouza massacre. The number of Algerian Muslims killed in mainland France alone had reached 3,889 by January 1962.[33] Establishing who killed whom begs further questions over what the Algerian War was about, and who it was between.

Was it a colonial-type war of counter-insurgency? Was it a war of liberation? Was it a revolution? Was it a civil war between Algerians?[34] Was it a civil war between French people? Was it a simple confrontation between oppressor and oppressed? Was it a struggle to assert an Algerian national identity – and reinvent a French one? This only serves to underline still further the central argument of this book, namely the diversity of experience. The war was a complex event whose character changed dramatically – and more than once – between 1954 and 1962. Bertrand Tavernier's documentary film *La Guerre sans nom* (1992) and Benjamin Stora's *Les Années algériennes* underline this. Together they show how torture was one experience among others.[35]

Experiences

Wars are always about killing. They are also inevitably about battles over statistics, their meaning and their use. As discussed above, this was emphatically so in the case of the Algerian war: the legitimacy of the new regime rested on the legend of 'a million martyrs', the rank-and-file Algerian people whose blood was the price paid for independence and the mythic coagulant for subsequent national identity.

Publications in the later 1980s and 1990s have cast doubt on the earlier typology of the Algerian struggle as a uniquely savage, pointless, futile 'war with no name'. That characterization suggested a singularity to the Algerian conflict, setting it apart as a lived experience for the French troops. This now appears unconvincing the more the war recedes and its points of similarity with other twentieth-century conflicts – and their soldiers' experiences – can be discerned more clearly. Comparisons with other conflicts in the era of the world wars, and in the period of Cold War and decolonization after 1945, point to what was common, in whole or in part, with the Algerian experience. Indeed, the gradual lessening of polemics about the Algerian conflict suggests that the war's salient characteristics were on the whole unexceptional. This appears particularly so in a context of many wars of counter-insurgency and national liberation in Africa and Asia from the 1940s to the 1970s.

Generic problems of wars

Historical triumphalism

If ever there was an example of history being written by the victors, the history of wars is a quintessential case. However, this is typically just the first phase of a cycle of historicization. Each generation has its own vantage point on a past that becomes inevitably and legitimately more contested with the passage of time. Wars often wear an appearance of decisiveness to the participating generation. To succeeding generations, on the other hand, the outcomes seem less durable. To take the example of France and the First World War, the survivors of Maurice Genevoix's *Ceux de 14* believed that their sacrifice had brought not only victory but an end to such slaughter – 1914–18 as the war to end all wars. Much of the peacemaking at Paris in 1919 turned around visions of a new international order founded on arbitration and conciliation. For survivors of the combatant generation their victory was viewed as a triumph not merely over Germany but over war itself.[36]

Few wars, however, could spawn such high-minded idealism from their combat veterans. Even in the case of the Great War, revisionism was well under way in less than a generation. The revival of a Europe arming to the teeth by the mid-1930s fuelled disillusionment, while the dissipation of the achievement of 1918–19 signalled the next cycle of historical perspective on the war.[37] For most French soldiers and civilians the war of 1914–18 was about defending all that was exceptional and noble about France and her universalist values. So, despite its unhappier course, was the war of 1939–45. The crux of these values was the so-called 'civilizing mission' linked to France as the originator and evangelist of the Declaration of the Rights of Man. Disastrously, however, such ideals were trampled under the boots of French soldiers when it came to war in Algeria.

For the Algerians, too, the war was historicized for a quarter-century in a triumphalist mode. Ageron has noted that the mythology of Algérie Française was replaced by a similar and equally powerful mythology, of Algérie algérienne. This in turn began to fracture from 1988 onwards. Now the war's losers, silenced for so long, could re-evaluate their experiences and present themselves in a different light. Martin Evans shows in his chapter here that the *harkis*, for so long rejected in both France and Algeria and condemned for having 'made the wrong choice', began to challenge the certainties of the Algerian independence narrative. The FLN's universalist or 'master' narrative began to fracture with the onset of the systemic crisis of the Algerian state signalled by the riots of October 1988. This permitted groups that had previously been dismissed, and silenced, as 'losers' to legitimately reclaim their history and thereby assert their group identity. An integral part of this process was the way the status of 'victimhood' became an empowering mechanism rather than an emblem of powerlessness. A shift took place into a new climate more sympathetic to pluralistic accounts of the war's experiences and postwar consequences. The shake-up of old certainties, not least in crisis-ridden Algeria in the 1990s, provoked new patterns of interpretation. This was perhaps most explicit in Stora's *Les années algériennes*, noteworthy for being based on inclusion of all perspectives, however divergent, however conflictual. It was indicative of a new climate of understanding in France.[38] The *harkis* were one example of how new technologies were used to document and commemorate a war record, and strengthen a group identity essential for claiming reparations, benefits and pensions from a begrudging French state.[39]

The question of memory and war

The issue of triumphalism leads into a further generic factor: the question of memory of war. The works of Jay Winter and Pierre Nora have pioneered the opening up of memory as a legitimate object of historical inquiry.[40] Henry Rousso makes the distinction between memory as the recreation of the past and the study of memory as an ongoing process – to the question 'what happened?' has been added the issue of how war has been remembered in monuments, personal testimony, film and fiction. The interest in remembering, and in the various, sometimes discordant, ways any past is remembered formed a starting point for this volume. A common thread is how the meanings and significance of the Algerian War have been subjected to continual reconstruction and reconfiguration. As the testimonies along with the chapters by Philip Dine and Martin Evans demonstrate, the memory of the Algerian War has been a battlefield with competing groups and individuals attempting to take possession of public space, print and broadcast media to project their versions of the past.

Cultures of killing

The work of Joanna Bourke has pointed towards the 'culture of killing' as a further general problem of war. She poses the question of how ordinary men are turned into killing machines.[41] Her work strikes important echoes with Christopher Browning's examination of the psychology of extermination among Germans on the Eastern Front in 1941–5.[42] Georges Mattéi's testimony here is powerfully revealing of similar pressures and processes that operated on the minds of French reservists and conscripts in Algeria: self-preservation, peer pressure, revenge, psychological conditioning by the army, prejudice, racism and the sheer discovered pleasure in killing.[43] Mattéi's recollections suggest how Algeria can be set in the generic context of anti-guerrilla warfare. Like Vietnam and like Britain's war against the Mau Mau in Kenya, Algeria witnessed a weakening of army morale accompanied by military frustration at constraining 'rules of engagement'. Like other counter-insurgency wars, Algeria was a conflict without front lines and without uniformed regular opponents. This increased the propensity of certain French units to perpetrate atrocities, further undermining the French claim to be fighting for a nobler cause and within the bounds of western norms and laws of war.

Civil–military relations

Tussles for control of war policy characterized both sides in Algeria. An ironic symmetry occurred the longer the war went on. In the French case, the army as a dissident force shot its bolt in Algeria, its excessively frequent and ill-judged interventions in politics being brought to an end by means of a thorough republicanization after the failed military coup of April 1961.[44] Conversely, on the Algerian side, the issue of the struggle for supremacy between the political and military wings was a source of tension throughout the war. In retrospect it is clear that by 1958 the 'civilian' leadership had been displaced by the military wing. It was a harbinger of the balance of power to come in the Algerian Republic. This split was not only civil and military, but also between the internal and external cadres. In a further irony, the very success of the Morice Line ensured the preponderance of the external over the internal because the six *wilayas* within Algeria were now isolated from the key bases of political power in Tunisia and Morocco.

Images of the enemy

Benjamin Stora has pointed the way towards 'image' as a rich seam for historians to exploit in respect of the Algerian War.[45] One significant aspect is how difficult it was for the French to construct images that would credibly demonize the FLN leadership. French propaganda sought early in the war to present ALN units as 'bandits', later as people led astray by unrepresentative 'agitators'. France's universalist tradition since 1789 equated soil to Frenchness – and all Algerians constitutionally lived on French territory. By contrast, French propaganda had been effective in the First World War and to an extent in 1939–40. Kaiser Wilhelm II and Adolf Hitler were easy objects for lampooning and for serious propaganda that stressed their contempt for international law, treaties, the sovereignty of small nations and human rights. The dearth of hate-figures inside Algeria forced the French into alternative tactics. They targeted the FLN cadres sheltering in neighbouring Arab states as the tools of pan-Arabism (especially those in Egypt, excoriated as 'the sons of Cairo') and the FLN's external patrons (notably 'the demagogue Nasser'). Yet there was no escaping the problem that the shadowy FLN-ALN lacked prominent personalities ripe for demonization. Therefore visual propaganda's traditional tools – caricature and the ridicule of instantly recognizable enemy leaders – were weakened by the difficulty for France's war managers in identifying and vilifying the enemy in Algeria. The task of the bureau of psychological warfare therefore became more ambiguous and infinitely more difficult. As Nacéra Aggoun explains, 'the *fellagha* Arab guerrilla, used to symbolise the enemy, was depicted either as a faceless dark bulk with a human outline or as some sort of vermin'. To the end, however, the French faced the inescapable dilemma that some Arabs were friends while others were foes – and many were not clearly one or the other.

The examination of the propaganda struggles waged within the wider war for Algeria reveals further noteworthy aspects.[46] One is the concern of French politicians and colonial administrators about the potentially 'contagious' effects on the rest of the empire of violent campaigns for independence in French North Africa. Martin Shipway indicates in his contribution here that administrators fretted over 'contamination', nervously watching for signs of rising nationalist discontent in their territories. Officials, especially in sub-Saharan Africa, vigilantly monitored the 'capacity for dissidence' among local populations. Of particular interest were the groups living on the Saharan frontiers of 'black' and 'white' Africa, nomads whose loyalties lay more naturally to the north but whose political destiny was bound up in the sub-Saharan colonies. Colonial functionaries also worried that the emergent political elites might draw an example from Algeria's nationalism. Paradoxically, the Algerian War benefited the rest of French Africa in the sense that colonial administrators felt compelled to accelerate a managed and comparatively peaceful decolonization south of the Sahara from 1956; yet at this very moment the resolution of Algeria's own political future became ever more violently determined.

A second is that a comparable problem in aligning the 'home front' unambiguously behind the war effort existed in metropolitan France. There a vocal minority expressed support for the settlers. But even more clamorous groups of *oppositionnels* took a courageous public stand against French state policy and army torture, and in favour of Algerian independence. These ranged from students and intellectuals such as Jean-Paul Sartre, Marcel Péju, André Mandouze, Maurice Audin and Francis Jeanson, to the secretive *porteurs de valise*.[47] In both the field of propaganda and the management of pressures for independence in Algeria, factors common to all wars were apparent. It is perennially difficult to gauge whether psychological/propaganda actions are having the intended effects on the target, and it seems that political solutions are often the children of contingent fleeting historical moments. Shipway cites the prescient words of the Ivory Coast leader Félix Houphouët-Boigny on 27 February 1956: 'Events in North Africa have revealed conclusively how a climate of confidence between metropolitan and overseas populations may be eroded almost irremediably [...]; they also demonstrate how difficult it was subsequently to promote reform once passions have been allowed to run high.' The Algerian case shares with propaganda activities in all wars – hot as well as cold – the methodological weakness of excessive attention to the message of the propaganda product and insufficient attention to its impact on the targeted population. The reception of French psychological offensives and propaganda among the Muslim population is, as Aggoun concludes, an aspect demanding further research.

Specificities of the war in Algeria

As they were sucked into the new war in Algeria, French army officers responsible for training troops sought to learn, integrate and apply the supposed 'lessons' from counter-insurgency warfare in Indochina.[48] But as the chapter here by Alexander J. Zervoudakis shows, this was problematic. The terrain and climatic conditions differed sharply, of course. So did the attitudes of French politicians and public opinion, in part because Indochina was a distant colony whereas Algeria was constitutionally a part of metropolitan France and comparatively close to home. In Indochina, furthermore, there had been hints that the grand and noble ideals underpinning the *raison d'être* and purpose of the French military in earlier conflicts were now luxuries and must be jettisoned. In Algeria issues became much starker, French retaliation after FLN-ALN actions typically taking the form of the retribution of the mailed fist undisguised by any velvet glove.[49]

Yet there was no existential threat to French civilization, no clear and present danger to Provençaux or Parisians. To be sure, certain French officers sought to portray *fellagha* bands in apocalyptic terms. Their discourse depicted the counter-insurgency effort as a new crusade on the outer rampart of the defences of the West. Nevertheless, French hearts and minds proved resistant in the main to such crude attempts to raise the stakes. In practice parliamentarians, press and protesters all discerned the absence of clearly defined French war aims. This contrasted with the ALN-FLN's short-term fixity of purpose (independence). However, it is clear that the Algerian War did have its own characteristics and peculiarities.

Disputed beginnings and endings

At the time, and for many years afterwards, no agreement existed on dating either the war's beginning or its end. There was no declaration of war. Indeed, as noted already, the French steadfastly refused to acknowledge a state of war at all. The disputed beginning had its counterpoint in the contested ending. For some – mostly French – the struggle began with the wave of bomb attacks on French installations and *pied-noir* settlements on the night of All Saints 1954. But for many Algerian nationalists, the armed struggle predated this by almost ten years, being recognized as starting in the Sétif massacre of May 1945. As regards the war's termination, Algerian nationalists have commemorated 19 March 1962 (the date of the ceasefire) and 1 July 1962 (Algerian independence). The French, however, have not yet officially found a date that commands any national consensus. Consequently the war's end goes unmarked by France – even if at regional levels, left-leaning local veterans' associations have had some success in securing commemorative ceremonies and even street name changes adopting the 'radical' date of 19 March 1962. Yet for other *départements* of a more conservative political cast, that date remains unacceptable, decried as a national dishonour and capitulation.

An undeclared war and a problem of morale

A further, connected specificity was that the lack of any declaration of war contributed to the demotivation of much of the French army. This was especially true among reservists and conscripts. It also hampered French authorities in their endeavours to mobilize public opinion in favour of the war effort, since officially there was no war.

Specificities of time, place and military branch

Several factors in the nature of the conflict defined individuals' experiences, as François Sirkidji's testimony explains. The war was multi-faceted. It can help to distinguish three major subdivisions in the nature of the experience for French combatants: first temporal; second spatial – urban counter-terrorism, mountains, plains; third formational – branch/type of service.

Taking the first of these, it is crucial to acknowledge the considerable variations that marked the phases of the war. Periodization is necessarily open to debate. But historians generally now agree on the existence of five distinct phases to the Algerian conflict. Phase one extended from 1954 (the outbreak of the 'rebellion') to the parliamentary elections of 2 January 1956. Phase two ran from Guy Mollet's call-up of the reservists in the spring of 1956 to the Battle of Algiers in 1957. Phase three extended from late 1957 to de Gaulle's sidelining of General Raoul Salan in the autumn of 1958. Phase four saw the Challe and Constantine Plans 1959–60 – the twin-track strategy of defeating the ALN through massive military operations while simultaneously using large-scale financial infrastructural investment to 'win hearts and minds'. Phase five was the endgame in 1961–2, when the key issue became the timing and the terms on which France would quit Algeria.

Periodization is a key to a more nuanced, convincing analysis of attitudes among each identifiable constituency with a stake in the Algerian War: French servicemen, the settlers and Algerians, both ALN and non-combatants. For French servicemen, as Jean-Charles Jauffret's chapter here suggests, periodization mattered intensely: the Algerian garrison that faced the first wave of ALN violence in 1954–5 was a professional force, but needed to learn counter-guerrilla tactics. Later, the reservists who arrived in 1956 had to polish up their rusty military skills and undergo fitness training to meet the arduous conditions. Conscripts, drafted for service in their hundreds of thousands from 1957 onwards, experienced the transient friendships of the troop train and the comradeship of basic training. Periodization mattered down to the war's very vocabulary – the discourse and expressions of Indochina, and even of 1914–18, were current in the first stages in Algeria. Little by little, however, the war generated its own terminology and slang. As the war dragged on into 1958–9 (the fifth year and beyond), it also became routinized. The length of compulsory military service turned the troops' minds to surviving the daily round and accustomed them to the normalization of active service. It also dulled consciences to the brutalization of relations with the Muslim population, as Mattéi, Roy and Jean-Jacques Servan-Schreiber, from their divergent political stances, all publicly lamented.[50]

For settlers, the passage of time also produced a radicalizing effect. *Pied-noirs* leaders gradually lost faith that an electoral-administrative settlement could be reached that would preserve their privileges and also restore tranquillity between Muslims and Europeans. They became angrier. In 1960, fearing a sell-out by de Gaulle, they founded the OAS (Organisation Armée Secrète) as a diehard body to fight ruthlessly to preserve French Algeria.[51] For Muslim Algerians the war was an itinerary, quite literally so for those force-marched from their villages to the resettlement centres. For FLN cadres the itinerary commonly saw a move from armed struggle in 1954–7 to wider and more sophisticated forms of political action at the national, and increasingly international, levels. Attention to period also suggests the Algerian nationalist leadership's skill in adapting successfully to the defeat of their initial campaigns, reliant as those were on guerrilla attacks and urban bombings. Hard pressed by ruthless and effective French counter-insurgency tactics, the FLN deftly reversed the sequence of revolutionary liberation struggles prescribed by Mao, the armed strikes of the earlier years giving way almost entirely to political, diplomatic and propaganda offensives by 1960–2. This radical, intelligent and unconventional reordering of the classical phases of revolutionary war was disconcerting in the extreme – indeed literally disarming – for the French.[52]

Taking the second specificity – that of space and place – it mattered enormously for the soldiers' experience whether they were in the front line or in garrison duties in 'quiet' rear areas, such as guarding civilian or military facilities (hospitals, electricity substations, etc). Some men saw action and guns fired in anger; others played soccer or rugby to while away their time. For some the predominant memory of the war is of boredom; for others it is terror and revulsion. The banality of some soldiers' experience is perhaps brought home by the little known fact that 4,500 troops from the metropole, 800 legionnaires and 900 Muslims in regular French units died not as a result of enemy fire but in accidents (in training, at target-practice and especially in road accidents).[53] At a less existential level, postwar memories were shaped by whether a soldier served in an urban setting, engaging in patrols, street searches and counter-terrorist missions, or whether he saw action in the Saharan desert or in the mountains. The war's character was not monolithic and singular. It was diverse and variegated. In place as well as in time, service in Algeria could separate veterans as often as bind them. In one respect, however, there was broad consensus: that the encounter with the *pied-noirs* settlers, whom the soldiers had been ostensibly sent to 'protect', was a disillusioning experience. Most reservists and conscripts were greeted coolly by the European community. This seems to have resulted from a deep-seated tension between the settlers' desire for greater security on the streets of Algeria's cities and their desire for a normal way of life to be restored, free from the disconcerting, visible militarization of their security.

Taking the third specificity, varieties of experience could be sharply differentiated according to the branch of service one was in – Foreign Legion, army, navy, air force, gendarmerie. Each service had its own culture and traditions, its own *esprit de corps* and military role. Inter-arm command existed at the highest level (the Algerian theatre of operations). Yet it was rarely reflected in genuine combined operations or shared tasks, other than for short-lived specific missions. The navy had a greater role than has been acknowledged.[54] It formed a 'northern barrier' to complement the frontier barrages facing Morocco and Tunisia, blocking the coastal ingress of supplies and arms to the ALN. The paratroops were generally France's most idealistically committed servicemen. Gilles Perrault joined them because of the pride he took in them as the vanguard of the

French army that had liberated the mother country in 1944. Hélie de Saint-Marc, too young to have fought in the defeat of 1940, had resisted the Germans in occupied France and been interned in Buchenwald. Toughened in these personal fires, he became an unyielding defender of what he regarded as French national interest and military honour – Algeria was French and he was ready to risk all to prevent another defeat besmirching the army's reputation.[55] For many officers, Algeria was the place to draw a line: no more retreats, no more defeats. For colonialist officers, memories of the key role played by the overseas territories in helping liberate metropolitan France in 1944 remained powerful. The empire's continuation was a sine qua non, for them, of French great power status. For ideologues motivated by anti-communism, the struggle in Algeria was about barring the road to a Red Tide sweeping across the emergent nations of the Third World. Algeria was therefore a struggle on behalf of 'Western Civilization', the French army acting as latter-day Roman 'centurions', in Jean Lartéguy's evocative term, to protect NATO and the West.[56]

In French political circles there were those who viewed Algerian issues through the prism of the appeasement era and the Second World War. Those like Mollet, the leader of the SFIO socialist party, believed that the French settlers should not be sold out as the Czechs had been in 1938. President René Coty in 1957 invoked the memory of Verdun as a rallying call to justify why France must win in Algeria: the French Republic's integrity was in danger. Similar sentiments motivated François Mitterrand of the UDSR, the minister of the interior. He shared the left's commitment to the unity of the Republic and declared, apropos the FLN, that 'one does not negotiate with rebels'. Even the PCF's stance was ambiguous in the early years of the conflict, not least because it believed in the army–nation bond and the obligations of citizenship.[57] Hence its opposition to army desertions. Some civilians-in-uniform – such as the reservist Georges Mattéi – experienced a queasy feeling of being 'on the wrong side' as their commanders made them routinely carry out arrests, torture, atrocities and war crimes ('everyday Oradours') in the name of the Republic.

There was another dimension too: French men growing up in the 1950s were acutely aware of the embarrassing record of their Second World War forebears. Most Frenchmen had been denied the opportunity to fight from 1940 to 1945. This left a generational caesura among males of a nation whose men had, in the main, previously defined their patriotism and masculinity by their status in young manhood as citizens-in-uniform (1870–1, 1914–18). The sons and nephews of the 'lost warriors' of 1940–5 were those called on to defend the Republic in Algeria. In the person of 'Marianne', republican France assumed a symbolic feminine embodiment. But national identity in the first half of the twentieth century was strongly influenced by a masculine, modernist norm in the specific shape of the man-in-uniform, the citizen-soldier. Awkwardly, however, the brevity of the campaigns involving mass French armies in 1940 and 1944–5 meant France possessed (in quite another sense to that meant by Marc Bloch, the originator of the phrase) a 'generation with a guilty conscience'.[58] Humiliations in Europe in 1940–4 and in Indochina ten years later placed a quasi-moral obligation on young Frenchmen to rise to the challenge of this new threat to the nation. The conventional way to do so was by the expression of their masculinity and power in undertaking military service in Algeria. Thus was born 'the Djebel generation'.[59]

The children of 1939–45 felt compelled to eradicate the stigma of inaction attaching to the generation of their fathers and uncles.[60] Prominent though the reservist and conscript protesters were, they remained a minority. If those going to Algeria risked physical emasculation, it was a moral emasculation to which those who refused the call to arms appeared destined. Georges Mattéi, a Corsican reservist who was served his call-up papers while in Italy in April 1956, testifies to this. He has explained elsewhere that: 'What prompted him to return was the wish to experience war for himself. He felt unmanly because he had missed out on World War Two. Now, through the Algerian War, he wanted to overcome this complex and prove his self worth.' Mattéi's thirst for action arguably assumed an alternative, subversive form in his subsequent fight against torture and the perversion of the ideals of the Republic that he witnessed in Algeria. Mattéi recounted years later that 'despite being fascinated by the idea of combat, he was at the forefront of such protests'.[61]

As in other respects, the Algerian War contained its ambivalences: this time Frenchmen went to war en masse but found themselves fighting the wrong war, a dirty war (albeit, as one embittered conscript reflected, 'examples of "clean" wars must be pretty rare').[62] It was paradoxical that young men of military age in 1956–62 felt angry at having to serve in an ignoble and increasingly controversial cause, whereas the previous generation had been angry at being denied service in the noble cause of French Liberation. As Brigitte Rollet's chapter here shows, the director André Téchiné used his film *Les Roseaux sauvages* to explore how young Frenchmen and women of the late 1950s and early 1960s had to define masculinity, explore their sexuality and ritualize their passage from teens to adulthood against the backdrop of Algeria.

By the fifth and final phase of the war, in 1961–2, conscripts were less inclined than ever to risk death merely to strengthen the hand of Louis Joxe, Bernard Tricot and Robert Buron, de Gaulle's negotiators at the ceasefire talks in Evian.[63] Veterans of Algeria felt they belonged to a 'sacrificed generation'. They discovered, on demobilization, that their country intended only to forget what they had gone through and sink into a collective amnesia.[64] This was encouraged from the highest levels of the Fifth Republic, for de Gaulle had no interest in remembering Algeria. In 1961–2 he turned his back on empire as the touchstone of French grandeur.

Political elites were similarly silenced: the Gaullist UNR loyally supported the general's policies of nuclearization and European leadership. The SFIO and its allies were discredited by their dismal record of about-turns and incompetence in directing the war effort. The PCF lacked credibility when, in 2000, it demanded an inquiry into the French army's conduct and the question of torture, and urged compensation for French victims of the war – for it had voted emergency powers to Mollet's government in spring 1956. This was the very act that had opened the way to the dispatch of some two million conscripts to Algeria over the six remaining years of war.

Isolation

A further specificity of the Algerian War, one particularly prominent in memoirs of French professional officers, is the feeling of 'France alone' (*la France seule*). France felt that she was fighting 'a war without allies'. This had much truth – although Yahia Zoubir has noted that the USA did not completely renounce support for France. Some Americans were aware of the sensitivities of their French allies. A National Security Council report of November 1959 noted:

> The French government and a large segment of French opinion bitterly feel that the United States fails to give all-out support to its NATO ally in a place where critical French interests are at stake and when Frenchmen are being killed daily. There is French resentment concerning the activities of the FLN representatives in the United States and there is some suspicion that the United States actually intends eventually to supplant French influence in North Africa.[65]

In the main, however, the ambivalence of American spokesmen and the periodic criticism of French policy in Washington – over and above the more predictable censure from Moscow – irritated and discouraged French military leaders.[66] After all, France had been supplied and assisted militarily by powerful coalitions in 1914–18, 1939–40, 1944–5. Even in the Indochina war the US bankrolled over 70 per cent of the financial costs of the French military effort.[67] Never in her modern wars did France have fewer friends than during the Algerian crisis.

Algerian experiences

Until the late 1990s and Ageron's path-breaking conference, *La Guerre d'Algérie et les Algériens*, North African experiences of the conflict were overshadowed by a mountain of memoirs and scholarship on the French side of the war. Political censorship in Algeria made publication of memoirs there at best risky and at worst impossible. Fear was a factor from the 1960s to the 1980s, with the murder of some key actors such as Belkacem Krim. Algerian scholars such as Mohamed Harbi occasionally published in France.[68] But others felt that to do so was an act of betrayal. A few memoirs were published such as those of the leaders Yacef Saadi and Si Azzedine. But little emerged about the experiences of rank-and-file ALN soldiers.

Recent research has attempted to redress the balance. Some work has appeared that sheds light on the recruitment, training, strategies and tactics of the *fellaghas*, the Algerian fighters.[69] Like the French, the Algerians found the war a variegated and shapeless experience, often determined by spatial considerations – in short, where in the country they found themselves at any given moment. The French frontier defences – the Morice Line erected in 1957–8 along the Algerian–Tunisian border in the east and the comparable barrier built on the frontier with Morocco to the west – effectively separated Algerian nationalists of the interior from those based externally. The various sects or 'clans' of FLN-ALN militants faced ever greater obstacles to close and frequent contact with one another.

At a military level, this affected operations and tactics during the war. It also prepared the way for postwar antipathies and political rivalries. While the conflict was still in progress, the sealing off of the 'Politico-Administrative Organization' (OPA) inside Algeria from the leadership cadres in Morocco, such as Colonel Houari Boumediène's 'Oujda clan', and those in Tunisia, gave a significant edge to those based externally. Reminding some observers of the experience of the French Resistance in 1940–4, the FLN-ALN resistance located outside Algeria enjoyed the benefits of several crucial assets. These included secure training camps, arms supplies from friendly powers (East Bloc countries, Morocco, Egypt), access to Third World diplomatic support, radio broadcasting facilities and coverage from the international media.[70] None of these assets was available to the hard-pressed ALN bands within Algeria. This became particularly true as the noose thrown around them by General Maurice Challe's operations tightened in 1959–60. Further undermining the integrity and military effectiveness of the internal OPA/ALN was the infiltration by Captain Paul Léger's undercover agents, 'les bleus', into the OPA in the Casbah during the Battle of Algiers in 1957. Léger's operatives were mostly former ALN militants whom he 'turned', often under coercion. He then sent them back among their erstwhile comrades to sow distrust by planting false documents, spreading rumours and provoking arrests. A bloody turmoil ensued. ALN leaders such as Amirouche responded by unleashing a wave of beatings, throat-cuttings and disembowellings to silence suspected double-agents – most of whom were loyal to the nationalist cause but could not prove it. Léger took satisfaction from watching the FLN-ALN cadres eliminate each other, effectively doing his work for him.[71]

Léger's operation was part of a larger tactical symbiosis between the French army and the ALN. This symbiosis saw the latter's tactics define those of their opponent in an ever expanding and ever more violent circle.

Grasping that ALN strategy and operational methods, and those of the French, were in a permanent state of interconnectedness is essential for an understanding of the war experiences of both adversaries. Each fed off the other. This created a pattern of action and reaction, challenge, response and counter-response that was one of the conflict's defining characteristics. The FLN emerged in 1954 from an impasse within the traditional nationalist organizations led by Messali Hadj and Ferhat Abbas. It represented a new generation of activists who rejected compromise with the colonial authorities. For them the armed struggle was the only way ahead. However, in espousing violence, the younger insurgent leaders, including Belkacem Krim, Mohamed Boudiaf and Yacef Saadi, retained a realistic appreciation of the military balance of power. They were pitting the *fellaghas* against the fourth largest army in the world in terrain that generally favoured the French. In contrast to the jungle of Indochina, which the Vietminh exploited so successfully first against the French then against the Americans, the open scrub and the vast desert expanses of Algeria offered few military advantages for guerrillas. The objective of most FLN leaders was, therefore, to win a political victory. They sought to create a climate of insecurity that would bring Algeria to the attention of the world, and assert a moral claim for independence that would isolate France diplomatically. Within this single-minded political strategy that recognized how favourable votes in the United Nations would matter as much as military successes, the FLN forged a unity of purpose that rejected attempts to lure them into even a 'paix des braves' as proposed by de Gaulle in 1958.[72]

Given that many FLN leaders were not only veterans from the French army, most famously Boudiaf and Ahmed Ben Bella, but also MTLD activists, it is not surprising that they synthesized these two experiences in order to organize the ALN militarily. Borrowing directly from the MTLD's organization, Algeria was divided into six *wilayas*. Subsequently, metropolitan France was designated the 'seventh *wilaya*' when the FLN stepped up its action and took the fight to the French mainland.[73] The substructures of the light company (*katibas* of 100 men) and section (*faileks* of 30 men) were modelled on French military practice. Rapidly the *wilayas* assumed the status of fiefdoms, fratricidal conflict plaguing ALN military strategy from start to finish. At the heart of this conflict were questions of arms, supplies and authority. In-fighting also arose from the issue of legitimacy – progenitors of the FLN versus the new wave of leaders, imprisoned versus free, military versus political. Later, with the Morice Line's construction, this translated into a split between internal and external resistance that continued beyond the war against the French into the power struggle within the new Republic of Algeria.

Yet across these internecine divisions the ALN maintained the dynamics of their strategy. In the first phase we have delineated, from November 1954 to August 1955, the ALN struggled to win support among the

Muslims and used selective attacks to sow hatred between settler and native all across Algeria. In the second phase, poor coordination between the *wilayas* played into the French army's hands and prompted the launch of the August 1955 uprising as the best form of defence. In the third phase, the expansion of French forces through deployment of the reservists put intolerable pressure on the rural ALN. In response to this crisis, FLN leaders conferred in the Soummam valley in August 1956 and decided to launch the Battle of Algiers.[74] The major strike called among Muslim workers in Algiers in January 1957 prompted discussion of the emergency at the United Nations. In the fourth phase the FLN response to de Gaulle's return to power in France in May 1958 was to proclaim the Provisional Government of the Algerian Republic (GPRA), along with which went the ascendancy of Boumediène as power shifted to the externally based militants in Tunisia and Morocco. To those who paused from chasing fugitive *fellagha* bands, it was clear that the war would be decided politically, not militarily.

In the military-operational cycle already discussed, these strategies framed the French response. Given the nature of guerrilla war, the hunt for ALN combatants became ever more refined and efficient. A vast and sophisticated French military effort was applied to intelligence-gathering and operations, especially in 1959–60 under Challe's command. The French isolated and destroyed any ALN units foolhardy enough to make a stand; greatly superior in mobility as well as firepower, they caught, trapped and annihilated others that sought refuge in flight. The cat-and-mouse game played out between ALN and French army units in 1954–5 had something of the sporting quality of the hunter and his quarry seen in France in 1944 between the collaborationist Vichy *milice* and the Resistance *maquis*. But there was no longer a contest during the latter phases in Algeria. If the discourse of field sports and the chase occasionally marked the vocabulary of France's counter-insurgency officers, the sport had by 1960–1 become a totally one-sided *chasse aux fells*.

The schism between internal and external FLN-ALN cadres, initially of a military nature, developed into a key legacy for subsequent Algerian politics and society. For, in a stroke of irony, the Algerian external resistance triumphed in 1962 (and more obviously after Boumediène's coup of 1965), just as de Gaulle had successfully exerted his leadership over the internal French Resistance in 1944–5. Yet even the ALN's problems contained certain advantages. For one thing, the French lost much goodwill by their practice of securing the Algerian civilian population by means of herding them into *centres de regroupement*. These were compared to the German concentration camps of the Second World War. As many as two million Algerians, it is estimated, were relocated – often to camps hundreds of kilometres from their homes, their villages, grazing or farmland.[75] So politically and socially shattering were the consequences that the French sociologist Pierre Bourdieu called the resettlements the 'End of a World' for Algerian social hierarchy and stability.[76] The experiences of the centres during the war turned many Algerians not previously active in – or even sympathetic to – the FLN/ALN into newly radicalized men and women forcibly pulled up from the roots in their own land. The 130 years of French rule had hitherto left most Muslim Algerians surprisingly untouched. This was underlined in a report published in 1957 by the ethnologist Germaine Tillion. She highlighted the chronically undeveloped condition and poor nutrition of the people, and how 94 per cent of Muslim men and 98 per cent of Muslim women were illiterate in French in 1954, with only one male Muslim child in five and one female Muslim child in 16 receiving any schooling.[77] The new social relationships thrown up by camp life were remarked on, as Nacéra Aggoun explains, by the sociologists Bourdieu and Abdelmalek Sayad. In their book, *Le déracinement*, published in 1964 after fieldwork in the resettlement villages, they showed how French population policy backfired disastrously.[78] The repression's severity and the Nazi-style forced relocations of so many people produced a paradox: France achieved a military victory in Algeria in 1959–60, but at the price of a massive alienation and radicalization of the Muslim population.[79] It was, of course, precisely the latter's support and loyalty to France that was the most crucial factor in determining Algeria's political future.

Images

Images of the Algerian War were multi-dimensional, overlapping and ambiguous. Three in particular were crucial: the pre-existing, subliminal image of Algeria as a country; the image of its Arab peoples; and the consciously manufactured image of the French soldier as friend, fighter and personification of France

Similarities between France and Algeria (constitutionally part of France) were evoked even in the sea-crossing for the troops who embarked at Marseilles. The vistas of the Vieux Port of Marseilles and the Rade d'Alger, the strikingly similar urban architecture, the shimmering, sunlit public spaces, all contrived to ease the transition from metropole to Maghreb. Even the voyage itself left a seamless sense of Frenchness undisturbed as soldiers moved ashore and saw sights of reassuring familiarity. Disembarking on the Mediterranean's southern shore, the impression and ambience was of having moved place but not country. This was exactly as officialdom intended, *une seule France* indeed.[80] As Soustelle, Governor-General in 1955, declared – his words a banner headline in the leading *pied-noir* newspaper, *L'Echo d'Alger* – 'France will no more quit Algeria than Provence or Brittany'.[81] This was given concrete expression – literally – by the network of small forts, blockhouses and strong points that the French scattered across Algeria as a 'symbol of territorial presence' and control.[82]

For the early reinforcements sent south in 1954–6, such prior mental images as they possessed of Algeria may have derived chiefly from impressions gained by watching cinema newsreels.[83] In this first phase of the war even North Africa's most distinctive elements – a camel caravan, Arab beggar boys, a souk and a *méchoui* – appeared charming, unthreateningly exotic. Just as the popular postcards on sale at the Marseilles dockside had hinted, Algeria appeared quaintly touristic and folkloric. Even beyond the settled coastal conurbations, once troops found themselves deployed inland, Algeria's landscape at first appeared harsh yet noble, almost a transplanted French civilization burnished by sunshine, luxuriant in its orange groves and palm trees.[84]

Moreover, and paradoxically, Algeria was presented in a Christianized mythologization not as an Arabo/Islamic land but, predominantly, as a foyer of Gallo-Roman Mediterranean civilization. In an extension of the myth embraced by professional officers, the fight in Algeria was depicted as a last-ditch defence of western civilization, barring the way to the latter-day 'Communist barbarians' at the gates. This imagery was made to do duty throughout the Algerian War. In this myth the majority Muslim population was peaceable, intrinsically loyal and needed only effective protection by France. This image altered sharply from 1959 onwards when the struggle became more desperate and slipped into appalling brutalities as Algérie Française diehards adopted the discourse of apocalyptic threats crashing against the ramparts of Eurafrica. But for as long as possible the French encouraged traders to sell postcards that depicted Roman ruins, classical architecture and the buildings of the Algerian cities with their sparkling, whitewashed façades. Much of this suggested to French troops and administrators, especially those from the Midi, ways in which Algeria was an extension of their own homeland with the aquaducts at the 'picturesque Roman ruins of Tipaza', for instance, evoking those of the Gard.[85]

Sooner or later, however, for most French troops, Algeria's spell as a romantic and exotic land of tourism rather than terrorism was shattered. The sight and sound of ambulances and police cars, sirens wailing as they raced to a bar torn apart by an FLN bombing, or the shock at seeing victims of throat-cutting or disembowelling, brought naive French soldiers face to face with an 'other' Algeria. This was a violent and terrifying place. The *fellagha* guerrilla replaced the street-vendors of jasmine and oranges as the 'new type Arab' in the visual imaginary of French troops. Furthermore, many French soldiers found the Algerian countryside wild and forbidding. Far from a land of sunshine, troops deployed into the higher ranges of the Aurès, Atlas and Collo mountains experienced bitingly cold winds, freezing nights and snow in a landscape severe enough to test the stamina of the fittest regular paratroops or legionnaires. Inhospitable terrain was regarded as a friend to the *fellaghas*, a foe to French troopers. All the same,

Philip Dine has noted that the experience of most conscripts in Algeria was 'singularly lacking in danger'.[86] Less than 10 per cent of French forces did much fighting. Most were dispersed in static duties, defending telephone exchanges, power stations, protecting property, public buildings and port facilities.

The second image, that of 'the Arab', cast its shadow naturally enough over the French soldiers who experienced the Algerian War. In the conflict's first phase the troops stationed in Algeria were accustomed to day-to-day contact with the indigenous Muslims. They had, after all, been on garrison duties in the Maghreb for months, even years; some had been on active service in Morocco and Tunisia during the independence struggles of those countries from 1952 to 1956. The deterioration of relationships between the indigenous peoples and Europeans, both settlers and troops, was gradual. It occurred in part from the crude conflation of all native North Africans into the increasingly pejorative term 'Arabs', distinctions between true Arabs and Berbers being lost. Even then the deterioration was neither linear nor universal. Some parts of the immense country continued to enjoy peacetime relations between colonized and colonizers for a year or more after the 1954 start to the FLN-ALN rising. Though requiring much more research into particular local experiences, and a sensitivity to the chronological dislocations, it seems that a kind of normality, or at least no worsening of relations, persisted between Muslims and French security personnel until the wholesale expansion of French forces in 1956.[87]

However, as Nacéra Aggoun demonstrates, things changed dramatically in 1956 and 1957 with the mass arrivals of the reservists and conscripts. These men did not know North Africa, and many did not wish to. Their preconceptions about Muslim customs and characteristics, indeed about the value of France's overseas territories as a whole, derived from pre-existing naive idealizations. These ideas were promoted in their primary schools in the metropole in the 1940s and early 1950s. The lingering images that the young conscripts carried in their minds were paternalistic and colonialist: the dutiful natives of France overseas, 'the children of Greater France'. Alongside this coexisted a commonplace romanticization of the Maghreb and its peoples as an 'exotic', 'Oriental other'.

Philip Dine reminds us of the well-established literary preoccupation in western culture with the supposed charms of the harem and the slave market. At a crude level French squaddies found Algerian service tantalizing: it hinted at masculine bonding and adventures abroad with the scarcely veiled prospect of sexual 'eastern promise'.[88] As it had done for the men of the British army in 1914, instructed by Kitchener on how to behave towards French civilians, for the British and Anzac troops in Egypt in 1915 and for US soldiers encountering the women of Vietnam in the 1960s, military duty overseas set pulses racing among young men posted far from home. The encounter between the French army's citizen-soldiers and Algeria contained paradoxes. Danger and boredom were offset by the possibilities of sexual adventure. In a more Islamic location such as Algeria, realization occurred only in soldiers' fantasies; yet incidents of rape were cited and the more predatory dimensions to Franco-Arab encounters require further research.

Civilians-in-uniform drafted to Algeria had some awareness of the overseas populations, left over from the Second World War (when colonial and North African detachments had played a high-profile role in the Liberation of France in 1944). But few had first-hand experience. The peoples of Algeria were a foreign 'other'. Dimly aware of this, and the potential for ignorant and often reluctant soldiers to worsen rather than ease tensions, the French military authorities sought to educate and prepare troops for Algerian service. They did so at a banal level by issuing simplistic cartoon manuals, providing simple phrases in Arabic thought likely to assist the soldier in daily dealings with the native inhabitants, instructing troops how to treat the Arab population and enjoining them to respect local traditions, customs and dress.

Of course many thousands of Muslims also served France, acting as its agents in the diverse operations to restore and preserve security in the face of the FLN-ALN operations. As Martin Evans's chapter explains, there were at least four main categories of Muslims in the French security services. These were the GADs (*groupes d'auto-défense*) or self-defence groups; the *mokhaznis* or local militias, charged with village security under the direction of the SAS teams; Muslim regular troops in the French army itself; and the *harkis*, the volunteer auxiliaries. The *harkis* were especially vaunted by officers strongly committed to French Algeria, who idealized them as the embodiments of French assimilationist policy. *Harkis* were said to personify a future for Algeria rooted in a mutually supportive and amicable Franco-Muslim partnership. The 'Algerianization' of the war in 1959 and 1960 was a cornerstone of Challe's strategy to assume the offensive, pacify the country and eliminate the ALN's capacity for action. To achieve this, a dramatic expansion of *harki* strength from some 26,000 to 60,000 occurred. For certain commanders, such as Challe, Massu and Hélie de Saint-Marc, praise for the *harkis* became sentimental and self-deluding.[89] At independence, these officers were tormented by a sense of betrayal – aghast that they could not honour their promises to safeguard the *harkis'* future, and convinced that their own honour had been sullied by de Gaulle's 'retreat' to 'the hexagon' that left the *harkis* at the mercy of the new masters of 'Algerian Algeria'.[90] In practice, as Evans notes, the settlers always had misgivings about confiding their security to thousands of armed Muslim auxiliaries, and the tactic got a much cooler reception among the *pied-noirs* than in the French army. In the war's aftermath, *harkis* were some of the most forgotten participants. Although 68,000 *harki* soldiers escaped to France between April and August 1962, about 100,000 more were left behind and killed within nine months. De Gaulle, 'in a hurry to close the Algerian file', officially discouraged the *harkis* from fleeing to France. Subsequent presidents were equally neglectful of the *harkis* and their families, reckoned by 1991, when they rioted in Narbonne and Carcassonne for rights and recognition, to number 450,000.[91]

The third image, the army's depiction of itself, was sedulously controlled and skilfully disseminated. At the heart of this enterprise was the army's own public relations office, the SIRPA, and photographic bureau, the ECPA. Commonplace illustrations included famous generals decorating infantrymen after action, presentations of new weapons and colours to Muslim auxiliaries, squads of heroic-looking soldiers (often atop rugged mountainous terrain), French superior technology in operation (typically helicopters) and the idealistic young SAS pacification officer surrounded by 'his villagers'.[92] These agencies, furthermore, worked closely with mass-circulation news magazines, notably *Paris-Match*: first to ensure the desired representation of the army's tasks and demeanour; second to market these images to the metropolitan taxpayer and voter – increasing numbers of whom were simultaneously parents of the troops.[93]

Many of these images were, inevitably, caricatures. The army command offered a demonic portrayal of the FLN as a fanatical minority, the tools of Nasser and of Communism. Against their barbarous nihilism, the army propagandists sought to make young French troops feel themselves to be the shields of civilization, bulwarks against militant Islam and the obscurantism of the Orient. This state of mind was apparent quite early in the war among the professional and elite units. Pierre Hovette, a company commander in the 3rd Colonial Parachute Regiment operating in the Constantinois and the Kabylie hills in late 1955, welcomed the challenge of restoring a French physical presence and a climate of security in what had, since November 1954, become a 'no-go' area. He recalled how his men relished their 'chance to show [...] critics that the paras are capable of succeeding at something besides war'.[94]

If oversimplified, monochrome images of friendly Muslims tended to prevail on the French side, FLN mythmakers also presented a one-dimensional tableau of an 'Algerian people' united to expel the French. Gillo Pontecorvo's film, *The Battle of Algiers* (1965) did not deal in caricatures. As Hugh Roberts notes, its documentary style recreates the struggle in the Casbah among the labyrinthine, dark, narrow streets from January to September 1957 – arguably the pivotal event of the Algerian War. The film-maker sought to convey the motivations of all sides in the conflict; in this, however, Pontecorvo was making an exception that proved the rule.

In the treatment of gender as a dimension to the conflict, Pontecorvo showed how burdensome a myth the French had constructed for themselves in envisioning Algeria's women as passive and submissive bystanders in the struggle for its political future – and their own. French 5e Bureau psychological warfare leaflets and posters, notes Nacéra Aggoun, glorified women as the hope of the new, modern, peaceable Algeria. In the slogan of one hoarding, women would be 'the cornerstone in the construction of the new Algeria'. The key theme of the year 1959 was that of peace and the restoration of order: 'it is through us that peace will be reborn and peace is the traditional and sacred vocation of women'. The theme of women as modernizers was reflected in the campaign of the French to discourage Algerian women from wearing the veil (*le dévoilement*). Yet young French citizen-soldiers found what they saw and what they experienced was far removed from the nostalgic and romanticized preconceptions of Arab women with which they arrived in North Africa. Pontecorvo reminds us that Muslim women fought actively in the battle. Many passed secret documents and gathered intelligence. Some, such as Hassiba Ben Bouali, placed handbag bombs under bar stools. Far from remaining docile and passive, Algerian women assumed vital combat roles in prosecuting the struggle for national liberation. But there is much to be done to recover their memories of wartime experience and build these satisfactorily into an Algerian war historiography largely dominated, thus far, by masculine narratives.[95]

French troops' morale in face of the widening Moslem participation in the FLN cause ebbed and flowed according to the professional or drafted quality of the soldiers and according to the phases of the conflict. In the early stages, even the legendary Foreign Legion suffered flagging morale. Eckard Michels discusses the lack of enthusiasm among aggressive legionnaires disillusioned by defeat and withdrawal from Indochina – a 'hot war' of the sort the Legion trained for – and from Morocco in 1956. Even this elite corps experienced a dangerously high level of desertions. No fewer than 604 legionnaires were posted as 'missing – deserted' at the end of 1957. This was equivalent to an entire battalion. In response, the legionnaires' training was lengthened to 20 weeks, morale and combat effectiveness recovering markedly from the turn of 1957–8. The revived spirits of the legionnaires resulted from the increasingly effective frontier barriers, the decline in ALN activity and improved rates of pay. By 1958 Salan, then the army commander-in-chief in Algeria, could state confidently that 'The Legion remained the very personification of high morale'. Legionnaires were appalled by the decisions in Paris to quit Algeria: the 1st REP (Foreign Legion Parachutist Regiment) backed the abortive generals' coup of April 1961 and was disbanded by de Gaulle as a punishment. As the war ended, the Legion had to uproot itself from its headquarters at Sidi-bel-Abbès and, in a very physical mark of French retreat, move to a new base at Orange in southern France. Legionnaires felt that their comrades had died in vain.[96] Paradoxically, therefore, the morale of professional troops strengthened the longer hostilities continued, while the morale of reservists and conscripts – though they came later to the war – tended progressively to weaken.

Part of the explanation lay in the peculiarly 'dirty', dishonourable kind of war it became. Bringing the war's brutalities home to a reading public in France were articles published from 1956–7 in Sartre's journal *Les Temps Modernes* and in semi-autobiographical narratives by reservists such as Mattéi and Daniel Zimmerman.[97] Their accounts make plain that neither side had a monopoly on cruelty and 'dirty tricks'. Mattéi, for example, confessed that men in his squad 'had a shack where systematically ... nearly all enemy prisoners were tortured and interrogated'. He also recounts the occurrence of unauthorized summary executions. Yet he reminds us too of how horrifying were many encounters by young French civilians-in-uniform with the violence of the war. Ambushed by a well-concealed ALN commando hidden in an olive grove that raked them with fire at 20 metres' range, Mattéi's squad lost five killed and three wounded. One of the latter was horrifically emasculated as a lesson to the colonial oppressors. Another soldier, this time a conscript private in the 14th Tirailleur Battalion from July 1958 to early 1961, Gerard Périot, frankly admitted that 'rank-and-file morale had never been very brilliant in Algeria'. The men were 'under-fed, disgusted by our frequent about-turns and errors, and appalled by the attitude of too many officers and NCO's more interested in medals and money than in pacifying Algeria'.[98]

For metropolitan conscripts the tour of duty was extended to 28 months in 1959, a month more than the tour for those from the Algerian settler community. This caused rancour. So, too, did the fact that metropolitan conscripts were allowed only a single 23-day leave to visit their families during their service in Algeria. Périot confessed that 'the length of the tour terrified the men'. He also noted a widespread suspicion among his comrades-in-arms that the *pied-noirs* draftees were privileged with safer staff and garrison duties.[99] This corroded the unity of the army and helped undermine the commitment of the mainland French to the cause. These perceptions were transmitted home in letters to families and friends. They fuelled the sense that the risking of life and limb by reservists and draftees to preserve Algeria for the settlers went unappreciated.

With their war lost by 1962, a million settlers fled to France in a few months, most travelling with 'nothing... but a couple of cheap suitcases and bitter memories.'[100] However, in the current state of research the complexities of the *pied-noirs'* existence in Algeria is obscured by caricatures of them as small-town traders, petty functionaries and racist bigots. This crude portrait of the community needs to be redrawn. At one extreme the case of the *pied-noir* writer Jules Roy illuminates a more idealistic and heroic type. Resigning in the rank of colonel in 1953 in protest against French brutalities in Indochina, he spoke out in the late 1950s against the French and felt that Muslim Algerians 'were right to rebel against their oppressors'.[101] More ambiguous was the position of the even better known Nobel prize winner, Albert Camus. In truth, the settler community's diverse roles and culture awaits its historians.[102]

In the longer term the awkwardness and suspicions felt by metropolitan conscripts and reservists towards the settler community they were in Algeria to protect placed a question mark over the whole French effort in North Africa. In terms of modest financial investment, faltering industrial development policy and the low-level of migration from France to Algeria, perceptive French commentators remarked on the eve of the outburst of violence that metropolitan efforts were not remotely commensurate with the challenges arising in North Africa.[103] After the FLN's insurrection was under way the Anglo-Saxon press and media, as Michael Brett's chapter points out, tended to echo the concerned French critiques about the conduct of the Algerian War. Journalists such as Edward Behr and Michael Kettle spent lengthy periods in Algeria covering both politics and the military operations for American and British news magazines and papers.[104] British commentators particularly latched onto Servan-Schreiber's *Lieutenant in Algeria* (published in English translation in New York in 1957 and London in 1958), and Henri Alleg's searing indictment of torture, *The Question*, with its preface by Sartre, published in 1957. In the eyes of some of the French, Anglo-American writers and media commentators on the struggle legitimized the FLN's motives in seeking to internationalize the dimensions of the struggle. Paradoxically the FLN skilfully seized the moral high ground of universalism so often claimed by France. As they preached engagement in a revolution for the rights of Algerian men (and women) as citizens, the FLN benefited from Anglo-Saxon writers' help in drawing world-wide attention to the irony of France perpetrating appalling human rights' violations in Algeria.

International dimensions

In France's international relations after 1871 her statesmen sought in peace and war never again to face isolation. Possession of powerful friends and membership of alliances became a cornerstone of French geo-strategy. The crisis in Algeria at first seemed unlikely to deviate from this pattern. From November 1954 to the Suez debacle of November 1956 France, broadly speaking, succeeded in depicting the conflict as a general threat to her western allies. In Washington, President Dwight D. Eisenhower's Republican administration was receptive to imagery of a 'Red Tide' of global communism sweeping west from the Middle East around the Mediterranean shoreline. Anthony Eden, the British Prime Minister (1955–7), was even more convinced of the existence of an Arabo-Communist conspiracy. This was orchestrated, he thought, by the Egyptian leader, Gamal Abdul Nasser. For the obsessive Eden (who had been Foreign Secretary during Hitler's diplomatic 'march of conquest' in 1936–8) Nasser and Arab nationalism amounted to a 'new Nazism'. Such attitudes in Washington and London fed an illusory French expectation that the war they were waging in Algeria would enjoy major Allied assistance.[105] French leaders did have early success when they appealed to the NATO obligation to defend the territorial sovereignty of one and all. Suez, however, shattered French hopes.

After 1956 the Eisenhower administration stepped back from an Algerian imbroglio that Americans now construed as 'imperialist'. Eden's successor, the more canny and pragmatic Harold Macmillan (1957–63), tacked in the wake of this American change of course. British policy cooled markedly towards French military resistance to nationalism in Africa, Macmillan himself famously speaking in 1960, at Cape Town, of a 'wind of change' blowing through the continent.[106] In February 1958 the French air force in Algeria mounted an unauthorized bombing of an unprotected refugee camp at Sakhiet, in Tunisia, after a story that the camp was sheltering an ALN commando unit. Not only was Sakhiet an outrage against international law, it unleashed a storm of condemnation from the world's media. This worsened France's relations with her allies and put her in the dock of the United Nations.[107] John F. Kennedy, on the campaign stump for the 1960 presidential elections, joined the chorus of criticism. After his January 1961 inauguration, condemnation of French actions in Algeria became official US policy. Hence, French image management through propaganda was defeated by France's own clumsy blunders and by the internationalization and 'mediatization' of the war. French policy-makers hoped to preserve hermetic partitions between overseas territories and handle each case of nationalism individually. But the spread of radio, newsreel and television coverage of wars and insurrections placed policy-makers in an unaccustomed glare of publicity, compressed their decision-making time and strengthened French sentiments that an end to the Algerian imbroglio could only come through withdrawal.

Paradoxically, the FLN thus imitated de Gaulle's own tactics for the wartime Resistance, whereby primacy was given to international and political campaigns over purely military action. After the Soummam Declaration, the FLN manipulated the world's media far more effectively than did their French opponents. Why then did this international opprobrium not induce France to retreat from its Algerian entanglement immediately? Three explanations suggest themselves. First, and paradoxically, France's international standing over the Algerian War plunged to its nadir just as the French armed forces were achieving military victory. This made influential generals determined to fight on: after all, the aim of military action had ostensibly been to create security conditions conducive to politico-electoral-economic reforms to keep France in Algeria.[108] Second, the weight of the settler community and its political allies in Paris kept a brake on metropolitan inclinations to cut and run. Third, as Jacques Frémeaux's chapter discusses, it was not just the coastal zone and the *pied-noirs* at stake. There were also the far-reaching strategic and economic assets in the Sahara: the missile and nuclear weapons facilities at Colomb-Béchar, Reggane, Hammaguir; the oil wells of, for example, Edjelé and Hassi Messaoud.[109]

During this time the Algerians played a deft diplomatic game, skilfully exploiting French mistakes. As the underdogs, FLN diplomats learnt from an early stage to make the most of the international card. The November 1954 Declaration of the FLN, issued in the aftermath of the All Saints' Day attacks, enlisted 'the diplomatic support of our Arab and Moslem brothers'. Subsequently, the internationalization of the struggle became a core FLN tactic. This often capitalized on French blunders and turned them into nationalist triumphs. In this way the FLN gained support abroad. It did so, firstly, by securing safe havens, training camps and propaganda outlets (Radio Cairo); secondly by winning diplomatic recognition for the Gouvernement Provisoire de la République Algérienne (GPRA), the nationalist provisional government, from a steadily-expanding list of eastern bloc and Third World nations from 1958 onwards. The French found, as a result, that they were swimming against a strengthening tide of international opprobrium.[110]

Testimonies

A deeper and more sophisticated understanding of the war depends upon recording and integrating personal narratives. Written documents are never the whole historical record; how much more is this so when we are dealing with clandestine organizations in which to write anything down could be a short step to arrest, torture and death. Now almost a half century after the conflict there is an urgency in assembling these unwritten memories of the participants. This volume makes a contribution. One of its most exciting and original dimensions is its achievement in bringing together disputed, sometimes confrontational, Franco-French narratives. But we recognize that this is a small and unscientific selection that can only hint at the rich seam of testimony. Still seriously under-represented are records of the views and experiences of women in Algeria from 1954 to 1962, Muslims as well as *pied-noirs*, along with the perspectives of mothers, wives, girlfriends, children of Frenchmen who served, and some of whom died, in Algeria. Part III of this collection presents perspectives from career army officers on the one hand, and from anti-war activists, both civilians-in-uniform and militant, politically engaged intellectuals. The testimonies are those of the late Major Paul Léger, Colonel Henri Coustaux and General Alain Bizard from the French officer corps of the Algerian war era, together with those of André Mandouze, François Sirkidji, Bernard Sigg, and the late Georges Mattéi from the broad-based French opposition to the war.

Conclusions – avenues for future research

Further research would illuminate relations between the home front and war front. In the former case too little has yet been done to elucidate public opinion and correlate attitudes to the ebbs and flows of the war.[111] Work is needed comparable to that of Stéphane Audouin-Rouzeau on front-line troops' daily preoccupations in the First World War. This has begun through the collection and publication of letters from drafted servicemen, giving a voice to an otherwise silent working class.[112] These men were not natural correspondents but, perhaps for the only sustained time in their lives, found that distance from home prompted them to pick up a pen. For these 20-year-olds, resentful that destiny had saddled them with the Algerian War, 'no-one could tell them this was the best time of their lives'.[113] The next stage in the recovery of memory produced surveys and interviews among veterans. This has pulled back the shroud that hid their experiences. As the 'Djebel generation' nears old age, mourning for dead comrades and their own lost youth complete, history and historians are at last helping them to some form of closure and to 'reintegrate History'.[114]

A key area for further research is the roles and attitudes of French and Algerian women to the war. Long-service professionals may have had wives and mothers imbued with a 'colonialist', maternalistic mentality. Older reservists typically were married men, some with families; younger conscripts often had girlfriends and fiancées in France. In short, this war impacted extensively on the women of the metropole. Finding their diaries, or letters exchanged between them to confide views on the war's progress and its politics, promises to reveal the outlooks of the 'second sex', the hitherto 'silent half' of the French population.

In conclusion, study of the Algerian conflict now draws at least as much from filmic and literary representations, from oral traditions and testimonies, as it does from the release of official papers – welcome though the latter is after the long 'silence'.[115] The essays here interweave multiple sources and diverse perspectives. They point to the varieties of experience and the legitimacy of the many memories of the war, even if these remain divergent and irreconcilable. The triumphalist narrative of a united Algerian people throwing off French colonialist shackles held sway in the 1960s and 1970s; but this served history no better than the 'Nostalgérie Française' that emanated from certain quarters of France at the sight of Algeria's descent into anarchy and bloodletting in the 1990s. It may still surprise that the Algerian War lasted as long as America's Vietnam War and that as many French troops served in Algeria as did Americans in Vietnam. It may also surprise that, by comparison, 25 per cent more French families were hit by the death of a serviceman in Algeria than American families who suffered a loss in Vietnam. However, the Americans openly confronted their Vietnam traumas, President Ronald Reagan dedicating the Memorial Wall in Washington in 1982 only seven years after the 'fall' of Saigon. By contrast, forty years after the 'fall' of French Algeria, French governments had offered no such cathartic gesture to the French people. Given the significance of the war for French society, coming to terms with such a scar in its past has become an international scholarly enterprise.[116] The contributions in the present volume have sought to avoid both colonial rehabilitation and the mythmaking of Algerian nationalism. The 'new history' of the Algerian War, multi-dimensional and open to previously silent voices, promises much. By working together for this project, rather than on separate tracks, historians of culture, the military, diplomacy and society suggest how a more rounded understanding of one of the most important but neglected wars of the twentieth century can emerge.

Notes

1. Simone de Beauvoir, *La Force des Choses* (Paris: Gallimard, 1963).
2. Quoted in obituary of Jules Roy, *The Times* 11 July 2000, p. 19.
3. J. Pouget, 'L'honneur des capitaines', in P. Héduy (ed.), *Algérie française, 1942–1962* (Paris: Société de Production Littéraire, 1980), p. 366.
4. See M. Cornaton, *Les Camps de regroupement de la guerre d'Algérie* (Paris: L'Harmattan, 1998); K. Sutton and R. I. Lawless, 'Population regrouping in Algeria: traumatic change and the rural settlement pattern', *Transactions of the Institute of British Geographers*, 3: 3 (1978), pp. 331–50.
5. See M. Evans, 'La Lutte continue...? Contemporary history and Algeria', *History Today*, 47: 2 (February 1997), pp. 10–12.
6. P. Oulmont, 'Patriotisme et nationalisme au miroir de la guerre d'Algérie', *Historiens et géographes*, 89 (1998), pp. 293–307.
7. By contrast, for less inhibited ways of teaching French colonial history in France, the USA and Britain, and for revealing how film, literature and history can be imaginatively combined, see A. L. Conklin, 'Boundaries unbound: teaching French history as colonial history and colonial history as French history', *French Historical Studies*, 23: 2 (Spring 2000), pp. 215–38.
8. See H. Remouan, 'Pratiques historiographiques et mythes de fondation: le cas de la guerre de libération à travers les institutions algériennes d'éducation et de recherche' in C.-R. Ageron (ed.), *La guerre d'Algérie et les Algériens, 1954–1962* (Paris: Armand Colin, 1997), pp. 305–21 (esp. the section entitled 'L'insurrection du 1er novembre comme mythe fondateur', pp. 315–17).
9. As other recent 'inconvenient' aspects of French history had been, notably the Vichy period with its ambiguities of collaboration and survival. See H. Rousso, *The Vichy Syndrome: History and Memory in France since 1944* (Cambridge, MA: Harvard University Press, 1994). Rousso's approach has also influenced Benjamin Stora's methodologies in examining the Algerian case: see B. Stora, *La gangrène et l'oubli. La mémoire de la guerre d'Algérie* (Paris: La Découverte, 1992).
10. 'Officially in France, the Algerian war never took place: it was only a matter of "operations for the maintenance of order"', remarked Jean Planchais, who covered the war for *Le Monde*, in the opening to his article, 'La Guerre d'Algérie', the lead piece for an entire issue of *Le Monde: Dossiers et Documents* on the Algerian war, 146 (July–August 1987), p. 1.

11. François Mauriac, leading Catholic writer and journalist opposed to the war. *Le Monde*, 11 November 2000.
12. Quoted in R. Vinen, *France, 1934–1970* (Basingstoke: Macmillan – now Palgrave Macmillan, 1996), p. 163.
13. Cf. P. Éveno and J. Planchais, *La guerre d'Algérie. Dossier et témoignages réunis et présentés par Patrick Éveno et Jean Planchais* (Paris: Editions La Découverte and *Le Monde* Editions, 1989); also *Trente ans après: Nouvelles de la guerre d'Algérie* (Paris: *Le Monde* Editions, 1992).
14. See M. Touili, *Le retentissement de la révolution algérienne. Colloque international d'Alger (24–28 novembre 1984)* (Algiers: Entreprise National du Livre, 1985); also P. Bernard, 'L'Algérie trente ans après' *Le Monde*, 9 November 1984, p. 25.
15. See F. Bédarida (ed.), *La guerre d'Algérie et les chrétiens* (Paris: Bulletin de l'IHTP, 1988); J.-F. Sirinelli and J.-P. Rioux (eds), *La guerre d'Algérie et les intellectuels* (Brussels: Complexe, 1988); J.-P. Rioux (ed.), *La guerre d'Algérie et les français* (Paris: Fayard, 1990).
16. *Mémoire et enseignement de la guerre d'Algérie. Actes du colloque* (Paris: Institut du Monde Arabe/Ligue de l'Enseignement, 1993).
17. See the illustrated commemorative 30th anniversary album by A. Tristan, *Le silence du fleuve: octobre 1961* (Bezons: Au nom de la mémoire, 1991); also *17 octobre 1961. Mémoire d'une communauté* (Paris: Editions d'Actualité de l'Emigration/Amicale des Algériens en Europe, 1987).
18. For example, the cover-photograph and headline 'Nuit de Troubles à Paris', and photo feature-article entitled, 'Le drame arrive en métro', *Paris-Match*, 655 (28 October 1961), pp. 40–9.
19. G. Boulanger, *Papon, un intrus dans la République* (Paris: Seuil, 1997), p. 240. Cf. R. J. Golsan, 'Memory's *bombes à retardement*: Maurice Papon, crimes against humanity and 17 October 1961', *Journal of European Studies*, 28: 1 (1998), pp. 153–72; N. MacMaster and J. House, '"*Une journée portée disparue*": the Paris massacre of 1961 and memory', in K. Mouré and M. S. Alexander (eds), *Crisis and Renewal in France, 1918–1962* (New York: Berghahn, 2002), pp. 267–90; J.-L. Einaudi, *La Bataille de Paris, 17 octobre 1961* (Paris: Seuil, 1991); M. Levine, *Les ratonnades d'Octobre. Un meurtre collectif à Paris en 1961* (Paris: Editions Ramsay, 1985); B. Violet, *Le Dossier Papon* (Paris: Flammarion, 1997), pp. 107–37.
20. See P. Vidal-Naquet, 'Il se manifeste une gigantesque envie de vérité à propos de l'Algérie', *Le Monde*, 28 November 2000, p. 18; J.-M. Bezat and A. Chemin, 'Lionel Jospin écarte l'idée d'une commission spéciale sur la guerre d'Algérie'; J. Isnard, 'Les historiens français et algériens face au maquis des archives'; J.-M. Bezat and J.-L. Saux, 'Les politiques d'accord pour le travail de mémoire mais pas sur la repentance'; A. Garcia, 'Les anciens combattants accusent les gouvernants de l'époque', all in *Le Monde*, 29 November 2000, p. 6; C. Tréan, 'Guerre d'Algérie: juger les tortionnaires?', *Le Monde*, 2 December 2000, pp. 1, 16.
21. P. Bernard, 'Les recherches historiques sur la guerre d'Algérie seront facilitées', *Le Monde*, 28 April 2001, p. 4. The Circular was promulgated in the *Journal Officiel* of 26 April 2001, and applies to the Ministries of Employment, Justice, the Interior, Foreign Affairs, Defence and Culture.
22. Einaudi, quoted in *Le Monde*, 28 April 2001, p. 4.
23. *El Watan*, 6 November 2000.
24. See M. Evans, 'From colonialism to post-colonialism: the French empire since Napoleon', in M. S. Alexander (ed.), *French History since Napoleon* (London:

Arnold, 1999), pp. 391–415. Cf. D. Schalk, 'Has France's marrying her century cured the Algerian syndrome?', *Historical Reflections*, 25 (1999), pp. 149–64.
25. P. Aussaresses, *Services spéciaux: Algérie, 1955–1957* (Paris: Perrin, 2001). This was extensively discussed on publication: see G. Elgey, 'Crimes de la guerre d'Algérie: divulguer pour ne pas répéter', *Le Monde*, 5 May 2001, pp. 1,16; M. Tubiana, 'Plus de décorations pour Aussaresses et ses pareils', ibid., p. 16; P. Georges, 'Pour la France', ibid., p. 34; also (unattrib.), 'Les aveux du général Aussaresses suscitent une grande émotion en Algérie'; N. Weill, 'La torture en Algérie entre tabou, occultation et mémoire'; J. Isnard, 'Le Service historique des armées veut protéger les militaires qui se confient à lui', all in *Le Monde*, 8 May 2001, p. 5; P. Vidal-Naquet, 'Amère victoire', *Le Monde*, 12 May 2001, pp. 1, 14; M. Harbi, 'Un passé de tortures qui ne passe pas', ibid., p. 14
26. *Le Monde*, 23 November 2000; also S. Thénault, 'Armée et justice en guerre d'Algérie', *Vingtième Siècle*, 57 (1998), pp. 104–14. Cf. J. Massu, *La vraie bataille d'Alger* (Paris: Plon, 1971); A.-G. Minella, *Le soldat méconnu. Entretiens avec le général Massu* (Paris: Mame, 1993); J.-J. Jordi and G. Pervillé (eds), *Alger 1940–1962. Une ville en guerre* (Paris: Autrement, 1999), pp. 126–85.
27. A. Horne, *A Savage War of Peace: Algeria 1954–1962* (London: Macmillan – now Palgrave Macmillan, 1977), p. 538; J. Talbott, *The War Without a Name. France in Algeria, 1954–1962* (London: Faber & Faber, 1981), p. 246.
28. See E. Michels, *Deutsche in der Fremdenlegion 1870–1965. Mythen und Realitäten* (Paderborn: Ferdinand Schöningh, 1999).
29. See M. Faivre, 'Les Français musulmans dans la guerre d'Algérie. 1. De l'engagement à la mobilisation', and M. Bodin, 'D'une guerre à l'autre: l'évolution de l'état d'esprit des soldats algériens (1947–1956)', *Guerres mondiales et conflits contemporains*, 177 (January 1994), pp. 139–65, 166–83 respectively; also M. Faivre, *Les combattants musulmans de la guerre d'Algérie, des soldats sacrifiés* (Paris: L'Harmattan, 1995), pp. 159–61.
30. P. Messmer, *Les Blancs s'en vont. Récits de décolonisation* (Paris: Albin Michel, 1998), p. 172.
31. Talbott, *War Without a Name*, p. 246.
32. See, however, the contemporary photo-report entitled 'Rue d'Isly: 10 minutes sanglantes', *Paris-Match*, 678 (7 April 1962), pp. 54–61.
33. Statistics in C.-R. Ageron, 'Les Français devant la guerre civile algérienne', in Rioux (ed.), *La Guerre d'Algerie et les français*, pp. 53–62; also Vinen, *France, 1934–1970*, p. 159.
34. See C.-R. Ageron, 'Complots et purges dans l'armée de libération algérienne (1958–1961)', *Vingtième Siècle*, 59 (1998), pp. 15–27.
35. The personal testimonies recorded for the film are published in P. Rotman and B. Tavernier, *La guerre sans nom. Les appelés d'Algérie, 1954–1962* (Paris: Seuil, 1992).
36. F. Field, *Three French Writers and the Great War: Studies in the Rise of Communism and Fascism* (Cambridge: Cambridge University Press, 1975).
37. See R. Dalisson, 'La célébration du 11 novembre ou l'enjeu de la mémoire combattante dans l'entre-deux-guerres (1918–1939)', *Guerres mondiales et conflits contemporains*, 192 (1998), pp. 5–23.
38. See A. Thomson, *Anzac Memories* (Cambridge: Cambridge University Press, 1994), which explores the way in which the image of the damaged Vietnam veterans facilitated a more receptive mood to alternative perspectives on the impact of war experiences in place of previously dominant masculine

narratives. Cf. D. M. Shafer, 'The Vietnam combat experience: the human legacy', in Shafer (ed.), *The Legacy: The Vietnam War in the American Imagination* (Boston: Beacon Press, 1990); and S. Hoffmann, 'Algérie et Vietnam', *Le Monde*, 11 May 1990, p. 27.

39. See M. Evans 'Rehabilitating the traumatized war veteran: the case of French conscripts from the Algerian War, 1954–1962', in M. Evans and K. Lunn (eds), *War and Memory in the Twentieth Century* (Oxford; Berg: 1997), pp. 73–85; also Internet site 'Collectif National "Justice pour les Harkis" et leurs familles', http://www.chez.com/justiceharkis.
40. J. Winter, 'The generation of memory: reflections on the "memory boom" in contemporary historical studies', *Bulletin of the German Historical Institute*, 27 (Fall 2000), pp. 69–92; P. Nora, *Realms of Memory: The Construction of the French Past* (New York: Columbia University Press, 1996); see also G. Eley, foreword to Evans and Lunn, *War and Memory*, pp. vii–xiii.
41. See J. Bourke, *An Intimate History of Killing: Face to Face Killing in 20th Century Warfare* (London: Granta, 1999); also J. Bourke, *Dismembering the Male. Men's Bodies, Britain and the Great War* (London: Reaktion Books, 1996).
42. See C. R. Browning, *Ordinary Men. Reserve Police Battalion 101 and the Final Solution in Poland* (New York: HarperCollins, 1992).
43. See M. Evans, *The Memory of Resistance. French Opposition to the Algerian War (1954–1962)* (Oxford: Berg, 1997), pp. 105–8.
44. See M. S. Alexander, 'Seeking France's "Lost Soldiers": reflections on the French military crisis in Algeria', in Mouré and Alexander (eds), *Crisis and Renewal in France*, pp. 242–66; M. S. Alexander, 'Duty, discipline and authority: the French officer elites between professionalism and politics, 1900–1962', in N. Atkin and F. Tallett (eds), *The Right in France since 1789* (London: I. B. Tauris, 1998), pp. 129–59.
45. B. Stora, 'Quelques réflexions sur les images de la guerre d'Algérie', in Ageron (ed.), *La guerre d'Algérie et les Algériens*, pp. 333–40.
46. See Z. Ihaddaden, 'La propagande du FLN pendant le guerre de libération nationale', in Ageron (ed.), *La guerre d'Algérie et les Algériens*, pp. 183–99.
47. FLN supporters in France who clandestinely smuggled documents, leaflets and money between the metropole and Algeria. See D. Djerbal, 'La question des voies et moyens de la Guerre de libération nationale en territoire français', in Ageron (ed.), *La guerre d'Algérie et les Algériens*, pp. 111–35; and L. Hamon and P. Rotman, *Les porteurs de valise* (Paris: Albin Michel, 1979).
48. See J.-M. Marill, 'L'Héritage indochinois: adaptation de l'Armée française en Algérie (1954–1956)', *Revue Historique des Armées* (hereafter: *RHA*), 187 (June 1992), pp. 26–32.
49. See M. Thomas, 'Order before reform: the spread of French military operations in Algeria, 1954–1958', in D. Killingray and D. Omissi (eds), *Guardians of Empire* (Manchester: Manchester University Press, 1999), pp. 198–220.
50. Cf. G. Mattéi, *La guerre des gusses* (Paris: Balland, 1982; reissued by Editions de l'Aube, 1995); J. Roy, *La guerre d'Algérie* (Paris: Julliard, 1960); also J. Roy, *Mémoires barbares* (Paris: Albin Michel, 1989); J.-J. Servan-Schreiber, *Lieutenant in Algeria* (London: Faber, 1958); also J.-J. Servan-Schreiber, *Passions* (Paris: Fayard, 1993).
51. See A.-M. Duranton-Crabol, *Le temps de l'OAS* (Brussels: Complexe, 1995); J.-J. Susini, *Histoire de l'OAS* (Paris: La Table Ronde, 1963); R. Kauffer, *L'OAS. Histoire d'une organisation secrète* (Paris: Fayard, 1986).

52. A. Derradji, *The Algerian Guerrilla Campaign Strategy and Tactics* (Lewiston, NY and Lampeter: Edwin Mellen Press, 1997); cf. J. G., 'L'organisation de base de l'Armée de Libération Nationale', *Les Temps Modernes*, 175–6 (October–November 1960), pp. 531–7.
53. B. Stora, *Histoire de la guerre d'Algérie (1954–1962)* (Paris: Editions La Découverte, 1993), p. 89; the high mortality from accidents is also drawn out in the film *La Guerre sans nom*.
54. See J. Kessler, 'La surveillance des frontières maritimes de l'Algérie, 1954–1962', *RHA*, 187 (June 1992), pp. 94–101; B. Estival, *De Port Saïd à Port Say* (Paris: Editions les 7 Vents, 1991), pp. 129–41; also B. Estival, 'The role of the Navy in littoral defence in the Algerian War', *Journal of Strategic Studies*, 25: 2 (2002); P. Boureille, 'La marine et la guerre d'Algérie: périodisation et typologie des actions' in J.-C. Jauffret and M. Vaïsse, *Militaires et guérillas dans la guerre d'Algérie* (Brussels: Editions Complexe, 2001), pp. 91–114.
55. On Perrault see the interview in Stora's documentary *Les Années algériennes* broadcast on TFI in 1991; on de Saint-Marc see his *Mémoires. Les champs de braises* (Paris: Perrin, 1995); Helie de Saint-Marc, *Les sentinelles du soir* (Paris: Editions des Arènes, 1999); L. Beccaria, *Hélie de Saint-Marc* (Paris: Perrin, 1988).
56. J. Lartéguy, *Les Centurions* (Paris: Presses de la Cité, 1959).
57. See D. Joly, *The French Communist Party and the Algerian War* (Basingstoke: Macmillan – now Palgrave Macmillan, 1991).
58. See M. Bloch, *L'Etrange Défaite. Témoignage écrit en 1940* (Paris: Editions Franc-Tireur, 1946); English trans. by G. Hopkins as *Strange Defeat: A Statement of Evidence Written in 1940* (New York: W. W. Norton, 1968).
59. X. Grall, *La Génération du Djebel* (Paris: Editions du Cerf, 1962).
60. Evans, *The Memory of Resistance*, p. 105.
61. Ibid., pp. 106–7.
62. M. Matéos-Ruiz, *L'Algérie des appelés*, (Biarritz: Editions Atlantica, 1998), p. 48.
63. See M. Péju, 'Mourir pour de Gaulle?', *Les Temps Modernes*, 175–6 (October–November 1960), pp. 481–502.
64. See R. Delpard, *20 ans pendant la guerre d'Algérie: générations sacrifiées* (Neuilly-sur-Seine: Editions Michel Lafon, 2001).
65. NSC Policy No. 5911/1, 4 November 1959, National Archives, Suitland/College Park, Maryland, in Y. H. Zoubir, 'The United States, the Soviet Union and decolonisation of the Maghreb, 1945–1962', *Middle Eastern Studies*, 31: 1 (January 1995), pp. 58–84 (quotation p. 75).
66. See Y. H. Zoubir, 'US and Soviet policies towards France's struggle with anti-colonial nationalism in North Africa', *Canadian Journal of History*, 30: 4 (December 1995), pp. 439–66.
67. See L. S. Kaplan, D. Artaud and M. R. Rubin (eds), *Dien Bien Phu and the Crisis of Franco-American Relations, 1954–1955* (Wilmington, DE: Scholarly Resources, 1990).
68. M. Harbi, *Aux origines du FLN* (Paris: Editions Bourgois, 1975); *Le FLN: mirage et réalité, des origines à la prise du pouvoir (1945–1962)* (Paris: Editions Jeune Afrique, 1980); *Les Archives de la Révolution algérienne* (Paris: Editions Jeune Afrique, 1981).
69. See A. Derradji, *The Algerian Guerrilla Campaign*, cited above, n. 52.
70. C.-R. Ageron, 'Un aspect de la guerre d'Algérie: la propagande radiophonique du FLN et des Etats arabes', in Ageron (ed.), *La guerre d'Algérie et les Algériens*, pp. 245–59; R. J. Bookmiller, 'The Algerian war of words: broadcasting and revolution, 1954–62', *Maghreb Review*, 14: 3–4 (1989), pp. 196–213.

71. See P.-A. Léger, *Aux carrefours de la guerre* (Paris: Plon, 1983).
72. See M. Thomas, 'France accused: French North Africa before the United Nations, 1952–1962', *Contemporary European History*, 10:1 (March 2001), pp. 91–121; also M. Vaïsse, 'La Guerre perdue à l'ONU ?', in Rioux (ed.), *La Guerre d'Algérie et les Français*, pp. 451–62.
73. See A. Haroun, *La 7e wilaya. La guerre du FLN en France* (Paris: Seuil, 1986).
74. On the Soummam Congress see M. Kettle, *De Gaulle and Algeria 1940–60* (London: Quartet Books, 1993), pp. 67–9.
75. See C.-R. Ageron, 'Une dimension de la guerre d'Algérie: les "regroupements" des populations', in Jauffret and Vaïsse (eds), *Militaires et guérilla dans la guerre d'Algérie*, pp. 327–62; K. Sutton, 'The influence of military policy on Algerian rural settlement', *Geographical Review*, 71: 4 (October 1981), pp. 379–94; also K. Sutton, 'Army administration tensions over Algeria's *Centres de Regroupement*, 1954–1962', *British Journal of Middle Eastern Studies*, 26: 2 (1999), pp. 243–70; and K. Sutton, 'The *Centres de Regroupement*: the French Army's final legacy to Algeria's settlement geography', in A. G. Hargreaves and M. J. Heffernan (eds), *French and Algerian Identities from Colonial Times to the Present* (Lampeter: Edwin Mellen Press, 1993), pp. 163–88.
76. P. Bourdieu, *The Algerians* (Boston: Beacon Press, 1962, preface by Raymond Aron), p. 184; this book is a translation of Bourdieu's *Sociologie de l'Algérie* (Paris: Presses Universitaires de France, 1958).
77. G. Tillion, *L'Algérie en 1957* (Paris: Editions de Minuit, 1957), esp. pp. 68–9.
78. Bourdieu, *The Algerians*, pp. 134–44, 163–88.
79. See *Le Procès des généraux Challe et Zeller. Texte intégrale des débats* (Paris: Nouvelles Editions Latines, 1961), pp. 22–9.
80. See Talbott, *War Without a Name*, pp. 10–36; J. K. Gosnell, *The Politics of Frenchness in Colonial Algeria, 1930–1954*, (Ann Arbor, MI: UMI dissertation services, 1999); B. Stora, *Histoire de l'Algérie coloniale 1830–1954* (Paris: La Découverte, 1991).
81. *Algérie 1954–1962. Arrêt sur images inédites* (Paris: FNACA-GAJE, 1992), p. 12.
82. See photograph 'Le fortin au Bordj', in O. Hamon, 'Chronique du conflit algérien, 1954–1962', *Revue Historique des Armées* (hereafter: *RHA*), 2 (1992), p. 33.
83. See I. Backouche, 'L'Algérie et les actualités cinématographiques Gaumont: analyse et perception d'une crise', *Historiens et Géographes*, 89 (1998), pp. 373–90.
84. See Matéos-Ruiz, *L'Algérie des appelés*, pp. 25–49.
85. Hamon, 'Chronique du conflit Algérien', in *RHA*, 2 (1992), p. 38.
86. P. Dine, *Images of the Algerian War: French Fiction and Film, 1954–1992* (Oxford: Clarendon Press, 1994), p. 132.
87. For a pioneering methodological approach on this issue see, N. Aggoun, 'L'opinion publique algérienne du Chélif algérois à la veille de l'insurrection de 1954 par les sources orales ou la vision des colonisés', in R. Goutalier (ed.), *Mémoires de la colonisation: relations colonisateurs-colonisés* (Paris: L'Harmattan, 1994), pp. 35–47.
88. See the photographs such as 'Femme du Sud (Ouled Nail) à Bou Saada', in Hamon, 'Chronique du conflit algérien', *RHA*, 2 (1992), p. 36.
89. See G. Carreras, *On les appelait les Harkis ...* (Paris: L'Harmattan, 1997); *Algérie 1954–1962*, pp. 165–6; Minella, *Le Soldat méconnu*, pp. 213–17; G. Fleury, *Le Combat des Harkis* (Paris: Editions Les 7 Vents, 1989).
90. M. Challe, *Notre révolte* (Paris: Presses de la Cité, 1974).

91. See J. Phillips, 'Sons of France's forgotten Algerians demand to live in dignity', *The Times*, 13 August 1991, citing a 1964 Algerian government report.
92. See indicative photographs in *RHA* special issue, *Algérie 1954–1962*, 187 (June 1992), pp. 34, 35, 37; *RHA*, 3 (1995), pp. 49, 53, 55, 56; *Algérie 1954–1962. Arrêt sur images inédites* (Paris: FNACA-GAJE, 1992), pp. 57, 98, 170–9 and *passim*; J.-P. Lamy, 'Témoignage: 1959, Opération en Kabylie', in *Hommes de Guerre* (March 1988), pp. 36–8.
93. See the front covers of *Paris-Match*, 361, 10 March 1956; 364, 31 March 1956; 375, 16 June 1956.
94. P. Hovette, *Capitaine en Algérie* (Paris: Presses de la Cité, 1978), p. 12.
95. See, however, D. Amrane, 'Une femme algérienne dans la guerre', in *Nouvelles de la guerre d'Algérie*, pp. 121–7.
96. See V. Ortuno, *Mort pour une chose morte* (Paris: Julliard, 1971).
97. Mattéi, *La guerre des gusses*; D. Zimmermann, *Nouvelles de la zone interdite* (Paris: L'Instant, 1988).
98. G. Périot, *Deuxième classe en Algérie* (Paris: Flammarion, 1962), p. 219.
99. Ibid., pp. 220–2.
100. Vinen, *France, 1934–1970*, p. 171. See also the evocative front cover of *Paris-Match*, 686, 2 June 1962, a photograph of a tearful young family at the rail of their steamship, gazing in trepidation at the looming coastline of France, beneath the caption 'Does France still love us?'
101. J. Kirkup, obituary of Jules Roy, *The Independent* 17 June 2000. Cf. Roy, *La guerre d'Algérie*; also Roy, *Mémoires barbares*.
102. See, however, A. Figueras, *Les pieds-noirs dans le plat* (Paris: Les Presses du Mail, 1962); also Messmer, *Les blancs s'en vont*, pp. 159–69, 177–80; and A. Roche, 'Pieds-noirs: "le retour"', *Modern and Contemporary France*, NS, 2: 2 (1994), pp. 151–64.
103. See, for instance, J. Blanchard, *Le Problème Algérien. Réalités et perspectives* (Paris: Presses Universitaires de France, 1955); Tillion, *L'Algérie en 1957*, pp. 55–9, 71–4, 111–21.
104. See E. Behr, *The Algerian Problem* (London: Hodder & Stoughton and Penguin Books, 1961).
105. See M. Connelly, 'Taking off the Cold War lens: visions of North–South conflict during the Algerian War for independence', *American Historical Review*, 105: 3 (June 2000), pp. 739–69; also I. M. Wall, 'The United States, Algeria and the fall of the Fourth French Republic', *Diplomatic History*, 18: 4 (Fall 1994), pp. 489–511; also I. M. Wall, *France, the United States and the Algerian War* (Berkeley, CA: University of California Press, 2001); M. Thomas, *The French North African Crisis: Colonial Breakdown and Anglo-French Relations, 1945–62* (Basingstoke: Macmillan – now Palgrave Macmillan, 2000), pp. 158–78.
106. For a full examination of British policy on these matters, see Thomas, *The French North African Crisis, passim*.
107. Thomas, 'France Accused', pp. 109–111.
108. Thomas, 'Order before reform' (cited above, n. 49), esp. pp. 207–8, 211–17.
109. See J. Frémeaux, 'La guerre d'Algérie et le Sahara', in Ageron (ed.), *La guerre d'Algérie et les Algériens*, pp. 93–109; Frémeaux, *Le monde arabe et la sécurité de la France depuis 1958* (Paris: Presses Universitaires de France, 1995), pp. 13–15, 24–8, 34–49. Cf. T. Smith, *The French Stake in Algeria, 1945–1962* (Ithaca, NY: Cornell University Press, 1978); also T. Smith, 'The French economic stake in colonial Algeria', *French Historical Studies*, IX: 1 (Spring 1975), pp. 184–9.

110. See Thomas, *The French North African Crisis*, esp. pp. 138–56; and M. Thomas, 'The dilemmas of an ally of France: Britain's policy towards the Algerian rebellion 1954–62', *Journal of Imperial and Commonwealth History*, 23: 1 (January 1995), pp. 129–54.
111. See, however, C.-R. Ageron, 'L'opinion française à travers les sondages' in Rioux, *La Guerre d'Algérie et les Français*, pp. 25–44; J. Talbott, 'French public opinion and the Algerian War: a research note', *French Historical Studies*, IX: 2 (Fall 1975), pp. 354–61.
112. M. Lemalet, *Lettres d'Algérie, 1954–1962. La guerre des appelés. La mémoire d'une génération* (Paris: J.-C. Lattès, 1992).
113. P. Videlier, 'Tardive redécouverte de la guerre d'Algérie', *Le maghreb face à la contestation islamiste. Manière de voir*, 24 (November 1994), pp. 92–4.
114. C. Mauss-Copeaux, *Appelés en Algérie. La parole confisquée* (Paris: Hachette, 1998).
115. The French army, navy and air force archives of the Algerian War have been progressively released since 1992, while foreign ministry documents and many collections of private papers are also becoming steadily more accessible (albeit some still dependent on ministerial *dérogation*). See *Introduction à l'étude des Archives de l'Algérie* (Vincennes: Service Historique de l'Armée de Terre [SHAT], 1992); and J. Nicot, P. Schillinger and C. Obert, *Inventaire des Archives de l'Algérie. Sous-série 1H. Tome II (1945–1967)* (Vincennes: SHAT, 1994). Particularly helpful are the volumes of original documents appearing under the editorship of J.-C. Jauffret: *La Guerre d'Algérie par les Documents. Tome 1. L'Avertissement, 1943–1946* (Vincennes: Publications du SHAT, 1990); *Tôme 2. Les Portes de la Guerre, 1946–1954* (Vincennes: Publications du SHAT, 1998).
116. See G. Malaurie, 'Vietnam et Algérie: de l'imagerie à l'image', *L'Express* (17 April 1997), p. 114, reviewing B. Stora, *Imaginaires de guerre* (Paris: La Découverte, 1997); also S. Hoffmann, 'Algérie et Vietnam', *Le Monde*, 11 May 1990, p. 27.

Part I
Experiences

2

From Indochina to Algeria: Counter-Insurgency Lessons

Alexander J. Zervoudakis[1]

At the end of every war, armies attempt to learn the lessons of that conflict. Quite often there is a period of peace in which these 'reviews' can be conducted and lessons drawn and applied to doctrine organization and equipment. This exercise is carried out by both victor and vanquished, and during the last century it has always been of capital importance for the vanquished who have often followed the Clauswitzian dictum that in war no result is final. In all armies, to varying degrees, the filters of defeat or victory often distort this process. The French armed forces went through this process at the end of the war in Indochina, but unlike other armies, they did not have the time to fully digest or even dissect the Indochina conflict as France went straight from the one conflict to another. Also the very nature of the end of the war in Indochina, and the pivotal role of the defeat at Dien Bien Phu in France's departure from the Far East, distorted every attempt of 'learning the lessons' from that war.

As the war in Indochina ended, two major studies were produced by the Corps Expéditionnaire Française d'Extrême Orient (CEFEO). The first was by Colonel Nemo in January 1955, while the CEFEO was still in Indochina. This study comprised two parts, the first is the *Enseignements des Opérations*[2] and the second, by far the most voluminous, is the *Guerre en Surface au Tonkin de 1946 à 1954.*[3] This second part was produced under Colonel Nemo's auspices and is an all-encompassing study in three parts, with five annexes which cover all arms and types of operations.[4] The other study was produced much later, and the driving force behind it was the then C-in-C and High Commissioner, General Ely. In April 1955, he asked officers who had served in Indochina from 1946 to 1954 to write about the 'enseignements à tirer des méthodes utilise jusqu'ici, tant par l'ennemi que par les force de l'Union françaises'.[5] These reports were the basis of a single document known as *Enseignements de la Guerre d'Indochine*, otherwise known as 'Rapport Ely'.[6] The Rapport Ely and the *Enseignements des Opérations d'Indochine* were both influenced heavily by the shock produced within the High Command by the fall of Dien Bien Phu. Both documents are not thorough historical analyses of the war, but headquarters staff reports produced within a specified timeframe and lacking the luxuries of time and extensive archives usually afforded to historians. The Rapport Ely was translated by the US Department of Defense and was published by RAND in May 1967.[7] Since its declassification, it has been used by US historians to produce distorted images of the war in Indochina.[8] Despite their deficiencies, both reports, particularly the first one which was edited and supervised by Nemo, can provide the historian with a good insight into the 'lessons learned' as seen by the French armed forces in 1954.[9]

In trying to distil the lessons the French armed forces learned in Indochina, I will look briefly into the nature of their opponent and the type of war it fought. Then, before analysing the lessons at the strategic, operational and tactical level, I will examine an 'element' which can be found at the heart of every war and every conflict: intelligence. In the Rapport Ely, intelligence can be found under 'Essential Elements' (Part 2, Section 4) as a clearly identifiable 'element', if not the most important element, occupying over two-thirds of this section. Similarly 'la primauté du renseignement' permeates throughout the Nemo Report.

The nature of the war and the Vietminh

The war in Indochina can be divided into two periods. The first period is from 1945 to 1949, and is in reality a colonial war during which the French tried to reimpose their sovereignty after the Japanese occupation. The signing of the Paris Accords on 8 March 1949, giving independence to Vietnam, marks the end of the colonial war.[10] From mid-1949 to 1955, the war changes to an anti-communist war where, on the one hand, there were three independent Indochinese states of Vietnam, Laos and Cambodia supported by France, and on the other, the Vietminh and its communist allies, the Soviet Union and the PRC (China). As Jean Pouget put it in his book *Le Manifeste du Camp No. 1*: '... du rideau de bambou au rideau de fer, c'était le monde communiste, un empire de 15,000 km. Une masse d'un millard d'hommes.'[11] France was planning to stay in Indochina until the three Indochinese states were capable of defending themselves and also to protect French economic, diplomatic and cultural interests in the Far East.

From 1950 onwards, the French High Command knew that France's interests lay primarily in Europe and North Africa and that the defence of Indochina was only a secondary consideration for policy-makers in Paris. By 1950, France was fighting not a colonial war but a war where it was defending the independent states of Vietnam, Laos and Cambodia from an increasingly powerful communist insurgent army: the Vietminh. General de Lattre was the first but not the last to emphasize this point publicly, when he declared in front of a Vietnamese audience that 'Cette guerre est la vôtre, elle ne concerne plus la France que dans la limité de ses promesses envers le Vietnam'.[12] These were not idle words but the reality, especially if one sees that Vietnam was progressively being run by the Vietnamese government, starting from the southern end of the country, and both Laos and Cambodia were conducting their business often independently of France. Quite often this independence could create friction in the conduct of the war against the Vietminh.

From 1950 onwards, in the north of Indochina, there was also a switch from a guerrilla war to a total conventional war between what was in effect two states: the Etat du Vietnam and the Vietminh. In this total war, the population and the resources of each side were the objectives. The population was at the same time the 'friend' and the 'enemy'. Controlling the population and the resources was to be vital to the outcome of the war.

The opponent of the Franco-Vietnamese forces, the Vietminh, was a communist army, supplied mainly by Communist China (PRC) and supported by its own resources and the economy of the Vietminh country (Pays Viet). After its near annihilation in 1947, the Vietminh organized itself so as to win a conventional war. Colonel Ly Ban, one of the leading Vietminh figures, said during 1949 that: 'L'histoire de la guerre mondiale prouve que la guérrilla ne peut resoudre une guerre; c'est à la guerre mobile et aux batailles rangées qu'en revient l'honneur'.[13] There was no mystery or oriental wizardry in the tactics or operational strategy followed by the Vietminh. The Vietminh had a western ideology, Communism, which they adapted to incorporate Vietnamese nationalism. Other communist movements around the world did exactly the same, moulding a basic communist ideology to fit the national culture. A good example of this was the Greek Communist Party that tried by force to get to power from 1944 to 1949. The Vietminh High Command and officer corps were trained along western lines, adapting for their regular forces operational and tactical ideals taught to some of them at Wang Pao Military Academy in China.[14] Clausewitz was, for example, standard reading for officers.[15]

As the Vietminh forces developed after 1949, they were divided into the regular army (Ve Quoc Doan), the regional forces (Bo Doi Dia Phuong) and the popular or guerrilla forces (Dan Quan and Du Kich). Most of these units were equipped increasingly after 1949 with modern weapons. The Vietminh controlled a land mass that was in effect the de facto Vietminh country (Pays Viet). The Pays Viet Minh had a powerful and unassailable life support system and sanctuary: the Peoples' Republic of China. The weak points of the Pays Viet Minh were, firstly, the lines of communication connecting its two distinct parts: the Viet Bac and the Thanh Hoa. Secondly, it was the constant need for army recruits and food, in other words men and rice. It was, nonetheless, an impressive politico-military machine which had one objective: to capture power and impose its system on the country and society. Its objective never changed, and its strategy was equally unchanged and largely unchangeable. As of 1950, it also became the 'motor of the war', in other words having the strategic initiative most of the time. The Algerian insurgents never had all that. One can argue over ideology, sanctuaries and objectives, but they never had a fully armed, heavily equipped force like the Vietminh, nor was there ever a FLN/ALN country with resources and lines of communication to protect.

Intelligence

Intelligence is one of the forgotten successes of the French armed forces during this conflict.[16] Let us first clarify what intelligence is and is not. The report of a spy, the high resolution photograph taken by an air reconnaissance aircraft, the report of a patrol, the radio intercept, the captured document and the interrogation of a prisoner or of a defector are only pieces of information. Intelligence is the product resulting from the processing of all this information by military analysts. The intelligence officer works in many respects like a historian searching for different types of documentary evidence, then collating it and analysing it. Experience from at least the turn of the century in countless conflicts has taught us that it is only all-sources intelligence that can be accurate, in other words intelligence based on different types of information. The intelligence analysts produce the intelligence and are not the collectors of the information. The CEFEO developed at all levels a sophisticated intelligence apparatus that was able to feed the C-in-C and his commanders with good timely and accurate intelligence on the Vietminh, its organization, army and intentions.[17] The analytical effort of the CEFEO was as important as the collection agencies it had operating in the field. The Vietminh's bureaucratic tendencies and use of radio communications coupled with good French intelligence gathering provided an important part of the accurate information the 2 Bureau EMIFT could draw upon for its analysis. POWs, defectors and refugees from the Vietminh-controlled areas, as well as air reconnaissance both visual and photographic, added to the information the CEFEO's intelligence organizations, at the different levels, drew upon to produce their often accurate analysis. The strategic and operational intentions of the Vietminh were, as of 1949, accurately forecasted by the CEFEO's intelligence. CEFEO defeats were often results of either misuse of intelligence or complete disregard of accurate intelligence predictions and indications. What is known in French historiography as the 'RC4 disaster' in September/October 1950 is a good example of this. Before and during the autumn of 1950 intelligence was always available to the C-in-C and the local commanders.[18] However, they and their supporting operations staffs decided to carry out an operation based not on the known facts and intelligence reports about the Vietminh, but on their own highly subjective and inaccurate views about Vietminh capabilities. Deep and personal differences and disagreements as to future operations, and sheer incompetence by the frontier commanding officer, created the disaster.[19] Similarly Dien Bien Phu, despite the popularly held belief, was not an intelligence failure. The C-in-C, General Navarre, had planned the occupation of Dien Bien Phu based on an accurate picture of the Vietminh's reactions and plans for 1954. The Vietminh's plans changed when the strategic pictured was radically altered by a unilateral action taken by the French government. This change was never discussed or communicated to the C-in-C on the ground in advance and when it happened, Navarre was left to sort out a situation that was totally different from the one he had planned.[20]

The intelligence Navarre was receiving from his 2 Bureau in no way could have predicted the French government's actions. His 2 Bureau gave him good analysis and cogent arguments as to why Dien Bien Phu should be captured in the first place. The importance of Dien Bien Phu for Vietminh communications and its rice production[21] made the Dien Bien Phu cell an important objective for both sides, as Dien Bien Phu was identified as the last possible place Laos could be defended from in the event of a Vietminh offensive coming from the east.[22]

During the battle, a series of operational and tactical mistakes were made as a result of erosion in confidence, just before the start of the battle and due to the operational commander, General Cogny.[23] CEFEO intelligence provided extremely accurate predictions of Vietminh intentions throughout the battle. The 2 Bureau also provided an accurate picture of the increasing Vietminh capability around Dien Bien Phu. So, Dien Bien Phu was not an intelligence failure, but rather a typical example of what happens when the political leadership takes decisions in wartime without consulting or at least warning in advance the military commander.

During the period 1951–4 the CEFEO's intelligence capability was the vital ingredient behind some spectacular successes, such as the defeat of the Dong Trieu Vietminh offensive (Hoang Hoa Tham) in March–April 1951, the defence of Nghia Lo in October 1951, the attrition battles around Hoa Binh from December 1951 to February 1952 and also the successful defence of Na San in 1952–3. All these were successes based on all-sources intelligence. When parts of the CEFEO intelligence apparatus started relying on single-source intelligence then setbacks occurred like the loss of Nghia Lo and the eastern Thai country in the autumn of 1952.

With few resources – the French had to rely on force multipliers – intelligence was probably the most important as it provided knowledge of the Vietminh's world and intentions. Despite severe difficulties, the French intelligence apparatus in Indochina was able to provide most of this knowledge. Like other intelligence apparatus set up by other countries in other conflicts, the French faced its own internal crises, conflicts of interests, even turf fights over collection assets and information collected. It also had its fair share of single-source mistaken assessments. Some accuse it of lacking in good HUMINT (human intelligence) on the Vietminh and China (although one should also ask whether any country at that time had good intelligence on China). Good HUMINT on a close-knit communist regime is also difficult to collect. Whatever the failing, France had to build its collection networks and organizations from scratch in 1945 after Liberation. In the time and with the resources available France did build an effective collection organization in Indochina whatever its organizational and operational difficulties. But of course these collection sources would have gone to waste unless there was a good analytical community at all levels to analyse them. This all-sources analysis capability existed in Indochina and the analysis produced was often correct and showed the excellent capabilities of the 2 Bureau at the strategic, operational and even tactical level.

Strategic level

As already stated, the Vietminh had a single objective, a clear unbending line to follow: win the war at all costs, take power and install the Vietminh as the sole government in Vietnam. The CEFEO's objective, meanwhile, kept changing. It had started by being a restoration of French sovereignty, but it turned into giving autonomy, creating a Union Française and then the granting of some independence, which then transmuted into the granting of full independence. There was not such a clear line. To plan military operations a commander-in-chief needs to know the wider objectives at the strategic level. The strategic level in any democratic country was and still is decided by the government. In other words, there was a need for a policy towards Indochina which would define the objectives so that the commander-in-chief could prepare his operational strategy and task his forces. Between 1946 and 1954, there were as many policies about Indochina formulated in France as there were governments in Paris. This state of affairs could lead to only one outcome, failure.[24] Colonel Nemo commented bluntly in his report about the lack of any firm objectives from the French government.

> Une politique ne se fait pas au jour le jour ... La guerre d'Indochine a prouvé la nocivité du système qui consiste à n'avoir aucune idée politique ferme, sur de longues années. Son résultat actuel est le triomphe d'une volonté simple et continue sur des indécisions persistantes; c'est une lesson essentiel de retenir.[25]

Not only was there no central political direction, but at the theatre level there was no unity of command. During the war in Indochina there was only one commander-in-chief who was at the same time high commissioner and, therefore, responsible for political affairs, General de Lattre during December 1950 to December 1951. From the very beginning of the conflict, the posts of commander-in-chief and high commissioner were separate, producing confusion and at time conflict between the two, as was the case between General Leclerc and Admiral d'Argenlieu, Generals Blaizot and Bollaert, and Generals Carpentier and Pignon. In the last two years of the war, the lack of clear policy objectives or unity of command resulted in a world of unreal expectations which brought about the tragic end of French influence and presence in the Far East.

When, in May 1953, General Navarre was nominated Commander-in-Chief (C-in-C) of the CEFEO, he was told by René Mayer that the government was searching for a 'sortie honorable',[26] without specifying what kind of honourable exit this was to be. This was his only directive. He could decide on operations, but the direction of the war was not within his grasp.[27] Unlike all other C-in-Cs during the conflict, he was given the luxury of one month to prepare an overall plan.[28] He presented his plan to the Comité de Defense Nationale at the Elysée on 24 July 1953 and was then asked to leave the room, after being told by Vincent Auriol that: 'Le government vous fera connaître sa décision'.[29]

General Navarre received an answer four months later on 21 November 1953.[30] The plan was already two and a half months old and, because in war the enemy does not wait for you to decide on a plan, operations had already begun. Navarre's opponent, General Giap,[31] was not only the C-in-C but also presided over the politburo committee responsible for military matters and was a member of the inner circle that decided on every aspect of the Vietminh's world. The Vietminh, in fact, took some time to reach a decision, but when that decision was made, it adhered to it. Equally, the C-in-C was central to the decision-making apparatus and never became an outsider. In the Vietminh, political and military powers were blended into one. For the CEFEO at the strategic level, the most important lesson of the war was unity of command and clear objectives. 'Marcher droit vers un but clair', Lyautey used to say. This was, however, an impossible task in the unstable and corrupt system of the Fourth Republic in France.

Operational level

At the operational level, the CEFEO was reduced to fighting a war 'avec des ficelles' because of the lack of strategic direction. For the Vietminh, the logistics were virtually next door in China. For the CEFEO, the logistics stretched from France, and France was in a 'peace mode'. Worse still, because of reconstruction in the Metropole and the 'Europe first' policy, troops in Indochina, both CEFEO and Vietnamese, were never properly equipped for the war they were fighting. Already by mid-1951 and especially so by 1952, certain regular Vietminh units like the 308th Vietminh Division were better equipped in certain types of weapons than the CEFEO. A good example of this can be found, in June 1951, during the Quang

Trung offensive on the Day River: CEFEO units were amazed to find that Vietminh units of the 308th Division were equipped with 57 mm recoilless guns, which the CEFEO themselves lacked. The 7BPC commented bitterly about this in one of its morale reports.[32]

The US could not, despite what American historians sometimes claim, provide an immediate cascade of cash and weapons. It was not only the 'red tape' imposed by US legislation and diplomacy, but constant delays were also caused by the effects of the Korean war on a US not prepared for such a conflict.[33] A good example of this is the supply of aircraft to the CEFEO. B-26 light bombers were also needed in Korea, and US needs took precedence. During the summer of 1951, 25 per cent of the Bearcats sent to Indochina were grounded due to a lack of maintenance manuals.[34] CEFEO units in 1951 and 1952 did not always have good waterproofs or water-resistant radio sets. Newly created Vietnamese units, not yet fully operational, were sometimes equipped with such items, much to the annoyance of those units in the thick of the fighting.[35] The CEFEO was undoubtedly better equipped in certain types of equipment but was never a uniformly equipped force. Units often had a mixture of American, French, British and even German equipment, uniforms and weaponry, which of course did not improve the efficiency of the logistics support.

Apart from the difficulties with logistics, there was another important operational consideration, pacification. In a war where the population was the objective, both enemy and friend, Franco-Vietnamese forces needed political, economic and military weapons. In other words, they needed a pacification strategy. When, at the highest level, there was no strategy and no clear objective, it was very difficult to formulate a clear pacification strategy, because the political leg of pacification was missing. Despite this serious handicap, the CEFEO was able, by 1952, to find a successful key so as to conduct the pacification battle. This key was one of the unsung successes of the war on the CEFEO side, and this was the concept of GAMO – Groupement Administrative Mobiles Operationnel.

Without much central planning and on a trial and error basis, the CEFEO, by 1951, tried to pacify the Tonkin using three main procedures. Firstly, there was the 'carroyage' or quadrillage system, used by the Romans and by the French empire builders. This divided an area according to lines of communication and was reinforced by posts at major crossroads. It facilitated movements of troops into the defined area.[36] Secondly, there was the system of mobile reserves introduced by the colonial camel corps (the meharistes) centred at strategic locations and patrolling the territory either on specific search missions against the rebels or in order to show its presence.[37] Thirdly, under the pressure of the Vietminh's subversion units (Dich Van) and because of the constant shortage of manpower, self-defence militia were created for each village.[38]

All these tactics, either by themselves or in combination, were badly executed, and there was no uniformity or continuity. Road security, critical to the movement of troops, drained resources. Units stayed with the roads, leaving the surrounding areas unmolested. This meant that the road itself became insecure. The road, which was the most important tactical weapon in the quadrillage system, was an artery, and if this was not secured, the surrounding area it was supposed to service and secure ended up suffocating. Posts, the centrepiece of Franco-Vietnamese presence in the Tonkin, were also badly defended and often were blind to what was going on around them. Posts were supposed to defend roads, communities and the countryside. But the posts were badly defended against the modern equipment in Vietminh possession, and the post troops were too few or too lightly equipped to face the Vietminh in close engagements. These serious deficiencies and the lack of training meant that posts were lonely outposts in a hostile alien land ruled by the Vietminh politico-military structure. Patrols could not inhibit the Vietminh control of the population during either the day or the night, particularly the latter. The population was, thus, progressively left to the Vietminh. What the CEFEO was not securing until 1951 was the integrity of an area defence that would require roads, fields and villages to be under secure control. A total area defence would have convinced the local population to start providing information about the Vietminh, plus manpower for guard duties. During 1951, widescale pacification operations on the Tonkin Delta halted the deterioration of the security situation in the Delta by destroying regional and regular Vietminh units during operations such as 'Meduse', 'Reptile', 'Citron' and 'Mandarine'.[39] But these operations did not uproot the Vietminh infrastructure in the villages and the countryside. That infrastructure helped the reinfiltration of the Vietminh regular and regional units back into areas that were supposed to have been cleared during the 1951 operations.[40]

What was required to achieve a lasting pacification was to weed out the Vietminh infrastructure, protect the population so as to be able to have constant information on the Vietminh and establish a protected and well-equipped Vietnamese administration – in other words, a new infrastructure to replace that of the old colonial regime and that of the Vietminh. In 1952, General de Linares and his headquarters staff came up with the concept of the GAMO. After the end of the battle of attrition along the RC6 and Hoa Binh, Generals Salan and de Linares issued the 'Instruction on Pacification' on 11 March 1952.[41]

The politco-military plan for the Delta for the rest of 1952 was based on three points: firstly, to free the Delta from the infiltrated regular Viet Minh units, which was to be the purpose of the large-scale operations in 1951; secondly, to secure the blockade both from and to the 'Vietminh country', which was to be undertaken by sector units; thirdly, to undertake progressively the internal pacification by destroying the Vietminh infrastructure and establish a protected Vietnamese administration.[42] The instruction recognized that the third stage was a delicate and difficult one, as the administration was vulnerable during its early stages to the remains of the Vietminh infrastructure. In order to protect the population and secure the smooth functioning of the Vietnamese administration, the GAMO was introduced as the new tool of pacification.[43] Their task was to re-establish communal and provincial administration, provide social and medical aid to the rural population, while continually seeking out and destroying the Vietminh infrastructure. The GAMO personnel were all Vietnamese and under the authority of the province chief where the operations were taking place. (After 1950, provincial chiefs were always Vietnamese.) The GAMO moved alongside the units of the Mobile Groups undertaking the traditional role of pacification by chasing the Vietminh organized armed presence, while also protecting the GAMO from the return of regional Vietminh units. Operating alongside the regular troops, the GAMO provided them with vital assistance in identifying Vietminh cadres, providing support and advice to the unit's intelligence officers. Prisoners were screened exclusively by the GAMO's intelligence officers and the GAMO were the sole advisers of the officer commanding the operation on all matters relating to the population. The GAMO would, after the initial phase of the pacification operation, get on with creating an administration to provide social and medical aid, the latter being a function that the Vietminh could not provide. The administration would also provide IDs, a great benefit to any counter-insurgency effort, would undertake a census of the population, and would provide self-defence militias without any Vietminh influence. The GAMO also had their own protection force, the Bao Chinh Doan, which was also a completely indigenous force but lightly armed.[44]

Operation 'Mercure'[45] (25 March–12 April 1952) was the first use of the GAMO, but the experiment was not a total success as the GAMO units were taken out of the area too soon. It had been decided that the GAMO should be used in the corridor between Hai Phong and Hanoi, and expand from there to the rest of the Delta. Starting with operations 'Polo', 'Porto' and 'Turco'[46] in April 1952, the system of the GAMO came into its own. Operations 'Bolero' 1 and 2[47] in July and August 1952 were planned so as to support the GAMO in pacifying the area between Dong Trieu and Haiduong. Colonel Dulac, who had helped plan the 'Bolero' operations, described in his biography *Nos Guerre Perdues* and also in his reports at the time that the area was deserted when the troops moved in. As the work of the GAMO increased and bore fruit, the region became safe. It was slow and unspectacular work, but this is the nature of pacification. Dulac wrote in his report: 'It works, but no hurry.'[48] His fear was, firstly, that the protective screen of regular units would be taken away, and, secondly, that the GAMO itself would be moved before full normality returned to a region and the civil administration had taken root.

The GAMO did have their problems often associated with lack of resources. Another problem that did develop as time passed was the influence different Vietnamese political parties tried to gain in the GAMO by having their own members appointed in their ranks. But this was not a major problem and in a way proved beneficial as they were fiercely anti-Vietminh. By the beginning of 1953 the CEFEO had finalized its ideas on pacification. Pacification was to be based on four principles: firstly, military operations were not the objective of pacification but a tool; secondly, pacification was to be a Vietnamese task; thirdly, the principal objective was the population; and fourthly the planning for the pacification campaign was a combined Franco-Vietnamese task.[49]

In a pacification campaign there were to be three phases. Phase one was the military phase whose objective was the destruction of the Vietminh bases and units. Phase two was the politico-military phase with the objective to destroy the Vietminh infrastructure, prevent Vietminh elements from returning and build up the administration. This was the phase for the GAMO action supported by sector units and provincial police and Sureté (Security Service). Phase three was to be executed by the Vietnamese administration. It was at phase three that self-defence militias were to be introduced as a preventative measure and not as a solution, before Vietminh infrastructure and units were eradicated.

The tools necessary for these phases to be successful were: a good and competent Vietnamese administration; well trained and equipped GAMOs; good intelligence; sufficient roads and airfields; self-defence militias; light battalions specialized in pacification and finally, of course, agrarian reform (property and irrigation).

The most original of these tools was the GAMO. Without these two ingredients the GAMO could only be effective for a very short time. To achieve lasting pacification, what was also needed was time and protection by the CEFEO units. Without these ingredients, the efficacy of pacification would be short-lived. However, time and manpower were in short supply as far as the CEFEO in the 1950s was concerned.[50]

Tactical level

There are two tactical lessons that are common to both the Nemo and Ely reports and were very relevant to the new conflict which was about to start. Firstly, in both reports there was a strong emphasis on the quality required for territorial/sector units.[51] In Indochina, the best units were often considered to be those belonging to the Mobile Groups and the Intervention units of the General Reserve. This meant that sector units were not the best available. But a bad or mediocre sector unit would only damage pacification, its main duty, by its very mediocrity. Similarly, intervention units would often upset longstanding and painstaking pacification work by their clumsy and heavy-handed approaches.

Secondly, the CEFEO used extensively the method of vertical envelopment, that is sending troops into battle by parachute.[52] The use of paratroopers, first employed in the Second World War, was extensively used by the French in Indochina. The use of airborne forces alleviated the problem of providing quick reinforcements, and it allowed for the movement of troops to inaccessible parts of Indochina. The Vietminh sometimes took between 15 days and a month to move its divisions into position for an offensive. After 1950, the CEFEO could commit units from the General Reserve within 48 hours in some of the most inaccessible areas, such as Nghia Lo and Gia Hoi in 1951, where road communications with the Tonkin Delta were no longer available.

It was during their airmobile operations that CEFEO para officers increasingly advocated the use of the helicopter.[53] At this point, we must give credit where it is due. To a large extent, the CEFEO pioneered the use of helicopters for airmobile and search-and-rescue operations in Indochina. The problem was that the funds for large purchases of helicopters were very difficult to garner, and the row between the air force and the army as to who was to operate them effectively prevented the large-scale use of helicopters in Indochina. However, the doctrinal and operational foundation for their use was established during this conflict. The helicopter would increase the mobility of troops and cut down on the expense and wastage of parachuting units. Troops would also enter into battle without the nerve-wracking experience of a parachute drop. However, these ideas were implemented in Algeria, where the right equipment existed in large numbers, and airmobile operations became routine.

Army morale after Indochina

Finally, let us briefly deal with the morale of the officers and men of the CEFEO leaving Indochina. Most of them were destined to go and fight another war, this time in Algeria. Comments here focus on the officers and NCOs, since it was they who led the French armed forces in Algeria over the next eight years. It is very interesting that in both of the Enseignements documents (Nemo and Ely), there is no specific mention of morale as it applied to the officers and men of the CEFEO. This is surprising, given the fact that it was not unusual for someone to have done a tour in each of the two periods described at the beginning of the chapter.

Most of the personnel were discovering a new, largely unspoiled country and almost all of them fell in love with Indochina, and especially Vietnam, because this was the main theatre of operations. They loved the people, found the customs and cultures fascinating. They caught what became known as the 'mal jaune'. For a large percentage of the officers and NCOs in Indochina, their rank was well below the duties and responsibilities they had to bear.[54] All had seen the disaster in 1940 suffered under the German occupation and were elated by being one of the winners when the war ended in Europe. They were arriving in Indochina, confident of victory, and eager to avoid the type of humiliation they had suffered in 1940–4. The Resistance in France had also made many in the military more atuned to politics, and were, therefore, more sensitive to the political dimension of this conflict and to their responsibilities vis-à-vis the population they were going to protect from the Vietminh.

When asked to occupy a village by the Chinese border and raise a local militia, Helier de St Marc asked for the political dimension of this particular task, so that this could be conveyed to the local population to help gain their trust. His CO dismissed these concerns, asking St Marc instead: 'if Napoleon had ever explained the political dimension to his cavalry before they charged?'[55] St Marc, like all his colleagues who took part in pacification or commanded auxiliary, partisan or regular Vietnamese troops, gave promises to his men and, most importantly, to their families, and to the populations they were going to protect. It was because of these promises that thousands of Vietnamese, Thais and other ethnic groups joined the fight against the Vietminh.

The indigenous population – and by this I mean the Vietnamese – often commented to CEFEO troops how they provided information on the Vietminh to the CEFEO in 1945–6, but how the CEFEO did not stay to protect them from the Vietminh who came looking for revenge. They were not prepared to renew the experience. The CEFEO had to decide if they were going to be in a position to protect the population who supported the Vietnamese state in the long term. Because of that, many French officers and NCOs gave sincere promises, based on the promises of the French political leadership. Then in 1950 and in 1954, they were told to betray these promises. In a total war where the population was your target, your enemy and your ally, withdrawal from an area was not a mechanical move done in a Staff College war game, but a move that would destroy lives and villages and undermine and discredit the honour and trustworthiness of the armed forces who had the task of protecting the population.

The orders to evacuate and leave behind the population were always not only difficult to execute but traumatic for those who had to action them. St Marc was one of those officers who had to carry out such orders. In February 1950, he had to evacuate Ta Lung, taking only his legionnaires and the 'partisans' with their families. The local inhabitants and the militias were to be left behind. St Marc stayed with the rear-guard, and he was therefore to witness the panic and flight of the local populace.

> C'est la que j'ai vu ceux je n'avais pas voulu voir, auxquels je n'avais pas voulu penser. Les habitants des villages environnants, prévenus par la rumeur, accouraient pour partir avec nous. Ils avaient accepté notre protection. Certains avaient servi de relais. Ils savaient que, sans nous, la mort était promise. Nous ne pouvions pas les embarquer, faute de place,

> et les ordres étaient formels: seuls les partisans pouvaient nous accompagner. Les images de cet instant-la sont restées gravées dans ma mémoire comme si elles avaient été découpées au fer, comme un remords qui ne s'attenuera jamais. Des hommes et des femmes qui m'avaient fait confiance, que j'avais entraînés a notre suite et que s'accrochaient aux ridelles recevaient des coups de crosse jusqu'à tomber dans la poussière. Certains criaient, suppliaient. D'autres nous regardaient, simplement, et leur incompréhension rendait notre trahison plus effroyable encore.[56]

Those who lived through such traumatic events promised themselves never again to betray those they had promised to protect. It was sentiments such as these that would lead to the radicalization of the armed forces in Algeria and to eventual revolt when faced with similar decisions at the end of the 1950s and in the early 1960s.[57] St Marc remembers that when General Challe invited him to join the putsch of 1961, his choice was influenced by his 'Vietnamese past'.

> Pendant que le General Challe me parlait, je revoyais un poste de bambou en Haute Région le jour de 1948 où j'avais accepté de former des partisans à Talung. J'ai senti de nouveau le souffle de la honte ... Un homme qui trahit sa parole sans pouvoir faire autrement est un vaincu. Un homme qui trahit d'autres hommes en toute conscience est un criminal.[58]

There were also many officers and NCOs who went through a traumatic captivity at the hands of the Vietminh. During the whole conflict, the Vietminh took 39,888 prisoners, 29,954 of whom were never returned.[59] Vietminh POW camps had no barbed wire, only the jungle and hunger to keep the inmates in. In these camps, the Vietminh used Chinese brainwashing methods, attempting to turn the POWs into good 'fighters of peace' and, therefore, useful tools for Vietminh and communist propaganda. The main tools of leverage were food and hunger. The Vietminh hoped to achieve their aims through the prisoner's stomach and his instinct for survival. The mortality rate in Vietminh camps was between 65 and 72 per cent, depending on the period and category of prisoner. A comparison with POWs in the Second World War shows the enormity of the slaughter. The mortality rate among French POWs in German camps between 1940 and 1945 was only 2 per cent, that of Soviet prisoners in Germany 57 per cent; and among German POWs in Russia 37 per cent.[60]

The inhuman conditions and the constant attempts at brainwashing made those returning to France in 1954 willing to fight to the last in order to safeguard French soil and culture against hostile forces. Some of the best officers and NCOs in Algeria were men who had witnessed the full horror of the Vietminh prison regime, people such as Pouget, Graziani, Planet,

Tournet and Bizard. All those who fought in Indochina felt when they left it in 1954–5 that they had fought for justice and honour – the honour of France's promises vis-à-vis the three Indochina states. 'Je me suis battus', said Jean Pouget, 'pour quelque chose de plus précieux, une petite flame fragile survivant par miracle au vent de l'histoire au revolutions de notre siècle, que j'avais cru voir briller au bout du monde: une façon de vivre libre'.[61] In their hearts, they were feeling like Alexandre de Rhodes who, when he left Indochina in 1954, wrote: 'je quitte de corps la Cochinchine mais certes non pas de coeur aussi peu que le Tonkin. A la verité il est entier en tous les deux et je ne crois pas qu'il puisse jamais en sortir'.

Troopships returning from Indochina in 1954 often stopped at Algiers. In many of these ships, ex-prisoners of war were returning after four years of captivity. Three ex-POWs arrived in Algiers in the late autumn of 1954. Their troopship stopped for 24 hours. At night, during the curfew, they had permission to wander into the city. Alain Bizard, Jacques Planet and Jean Pouget saw the barbed wire in the streets, the public building protected by sandbagged machine-gun posts, the CRS in helmets and the Tirailleurs standing guard at checkpoints. They looked at each other, and even if they remained quiet, they all had the same thought. A new war had started on French soil. This war they could win; they had the expertise, the know-how and the will to win.[62]

Notes

1. The views expressed in this chapter are those of the author based on his personal research and do not represent current or past policy of Her Majesty's Government.
2. SHAT 10H985.
3. SHAT 10H2509.
4. SHAT 10H2509, *'La Guerre de Surface de 1946 à 1954' Annexe 1: Les Armes dans la Guerre de surface. Annexe II Cinq Types d'Opération.*
5. Inventaire des Archives de l'Indochine, Sous Série 10H (1867–1956) (SHAT, 1990), Vol. 1, p. 261.
6. SHAT 10H983.
7. Rand Memorandum, RM–5271-PR, 'A translation from the French: lessons of the war in Indochina, Vol. 2'.
8. One recent case of this is the distorted image of the Indochina war presented by Douglas Porch in *The French Secret Services* (Straus & Giraux, 1995). See chapters 12–14.
9. The air force also produced a document called *Synthèse sur l'Emploi des Forces Aériennes en Extrême-Orient, 1946–54,* and this offered a valuable air force perspective on the war.
10. Much ink has been wasted in discussing and often ridiculing the independence given because it was, to a certain extent, limited, and was to become complete only by stages. Looking back at the era of decolonization, the author believes that stages and progressive independence was the only responsible way for France, or even Britain, to proceed.

11. J. Pouget, *Le Manifeste du Camp No. 1* (Fayard, 1969), p. 11.
12. Maréchal J. de Lattre, *La ferver et le Sacrifice* (Plon, 1988), p. 286.
13. Notes d'Information sur les Forces Rebelles: No. 1 Organisation des Forces Armées Rebelles, 25 Sept. 1951, EMIFT 2 Bureau, Section Indochine, p. 8. The need for a conventional army and the fact that only a conventional total war will bring victory is very strongly reflected in Truong Chinh's *The Resistance Will Win*, written in September 1947 (Editions de Langues Etrangères, 1977).
14. *Biographies des Principaux Chefs Militaires du Viet Minh*, June 1954, EMIFT 2 Bureau.
15. Colonel Bui Tin of the 304th Division Training Cadre has testified: interview with the author, Paris, May 1994.
16. For a more detailed examination see 'Nihil mirare, nihil contemptare, omnia intelligere: Franco-Vietnamese intelligence in Indochina, 1950–1954' by Alexander Zervoudakis, in *Knowing Your Friends*, Martin Alexander (ed.), and 'Le renseignement aérien en Indochine' by Alexander J. Zervoudakis, in *Regards sur l'Aviation Militaire Française en Indochine 1940–1954* (SHAT, 1999).
17. See *Knowing your Friends*, pp. 200–4.
18. See, for example: 'Fiche au sujet de la menace Vietminh sur la RC4' (8 Sept. 50) SHAT 10H2517. Another good example is 7018/ZOT/2B. 'Situation Vietminh', 23–30 Sept. 50, (1 Oct. 50) SHAT 10H1142.
19. A. Zervoudakis 'Franco-Vietnamese Intelligence', in *Knowing Your Friends*, pp. 210–14.
20. Ibid., pp. 214–17.
21. Porch's idea of opium being the reason for the battle of Dien Bien Phu is easily countered by these facts. Dien Bien Phu, along with Nghia Lo, was an important valley, being the only substantial rice-producing area in the whole of the Thai country, i.e. north-west Tonkin. The locally produced opium was one of the few products of the Thai country used before 1950 by the Vietminh as a bartering tool to purchase weapons, but it was by no means the chief reason for Vietminh interest in the area. Elements of the GCMA and the leader of the Thais, Deo Van Long, were involved in opium transactions, but too much mythology is associated with the affair, which is only good for Hollywood-style conspiracy theories.
22. See, for example, SHAT 10H982, Note for C-in-C. Letourneau, 27 Oct. 1952.
23. If this sounds a little strong, one only needs to read the devastating recommendations for the further career employment of General Cogny by the Catroux Commission of Enquiry on the battle of Dien Bien Phu (Annex A, *Rapport Catroux*, full copy of the report to be found in *Histoire de la IV République* by Georgette Elgey (Fayard, 1993), Vol. II, pp. 641–722).
24. The extraordinary state of affairs is graphically described in the three-volume *Histoire de la IV République* by Georgette Elgey. For an Anglo-Saxon view, see Philip M. Williams, *Crisis and Compromise* (Longmans, 1964) and *Plots and Scandals in Post War France* (New York: Cambridge University Press, 1970).
25. 10H985, 'Enseignements Nemo', p. 1415.
26. General Yves Gras, *Histoire de la Guerre d'Indochine* (Denoël, 1992), p. 511. 'Rapport concernant la conduite des opérations en Indochine sous la direction du Général Navarre' (Rapport Catroux), Part 1, p. 4.
27. J. Pouget, 'Dien Bien Phu ... et si nous avions gague cette bataille', p. 4.
28. 'Rapport Catroux', Part 1, pp. 5–7; P. Rocolle, *Pourquoi Dien Bien Phu* (Flammarion, 1968), pp. 51–2, 109–11; J. Pouget, *Nous étions à Dien Bien Phu* (Presses de la Cité, 1964), pp. 45–66; Y. Gras, *Histoire de la Guerre*, pp. 511–14.

29. J. Pouget, 'Dien Bien Phu ...', p. 5.
30. Y. Gras, *Histoire de la Guerre*, p. 514; J. Pouget, *Nous étions à Dien Bien Phu*, pp. 123–4; 'Rapport Catroux', Part 1, p. 11.
31. It is important to remember that when we talk about 'Giap' it is not always a reference to the individual, but to the whole of the inner circle of the Vietminh's leadership.
32. Y. Gras, *Histoire de la Guerre*, p. 408. During the battles in the Dong Trieu (April 1951), the 7BPC commented on the fact that the Vietminh had 'recoilless guns before CEFEO units': SHAT 10H380, 'Rapport sur Moral 7BPC', 20 June 1951.
33. A. Zervoudakis, 'De Lattre et les Américains en Indochine en 1951: l'aspet militaire', in *Jean de Lattre et les Americains, 1943–1953* (Conference, Paris, 26–27 March 1994); R. Weigley, *The American Way of War* (Indiana University Press, 1977), pp. 382–98.
34. SHAT C1046. 'Compte Rendu Mensuel d'Opérations au Tonkin pour le mois de Juillet, 1951'; A. Zervoudakis, 'L'emploi de l'Armée de Air en Indochina, 1951–1952', *Revue Historique des Armées*, 1 (1992).
35. SHAT 10H380, 'Rapport sur le Moral 8 BPC', 16 Dec. 1951.
36. SHAT 10H2519, 'Etude relative à la Pacification dans le Delta au debut de 1952', Hanoi 23 Feb. 1952; Rapport Ely, Chapter V; Nemo Report, pp. 77–80.
37. Ibid.
38. Ibid.; SHAT 10H1120, 2 DMT/Cdt FTNV, Bureau de Liaison pour la pacification 'Historique'.
39. SHAT 10H946, 90/EMIFT/3, 11 March 1952. 'Pacification du Delta Tonkinois'.
40. This is the main reason why the Delta had been reinfiltrated during the early months of 1952.
41. SHAT 10H946, 90/EMIFT/3, 11 March 1952, 'Pacification du Delta Tonkinois'.
42. Ibid.
43. SHAT 10H2251, 'Instruction sur l'organisation et le functionnement des Groupes Administratifs Mobiles Operationnels', Hanoi, 8 Aug. 1952. Signed by Pham Van Binh, Governor of North Vietnam.
44. SHAT 2763, 261/B5 FTNV/Bureau Regional pour la Pacification, 'Note d'Information concernant l'action GAMO et ses résultats'. Hanoi, 5 Sept. 1952.
45. SHAT 10H1228, EMIFT/3B, 'Rapport d'Ensemple sur l'opération Mercure'; SHAT 10H1228, FTNV-GM No. 3, 'Enseignement tirer de l'opération Mercure'; SHAT 10H2763, 'Enseignements à tirer de l'essai du GAMO dans la Province de THai-Binh lors de l'opération Mercure'.
46. SHAT 10H1260, EMIFT/3B, Instruction, 'Opérations PORTO, POLO, TURCO', April 1952.
47. SHAT 10H1137, 503/GM7/3B, 'Rapport sur l'Opération BOLERO I' (28 June–29 July 1952); SHAT 10H1137, 59/ZN/3/OP, 'Compte Rendu de l'Opération BOLERO II' (27 Aug. 1952).
48. André Dulac, *Nos guerres perdues* (Fayard, 1969), pp. 45–51.
49. SHAT 10H176, 1003/ADC, 'Pacification du Nord Vietnam', 24 Mar. 1953.
50. SHAT 10H2763, 266/ZN/5B, 'Leçons à tirer de l'experience des GAMO – Col. Riner', 25 Sept. 1952.
51. Nemo Report, pp. 33–5 (Part 1); Report 'Ely', pp. 55–70, 150–2.
52. Rapport Ely, pp. 161–71, and Part 2, pp. 37–43; SHAT 10H988, 'Enseignements à tirer de la guerre d'Indochine', 10276/BAPEO/3B.
53. Rapport Ely, pp. 201–5; SHAT 10H653, Colonel Charatte, 'Considérations sur les opérations Aéroportées du Théâtre d'Opérations Indochinois', 1952; Colonel

P. Gaujac, 'L'ALAT', *Revue Historique des Armées*, 189 (Dec. 1992).

54. A good discussion of this question of morale and the way French officers saw Indochina can be found in Raoul Girardet's work *La Crise Militaire Française* (Armand Colin, 1964), pp. 159–85.
55. L. Beccaria, *Helier de Saint Marc* (Presses Pocke, 1988), pp. 92–3; Helier de Saint Marc, *Mémoires* (Perrin, 1995), pp. 102–22. In Saint Marc's *Mémoires* there is a fuller description of his life at Ta Lung.
56. Ibid., p. 123; L. Beccaria, *Helier de Saint Marc*, pp. 101–2.
57. Ibid., p. 102.
58. Helier de Saint Marc, *Mémoires*, p. 265.
59. Of these POWs, 9,404 were from the Indochinese states; 9,247 never returned. These numbers speak for themselves. The best description of life in Vietminh POW camps can be found in J. Pouget, *Le Manifeste du Camp No. 1* and L. Stein, *Les Soldats Oubliés* (Albin Michel, 1993). See also Col. Bonnafous, 'Les Prisonniers du Corps Expéditionnaire Français dans les Camps Viet Minh (1945–1954)', *Guerres Mondiales*, 147 (1987).
60. L. Stein, *Les Soldats Oubliés*, p. 310; 'Rapport du Médecin Capitaine G. Armstrong, 3BCCP', Saigon, 26 Sept. 1954.
61. J. Pouget, 'Nous étions à Dien Bien Phu', p. 80.
62. This incident was described to the author by Jean Pouget and General A. Bizard independently. A published summarized version exists in P. Heduy (ed.), 'Jean Pouget L'honneur des capitaines', in *Algérie Française*, p. 366.

3
Algeria and the 'Official Mind': the Impact of North Africa on French Colonial Policy South of the Sahara, 1944–58

Martin Shipway

What were the implications of Algeria's special and distinctive status for colonial policy-makers in the postwar period leading up to decolonization? It is a commonplace of French imperial history that Algeria was a case apart, bigger, more important and more problematic than any other French dependency, even before the FLN's declaration of war in November 1954. Its constitutional status as an assimilated extension of metropolitan France lent superficial plausibility to the French political class's frequent affirmation that 'l'Algérie, c'est la France'; its powerful and vocal settler community ensured that this sentiment remained an article of faith; and the distinctiveness of Algerian administration was maintained by an informal system of 'sealed partitions' (*cloisons étanches*), which prevented interference from those administrative services responsible for other parts of the French empire.[1]

This chapter explores official attitudes to North Africa, and to Algeria in particular, within the Ministry of Colonies (renamed the Ministry of Overseas France in January 1946), which oversaw the administration of French colonial dependencies outside North Africa. In particular it examines two broad, overlapping approaches to Algeria, Morocco and Tunisia adopted by postwar colonial policy-makers. The first, largely abortive approach comes under the heading of what might be called imperial coordination. By this is meant the attempt by dynamic, liberal officials, initiated at the 1944 Brazzaville Conference, to restructure and rationalize the French empire in order to pre-empt a perceived nationalist challenge to the imperial order. Although grandly renamed the French Union (Union Française) in March 1945, the new structure never really cohered in the manner intended by the visionaries at Brazzaville. Indeed, as France's largest and nearest overseas dependency, Algeria might have been thought the *sine qua non* for any general restructuring of the French Union, and yet reform in Algeria was largely pursued (or not) on a parallel and quite separate track, a development confirmed at the latest by the time of Gaston Defferre's epoch-making Framework Law (*loi-cadre*) of June 1956, which overhauled the political and administrative structures of the great colonial federations of French West Africa (Afrique Occidentale Française – AOF), French Equatorial Africa (Afrique Equatoriale Française – AEF) and Madagascar, and which set France's sub-Saharan dependencies on the road to decolonization.

The second approach is encapsulated in the political report-writer's stock phrase 'repercussions of events in North Africa'. How did colonial officials view the impact of events north of the Sahara on the peoples of Black Africa and Madagascar? Impact will be taken here in three senses. First, officials were vigilant for any indication that local populations or the new political elites were drawing inspiration from the rise of nationalism in Algeria, or in the North African protectorates. Secondly, impact might mean more direct involvement, for example in the form of propaganda from Algerian or Moroccan sources. Thirdly, what was the capacity for 'dissidence' among those groups living on the Saharan frontiers of 'Black' and 'White' (i.e. in French racial terminology Arab or Moorish) Africa, nomads whose loyalties lay more naturally to the North, but whose political destiny was bound up in the sub-Saharan colonies of AOF and AEF?

Two preliminary observations need to be made here. The first concerns the extent to which 'the system worked': notwithstanding the recurrent anxieties of officials in Paris and the colonial capitals, the sealed partitions stayed in place until the bitter end, so that this is rather a case of 'the dog that didn't bark'. There was no great Fanonian revolt against the French colonial presence south of the Sahara, where the transition to independence was orderly albeit effected against the background of violence and insurrection in Madagascar, Cameroun and elsewhere. The second, related, observation concerns a more subtle consequence of the 'sealed partitions' for the researcher, which is that the problem of Algeria was often hidden or distorted by a screen of discretion and euphemism.[2] What, then, was understood exactly by 'North Africa' or the 'events' which took place there? One thing is clear, which is that officials often referred to Tunisia and especially Morocco, which for most of the period concerned posed a far more serious and tangible threat in Black Africa. In this sense, Algeria's separate status and history turn out to be more a problem for the historian than for French policy-makers. For the sake of completeness, the scope of this chapter has been widened to encompass the wider picture in North Africa.

The period covered extends from the Brazzaville Conference in 1944 to the end of the Fourth Republic 14 years later, but the main focus is on two periods of 'crisis'. The first is that from the Brazzaville Conference until the passing of the new Constitution in October 1946. The second period of crisis is around late 1955/early 1956, in the run-up to the Framework Law; this is also the moment at which the flare of insurrection in Algeria could be distinguished alongside the greater conflagrations in Tunisia and

Morocco, and provides a useful moment at which to take a 'snapshot' of the broader picture. But this moment also necessarily looks forward to de Gaulle's return to power in May 1958 and to the September 1958 referendum in Black Africa, at which point the colonial histories of Black Africa and Algeria were definitively separated out one from the other.

Sealed partitions

The structures of colonial administration, like so many aspects of French public life in the aftermath of defeat, occupation and liberation in the years 1940–4, underwent a period of intense scrutiny and restructuring, only to fall back into substantially the same pattern as before, as the pressure for continuity outweighed the desire for change.[3] According to the traditional pattern, imperial policy had to be coordinated between three ministries: Colonies, Foreign Affairs (responsible for the North African protectorates and the Levant Mandates) and Interior (which oversaw the Algerian civil administration). Within the latter two ministries, a powerful and entrenched department blocked out ministerial or parliamentary interference: the Africa-Levant Department at the Quai d'Orsay and the Algerian Sub-Department at the Interior. Further responsibility fell to the Ministry of War, especially concerning the Algerian Southern Territories. This pattern was necessarily disrupted by the defeat of France. With the establishment of the French National Liberation Committee (Comité Français de la Libération Nationale – CFLN) in Algiers in 1943, a Commissariat for Muslim Affairs was created, headed by the liberal and authoritative General Georges Catroux. Catroux also chaired a Commission for Muslim Reforms, which met in Algiers over the spring and summer of 1944; its ambitious recommendations were reflected in the 1947 Algerian Statute, but were subsequently sidestepped by the Algerian Assembly, dominated as it was by settlers and pro-French Algerians, the so-called *béni-oui-oui*.[4] Catroux's Commissariat was transmuted to a Ministry for North Africa in liberated Paris, with joint responsibility for Algeria alongside the Ministry of the Interior, but this was rapidly disbanded in January 1945. This drew a line under the institutional innovations of the preceding period.

The main impetus for reform at this early period came from the Colonial Commissariat headed by René Pleven, and in particular from his dynamic Director of Political Affairs, Governor Henri Laurentie. As Secretary-General at the Brazzaville Conference, Laurentie was also the principal author of the bold new scheme for a federation of all imperial territories, an idea subsequently realized in diluted and less radical form in the French Union. The ambitious, indeed unrealistic, scope of Laurentie's scheme contrasted sharply with the caution of the deliberative body at Brazzaville, composed of the governors and governors-general of French Black Africa.

The original plan for a grand imperial conference was scaled down, for ostensibly practical reasons, and the Moroccan and Tunisian Residences as well as the Algerian Government-General sent only observers to the conference. Nonetheless, the Conference's recommendations were intended to have wide resonance north of the Sahara, as René Massigli, Commissioner for Foreign Affairs, explained in a letter to officials in Rabat and Tunis.[5] In fact, Massigli's advice seems to have been interpreted as enjoining caution and, while the Algerian observers left little trace in the official records of the conference, those from Rabat in particular took upon themselves the task of curbing the enthusiasms of Laurentie and his colleagues. Moreover, where the Conference addressed themes of relevance in North Africa, in particular those relating to Islam or the use of Arabic in schools, passages were struck from the record, and were left out in the roneotyped transcripts later distributed; this was a customary, but nonetheless striking, instance of official discretion.[6]

The pattern of interaction established at Brazzaville was to be repeated in the ensuing discussions surrounding the proposed French imperial federation, in which the three North African territories had a theoretical key role. In a series of committees, meeting in Algiers in 1944 and in Paris in early 1945, Laurentie and his colleagues at the Ministry of Colonies argued for a multi-tiered hierarchy in which Morocco and Tunisia, and perhaps Algeria, were to be included as 'Associated States' with limited autonomy but extensive deliberative powers. The response of Algerian representatives was one of mild but non-committal approval; in one meeting of the Commission of Experts which met in 1944 to take forward the rather inconclusive discussions at Brazzaville, a young Jacques Berque, representing the Algerian Government-General, commented that Algeria had suffered too long from metropolitan supervision and from what he called the 'universalising tendency of the French spirit'.[7] Initially also the Commission which met in the spring of 1945 under the presidency of Gaston Monnerville was meant to have a wide brief: the Interior Minister, the Socialist Adrien Tixier, conveyed his wishes that the Commission extend its brief to cover the institutions of every overseas territory.[8] This was also the intention of Pleven's successor as Colonial Minster, Paul Giacobbi, who had recently presented the March 1945 Declaration on Indochina, offering in some respects a blueprint for the idea of the Associated States. As he suggested in a letter to Georges Bidault, Foreign Minister, the Declaration was intended to unite the Metropole with all member countries of the French community (*communauté*), and that the Constitution of the French Union, and at the very least the composition of an eventual Constituent Assembly, 'could not fail to affect Morocco and Tunisia'.[9] At the first session of the Commission, however, the Quai d'Orsay's representatives remained unmoved. As one pointed out, the Africa-Levant Department had no objections to the eventual inclusion of

Tunisia and Morocco in the French Union, but maintained that this should first be studied in depth by its own services. As Laurentie commented, did the Quai d'Orsay really think that it could make 'a little constitution all on its own'?[10] There was, however, little that Laurentie and Monnerville could do, and Giacobbi duly confirmed that the Commission's field of study should be confined to the relatively minor question of African representation in the forthcoming Constituent Assembly. Algeria was discussed separately, the protectorates apparently not at all, and the question of Indochinese representation was suspended pending Indochina's 'liberation'.

In a sense, this inter-service wrangling was of little consequence in the face of the real issues of colonial policy faced on the ground. This much at least was clear to Laurentie, for whom matters came to a head with the crises which erupted in Syria and Eastern Algeria in May–June 1945. As he argued in a cogent, if somewhat alarmist, confidential memorandum to Giacobbi, France was faced with a general colonial crisis in which increasingly the forces of nationalism would combine on all sides to threaten France's very survival as an imperial power. At the heart of Laurentie's analysis was a plea for administrative rationalism, as he and his 'colonial' colleagues looked on helpless:

> ... this urgent and dangerous conjuncture is confronted by an incoherent and incompetent administrative system. The obvious need for united action is confounded by the overlapping responsibilities of two ministerial departments, each of which devotes to North Africa only a residue of its energies.[11]

Although a North Africa Committee existed to coordinate policy, it was, as Laurentie commented, direction rather than coordination that was needed. Laurentie envisaged a reformed administrative system which would combine the virtues of regional specialization and central metropolitan control, with separate ministries for Indochina, North Africa and at least one other for Black Africa, Madagascar and the remaining colonies. At the same time, the need for political unity and governmental efficiency remained imperative; Laurentie proposed the creation of a colonial 'super-Minister' who alone would sit in the Council of Ministers and would be constitutionally responsible for colonial policy overall.[12]

It would be easy to condemn Laurentie's rhetoric as 'protesting too much', but the fear of European 'eviction' from the colonies was a recurrent theme in the Colonial Ministry, especially after the war in Indochina and the Malagasy insurrection served to 'confirm' the thesis of a concerted nationalist strategy. Thus, in August 1947, Gustave Moutet, nephew and private secretary (*chef de cabinet*) to the vetern minister Marius Moutet, detected the:

> ... warning signs of a vast enterprise aiming to pull the Overseas Territories apart, which, after Indochina and Madagascar, will lead to the creation of new fronts of agitation and combat.[13]

The thesis of communist conspiracy added a further element of what passed for realism in the late 1940s. For example, in a circular produced by the military intelligence services (Service de Documentation, d'Etudes et de Contre-Espionnage – SDECE) in May 1950, explicit support was given to the British catch-all thesis of Communist involvement in Black Africa, for, as the document explained:

> Communism in Africa is not doctrinaire in character and the movement is not based on considerations of dialectical materialism. In fact, its essential tendency is to exploit nationalist or even racialist sentiments, the first and fundamental aim of which is the expulsion of the white races.[14]

In this way, a cast-iron justification was provided for applying the 'Communist' label to any uncongenial movement on French-held territory. Moreover, North Africa could also quite readily be brought within the scope of anti-communist geopolitics, as a further intelligence document for 1955 demonstrated:

> A key area for any 'peripheral' strategy, North Africa remains a focus of interest for leaders of the international communist apparatus, whose hand is behind various destabilising activities ranging from agitation and propaganda to support for nationalist and separatist movements ...
>
> Islam at present may be considered to be at the stage of bourgeois nationalist revolution, which is where the most direct and dangerous contact with communist doctrine occurs.[15]

It was against the background of such received wisdom that policy-makers operated throughout the period of decolonization.

The wearied parliamentary and public acceptance of the October 1946 Constitution, however, more or less brought to an end official initiatives to rationalize the structure of empire. Although the institutions set out in the Constitution were more rigid and less ambitious than Laurentie's original, probably unworkable, schemes for a federal French Union, the High Council of the French Union at least provided a framework within which the new 'Associated States' of Cambodia, Laos and, eventually, Bao Dai's Vietnam could be accommodated. In 1952, Cambodian representatives on the High Council, with the tacit approval of President Vincent Auriol (as President of the French Union), made a last-ditch attempt to persuade the French government to incorporate Tunisia and Morocco as Associated States. The Ministry of Foreign Affairs prevaricated in time-honoured fashion, insisting on the protectorates' inviolable international status, until a change of government brought a change of heart and the project was shelved.[16]

The question of changing Algeria's constitutional status continued to elude serious discussion, largely by default: it was apparently in no one's interest to disturb an uneasy status quo by examining too closely the anomalies of French Algeria. On the other hand, the innovation represented by the presence of the sub-Saharan colonies in the Constituent Assembly, and thereafter in the National Assembly, set out a separate path for African development confirmed by Gaston Defferre's Framework Law in 1956, which, as François Borella suggests, represents the culminating official expression of what had been meant by the Brazzaville 'spirit' (*esprit de Brazzaville*).[17] After Dien Bien Phu and the explosion of nationalism in Tunisia and Morocco, and perhaps already in the face of events in Algeria, unrest in Black Africa, Madagascar and elsewhere was now to be pre-empted by extensive reforms which would match those in neighbouring British colonies.[18] For presentational purposes at least, North Africa was already, in a sense, being written off by the authors of this legislation. Thus, in a letter to Defferre before the National Assembly debate, Félix Houphouët-Boigny, a Minister in the Mollet government, suggested that Defferre's opening speech need not include reference to the 'troubles' which had rocked Madagascar and, more recently, Cameroun; rather it should be suggested that there was still time for the government to act free of any pressure for reform. As he continued:

> Events in North Africa have revealed conclusively how a climate of confidence between metropolitan and overseas populations may be eroded almost irremediably, even during periods of apparent calm; they also demonstrate how difficult it is subsequently to promote reform once passions have been allowed to run high.[19]

Although, as so often, 'North Africa' mostly meant Morocco and Tunisia in this context, the sense of Black African reform being a last chance for the French to instigate successful reform is palpable, and the hint was taken up readily by Defferre in his presentation to the National Assembly.[20] Hereafter, perhaps, there was a new sense of mission to the protection of Black Africa from outside contamination, and it is with this perception in mind that we turn to the question of North African influence across the Sahara.

Repercussions

Senior officials in France's sub-Saharan dependencies could be forgiven the nervousness which is conveyed by their correspondence in the mid-to-late

1950s. Independence in Morocco and Tunisia, insurrection, massacre and the threat of military takeover in Algeria certainly contrasted with the sense of purpose and order induced by the implementation of the Framework Law. And yet, as they knew well, their administration was understaffed and under-resourced, their territory was vast and largely under-policed. Madagascar and Cameroun were recovering still from the aftermath of insurrection and French military repression. Political and trades union activism and a burgeoning nationalist press in Dakar and Tananarive especially promoted a new-found sense of challenge to French rule among an elite which, ten years before, had almost universally been described as loyal. To be sure, official anxiety was concealed to a large extent by the bland accounts of local morale (*état d'esprit*) reported back to Paris and further synthesized there for internal consumption.[21] What is perhaps remarkable in these circumstances is that the line held, there was no explosion and the reforms set in train by the June 1956 Framework Law led to peaceful decolonization. In what follows, the cases of Madagascar and AOF are briefly examined in order to assess the resonance of events in North Africa.

Reports from Tananarive give perhaps the clearest instance of official reassurance in response to Parisian predictions of imperial crisis. Of chief significance for the Malagasy nationalist press was the Moroccan and Tunisian example of independence achieved by violent defiance of French rule. As was reported in March 1956:

> Moroccan and Tunisian independence is presented as proof of the death-throes of the colonial system, which will soon no longer be able to resist the claims of other 'dependent' peoples. Terrorism is represented as the expression of popular despair in a nation deprived of its rights by the colonialists. Some articles in the extremist press suggest terrorism as an option but are careful not to conclude in its favour.[22]

However, such analysis needs to be understood in the light of Malagasy political particularities. Malagasy nationalists looked more readily to models of independence than did their Black African counterparts at this period, given their own remembered history of national independent statehood until annexed by France in 1896. Moreover, the trauma of the 1947 insurrection was vividly recalled by the amnesty law of March 1956, which released the Malagasy former *députés*, accused of fomenting the insurrection, but left many insurrectionaries in detention.[23] In this context, the Framework Law was seen more as a trap than as an opportunity.[24] Associated State status was discussed and rejected in favour of independence. Nationalists also sought Malagasy representation at the Bandoeng Conference and membership of the emerging Non-Aligned Movement. On the other hand, such reports were invariably accompanied by official health-warnings, to the effect that the broad mass of Malagasy opinion was unmoved by news from North Africa, and that Malagasy nationalism was dominated by the Merina elite whose forebears had dominated the island before the advent of the French. These were standard themes of the 'official version' of the French mission in Madagascar, from which it may be concluded that business continued much as usual.

The significance of Algeria to Malagasy opinion, as also generally in French Africa, was of a different order, as nationalists feared that the European settler population of Madagascar, the most numerically powerful and politically vocal in any colony outside North Africa with the possible exception of New Caledonia, would draw inspiration from the example of settler activism. This possibility is first mentioned in a report for March 1956, following the Philippeville massacre and its aftermath the previous August, and perhaps reflecting the flexing of *pied-noir* political muscle which accompanied Guy Mollet's visit to Algiers in February 1956.[25] More significantly, it recurs in a report for May 1958, which recorded that nationalist parties were hiding their archives for fear that the crisis in Algiers would provoke copycat settler activity in Tananarive. Official fears of settler unrest proved groundless, although Committees of Public Safety were formed in Madagascar and elsewhere. But reports do not mention the enthusiasm in various military garrisons for the insurrectionary stance of the army in Algeria. Here too the garrison in Madagascar seemed poised to take the lead, and the High Commissioner André Soucadaux could not rely on the support of local organizations, as was the case in Dakar, given the continuing fragmentation of Malagasy politics. Relief at de Gaulle's acceptance of power was thus quite palpable, even setting aside the fact that the three High Commissioners, Cusin at Dakar, Messmer at Brazzaville and Soucadaux, were all Gaullists with wartime experience.[26]

While North Africa consoled or inspired Malagasy nationalists coming to terms with the defeat of 1947, developments in Algeria and Morocco were potentially of far more direct impact in French West Africa. Reporting to Paris in April 1956, High Commissioner Bernard Cornut-Gentille saw the possible North African impact on the Federation in two ways: frontier problems and those affecting the heart of the Federation rather than its periphery.[27] Cornut-Gentille summarized the intangible nature of North African impact, in a characteristic biochemical metaphor, as a 'pernicious ferment'. Among more specific questions, the High Commissioner's principal concern was that demands for West African troops (*tirailleurs sénégalais*) for service in Algeria would deplete numbers stationed in AOF below advised levels. In March 1956, Cornut-Gentille had relayed the reservations of the Commander of Troops in AOF-Togo, General Garbay; the latest detachment of ten thousand men ordered by Paris brought the total to be sent to Algeria to half the available manpower, including troops drawn from the essential garrison (*bataillons de souveraineté*). But Cornut-Gentille had two more general points to make. First, deployment of Black

African troops in Algeria could be exploited readily in propaganda, which was likely in this case to take the form of a 'appeal to Islamic solidarity', or a more general call for the 'fraternity of coloured peoples'.[28] Indeed, this prediction was confirmed by what was described as the first Algerian propaganda tract to reach Dakar from Cairo, though it presumably never got further than the intelligence services of the Government-General.[29] Cornut-Gentille's second concern was for the adverse effects on public opinion in Dakar. The despatch of *tirailleurs* to Madagascar and Indochina had already been controversial; now, although there had been no public demonstrations, the matter was the subject of extensive press and political commentary. Even traditionalist moderate parties (BDS, SFIO) had adopted positions interpreted as hostile to the French presence, while more extreme groups, including the Communist-dominated trades union movement (Confédération Générale du Travail – CGT) and some youth groups were stressing the theme of Muslim solidarity in the belief that this was mostly likely to reach ordinary people (*la masse*) and to impress the elites for whom 'panislamism' was all the rage.[30] Cornut-Gentille played down the significance of these reports in his conclusion, however: with the Framework Law imminent, the much-scrutinized intelligentsia ('les milieux évolués') would soon have more immediate concerns to occupy their newly awakened political consciousness.

If the prospect of political integration offered by the Framework Law was comforting in the Black African heartlands of Dakar and points South and East, the same could not be said for the North. Here a long, poorly defined border with Morocco, Algeria and the Spanish Sahara bound the Saharan districts of three AOF colonies (Mauritania, French Sudan, Niger) and a fourth, Chad, ruled from Brazzaville. The sparse populations of these territories were typically nomadic groups of uncertain loyalties, one of whom, the Regueibat of the Western Sahara, had been 'pacified' as recently as 1934, and whose cultural, religious and commercial affinities pulled them to Rabat and Tamanrasset rather than to Dakar and Saint-Louis.[31] Moreover, the political reforms of 1946 had further sidelined these 'white' nomadic groups, since the prize of political representation in Paris and Dakar had tended to fall to 'assimilated' Black Africans.[32]

Dakar's policy with regard to these groups was to improve intelligence in the hope of detecting possible infiltration and/or the potential for 'dissidence'.[33] In fact, calls from Paris for improved intelligence-gathering were largely otiose given the shortage of personnel and the paucity of resources available. This was a recurring theme, but the central point could be simply stated: an average administrative district (*cercle*) in AOF, more than four times larger than a metropolitan *département*, was typically overseen by a single Administrator. Increasingly tied down by bureaucracy, an Administrator found less time to tour his district, and leave was frequently postponed beyond reasonable endurance because of staff shortages.

Moreover, his capacity for extracting valuable intelligence from local informers was restricted by limited political funds to distribute 'gifts'; according to one report, the monthly political budget for a district in French Sudan was a 'derisory' 5,000 francs.[34] To compensate for these insufficiencies, Arab-speaking liaison officers were deployed in Mauritania and French Sudan with the specific task of gathering intelligence, and the same was proposed for Niger and Chad.[35] Steps were also taken to improve coordination between officers in AOF and their opposite numbers in Algeria. It was a significant comment on the rigid administrative hierarchy, which ensured efficient communication in the upper echelons but not in the field, that specific measures had to be taken to ensure regular meetings across the frontier and routine radio contact to exchange information.[36] Personal contacts were often limited by distance: by 1956 a new road had reduced the journey time between Koulouba, administrative capital of French Sudan, and Tamanrasset to a mere six hours.[37]

Despite these difficulties, political crisis of the kind feared by Paris was largely confined to an indeterminate future, with the notable exception of Mauritania, and here the threat came not from Algeria but from Morocco. Certainly in April 1956, Cornut-Gentille's report on North African impact foresaw few immediate difficulties that the palliatives of improved intelligence and resourcing could not remedy: the Governor of Niger reported only latent danger, while the Governor of Soudan's contacts with the military authorities of Tamanrasset provided firm reassurance concerning Tuareg disinterest in unrest further North.[38] Even in Mauritania, local opinion was 'attentiste' rather than actively hostile; Governor Parisot underlined the keen interest with which the Regueibat followed news from North Africa, noting that battery-operated radios had even been reported in their camps. What was chiefly puzzling, therefore, was their silence, which Parisot's hugely experienced liaison officer, the near-legendary Colonel Borricand, explained romantically in terms of 'Moorish politeness, which forbids any mention in our hearing of subjects thought to be unpleasant to us'.[39]

Subsequent events in Mauritania and the Western Sahara, which have been covered elsewhere, constitute the exception proving the rule of minimal impact of developments across the Sahara. The emerging scenario was one which, on a more general scale, would have spelled disaster for sub-Saharan French policy.[40] Of particular interest in the present context are the following elements of the affair. First there was the capacity for 'dissidence' by the former *député* for Mauritania, Horma Ould Babana, who, elected in 1946 backed by René Pleven's UDSR, defeated honourably in the 1951 elections and trounced by the 'official' candidate in the 1956 elections, emerged as the champion of the pro-Moroccan camp in Mauritania and, subsequently, in Rabat: here was living proof of the need to keep the new African elites 'on side', and of the fragility of pro-French loyalties.[41]

Secondly, Allal el-Fassi's 'thesis' of a Greater Morocco, finally mapped out following the Istiqlal leader's speech at Cairo on 3 July 1956, was a direct challenge to French territorial integrity. Indeed, in many ways, el Fassi seemed to present Morocco as the direct successor to the French colonial presence, since his plans incorporated the whole of Mauritania and even extended across the Senegal River to include the old Mauritanian administrative capital at Saint-Louis, which was by no stretch of the imagination ethnically or historically Moroccan.[42] Thirdly, the military operations of February 1958 which threw the Moroccan National Liberation Army back beyond a militarily and legally defensible South Moroccan frontier, Operation Ecouvillon (Eng.: *swab* (rifle)), showed the willingness of the French to defend an entrenched position by force, the more so because the campaign involved a politically sensitive, indeed distasteful, alliance with the Francoist military forces of the Spanish Sahara.[43] Fourthly, the shifting loyalties of the Regueibat, while providing some encouragement to Allal el Fassi, were nonetheless finally won over to the French – or Mauritanian – cause by the decisive use of force in Operation Ecouvillon, thus ensuring that the French colony of Mauritania had a future as a distinct and sovereign Islamic Republic of Mauritania. In effect, the French were defending the concept of the West African Federation, with all its historic arbitrariness, at precisely the moment when its future was being called into question by the 'balkanizing' thrust of the Framework Law reforms, and the wider momentum of the decolonization process. To put it another way, the compartmentalized colonial system in French Africa was now being transformed within an emerging Africa of independent states.

May we conclude, therefore, as suggested above, that 'the system worked', and that the elaborate and cumbersome imperial system in French Africa persisted to the very end? If so, it was perhaps more by luck than by good judgement, as far as French West Africa was concerned, although decisive action at the eleventh hour in Mauritania served to shore up the French system at its weakest and most permeable point. On the other hand, the 'sealed partitions' were maintained in many ways at the expense of the Algerian national cause, for the transition to independence in the colonies of sub-Saharan Africa, which was probably irreversible by the time of the September 1958 referendum at the latest, coincided merely with the beginning of the end north of the Sahara. Furthermore, the separate paths to independence trodden by Black Africans and Algerians were as much a matter of separate perspectives and separate histories as of French agency. Certainly, the concept of Algeria as the champion of African anti-colonialism was still in its infancy in the period under consideration.[44] Part of the reasoning for this was plausibly, if rather sanctimoniously, explained by a confidential SDECE report in early 1959:

> The nationalist leaders of Black Africa have sentimental ties to the F.L.N. However, given their support for non-violent methods of African liberation, they fear the contagious effect of F.L.N. brutality and therefore do not go beyond moral support.[45]

But the separate perspective and history of the French 'official mind' is also at issue here: if the system 'worked' it was in large measure only with the benefit of hindsight, as officials, rewriting history even as it was made, sought retrospectively to impose order on the muddle of decolonization.

Notes

1. The author gratefully acknowledges research funding from the Humanities Research Board of the British Academy and from the French Department of Birkbeck College, University of London. A *dérogation* was granted by the Directeur-Général des Archives de France allowing access to papers at the Centre des Archives d'Outre-Mer, Aix-en-Provence. Mme Edmonde Charles-Roux kindly granted permission to consult the Fonds Gaston Defferre in the Archives communales de Marseille.
2. See Benjamin Stora, 'Algeria: the war without a name', in R. Holland (ed.), *Emergencies and Disorder in the European Empires after 1945* (London, 1994), pp. 208–16.
3. For an elaboration of this theme, Andrew Shennan, *Reshaping France: Plans for Renewal, 1940–1946* (Oxford, 1989).
4. Guy Pervillé, 'La commission des réformes musulmanes de 1944 et l'élaboration d'une nouvelle politique algérienne de la France'; Tayeb Chenntouf, 'L'assemblée algérienne et l'application des réformes prévues par le statut du 20 septembre 1947'; in IHTP, *Les chemins de la décolonisation de l'empire français, 1936–1956* (Paris, 1986), pp. 357–65, 367–75.
5. Massigli à Maroc (pencilled in), 9 Dec. 1943, MAE, Alger/683.
6. Compte rendu, 'RABAT le 23 février 1944', MAE, Alger/683; the transcripts of the Conference proceedings, showing the blue-pencilled deletions are in AOM, AP/2295. For a fuller account of the conference and of Laurentie's federal idea, see M. J. Shipway, *The Road to War: France and Vietnam, 1944–1947* (Oxford and Providence, RI, 1996), chs 1–2.
7. Minutes in AOM, AP/214 and MAE, Alger/683. This Commission had been called by the delegates at Brazzaville.
8. P.v. de la séance du 11 avril, AOM, AP/214.
9. Giacobbi to Bidault, no.10RC 6, 3 Apr. 1945, AOM, AP/215. All translations are by the author. On the March 1945 Declaration, see Shipway, *Road to War*, chs 2, 5.
10. P.v. de la séance du 11 avril, AOM, AP/214. The Quai d'Orsay's position is set out in Comité de l'Afrique du Nord, 'NOTE relative à l'intégration des Protectorats Tunisien et Marocain dans l'Union Française', 4 Mar. 1946, AOM, AP/214.
11. NOTE, 20/21 juin 1945: AN, Papiers Henri Laurentie, 72AJ535. This memorandum is analysed in Shipway, *Road to War*, pp. 74–5.
12. Ibid.
13. Note pour M. le Président du Conseil, no. 633, Très Secret, 1 Aug. 1947, AOM, AP/2255/1.

14. 'Communisme en Afrique Noire', SDECE doc. no. 21.1.-N.650-A.01.474, 19 May 1950, AOM, AP/2246/B.
15. 'Le Communisme et l'Afrique du Nord', Groupe de Travail Permanent, Commission des Informations Musulmanes, Conseil Supérieur de Renseignements, Secrétariat-Général du Gouvernement, n.d. (1955), AOM, AP/2246/B3.
16. See Georges Chaffard, 'Comment la Tunisie et le Maroc n'entrèrent pas dans l'Union Française', in *Carnets secrets de la décolonisation*, Vol. I (Paris, 1965), pp. 133–43.
17. 'La Conférence de Brazzaville dans le débat politique français après 1944', in Institut Charles de Gaulle, IHTP, *Brazzaville, Janvier–Février 1944: Aux sources de la décolonisation* (Paris, 1988), p. 339.
18. The possible impact of the British model is evoked in the 1950 SDECE document on 'Communisme en Afrique Noire' quoted above (see note 14): 'Ever faithful to her policy of old, Britain is attempting to stem the flow by granting "self-government", at least in principle. Time will tell whether or not this will entail serious repercussions for her African neighbours.'
19. Houphouët-Boigny, Ministre Délégué, Présidence du Conseil, to Defferre, Ministre FOM, 27 Feb. 1956, Archives Communales de Marseille (ACM), Fonds Gaston Defferre, 100 II 134.
20. JO, débats Assemblée Nationale, séance 21 mars 1956, 1108ff.
21. See the series of 'Synthèses politiques' for 1955–8 in AOM, AP/2162.
22. Synthèse politique, Mar. 1956, AOM, AP/2162.
23. On the 1947 Insurrection, see Jacques Tronchon, *L'insurrection malgache de 1947* (Paris and Fianarantsoa, 1974, repr. 1986); and see M. J. Shipway, 'Madagascar on the eve of insurrection, 1944–1947: the impasse of a liberal colonial policy', *Journal of Imperial and Commonwealth History*, 24/1 (Jan. 1996), 72–100.
24. Synthèse politique, Apr. 1956, AOM, AP/2162.
25. Synthèse politique, Mar. 1956, AOM, AP/2162.
26. Synthèses politiques, May, June 1958, AOM, AP/2162. See also Georges Chaffard, 'Le 13 Mai, Outre-Mer', in *Carnets secrets*, vol. I, pp. 331–46.
27. Haussaire AOF to Ministre FOM, no.0886/AP, 10 Apr. 1956, AOM, AP/2172/3.
28. Haussaire AOF to Ministre FOM, no.806. 10 Mar. 1956, AOM, AP/2148/5.
29. Haussaire AOF to Ministre FOM, no.1555 DSS/PG, 4 Jul. 1956, AOM, AP/2148/5.
30. Haussaire AOF to Ministre FOM, no.0886/AP, 10 Apr. 1956, AOM, AP/2172/3.
31. See Olivier Vergniot, 'Tindouf: un point d'équivoque, 1926–1934', in *Revue de l'Occident musulman et de la Méditerranée*, 41–42 (1986), pp. 119–35.
32. See Ministre FOM (DAP 2e bureau) to Haussaires AOF, AEF, 23 Jan. 1956, AP/2148/5.
33. Ibid.
34. Rapport sur la situation des Territoires français de l'Afrique noire, n.d. (1955), ACM, Fonds Gaston Defferre, 100 II 164; Ministre FOM to Haussaires AOF, AEF, 23 Jan. 1956, AP/2148/5; Note pour M. le Gouverneur-Général, Directeur des Affaires Politiques, 17 Feb. 1956, AOM, AP/2148/5.
35. Ministre FOM to Haussaires AOF, AEF, 23 Jan. 1956, AP/2148/5.
36. Note no.4083, a/s l'échange des renseignements entre l'Afrique Noire et l'Afrique du Nord, à l'attention du Lieutenant-Colonel AURIOL de l'Etat-Major particulier de la Défense Nationale et des Forces Armées, 23 May 1956, AOM, AP/2148/5.

37. Gvr Soudan to Haussaire Dakar, n.d., annexe to his no.0886/AP, 10 Apr. 1956, AOM, AP/2172/3.
38. Haussaire AOF to Ministre FOM, no.0886/AP, 10 Apr. 1956, AOM, AP/2172/3.
39. Gvr Mauritanie to Haussaire Dakar, no.170/CAB, 24 Apr. 1956, AOM, AP/2148/5.
40. See Pierre Robert Baduel, 'Mauritanie 1945–1990 ou l'Etat face à la Nation', in *Revue du Monde Musulman et de la Méditerranée*, 54 (1989/4), pp. 11–51; Olivier Vergniot, 'La question du Sahara occidental: Autodétermination et enjeux référendaires (1956–1989)', in *Annuaire de l'Afrique du Nord*, XXVIII (1989), pp. 385–418; Georges Chaffard, 'Une alliance militaire franco-espagnole sous la IVe République', in *Carnets secrets*, vol. I, pp. 252–93.
41. Baduel, 'Mauritanie 1945–1990', pp. 14–18.
42. Vergniot, 'La question du Sahara occidental', pp. 389–91.
43. Chaffard, 'Une alliance militaire'.
44. Cf. Slimane Chikh, 'La politique africaine de l'Algérie', *Annuaire de l'Afrique du Nord* (1978), pp. 1–54.
45. 'L'Afrique noire et le F.L.N.', SDECE, 16564/IIA, 26 Feb. 1959, AOM, AP/2246/A.

4
The Sahara and the Algerian War

Jacques Frémeaux

The Sahara was not an important battlefield during the Algerian War. Historical accounts of this period give it little prominence. The distances involved, the fact that inhabited zones were widely dispersed and the difficulties in concealing population movements from aircraft created conditions that did not favour guerrilla warfare. The ALN did not have at its disposal the sort of motorized transport which, twenty years later, mobile units in Morocco and Chad were to be able to call upon. These units, moreover, were at the service of nomadic peoples who had retained much of their traditionally warlike nature. Through tradition and coercion, the French effectively succeeded in keeping the majority of tribal warriors under control.

Nevertheless, even a superficial examination of the Sahara during the Algerian War shows the extent to which that region cannot be dissociated from the study of the conflict as a whole. It actually constituted a significant economic and political challenge throughout that conflict, to which, at least on the French side, considerable effort was devoted.

The situation in 1958

Before 1954, the Sahara was not, for the French, simply the hinterland of Algeria. The thinking of national leaders was guided principally by the goals of organizing and defending the French empire. From the 1890s onwards, the conquest of the desert, from the Atlas to Niger and from the Atlantic to Chad, legitimated by a set of international conventions and put into effect by a series of expeditions, had above all sought to construct a 'French African bloc', these ambitious visions coming accompanied by grandiose projects, of which the most famous remains that of the construction of a trans-Saharan railway, of which only a handful of short sections towards the interior were ever built. During the interwar period this strategic interest in the role of the Sahara as an imperial colony was enhanced. Strategists had underlined the benefits of developing land links between

North Africa and Black Africa, ensuring that Senegalese infantrymen could be sent to France without undergoing the dangers of a sea journey in the event of a military mobilization. Other strategists had thought of using the area to allow room for manoeuvre in the direction of the Italian colony of Libya, or even occupied Ethiopia. Some visionaries, for example the historian and geographer E. F. Gautier, imagined the construction of a vast 'inter-Saharan grouping' with economic ends, while certain individuals, such as the geologist and explorer Conrad Kilian, who travelled throughout the area between 1922 and 1943, dreamed of discovering great mineral riches, particularly oil.[1] For a nation which imported almost all of its oil (about 7 million tonnes), then essentially a strategic raw material, this would have represented a considerable boon.

These perceptions, far from being weakened, were reinforced after the Second World War. A number of French leaders then saw the control of the Sahara as a means of maintaining the defence of Western Europe's southern flank. This outlook is clearly summarized in a work by Captain Thomas, Chief Administrator of the Air Force, published in 1957, with a foreword by Jacques Soustelle:

> Measuring 2000 km from North to South and 4000 km from East to West, the Sahara constitutes an immense platform for the dispersal of all the vital organs of Europe, which are at present extremely vulnerable due to the very fact of their concentration. The desert offers Europe the space for strategic retreat which is lacking to it and, thus, reestablishes the balance of power. Due to its vitally important location, however, it is at present particularly under threat. In the struggle between East and West, the Sahara occupies an essential position as it is by this route that Europe can be outflanked. The communist bloc has established its influence over Eastern Europe and the Middle East and it has access to the Mediterranean. If it succeeded in getting hold of the Sahara, Europe would find itself threatened on two fronts.[2]

The military means to be put in place for a potential battle for the Sahara were designed in an ultra-modern form, representing the arrival of sophisticated warfare, the model for which was provided by the military operations of 1941–2 in the Libyan and Egyptian desert. The elements of this were the dispersal of forces, underground organization, a strong network of surface communications, the use of deception (dummy installations, oil production sites, camps and manufacturing facilities, and dummy armoured columns intended to deceive the enemy), the search for aerial supremacy and a massive military commitment designed to achieve a rapid military victory.[3]

At the same time some new visions of the future were born that were characteristic of the state of mind then driving the top state 'mandarins', the force behind the economic recovery, who strongly favoured the idea of rapid and planned growth. Erik Labonne, a diplomat who fervently advocated 'optimizing development', worked tirelessly to create an inventory of the mineral riches of the territories under French control. He gained the enthusiastic endorsement of General Catroux. At the beginning of 1952 the Bureau d'Organisation des Ensembles industriels africains (African Industrial Bodies' Organizational Bureau) was set up, with the goal of providing French Africa with the means of production of which it had been so cruelly deprived during the war. In October 1952 the first Saharan areas for oil prospecting were allocated to French companies. On 11 January 1956, for the first time, oil gushed forth at Edjeleh, near the Libyan border. This was seen as perhaps finally offering France the prospect of achieving autonomous control over her future energy supplies. At the start of 1957 it was estimated that within two years it would be possible for France, thanks to Saharan oil, to satisfy a quarter of her own energy requirements and that, within a period of 15 years, that is to say by 1972, it ought to be possible to achieve complete energy self-sufficiency.[4] Such prospects were most enticing given that 85 per cent of crude oil imports were from the Middle East (a proportion which had been increasing, furthermore) and that this trade was essentially controlled by Anglo-American companies which, in 1958, were producing 90 per cent of the region's oil.[5] The Suez Crisis, resulting in the blockade of the Canal and the cutting-off of supplies by the Syrian and Lebanese governments who controlled the IPC's oil pipeline access, demonstrated the vulnerability of French and British oil purchases from this source of supply. Rationing had to be introduced for several months and oil from America, and above all Venezuela, had to take the place of this lost source of supply. Furthermore, it did not seem at all a bad idea to give French companies complete control over certain zones of production, given the monopoly still enjoyed by the 'Majors'. In 1958, then, French capital owned almost 80 per cent of the Algerian mining area (almost half of this French capital, furthermore, being of public sector origin).[6]

In addition, the Sahara was to become the location for French space and nuclear research experimentation, the decisive step in a whole series of efforts undertaken from 1945 onwards (with the creation of the CEA (the Atomic Energy Commission)) and speeded up by the government of Pierre Mendès France after 1954. In 1953, the Colomb-Béchar Centre of Experimentation was created, a number of tactical missiles being developed there, in particular, by Nord-Aviation. The Suez Crisis only accelerated this process. While they were not very credible, Soviet threats of resorting to the use of atomic weapons nonetheless underlined the danger that could be posed in the near future to a politico-militarily isolated France by the Soviet nuclear threat, a threat that would not be counterbalanced by an American guarantee of security. Le Tanezrouft was retained in preference to other sites (Kerguelen, Touamotou) which were judged too impractical and too distant. From the start of 1957 the first assessments were carried out so as to decide upon the location of a testing centre, for which it was anticipated that responsibility would be given to the mixed Armed Forces-CEA nuclear experimentation group, which had been set up in March of the same year. In July the decision was taken to locate the testing site at Reggane, 150 km from Adrar, the capital of the Touat region. On 22 April 1958 prime minister Félix Gaillard decided that a first test would take place from the first quarter of 1960, a decision that de Gaulle was to ratify on taking office.[7] It should be emphasized that de Gaulle went to the Sahara in March 1957, attending missile tests at Hammaguir and visiting the oil production facilities of Edjeleh and Hassi Messaoud.

The political trends associated with these changes tended more and more to confirm the distinction between Algeria and the Sahara. Since 1902 the Sahara and its Northern fringes had possessed, under the name of 'the Southern Territories', a separate organization from that of the three *départements* of Northern Algeria.[8] The 1947 statute anticipated the abolition of the Southern Territories or appeared to herald their rapid assimilation into Algeria, given the fact that a special law would lay down the exact conditions under which these territories would be assimilated into the *département*-based organizational system (Title VI, article 50).[9] However, similarly to the statute as a whole, these measures were not in reality put into effect. It was not until 1957, and the decree of 7 August, that the creation of the two new *départements* of Les Oasis (with its capital at Laghouat) and La Saoura (with Colomb-Béchar as its capital) took place. These new *départements* did not put an end to the division between northern Algeria and the Sahara. The future of the Saharan *départements* was, in fact, to depend upon the OCRS (the Common Organization of the Saharan Regions), created through the legislation of 10 January 1957 which put the Algerian Sahara, together with the Saharan regions of Sudan, Nigeria and Chad, under the control of a General Representative whose powers, at this time, were not only economic in nature, but also administrative and political. Shortly afterwards, in June 1957, a Ministry of the Sahara was created, on which the *départements* of southern Algeria were to be dependent. Max Lejeune, the Minister, combined his responsibilities with those of General Representative of the OCRS. Working in the High Commission of the latter body were Marius Moutet (Chairman of the Department), François Mitterrand (Vice-Chairman) and former Governor Naegelen.[10] Certain individuals even put forward the idea of involving Tunisia and Morocco in this enterprise, as part of a French-North African federation, an undertaking suggested at the same time by armed forces chiefs of staff.

Essentially, all these strategies converged and one man symbolized perfectly their unity of outlook: Pierre Guillaumat. The son of a general who had been Minister of War under Poincaré, Guillaumat had been appointed before the war to the Moroccan and Tunisian mines service, where he served under Erik Labonne. An eminent member of the Free French information service, director of the Oil Research Bureau and of the Fuels Service (1951–8), General Administrator of the CEA (Atomic Energy Commission) (1951–8) and President of Electricité de France (the French Electricity Board) (1954–9), this graduate of the School of Civil Engineering of the École Polytechnique (a prestigious higher education institution) had a certain resemblance to the Saint-Simonians who, a century earlier, had been the inspiration behind the achievements of Napoleon III's industrial policy, such as the construction of the Suez Canal.[11]

These future plans did not appear to contradict the European projects under construction from 1950 onwards and confirmed at the Messina Conference of June 1956, which laid the ground for the signing of the Treaty of Rome in March 1957. Quite on the contrary, the growth in power which would accrue to France from the realization of Africa's immense potential was seen as allowing her the chance to occupy an important place in this future European community, as a key pillar of what would be the construction of a true 'Eurafrica'. It seemed, however, that Algeria was to remain the business purely of the French. As General Augustin Guillaume, Resident General of Morocco, candidly emphasized in 1953: 'Even if the Allies have to provide financial assistance so as to ensure an investment in plant which, furthermore, is in their interests as much as ours, it is indispensable that such assistance should not provide the excuse for overt or covert control over the political and administrative conduct of the affairs of our territories, nor for the arrival of significant numbers of foreign personnel.'[12] This mistrust was addressed, obviously, towards the Americans and the British, and particularly towards their oil companies, which were accused of wishing, at whatever cost, to retain their monopoly, causing a degree of anxiety that rose even further during the Algerian War.[13] It was also, however, a shot across the bows of the EEC, which was not to be allowed to take the place of France. The collection of legislation known as 'the Saharan oil code' had as its goal, indeed, to ensure the tight control of the French state over the allocation of concessions (something which was subsequently to facilitate greatly the actions of post-independence Algeria).

It was even more indispensable to ensure the territory was defended. Up until autumn 1957, the activities of the ALN in the Sahara had been low-key and limited. During this period, Tunis and Cairo radio announced the opening of a 'Saharan front', even if the statistics of operations on this front were far from earth-shattering: 9 civilians and 15 soldiers killed, plus the desertion of 63 soldiers of the French Camel Corps. It was rapidly crushed after the intervention of two parachute regiments, the 3rd Colonial Parachute Regiment under Lieutenant-Colonel Bigeard which operated between the end of October and the end of December in the large erg (area of dunes) to the North of Timimoun, and the 1st Parachute Regiment under Lieutenant-Colonel Jeanpierre which destroyed an ALN group near Sidi Okba. At the start of 1958, 'Operation Ouragan', a joint operation with the Spanish targeted against the Moroccan Liberation Army guerrillas in the Western Sahara, was designed to counteract Moroccan claims on the western part of the Algerian Sahara, Spanish Sahara and Mauritania, claims announced by the Istiqlal leader Allal el-Fassi in January 1956 and in part taken up with the UN by the Moroccan government in October 1957. These operations were sufficient to re-establish French control over the whole of the Algerian Sahara. Having only very weak resources at its disposal (it could only count on 80 men in the attacks of autumn 1957), the FLN was further hampered by the deterioration in its relations with the Moroccan and Tunisian authorities, particularly from summer 1958 onwards. The Moroccan government, which had negotiated the restriction of French garrisons to coastal bases at the same time as the Tunisian government had done so, seemed to want to negotiate directly with France over the question of its frontiers. On 30 June 1958, the Tunisian government agreed to sign an agreement allowing the construction of the Edjeleh-La Skhirra oil pipeline, an agreement which was followed, in July 1958, by the withdrawal of French forces, most notably the GSST (the Saharan Group of the Tunisian South), from southern areas of Tunisia. For this reason, or because they were asking for a redrawing of their national frontiers at the expense of those of Algeria, the Tunisians opposed all ALN operations to the south of Bir el-Ater, that is to say on the southern side of the Nemencha mountains. As for the Libyan government, it continued to take a prudent approach and banned the launching of any military offensives from its national territory.

The Fifth Republic and the Sahara

At first it appeared that the arrival in power of General de Gaulle would not require any revision of the principal planks of existing policy. Michel Debré, his prime minister, underlined the importance of the Sahara: 'The work of France [in Algeria], the security of the Mediterranean and the potential of the Sahara, not to forget the nature of our political principles, in my eyes justify French sovereignty, a sovereignty legitimised as much by the past as by the imperatives of the future.'[14] The Fifth Republic was prolonging and deepening the involvement of the Fourth Republic in the region. Paul Delouvrier, the General Representative of the government in Algeria and a man who had formerly been head of the financial division of the European Coal and Steel Community, proclaimed in 1960 that 'the Sahara is going to become a Euro-African home of energy. France will find herself at the centre of this evolving global construct'.[15] The Sahara could thus be seen as the central element of an ambitious political and economic project which was in the process of being turned into a reality. The oil wealth of the country was now recognized. The fuel reserves discovered were put into production extremely rapidly: the Bougie terminal, linked to the oil wells of the Hassi Messaoud region, was inaugurated in November 1959; in 1960, oil from the Polignac basin was piped to Tunisia via the Skhirra pipeline; and, in 1961, gas from Hassi R'mel-Arzew started to come on tap. These operations, brought about essentially by French engineers, technicians and capital (56 per cent from the public sector, 26 per cent from the private sector) seemed to symbolize a renewal of the spirit of enterprise in a nation apt to accuse itself of getting cold feet. Twenty million tonnes were produced in 1962, accounting for a third of the nation's supplies.

The essential role played by the Sahara in the development of what is now conventially referred to as the 'force de frappe' (the 'strike force', France's nuclear deterrent), a concept which includes both 'the bomb' and its carriers, should also be recognized. Pierre Guillaumat was appointed to the Armed Forces Ministry (June 1958 – February 1960) and then to the Atomic Energy Ministry (until April 1962). General Ailleret, another loyal supporter of de Gaulle, supervised testing on the ground.[16] The first above-ground test explosion (*Gerboise bleue* – blue jerboa) was successfully carried out on 13 February 1960 and the fourth in April 1961, on the eve of the putsch. Subsequently, from November 1961 onwards, underground tests were undertaken at In Ekker.[17] At the same time, the Sahara had been chosen for the development of French ballistic systems, planned to begin from August 1958. In September 1959 the SEREB (Society for the Study and Production of Ballistic Missiles) was created. The base of Hammaguir, about a hundred kilometres south-west of Colomb-Béchar, had to serve as the site for tests designed to perfect military hardware (Saphir, Topaze and Emeraude – Sapphire, Topaz and Emerald), but also for civil applications (Véronique and Diamant), for which the first tests started in 1961.[18]

Given this background, it was by no means inevitable that the future of the Sahara should be tied in with that of Algeria. General de Gaulle retained the Ministry of the Sahara, authority over which was given to Max Lejeune, the sole holder of this portfolio since its creation in June 1957, until January 1959, when it was conferred upon Jacques Soustelle, Minister of State with responsibility both for the Sahara and for atomic energy. Then, after Soustelle's departure in February 1960, responsibility passed to the Minister for Overseas Départements and Territories (the DOM-TOMs), initially Robert Lecourt, subsequently Louis Jacquinot.[19] As regards the organization of the wider region, the OCRS's sphere of influence was limited in February 1959 to the two Algerian *départements* of Les Oasis and La Saoura (which since 1957 had taken the place of the former territories of the South), then was enlarged through a series of agreements made with the other Saharan states. In his speech of 16 September 1959, announcing self-determination, de Gaulle spoke only of 'the twelve Algerian *départements*' of the North, excluding the Sahara. Soon afterwards, Olivier Guichard, one of the leading lights of the Gaullist movement, was given the office of Representative to the OCRS, henceforth a separate position from that of Minister for the Sahara, a development which may be seen as the expression of a strong desire to make this body into a distinctive and representative regional organization.[20]

In addition, the defence of the Sahara was very rigorously reinforced. There were 25,000 army troops there at the beginning of 1959 and 30,000 by the start of 1962. There were 26,000 men divided between two commands, the east and west zones of the Sahara, and placed under the command of generals, each of whom also fulfilled the role of Prefect of one of the two *départements*, that is to say Les Oasis and La Saoura. The remainder (about 4,000 men) was made up of the various units responsible for ballistic and nuclear testing. To this should be added 1,300 *harkis* and troop contingents provided by the Reguibat and Hoggar nomadic tribes. Mobility was provided by Saharan motorized transport companies, which ensured the security of the routes, while mixed units of the French Camel Corps had responsibility for providing a patrols service, a part of which was undertaken on camels. The responsibility for the security of so-called 'sensitive areas' was allocated to companies of Saharan infantry. In addition, the oil companies contributed to the defence of installations, reinforcing passive protection systems (fencing, gates, etc.) and recruiting security guards, the majority of whom were former members of the Foreign Legion. Alongside this there were rapid deployment forces: in Mauritania the Fort-Trinquet operational group, which was in close liaison with Tindouf; in northern Algeria airborne elements on permanent alert at the Telergma base and who were in a position to reinforce the air force commandos stationed at Colomb-Béchar. The external security of the forces comprised a series of zones that were out of bounds to civilians, and which extended from the western frontier blockade (which, de facto, prohibited access to the Oujda–Méchéria–Figuig triangle) to the greater part of the Ksour mountains, from the Amour djebel and the Ouled Naïl (including the Laghouat-Aïn Mahdi region), then essentially to the south and east of Négrine. In the Sahara itself, the Moroccan border areas (Hammada du Guir, Hammada du Draa) were off-limits, as were the area fringing Tunisia along the Eastern erg and the Libyan frontier in the Edjeleh oil pipeline sector. Political and administrative information and activity on a regional basis were provided by 42 Specialized Administrative Sections (SAS), around 120 officers and about a hundred NCOs.

It remained, then, difficult for the FLN to bring war to the Sahara. The ALN contented itself with seeking to use the Sahara as a means of skirting round the southern side of the military barriers and launching feeble commando raids that left the most sensitive French installations untouched. Did the FLN leadership look after the interests of the oil companies? This idea has often been put forward, without any precise evidence. Certainly it was a lot less easy to do lasting damage to the oil installations than is generally realized. In any case certain areas, such as that of Hassi Messaoud, seemed to pay no attention to the war that was going on around them. This situation which, for all the French government's practical purposes, allowed the separation of the destiny of the Sahara from that of Algeria to be envisaged, could only reinforce a defensive stance. Responsibility for this fell, after September 1959, to an inter-forces commander in the Sahara, then from December 1961 onwards, to a senior commander in the Sahara who came directly from the Armed Forces Ministry.

The attachment of the French government to separating the question of the Sahara from that of Algeria was shown at the time of the first Evian and Lugrin negotiations with the GPRA (provisional government of Algeria), from May or June to July of 1961. The French government expressed at this time its desire for the Sahara to be excluded from the area covered by the referendum, the future of the Sahara being decided, in due course, through consultations between all states in the region. For the FLN, on the other hand, having always proclaimed its commitment to a 'united and indivisible' Algeria, there was no question of a compromise on this matter.[21]

Forcing the Algerian negotiators to make do with the twelve northern *départements* was not an impossibility, but it could only have been achieved at the cost of a brutal split which would have compromised the future of the Sahara even if it had remained under French control. If it is true that the military resources of the FLN in the Sahara were extremely limited, it seems on the other hand that, particularly in the principal population centres (Oasis, Mzab, Ziban, Oued-Rhir), its political agents had a very strong influence, something which would present a risk of perpetuating insecurity. Furthermore, the Sahara had a 90 per cent dependence on the transport networks of northern Algeria for its supplies, which would have necessitated the establishment of costly alternatives which, in addition, would have had to pass through other African nations, and not ones which were or could be relied upon to remain very stable. Last but not least, it was clear that the imposition of such a policy on the GPRA would have meant sudden and immediate secession, and so the immediate loss of French positions in Algeria.

Thus, in his press conference of 5 September 1961, General de Gaulle, wishing to break the impasse in negotiations, decided to cut his losses. He recognized that, in return for the establishment of an association to safeguard French interests ('the freedom to benefit from the oil and gas which we discovered and which we discover in the future, the provision of airfields and the right of passage for all our communications with black

Africa'), France would not oppose the recognition of Algerian sovereignty over the Sahara.[22] From this time on he seemed to lose interest in the OCRS.[23] The governmental declarations of 19 March 1962 (inappropriately called the Evian Accords) authorized France to retain its nuclear and space research installations in the Sahara for a period of five years.[24] Thus, France's future as a nuclear power was protected, a condition which de Gaulle considered essential for the nation to recover its international status. In the same way, a 'declaration of agreed principles for co-operation in the development of the mineral wealth of the Sahara' safeguarded the most important elements of France's oil interests. For de Gaulle, unless these hydrocarbon fuels could be, in future, produced on French soil, the best option available would be for them at least to be paid for in francs, thus avoiding currency outflows and not 'subsidising the dollar or the pound'; also these fuels continued to be extracted by French companies, who benefited in terms of savoir-faire and profits. The economic merit of the first argument is debatable, to the extent that the counterpart of these foreign exchange savings was a degree of cooperation which relied upon significant financial transfers. The second argument is more solidly grounded, since it relates to working on the development of the French public sector.

Epilogue

The withdrawal from the military bases took place within the planned timescale. The final nuclear experiment took place on 16 February 1966, the continuation of the programme being handed over to the CEP (Pacific Experimentation Centre), whose setting up had been approved in 1963. France withdrew from the Hammaguir aerospace centre on 1 July 1967. The Les Landes test centre for the development of missiles, whose creation had been approved since July 1962, became operational in 1966, while the Kourou base in French Guyana, the developmental planning of which had begun a little later (in April 1964), took up the baton as regards civil aerospace research. Besides their better technical possibilities (a range of 8,000 km against 4,000 km for missiles launched from Les Landes, and the possibility of orbiting the equator for satellites launched from Kourou), all these new sites offered the advantage, at the time, of being located on French national territory.

Something similar happened with French oil interests. Saharan oil production, guaranteed by the provisions of the Evian Accords and then by the 1965 Treaty, had accounted for a third of French supplies in 1963, and still considerably more than a quarter in 1970.[25] In competition with CFP (which had been trading its oil under the Total brand-name since 1954), UGP (General Union of Petroleum), which had been created in 1960, became the nucleus of a company which, in 1966, gave birth to the

Elf-Erap group, through the agglomeration of a whole series of businesses created by the state down the years. With the support of the state which, by means of the allocation of export licences, assured it of 15 per cent of the domestic market, the new business was able to play a dynamic role in the sectors of refining, research and production.[26] A vigorous policy aimed at diversifying sources of supply allowed France to progressively lessen her dependence upon Algerian resources, while, on the other hand, the Algerian authorities became more and more demanding. While the nationalization of the Algerian oil industry in 1971, therefore, did not help to facilitate Franco-Algerian cooperation, it did not constitute a catastrophe for French companies. Elf-Erap, which had made the greatest degree of financial commitment to Algeria, preferred to withdraw in 1975 so as to complete a transformation started with its production in the North Sea and in Black Africa. Even if its great ambitions to obtain significant production concessions in Iraq, or even in Saudi Arabia, were to fall through in the end, its engineering capabilities allowed it to carve itself an important niche in the Middle East at a time when the provision of services was becoming an ever more important commercial factor. CFP preferred to retain a certain level of investment in Algeria, as a symbol of a form of cooperation in production which the company then wished to develop in the Middle East, where its activities remained at a significant level.

Did the attachment of the French governments of the period to oil, or indeed to the development of nuclear weapons, prolong the conflict, as has sometimes been suggested? This is far from clear as it seems that the question of the Algerian French (and, for many officers, of the Algerian people as a whole), may have carried a lot more weight than that of the Sahara's economic potential. It is true, however, to the extent that it may have appeared to be an essential element in France's future status on the world stage, that the Sahara constituted a considerable opportunity for a nation which, since 1945, had been trying to reconstruct its national power base. This task may be considered to have been accomplished by the 1970s, which explains why the French governments of the time should have been so prepared to accept the inevitable. It would be most interesting to examine how, since independence, the Algerian state, in this matter a faithful follower of the example set by the French state, has attempted to conduct an almost identical policy in the Sahara.

Notes

1. R. Valet, *Le Sahara algérien, étude de l'organisation administrative, financière et judiciaire des Territoires du Sud* (Algiers: La type-litho, 1927), pp. 321–4.
2. M.-R. Thomas, *Sahara et Communauté* (PUF, 1960), p. 260.
3. Ibid., p. 265.
4. Pierre Guillaumat, 'D'ici quinze ans, le pétrole saharien pourra couvrir tous les besoins', *Industries et travaux d'Outre-Mer* (Feb. 1957), pp. 59–60.

5. J.-J. Berreby, *Le golfe persique, mer de légende, réservoir de pétrole* (Payot, 1959), p. 215.
6. M. Brogini, *L'exploitation des hydrocarbures en Algérie de 1956 à 1971* (Masters dissertation, University of Nice), pp. 113–14.
7. Yves Le Baut, 'Les essais nucléaires français de 1966 à 1974', *Relations Internationales*, 59 (Autumn 1989), pp. 359–70.
8. J. Frémeaux, *L'Afrique à l'ombre des épées (1830–1930)*, Vol. 1: *Des établissements côtiers aux confins sahariens* (Service Historique de l'Armée de Terre (French Army Historical Service), 1993), pp. 82–4.
9. Legislation of 20 September 1947 conferring organic status on Algeria, as reproduced in P. E. Sarrasin, *La crise algérienne* (Editions du Cerf, 1949), pp. 224–44.
10. *Nouvelle revue française d'outre-mer* (March 1958), p. 122.
11. Obituary in *Le Monde*, 30 August 1991, and P. Péan, *Les émirs de la République. L'aventure du pétrole tricolore* (Seuil, 1982), p. 23.
12. General Guillaume, acting commander-in-chief of the strategic zone of North Africa and General Inspector of North African Land, Sea and Air Forces, 'Importance stratégique de l'Afrique du Nord', *Revue de Défense nationale* (November 1953), pp. 423–30.
13. P. Mélandri, 'La France et le "double jeu" des Etats-Unis', *La guerre d'Algérie et les Français* (Fayard, 1990), p. 434.
14. M. Debré, *Gouverner, mémoires 1958–1962* (A. Michel, 1988), pp. 193, 197.
15. Ch. R. Ageron, 'L'Algérie, dernière chance de la France', *Relations internationales*, 57 (1989), pp. 113–39, p. 134.
16. General Charles Ailleret, *L'aventure atomique française* (Grasset, 1968).
17. Yves Le Baut, 'Les essaies nucléaires français'.
18. Pierre Usunier, 'Les vecteurs sol-sol balistiques stratégiques', *L'Arme nucléaire et ses vecteurs* (Centre d'histoire de l'Aéronautique et de l'Espace, conference 1989), pp. 171–208.
19. Thomas, *Sahara et Communauté*, pp. 220–2, 233–48.
20. O. Guichard, *Mon général* (Grasset, 1980), pp. 379–80.
21. M. Cointet, *De Gaulle et l'Algérie française 1958–1962* (Perrin, 1995), pp. 217–22.
22. X. Yacono, *De Gaulle et le FLN* (ed. De l'Atlanthrope, 1989), pp. 42–6.
23. Guichard, *Mon général*, pp. 379–80.
24. Robert Buron, *Carnets politiques de la guerre d'Algérie* (Plon, 1965), p. 214.
25. Brogini, *L'exploitation des hydrocarbures en Algérie*, p. 438.
26. Henri Madelin, *Pétrole et politique en Méditerranée occidentale* (Presses de la FNSP, 1973), pp. 114–22.

5

From One Crisis to Another: the Morale of the French Foreign Legion during the Algerian War

Eckard Michels

Any analysis of the morale of the Foreign Legion during the Algerian War,[1] as with any other military conflict, has to take into account the singular nature of this elite corps of the French army. At least in theory, the Legion is exclusively composed of foreign mercenaries, but is commanded entirely by French officers. At the start of the Algerian War, about 45 to 50 per cent of the troops of the Legion were German, followed by about 15 per cent who were French and 10 per cent Italian.[2] Nationality, however, matters little for the purposes of assessing the morale of members of the Legion as, once they joined, their attachment to their homelands generally dissipated very rapidly. The motto of the Legion, 'legio patria nostra', was well chosen given the relatively easy integration of the various nationalities over the course of more than 150 years. In speaking about the morale of the Legion and the factors that influenced it, though, we must distinguish between, on the one hand and alongside the rank-and-file troops, the non-commissioned officers, who during the period we are examining were mainly foreigners, and, on the other hand, the French officer corps of the Legion. In the way that they reacted to events in Algeria, the officers of the Foreign Legion were by and large similar to their comrades in other elite French army units. They nurtured the same beliefs about the importance of the colonies and of wars of decolonization for the future role of France on the world stage and of the armed forces in the French nation. They viewed themselves as a national elite with a particular vocation, while the foreign mercenary did not concern himself with issues related to French domestic or foreign policy. The mercenary had been attracted to the Legion by his vocation for a life of military adventure or, more often, due to economic or social problems from which he wished to escape. In general he was interested neither in the goals of the war in which he was fighting under French colours nor in the destiny of France. As with all mercenary troops, his morale depended more upon material questions such as food, clothing and, above all, pay. For soldiers of the Legion the only points of reference were the Legion itself with its strong *esprit de corps* and, to a lesser degree, their own homeland. At the same time, however, the troops of the Legion were, like their officers, professional soldiers and volunteers, something that distinguished them from the great majority of French soldiers who fought in the Algerian War as conscripts. In contrast to these conscripts, for soldiers of the Foreign Legion the war wasn't a cruel and unpleasant episode in a life lived on Civvy Street; rather it was an adventure they had sought out and deliberately chosen. They had often experienced problems fitting into civil society in their home countries and could now consider themselves part of an elite military unit.

When the Algerian War broke out on 1 November 1954, the Foreign Legion, like the rest of the French army, was still deeply dismayed by the defeat suffered in Indochina. At the beginning, the Legion was still more involved in the disturbances in Morocco and Tunisia than in what was happening in Algeria. Most combat units of the Legion, which, due to the swelling of troop numbers during the war in South-East Asia, totalled about 32,000 men in autumn 1954, were either still in the Far East or were on their way back to North Africa. The last Foreign Legion troops returned to Algeria only in the spring of 1956. Apart from the three (1st to 3rd) Foreign Paratroop Battalions (which had been founded between 1948 and 1951), its two (1st and 2nd) Foreign Cavalry Regiments and its four Compagnies Sahariennes Portées (Motorised Saharan Companies), the Foreign Legion remained largely a heavy infantry force throughout the Algerian War, as it had been during the campaign in Indochina. At the end of 1954, it had the following infantry units: two battalions of the 1st Foreign Regiment, the 2nd, 3rd, 4th and 5th Foreign Infantry Regiments and the 13th Demi-Brigade of the Foreign Legion. In autumn 1954, the central services of the Legion were principally based in Algeria, the homeland of the Foreign Legion since its foundation in 1831. These included the Foreign Regiments' Common Depot, the Foreign Legion Autonomous Grouping and the 1st Foreign Regiment, that is to say all those sections of the Legion providing members of the Legion with administration, training, propaganda, recruitment, officer management and social support services, representing nearly 8,000 men in total. However, only about 2,300 men from the 3rd Foreign Paratroop Battalion, three Compagnies Sahariennes Portées and a battalion of the 1st Foreign Infantry Regiment were available as rapid deployment units for immediate action against the insurrectionaries. Some 3,200 soldiers from the 2nd Foreign Cavalry Regiment and the 4th Foreign Infantry Regiment, together with one Compagnie Saharienne Portées were stationed in Morocco and almost 800 men (one battalion of the 1st Foreign Regiment) were in Tunisia.

Compared to Indochina, which had always been a favourite posting and battlefield of the Foreign Legion, the prospect of returning to Algeria after the ending of hostilities in the Far East scarcely aroused enthusiasm. Even during wartime, South-East Asia had many attractions for soldiers of the

Legion, including higher pay, less strictness of discipline and the possibility for many of them to form alliances with native women. After an initial degree of relief, reports on the morale of units still present in the Far East following the ending of hostilities in July 1954 noted that a certain 'nostalgia for action' very rapidly grew up among Foreign Legion soldiers. Disappointment spread among reinforcements who had been happy to leave Algeria after undergoing a period of tough training on a very modest wage, but who were now forced to recognize that they had arrived too late to be able to take part again in active combat.[3] The ending of the vicious fighting in Indochina, which had cost the lives of 10,500 members of the Legion, and the prospect of a return to North Africa, which was still relatively peaceful in comparison to recent events in Indochina, did not raise troop morale at all.

Officers of the Legion, like the majority of their comrades in other units in 1954–5, feared that French policy vis-à-vis the problems in North Africa might be characterized by the same lack of firmness as during the war that preceded it and that this could lead to another political and military defeat. At the end of 1955, for example, the 3rd Foreign Infantry Regiment summed up the state of mind of its officers as regards the previous 12 months as follows: 'It must be noted that the conflict between the French nation and the French army that dogged officers during the Indochina campaign is being continued at present in North Africa.' The 1st Foreign Regiment's judgement at the end of 1955 was similar: 'Many, if not all (officers and staff) conclude that the Indochina business is being repeated and express unequivocal hostility towards the politics of surrender being followed by the government,'[4] whereas the concerns of the Foreign Legion troops were above all that garrison life would be too monotonous and that, given the lack of military operations, they would see a fall in their pay. As a consequence, the Legion found itself facing a wave of desertions during the return of its units from South-East Asia, units that had fought courageously against the Vietminh but which now feared the prospect of a boring and monotonous life in the garrisons of North Africa. Since the nineteenth century, the narrow Suez Canal, where the use of firearms was forbidden under international law, had offered the best chance for deserters to escape by jumping into the water. Between the autumn of 1954 and the start of 1956, more than 600 Foreign Legion soldiers, including 420 Germans, deserted from French vessels carrying veterans of the Indochina conflict.

Furthermore, in 1955–6, recruitment bureaux in France noted a significant decline in the number of volunteers compared with the period of the Indochina war, which was not solely due to the fact that, with West Germany regaining her national sovereignty in May 1955, the Legion had to close its recruitment posts on German soil. Paradoxically, the war in South-East Asia hadn't scared off potential volunteers, rather it had attracted these young men. The FLN uprising in Algeria, in contrast, was not, at the beginning, seen as a real war by the general public in Western Europe, so that fewer young adventurers felt attracted by this conflict. In addition, during the first 18 months of the Algerian War, the number of re-enlistments of former members of the Legion whose contracts had come to an end, which had remained high throughout the bitter fighting in the Far East and which, between the years 1952 and 1954, had been more important to the maintenance of troop levels than had the recruitment of new volunteers, fell to a significant degree. The comparative levels of re-enlistments and desertions were always an indicator of the state of mind of the *légionnaires*. After the defeat in Indochina and in anticipation of France probably soon withdrawing from her North African protectorates, many veterans lost faith in the possibility of pursuing a long-term career in the ranks of the Foreign Legion. As Colonel Lennuyeux, adviser to the French General Staff on all questions relating to the Foreign Legion, wrote in June 1956: 'Soldiers in the Legion, however, have only a limited degree of confidence in their future even in this country [i.e. Algeria] so the majority of them wish to return home first to follow the development of France's political and military situation from a distance.' In this report he judged the morale of those units of the Legion that were in Morocco, in particular, to have declined greatly, as shown by the dangerously high level of desertions. He finished the report by stating that 'it follows, from all viewpoints, that the Legion will be facing a crisis'.[5] Furthermore, with the end of the war in Indochina, many German *légionnaires*, considered since the end of the nineteenth century to be the best soldiers in the Legion, started to dream of returning to Germany. This has already been shown by the high proportion of Germans among deserters at the Suez Canal. For many of them in 1955–6, the prospects of the German economic miracle and of German rearmament appeared more attractive than a badly paid hunt for fellaghas (Arab guerrillas) in a land where traditionally it had always been difficult for foreign mercenaries to establish contacts with civilians among the native French or Muslim population. As a result, the percentage of Germans in the ranks of the Foreign Legion continued to decline throughout the Algerian War, from about 45–50 per cent in the autumn of 1954 to roughly 35 per cent in 1962.

Although, at the end of 1955, it was possible to see that a real new war had started in Algeria on 1 November 1954, bringing with it the prospect of a lot of military operations, in particular for units of the Foreign Legion, morale in all units remained fairly low up until the end of 1956. In general, the *légionnaire* was seen by his officers as a potentially unstable man, troubled and incapable of looking after himself, to the extent that a life of inactivity in the barracks could have a detrimental effect on his morale. The best remedy for counteracting any decline in morale was to carry out military offensives involving combat on different military fronts. Units of the Legion still stationed in Morocco, in particular, were hit by a wave of desertions from the end of 1955 because, after the negotiations on Moroccan independence, they were confined to barracks and, in consequence, were very sensitive to the propaganda of the Moroccan and Algerian nationalists. These latter groups incited them to desert and their propaganda was orchestrated by a German named Winfried Müller (alias Si Mustapha), head of the FLN's 'Foreign Legion Repatriation Service', which was based in Tetuan, in the former Spanish zone of Morocco. One particular goal of this service was to influence West German public opinion, which was traditionally very hostile to the Foreign Legion, in a way that would be beneficial to the cause of the FLN. From the spring of 1956, Colonel Lennuyeux pleaded for all Legion units still on Moroccan soil to be withdrawn so as to put an end to the wave of desertions from the 4th Foreign Infantry Regiment and the 2nd Foreign Cavalry Regiment, caused by the forced inactivity of French troops in Morocco. During the first ten months of 1956, for example, the 2nd Foreign Cavalry Regiment, which was based in Oujda, lost 71 *légionnaires* out of a total of 700 men due to desertions and, after the regiment had been transferred in autumn 1956, its commander noted that: 'troop morale has suffered due to the desertion crisis, which even put in doubt the loyalty of the most longserving veterans'. Its commander was optimistic, however, that with the prospect of new military assignments on Algerian soil, morale would improve.[6]

In March 1957, the last Foreign Legion soldiers finally left Morocco.

The situation in Foreign Legion units in Algeria was better because, immediately on returning from South-East Asia, all units that had been in Indochina were employed in operations against the ALN; nonetheless, it was far from satisfactory. Besides the officers' lack of trust in the government's commitment to fight the FLN right to the bitter end, they were critical of the military command's ability to adapt to the type of war being waged by the FLN. One example of this came from Pierre Sergent, who was a captain in the 1st Foreign Paratroop Battalion in 1955:

> Like all officers who served in Indochina, everywhere I am struck by our slowness to adapt our methods to those required in a counter-guerrilla campaign. At army staff HQ, they do not wish to admit that tanks are useless, as useless as these jets which are too fast to be practical in hunting down an enemy who is on foot. This type of a war requires an infantry response: infantry, infantry and more infantry. It requires a sort of 'super-infantryman' who is light, fast and similar to the paratroops or to the *légionnaires*, of whom there are far too few among the troops in Algeria.[7]

Certainly, in many regards, as colonial war troops unencumbered by heavy material and due to their tough training, professionalism and tradition of being highly mobile, Foreign Legion soldiers were better suited to a counter-guerrilla campaign than most other French troops. For the rank-and-file troops, however, their first experiences in Algeria, like those in Tunisia in 1954–5, were not very encouraging as, due to a lack of precise, up-to-date information, units would end up pointlessly wasting their time undertaking exhaustive – and exhausting – search operations involving the excessive use of men and material. The operations had been planned too far in advance and so allowed the small enemy units ample time to disperse before they could be caught by the French. Evidence of this is provided by the report for 1955 on the morale of the 3rd Foreign Infantry Regiment, which had been undertaking operations in the Aurès mountains since the beginning of that year: 'On a general level, the morale of the *légionnaires* is solid. Life on active service suits them well. However, they are becoming tired of having to face the same frustrations they have been facing for the past year. The lack of tangible results from operations to hunt down rebels is having a negative effect upon their morale.' The commanders of the 3rd Foreign Infantry Regiment, like those of the 2nd Foreign Infantry Regiment, which was still serving in Tunisia in 1955, challenged the lack of proportion between the resources used on the French side and the results obtained through these operations, something that could only prove to have a negative influence upon troop morale. In the 13th Demi-Brigade of the Foreign Legion, which, like the 3rd Foreign Infantry Regiment, had been used since its return from South-East Asia in early 1955 on exhausting and fruitless operations in the difficult terrain of the Aurès mountains, not a single re-enlistment was registered in ten months. 'It should be noted that nearly all the "major *a priori* operations" in which the Regiment has taken part have proved to be a disappointment,' wrote the commander of the 5th Foreign Infantry Regiment, even at the end of 1956.[8]

From the second half of 1956 onwards, however, morale in Foreign Legion units started to show a distinct improvement and this trend continued over the years that followed. The change in the climate of morale in the Legion was shown particularly by a rise in the rate of enlistments and re-enlistments and by a fall in the rate of desertions. After more than 18 months of military operations, at least the Foreign Legion soldier or potential recruit was able to get the impression that a real war was being conducted in Algeria, even if the results of military operations were not always satisfactory. However, the definite prospect of tough combat to come and, therefore, of a future role for the Legion as colonial warfare shock troops seemed to be assured. The sending of a battalion of the 3rd Foreign Infantry Regiment to Madagascar in autumn 1956, and plans and rumours indicating the possible deployment of certain units of the Legion in French Black Africa, were also given a positive welcome by members of the Legion, who were always enthusiastic about moving on to pastures new. The introduction at the end of 1955 of a 'maintenance of order bonus' in units of the Legion, while it was lower than pay had been in Indochina, naturally also had a positive impact on morale, as did a pay increase introduced from 1957 onwards.

In addition to this, from the end of 1956 onwards, units of the Legion had started to be used in a more mobile fashion, that is to say they would change their operational sector more frequently, something that was better suited to the restless wandering spirit of the *légionnaire*. Efforts were made to set up better equipped rest bases for units returning from South-East Asia, at which Foreign Legion units could rest for about a month after two or three months on operational duty. From the end of 1956, a sort of pattern became established whereby each battalion of the Legion would spend periods of time on active service interspersed with periods of rest. This pattern suited the character of the *légionnaire*, who wanted to be involved in active combat but who also wanted to be rewarded with free time back at barracks, time devoted particularly to drinking and to frequenting the military campaign brothels which each regiment had at its disposal, after time spent on tough military engagements. Furthermore, operational outcomes were becoming more positive due to a better use of information, often obtained through the systematic torture of persons suspected of having links with the FLN and due to the employment of smaller, more mobile units.

Morale was high particularly in regiments of the Legion serving as rapid deployment troops, as opposed to sectorial troops. At the start of the Algerian conflict, rapid deployment troop duties were the preserve solely of the three Foreign Paratroop Battalions, which, from autumn 1955, became the 1st and 2nd Foreign Paratroop Regiments. However, under pressure from Foreign Legion Command, which became the Foreign Legion Inspectorate from 1957 onwards, other units of the Legion were used as rapid deployment troops too. The officers of the Legion were convinced that sectorial troop duties did not suit the rather unsettled, restless, aggressive and often violent character of their troops and that, furthermore, assignment to these duties damaged their pride in being elite soldiers. In addition, the conscript mobilization from 1956 onwards provided enough troops to replace the soldiers of the Legion in their duties protecting the security of particular sectors. The Foreign Legion Inspector, whose responsibility it was to advise 10th Region Military Command and army staff HQ on all matters relating to the employment of the Legion, consistently emphasized the positive effect upon the morale of units of the Legion when they were used as rapid deployment troops: 'Accepting a tough lifestyle so long as it involves action and the risks of war, the Foreign Legion soldier considers himself to have been swindled and humiliated when he is given a static and subsidiary role', wrote Colonel Lennuyeux in February 1957. In the same report on the state of Foreign Legion units in

Algeria he contrasted the high morale of regiments used as rapid deployment troops, such as the Foreign Paratroop Regiments and the 5th Foreign Infantry Regiment, with the low morale of units used as sectorial or guard troops, such as the 3rd Foreign Infantry Regiment and the 13th Demi-Brigade of the Foreign Legion.[9] On 27th September 1958, a directive definitively freed the 3rd and 5th Foreign Infantry Regiments and the 13th Demi-Brigade of the Foreign Legion, like the two Foreign Paratroop Regiments, from all sectorial troop duties and they were attached to the general reserves deployed across Algeria, wherever battle fronts might be at a given time.

Foreign Legion inspection reports for the years 1958 and 1959, produced by General Gardy, head of Foreign Legion technical inspections, show evidence of the constant improvement in their state from 1957 onwards, something which corresponded with the general improvement in the military situation for the French armed forces in Algeria: 'Morale in general is excellent. The Legion, aware of its value and potential, had previously suffered through its use in missions that were too static'. Since July 1958, for the first time since the end of the war in Indochina, Foreign Legion recruitment and re-enlistments had reached a level sufficient to allow overall troop numbers to be stabilized for about three years at about 20,500 men, which corresponded to the theoretical figure laid down by armed forces high command in 1955. The continuous reduction in the overall size of the Legion, a constant since 1954, finally came to an end in 1959. The monthly rate of desertions, the official figure for which had been 2.69 per thousand, had still been rising in 1956, fell back to 1.29 per thousand in 1958 and 1.01 per thousand in 1959, meaning that at the height of the Algerian War there were even fewer desertions than there had been during the war in Indochina. Besides the recovery in the confidence the *légionnaires* felt in the future of their organization and the greater use of Foreign Legion units on active service, there were three further reasons for this fall in the level of desertions: the effectiveness of the French fortifications along the Tunisian and Moroccan borders completed in late 1957; the fact that the FLN, which had been inciting and supporting desertions on the part of Foreign Legion soldiers but which now found itself more and more isolated and under attack, had lost control of the terrain it had previously held; and the introduction of a higher rate of pay for those accumulating more than 18 months of service.[10] The report for 1958 on the morale of all troops in the 10th Military Region, that is to say for all French troops serving in Algeria, also made reference to the Legion in a positive way: 'The Legion remained', according to General Salan, 'the very personification of high morale'.[11]

The FLN's Foreign Legion repatriation service, which had been an effective weapon in the psychological war conducted against units of the Legion in Morocco until 1957, was no longer able to incite anything more than a handful of *légionnaires* to desert. From 1957–8 onwards, more than half of all cases of desertion took place from the 1st Foreign Regiment which, since 1920, had had responsibility for the training of all new recruits to the Legion. Desertion rates had always been higher in the Legion's training companies than in other units, since during the first few months of their lives as *légionnaires* many recruits had problems adapting to the tough discipline and were often disappointed by the ridiculously low pay they received during their first 18 months of service. In addition, those regiments charged with controlling the borders with Morocco and Tunisia, such as the 3rd Foreign Infantry and 1st Foreign Cavalry Regiments in 1958 and the 4th and 2nd Foreign Infantry Regiments in 1959–60, suffered more from desertions than other regiments of the Legion. Even these few isolated deserters were not, as the German Embassy in Tunis noted, motivated by any sympathy for the struggle of the FLN, rather they no longer wished to have to put up with the severe discipline of the Legion or were not happy with their pay.[12]

Having been assuaged for a while after the events of 13 May 1958, the distrust officers of the Legion, like their fellow-officers in other troops, felt towards the political authorities resurfaced in autumn 1959, the suspicion again being that the political leadership was seeking a political rather than a military resolution of the conflict. General Gardy, who was later to be one of those involved in the Algiers putsch of 1961, made two references to this in his inspection report of 18 November 1959, two months after de Gaulle's declarations that he wanted to solve the Algerian problem by applying the principle of self-determination. He wrote that the handling of the Algerian problem by the political authorities would lead to a crisis of morale among officers. The troops of the Foreign Legion were less affected by these fears as, for the most part, they had absolutely no interest in French politics and nor were they able to understand enough French to follow developments in France's Algerian policy in the media. The traditional isolation of soldiers of the Legion, who had little contact with civilians, was certainly another factor in this lack of any political consciousness. In general, the inspector was convinced that the state of the Legion was 'very satisfying' and that the morale of its troops was 'excellent', and in his view the employment and operational performance of the Legion's troops had improved still further on those of the previous year.[13] Besides improvements in the utilization of troops as a result of the Plan Challe, the success of the Foreign Legion was also due to the increase in enlistments and re-enlistments as well as to the fact that, at the same time, troop losses in Algeria were lower than those suffered in Indochina. This favourable situation with regard to overall troop availability allowed the Legion to increase the training period for recruits to six months, so that, for the first time since 1945, it was able to offer new recruits a thorough training programme. Furthermore, this training could also be undertaken using the equipment that would actually be used on military operations, another thing that had not been possible during the previous war.

Even though the distrust felt by officers towards de Gaulle's Algerian policy became even stronger during 1960 and early 1961, the morale of Foreign Legion troops remained excellent throughout this period and up until the April 1961 putsch, according to reports made by General Morel, the new Inspector. The sole cause for concern was the noticeable slackening off of enlistment from the second half of 1960.[14] This was probably due to the economic growth taking place throughout Europe, which drained the pool of potential *légionnaires* driven by economic hardship. Another reason might have been the fact that, since 1960, the general public on an international level had been getting the impression more and more that Algerian independence was bound to happen sooner or later and that it would be achieved through negotiations, that is to say that Algeria would not remain a war zone for much longer. Many potential mercenaries, therefore, were reluctant to commit themselves by enlisting. However, for the *légionnaires* in Algeria, who paid little attention to political developments, the war continued throughout 1960 and early 1961 and so the levels of re-enlistment remained very high and even rose.

Three Foreign Legion regiments took part in the Algiers putsch of April 1961. The 1st Foreign Paratroop Regiment formed the spearhead of the Algiers rebellion, but the 2nd Foreign Paratroop Regiment and the 1st Foreign Cavalry Regiment were also prepared to lend the rebel generals their support. General Challe and his co-conspirators were certainly able to count on the sympathies of the great majority of Foreign Legion officers as the Algerian War, like the Indochina conflict before it, had above all been a war of elite troops of the French army. Furthermore, the fate of the Legion seemed to be linked to that of Algeria, since the employment or stationing of the Legion on the mainland did not form part of its founding laws in 1831 and had never been undertaken, except for the purposes of defending French national territory during the Franco-German conflicts that took place between 1870 and 1945. There was reason to fear, therefore, that the end of the French colonial empire would also seal the fate of the Foreign Legion. It was probably only the aversion of Colonel Brothier, commander of the 1st Foreign Regiment, and of other officers of the Legion, to the idea of using foreign mercenary troops in an internal French conflict that prevented more Foreign Legion regiments from taking part in the putsch. According to two sources, this refusal to allow the Legion to meddle in French politics, expressed by Colonel Brothier in April 1961, was shared by non-commissioned officers of the Legion.[15] In April 1961, however, the decision on whether or not to take part in the putsch depended entirely upon the views of the officers of the Legion, as, for the non-French troops and NCOs, the only authority that counted was that of their superior officers. The non-French soldier of the Foreign Legion was an unaware and apolitical tool in the hands of his superiors. Although he was not in agreement with those who launched the putsch, Janos Kemencei, who was of Hungarian origin and at the time of the putsch was a warrant officer first-class in the 2nd Foreign Paratroop Regiment, testifies to this fact: "The soldiers in the two large and prestigious units of the Foreign Legion [the 1st Foreign Paratroop and 1st Foreign Cavalry Regiments] that joined the rebels obeyed their officers, as all Foreign Legion soldiers always obeyed their superiors. If I had been in their position, I would have followed orders to the letter in the same way, without the slightest equivocation'.[16]

After the failure of the putsch, the morale of the Legion was in freefall. The disbandment of the prestigious 1st Foreign Paratroop Regiment immediately after the putsch, the transfer or punishment of many officers of the Legion who were suspected of sympathizing with the rebels, the complete halt to recruitment for six weeks during May and June of 1961, and the negative image of the Legion not only in the French press but also among soldiers who had remained loyal during the putsch were all factors that gave the impression that the days of the Legion were numbered. It was probably only thanks to the fact that Pierre Messmer, a former officer in the 13th Demi-Brigade of the Foreign Legion and a Gaullist from the very beginning, was Minister of Defence at the time of the putsch that spared the Legion from being completely and immediately disbanded after what happened in Algiers. The ending of large-scale military operations from the second half of 1961 restricted Foreign Legion troops to boring guard duties and, together with the prevailing insecurity over the future of the organization, this was the cause of a large increase in the number of desertions and a fall in the number of re-enlistments. A typical example of this is provided by Mauro Carra, a warrant officer in the 1st Foreign Cavalry Regiment at the end of 1961 who, when asked by his captain whether he wanted to re-enlist for 1962, responded: 'I don't know if I'm going to go on with it anymore. That'll depend on the future of the Legion. I don't want to end up in a regiment of the "regulars"'.[17] Even after the resumption of recruitment in June 1961, the Legion could no longer enlist enough volunteers because, like many serving members of the Legion, the general public on an international level judged that the Legion no longer had a future. At first enlistments were limited to 180 per month from June 1961, then from April 1962 they were reduced to 120 per month, but the Legion couldn't manage to attract even this limited number of volunteers, whereas before the putsch a monthly figure of between 300 and 400 volunteers would be recruited. Desertions from Foreign Legion units became endemic after the ending of hostilities in Algeria in March 1962. Once again, as in Morocco in 1956–7, FLN propaganda encouraging Foreign Legion soldiers to desert was a great success.[18] After Algerian independence in July 1962, the German embassy in Algiers found itself flooded with German deserters.

Between 3 July and 25 October 1962, 76 such deserters were returned to their homeland.[19] Desertions did not only take place from units in Algeria, but continued too from the new garrisons in the south of France or on journeys to new postings overseas. As Simon Murray, a soldier in the 2nd Foreign Paratroop Regiment, which was guarding the French naval base of Mers-el-Kebir after Algerian independence, wrote in his diary on 2 September 1962: 'Morale is in freefall. Nothing happens to break the daily monotony.'[20]

The Legion, however, was not really over-concerned at this wave of desertions and at the lack of potential new recruits as, after the end of the Algerian War, a reduction in troop numbers from 19,000 men at the start of 1962 to 7,500 in 1965 was planned. At least the Legion, which had been at the forefront of every colonial campaign France had conducted since 1831, could console itself with having survived the end of the French colonial empire.

To sum up, the troop morale of the Foreign Legion during the Algerian War was closely linked to the general progress of this, France's last, colonial war. A period of doubt and pessimism among non-French men in the ranks, as well as among the French officers, at the start was followed, due to the intensification of the war and the greater efficiency of military operations, by a period of stabilization in the morale of the legionnaires between 1957 and 1961.

Whereas the officers' fears about the outcome of the war had already started to emerge in 1959, the morale of the rank-and-file troops of the Legion was only to suffer in the period following the failure of the 1961 Algiers putsch. However, the failure of the putsch and the final French withdrawal from Algeria resulted in a crisis in the morale of the Legion and a decline in the attractiveness of this elite corps to foreign volunteers. The consequences of this continued to be felt up until the late 1960s.

Notes

1. The best work on the history of the Foreign Legion is that written by Douglas Porch, *La Légion Etrangère 1831–1962* (Paris, 1994); chapters 27 to 29 are devoted to the Algerian War and give a good overview of the role of the Legion between 1954 and 1962. Unfortunately, however, they were completed prior to the opening up at the French Army Historical Service (Service Historique de l'Armée de Terre – SHAT) in Vincennes of the files on the Algerian War. Alain Gandy's book, *La Légion en Algérie 1954–1962* (Paris, 1992), is very detailed with regard to the Legion's battles in Algeria, but has a tendency to be too one-sided and uncritical.
2. On the proportions of different nationalities in the Foreign Legion see Jean Hallo, *Monsieur Légionnaire. L'homme et ses traditions* (Paris, 1994), pp. 152–3; on Germans in the Foreign Legion see Eckard Michels, *Deutsche in der Fremdenlegion 1870–1965: Mythen und Realitäten* (Paderborn, 1999).
3. SHAT 10H375, Report on the morale of the 2nd Foreign Infantry Regiment for

the second semester of 1954 ('nostalgia for action') 10H377, Report on the morale of the 1st Foreign Cavalry Regiment for the second semester of 1954.

4. SHAT 7U641, Report on the morale of the 3rd Foreign Infantry Regiment 1955; 7U618, Report on the morale of the 1st Foreign Regiment 1955.
5. SHAT 6T574, Report of 20th June 1956: 'Moral des unités de la Légion Etrangère au Maroc.'
6. SHAT 7U1029, Report of 28 October 1956 on the morale of the 2nd Foreign Cavalry Regiment for 1956.
7. Pierre Sergent, *Ma peau au bout de mes idées* (Paris, 1967), p. 158.
8. SHAT 7U653, Report on the morale of the 5th Foreign Infantry Regiment for the second half of 1956; 7U641, Report on the morale of the 3rd Foreign Infantry Regiment 1955; 7U623, Report on the morale in 1955 of the 2nd Foreign Infantry Regiment.
9. SHAT 6T573, 'Situation des unités de la Légion Etrangère en Algérie' (report by Colonel Lennuyeux, dated 8 February 1957).
10. SHAT 1H1348 d. 4, 'Rapport d'inspection des unités de la Légion en Algérie en décembre 1958' (report dated 5 January 1959, written by General Gardy).
11. SHAT 1H2415, Report on the morale of the 10th Military Region for 1958.
12. Political archive of the Auswärtiges Amt Bonn (PA) Referat 502/V3, Vol. 587, Reports from the German Embassy in Tunis to the Auswärtiges Amt, dated 14 September 1957 and 10 July 1958.
13. SHAT 30T 18, Inspection Report on the corps of the Foreign Legion, dated 18 November 1959.
14. SHAT 30T18, Inspection Reports, dated 13 June 1960 and 22 February 1961.
15. Charles Hora, *Debout la Légion!* (Paris, 1971), p. 260 and Janos Kemencei, *Légionnaires avant!* (Paris, 1984), p. 336.
16. Kemencei, *Légionnaires avant!*, p. 336.
17. Mauro Carra, *Une vie de légionnaire* (Paris, 1990), p. 69.
18. SHAT 1H1237, Report by the commander of the Algiers army corps to the general staff command, dated 12 April 1962.
19. PA Referat 708, Vol. 1922, Note made on 26 October 1962.
20. Simon Murray, *Légionnaire 22/2/1960–12/2/1965* (Paris, 1984), p. 202.

6
The War Culture of French Combatants in the Algerian Conflict

Jean-Charles Jauffret

Due to its eight year duration, did the Algerian conflict generate its own war culture? Based upon a national survey which we set up as part of CNRS (Centre National de la Recherche Scientifique) mixed research unit no. 5609 ('States, Societies, Ideologies, Defence'), commissioned by the University of Montpellier III, this study draws upon the analysis of 430 responses (and oral interviews) received over a four-year period to a questionnaire comprising 152 questions related to the Algerian War. This analysis is supplemented by the scrutiny of about forty private sources (contemporary letters, personal diaries of veterans) principally originating from the southern regions of France. Lastly, in addition to published personal accounts, the archives of the historical services of the French army and air force constitute the final, indispensable element of the work.

As soon as one starts to take an interest in the Algerian conflict, the problem becomes reduced to one central question for the French combatant, whether born in mainland France or in Algeria (and thus living through a different experience from the Algerian Muslims for whom this was a civil war): did this unrecognized war give birth to the last real wartime generation? To answer this question, the study of the culture of war, in the narrow sense of habits and customs,[1] offers a great deal. As there was no distinctive, declared enemy, the nationalist sentiment, which one might normally have anticipated, was not apparent. Nonetheless, Algerian War combatants, who were essentially national service conscripts, were distinguished from the professional soldiers of the war in South-East Asia or from their predecessors in the two world wars by their distinctive language, attitudes and feelings, and this for a mass army whose numbers, in the army alone, reached an average of 390,000 men in 1958.[2]

Esprit de corps

As the months went by, the section in which one was serving would become a mould. The distinctive elements of the uniform, the section's own vocabulary, the need to emulate the achievements of the other constituent bodies, not to forget the proliferation of badges and the nicknames given to unit commanders with strong personalities, all these were the outward symbols of the phenomenon of *esprit de corps*.

On 10 July 1957 a ministerial decree ordered that all airborne troops, with the exception of the Foreign Legion, should wear a red beret. This order delighted the *paras-colos* (Colonial Parachute Regiment), since this was their section colour, but the other regiments, such as the paratroop chasseurs, with their loyal commitment to their blue berets, disdainfully ignored it. A new call to order had to be issued on 1 October 1957 for the decree finally to be complied with.

Accepting the rules as regards uniform and rapidly applying them, the 3rd Colonial Parachute Regiment adopted 'leopard-skin' uniform and the famous 'Bigeard' cap. This battle dress, a variant on the classic canvas battle dress, became a parade uniform as well. It would be accompanied by accessories such as a dagger slipped into the jump boots which were themselves laced up in an elaborate manner.

Esprit de corps led to the expression of differences. For the army squaddies, the sailors were mere 'rowers', the air force 'runway sweepers' and the anti-aircraft artillerymen 'piss-in-the-airs'. Members of the air force, themselves divided into two different classes, of which the non-flying class was made up of the 'rampants' ('crawlers'), 'basiers' ('baseboys') and 'pailleux' ('strawboys'), referred to ground troops globally by the radio code-name 'trosols' ('groundies'), of whom the largest group were the 'mobile slugs' (or infantrymen). As for the navigators, of whom the most experienced were known as 'moustachus' ('beardies') even if they flew light aircraft (nicknamed 'trapanelles' ('mini-flaps')), they had a jargon in which sexual references played a leading role: a 'willy' was the term used for the wind-sock indicating wind direction on each aerodrome and 'ballsack' was the fine self-adhesive film covering navigation maps to prevent their getting damaged.

As a facet of military society, and indicating a technical savoir-faire, then, each troop developed its own vocabulary for the use of initiates only. The language of the air and naval service, and of the 'khaki marines' (shoreside naval troops such as the Marine Fusiliers Demi-Brigade) was particularly rich in this regard. 'The dinghy's at the gangway' meant that the jeep was waiting below the helicopter; and to be 'going overboard' meant that you were out of breath. On the western frontier barrier, all the marines would say, 'I'm going ashore' when they went off duty, while for the paratroops all those who did not jump were 'lead-arses'.

A specific vocabulary

The citizen-soldiers participating in the Algerian War also used a common slang, a mark of professional necessity and of complicity between veterans.

A certain 'L'ami Bidasse' ('Our friend the Squaddy') vocabulary was still around from the days of '8.47 Train'. The arrival in 1954 of the first units in NATO uniform (including white gaiters) reinforced, in this African land, the presence of the traditional language of the barracks. The names for the different ranks remained unchanged: a 'leek' (green body but white on top) was a general, while a 'cap de veau' ('veal-cap'[3]) was the captain of a vessel who, like a 'full colonel' (five unmixed stripes), was experiencing a 'stripes pregnancy' if he was waiting for a promotion. Sometimes a pejorative tone was added to the traditional cheeky humour. A 'second dick' was a second lieutenant fresh out of training school, and a 'bootlicker corp' was a corporal who still hadn't 'toasted his stripes'. As for weapons, timelessness was guaranteed: 'pélot' ('sou') was the name for a mortar shell, 'miteuse' ('mashy') was the abbreviated version of machine-gun, with some San Antonio-inspired variants such as 'crop sprayer'. Nevertheless, some expressions disappeared or were replaced. During the First World War, a 'yarn' or false piece of news was known as a 'latrine'. In Algeria this was to become a 'bouteillon'[4] (literally a 'bottle', though the equivalent in English-speaking military jargon is a 'Dixie'), particularly in the 15th Regiment of Senegalese Infantrymen and in other colonial units.

On returning from South-East Asia, the 'Centurions' (Foreign Legion) added another layer to this. The recruits of colonial regiments were completely astonished to hear them refer to members of the ALN as 'Viets'. This nostalgia was part of an amalgamation between the two wars whereby, after 'quitting 'Nam', the soldiers would continue the fight against world communist subversion in Algeria. The use of the term 'git' for a 'geezer' was carried over from South-East Asia to Algeria.

From the distinctive history of Algeria there was a double inheritance. The Algerian French contributed the colourful 'malapropism' (mixture of words). They also bequeathed distinctive hand gestures such as putting their hands together with their elbows raised to express complicity. Taken from Arabic or acquired via the African Armed Forces, certain items of vocabulary transformed the language of the recruits into jargon: 'chouf' for watchman or sentry, 'kawoua' for coffee, 'chrab' for wine and 'mektoub' for fate or destiny. The exclamations inherited were even more prevalent: 'Fissa!' for 'Quick!', 'Labbès chouia!' for 'that's really great!' (or 'that's really moving!'), 'Bezef!' for 'a lot' and 'Kif-Kif!' for 'the same old thing!' 'Finding a needle in a sheaf of straw' was one particularly imaginative mixture.

In fact, this inheritance gave added richness to a completely new range of vocabulary that was at the heart of war culture. Firstly, one must distinguish that part of the vocabulary that came from particular branches of the services. The navy bequeathed the Anglicism 'beacher' as a generic term for any disembarkation or landing. The 'servoes' of the Army Service Corps were particularly appreciated when they carried out 'EVASANs' sanitary evacuation duties on their 'castors' (GMC lorries). The T6 or 'Piper' pilots of the army light aircraft section would be understood by everyone when they referred to 'RAV' for *reconnaissance à vue* (visual reconnaissance). The following terms and phrases were adopted from the jargon of the parachute regiments: 'putting the buoys out' for marking out a jump area or acting carefully/being concerned) and 'crapahuter' ('yomping') for toiling up and down the djebels (ranges of hills). To be 'en stand by', that is to say to be on alert on the ground, became a metaphor meaning to be available or to be waiting for a posting. The transmissions section contributed a great number of expressions. As a remote control war, the Algerian War, even more than the South-East Asia conflict that preceded it, was the war of radio transmitter slang and of its semantic abbreviations. The international phonetic alphabet turned the classic 'PC' (for 'command post' or HQ) into 'Papa Charlie', while 'SCR 300' and 'PRC 10' posts were operational.

The presence of new equipment, in the shape of helicopters, also illustrated the linguistic inventiveness that was prevalent. This started off as coded language designed to deceive the enemy. The 'biffins' (infantrymen) ignored the term 'trap', used by the air force men to refer to the helicopter, in favour of 'ventilateur' or 'ventilo' (fan), of which one particular type, the twin-rotor Piasecki H 21, was known as the 'banana'. From this there came the expression 'to be banana-ed', meaning to be dropped by helicopter. The 'Barlu-canon' ('gun-Barlu') and other 'mammoths' were armed helicopters, most often the Sikorsky (the famous 'Siko') H 34.

Yet another variety of Algerian War-specific jargon made its appearance. Originating in operational reports, 'locking up' and 'combing' sat alongside DZs (dropping zones, that is to say landing areas for airborne troops, including those carried by helicopter). The modernity of the Algerian conflict was demonstrated by the employment of a formal jargon that made extensive use of bland clinical euphemisms. In this way 'launch an attack' was no longer used, but rather 'dealing with an objective'. Napalm bombs were chastely referred to as 'special delivery tins'. One didn't torture, one employed 'forceful interrogation' techniques, seen as a 'lesser evil', even if 'rock 'n' roll' (torture using electricity), 'breast stroke' (immersion in a bath tub) or 'sunbathing' (at 65 degrees centigrade) were 'against the traditions of the Armed Forces'. In marching and operations logs, 'wood duty' (the execution of prisoners too badly 'messed up' after their interrogation) was generally camouflaged under the standard phrase: 'the suspects apprehended were shot trying to escape'.[5] Doing 'creative accounting' meant being sure to write in the operational reports that the troops involved achieved a positive outcome, whatever the truth of the matter. In this manner, the discovery of a simple toolbox in a 'fell' (ALN) hideaway could be transformed into a 'repairs workshop'. This primly calculating use of language had the opposite effect on the men on the ground, who showed imagination beyond the call of duty in finding alternatives to the verb 'to kill' or 'to be killed'. Furthermore, this vocabulary was influenced by the assiduous reading of whodunnits as the level of boredom implicit in the Algerian War meant it became the golden age of detective stories.[6] Getting 'bumped off' seems very bland next to the ear-pleasing alternatives of being 'unsoldered' or 'dezinc-ed', a fear of sentries who were liable to get 'lit up' by a shot. In everyday language, new words appeared, such as 'beans', taken from the English and used in the plural with multiple meanings expressing disorder, an abnormal situation, etc.

One final word summed up the Algerian War through its ambiguity; used in preference to the alternative of 'gas(man)', this word was '*gus*' (in the plural, '*gusses*'[7]), meaning 'the bloke'. This word was used for any non-identified military unit as, from a distance, the 'fells' (FLN) had a tendency to resemble *harkis* or commandos. Originating in Montmartre slang, Auguste, *le rigolo*, was one of the euphemisms used by conscripts to designate the male member, while at the same time referring to a symbol of liberation from active service. This was ... *la quille* (the skittle).

La quille

The demob symbol of the skittle illustrated the aimless enlistment of conscripts in Algeria. To ease their embarrassment some veterans tried to 're-remember' their service, blotting out this puerile humour; but letters and notebooks of the period relate another narrative. Norbert Giraud, 58–1/D[8] class of the 1/408th[9] Regiment of Anti-Aircraft Artillery summed it all up in simple words: 'One day to do it, 28 months to earn it!' Some conscripts have religiously kept their skittle. The one belonging to Georges Carlevan of the 1/15th Regiment of Senegalese Artillerymen is made of eucalyptus wood and inscribed on its top end is the number of his class, 57–2/C. On the body of the skittle, which is painted in coloured bands, the names are written of the venues for training (Le Lido, Algiers) and of the locations in which he served (Phillipeville, Collo, Tamalous, Constantine, Télergma, etc.).

The skittle was the real cult object of the Algerian War for the conscripts. The term 'quillard' ('skittler'), used for someone who had completed his period of service, replaced the term 'classard'. According to edition 93 (22 January 1958) of the newspaper *Le Bled*, the term originated with a boat called *La Quille* which, up to 1939, used to go and look for convicts on Cayenne after they'd served their sentence. The citizen-soldier of 1954–62 was less a 'war worker', to revive an expression dear to the French soldiers of the First World War, than a 'war castaway' condemned to serve his period of purgatory on a battlefield which did not concern him. Undeniably, this ambiguous war for Algeria lacked a clear-cut and snappy slogan of purpose to rival 'La Patrie en Danger'.

On waking up, one of the first actions of the conscript would be to cross out on his wall calendar the date of the day before, exclaiming, like conscripts down through history: 'That's one less day for shooting!' The use of coded language would give the precise figure as to how long he had to go before getting his freedom: '241 to the juice!' meant that he still had 241 days to serve before being freed from active service (*le jus* was widely used for 'demob'). In an era when the cult of heroes in uniform had gone out of fashion, one can understand why the military authorities did all in their power to counteract the proliferation of these skittles with their seditious connotations. From 1957 onwards, repeated decrees threatened all those who wore a skittle hung on a string around their necks or attached to their suitcases with punishment, in particular through an extension of the period of service. Such measures caused the popularity of the skittle and its mythical links with freedom to spread, until it became a wider social phenomenon. In 1956, the weekly magazine *Regards*, a mass audience publication about the cinema, dedicated its front page, in issue 398, to a recalled soldier smiling at achieving 'La Quille', that is 'earning his skittle' on demobilization. As early as issue no. 3 of 'Hara-Kiri', Cabu, the former conscript cartoonist on *Le Bled*, was producing a page titled '*La Quille*, girls!' and in 1962 Jean Herman's French new wave film *La Quille* was a real pacifist declaration of faith. Even those responsible for the April 1961 putsch tried to win the support of the *quillards*, the Generals promising to return the duration of active service to its legal limit of 18 months and organizing the triumphant return to France on board the liner *El Mansour* of 800 men who had completed their military service, while the people of Algiers handed out cigarettes and presents.

The cry '*La quille*, for fuck's sake' was simultaneously a demonstration of discontent with anti-militarist connotations and an acceptance of the need, grudgingly, to do one's duty. The attitude of resignedly waiting for the liberation of *la quille*, which did not favour political commitments or the open expression of criticism, predominated over attitudes of protest or of demanding that same liberation. The latter could even involve insulting the flag on occasions.[10] The phenomenon of *la quille* as a sort of test of manhood from which they had not been able to escape was something held in common by operational troops, while the associations of *la quille* with camaraderie were, no doubt, common to all. When conscripts from the same class reached the end of their period of service, they'd first have a good meal, remembering the names of those who had fallen, and then 'get the hell out' for a no-holds-barred party. More or less implicitly, in fact, a large proportion of the conscripts shared the same loathing for the betrayal of the politicians. Based upon a strong sense of injustice, this accusation was not too strong. The key to it is contained in a dossier from the military archives.[11] In this dossier, dozens of letters of protest, which were never published, can be found, written by 'ordinary blokes doing their military service' challenging *Le Bled* about the false promises of the various prime ministers. In June 1957, shortly after being sworn in, Maurice Bourgès-Maunoury followed the example of his predecessor Guy Mollet in committing himself to returning the period of national service to 24 months. Sapper J.C., from the 55–1/C class, sent this response to the editor of the paper:

> [All my comrades] have done the duty that was theirs to do by the nation. Sometimes they may have grumbled a bit, but THEY HAVE NEVER SHIRKED [*sic*]. They were full of hope that, finally, they'd be able to return to their homes in order to enjoy a well-earned rest. Only now I find, and I am not the only one to find this, that we are being TREATED LIKE FOOLS [*sic*] a little more every day.

When, in 1958, the 56–1/B class were kept on active service for a full 30 months, the scale of protest was such that, to maintain its credibility, *Le Bled*, in issue no. 108 dated 7 May, published a letter from a conscript. In very moderate terms he asked: 'Why is 56–1/B troop still being kept on active service?' It was only in the final edition of the paper, issue no. 172 dated July 1962, that the conscripts were to be informed clearly of the exact date when the classes of 1960 would be demobilized from active service. As a cause of poor morale among the conscripts, then, the extension of the period of time served by the 'ADLs' (those serving beyond the statutory period of military service, that is to say more than 18 months) was a major source of discontent. From this, one can understand the attachment the conscript troops felt to this object, the skittle, which symbolized an end at last to their suffering and disappointments.

The need to remember

By offering modestly priced cameras, *Le Bled* promoted a need for memories to be retained in photographic form, a need peculiar to the Algerian War. Armed with their 'Foca Universals' or 'Kodak *rétinette* 24*36s', the conscripts devoted themselves to things exotic. For many of them this mass migration, class by class, to an African land retained the scent of adventure. Certainly there were photographers, all conscripts, with official accreditation from the military authorities, such as Marc Flament, attached to Colonel Bigeard's 3rd Colonial Parachute Regiment, and sectorial photographers like Marc Garanger who had particularly tightly defined objectives.[12] After their anthropometric ID photo sessions, an essential part of the pacification process through the establishment of an identity card system, they were often asked to 'take a picture' of soldiers on their own or with their mates, when those soldiers didn't possess an 'ST 280' or 'Tiranty' themselves. In confirmation of the findings of other researchers,[13] those of our sources who did possess a camera, which became faithful companions for the duration of the war, wanted above all to preserve the memory of their friends. On little 7.5 by 7.5 or 6 by 6 centimetre black and white squares of shiny paper, they'd keep a picture of their first view of the port of Algiers, of a bivouac, etc. The pictures of the countryside, especially those printed on slides, confirm the attractiveness of this beautiful but cruel land. As tourists in uniforms, the conscripts were also attracted by sights of native markets, women in veils, etc.

This need to preserve memories can also be seen in the custom of marking one's presence through graffiti. Like the Desaix grenadiers in Upper Egypt, the 'gusses' of the 10th Military Region (Algeria) were quick to make use of their pocket knives and charcoal. It should be added that the example was set from the top, being a favourite tool of the Psychological Action Service, the FLN and the OAS. A sign of the modernity of the Algerian War, the first war outside Europe to feature the use of 'tagging' (autographing using graffiti), was that in Algerian towns, and even under bridges, sites were swamped with a variety of slogans, even extending to abuse. It should come as no surprise to find that the charred walls of the Fedz Zénati forest building were covered with two phrases current with conscripts since 1954: *La quille* and 'Up your arse', this latter slogan being accompanied, in September 1959, by a charcoal drawing of a couple having sex. The carriages of *La Rafale*, the narrow-gauge train that ran between Oran and Colomb-Béchar, were covered in graffiti. Troop class numbers were written there, perpetuating the memory of the different troop contingents that had taken that train. The mania for graffiti-writing was such that, in May 1959 at Aïn Séfra, the Foreign Legion were given orders to put a grille around the *Pierres écrites*, rocks covered with ancient paintings, to protect them from the attentions of the *quillards*.[14]

The feelings of the combatant

When one interviews veterans of the Algerian War, the feeling that dominates their recollections of what they experienced remains a powerful spirit of solidarity between mates. In contrast to the combat generations of other wars, where there had been a mixture of territorials and young recruits, the combatants in Algeria had a homogeneity based on age groups. The fact that they were all in uniform and were all in the same boat led them to abandon social prejudices. They shared the same anxieties, the same parcels, the same joys and the same difficulties according to their postings. The rare minority who did sometimes find themselves isolated were those having deferred their service, who would be four to six years older than their comrades, and this downside could be erased by a stronger degree of commitment to the service of others for those who opted to become officer cadets or reserve second-lieutenants. Those with the warmest character among this conscript officer class found, in the small communities of isolated military posts, that same old impulse to create a military family that had been so familiar to platoon commanders in the First World War. In the parachute regiments, the split between active and reserve troops was made more hazy by an *esprit de corps* and degree of solidarity due, in many cases, to their 'superb officering'. Nonetheless, comparisons with previous wartime generations can only go so far due to the length of time that the troops spent living together, no more than 24 to 26 months at the very most, not including training classes.

This solidarity was the fruit of a learning process. This started, in the first instance, with the disappointments of brief friendships made on the train to Marseille or on board the ferry to Algiers, where there would be promises to write to one another that would be quickly forgotten. Following these first meetings, there would be the training classes, the first stage in friendships between young men of the same age, assigned to the same section, who 'sweated it out together'. Then there would come the deep influence of communal living, where the security of everyone depended on everyone else, whether on a deserted peak of the Atlas Mountains or in a parachute regiment continually moving between locations. As a cornerstone of good morale in a unit, as had been the case in the two world wars, military command would try to avoid changing the unit to which a soldier was assigned. Such changes were rare and came about largely back on the French mainland. As in the First World War, any change of unit was a punishment applied only on the authority of the corps commander, a decision taken where serious misconduct had taken place, in accordance with article 50 of the general disciplinary code of April 1933.[15]

This solidarity was a counter-force against misfortune, and part of this code was that you did not leave a comrade isolated or in difficulties. It is easy to understand the subsequent strength of paratroop associations, which were to become real mutual assistance societies.

Whether it suddenly appeared in brutal fashion on some hot dry day when the dusty sirocco wind was blowing across the desert, or whether it slowly matured like the boredom of a Buzatti hero staring vainly at his *Désert des Tartares*, *le cafard* (a complex feeling that is difficult to explain but is akin to a boring, frustrating version of the blues) was a multi-faceted phenomenon. Life in the open air and the constraints of operations alleviated the strongly felt emotion caused by the brutalization of life on a military base characterized by its obscure and continuous treadmill of watch duties, fatigues, ambushes, etc. Isolation also contributed a degree of nervous tension and difficulties in sleeping which fuelled *le cafard*, sometimes brought on by the soldiers themselves as they thought of their homeland, of girls, of social events in their home village, or of the number of months still to 'be shot of' before the end of their period of service and *la quille*. This poor morale could become contagious between conscripts in the same group, condemned to the incestuous life of small, uncomfortable military posts. Chronic boredom, the benign form of this, could sometimes lead to stupid bets, such as the one who could take the most beer or the one who could urinate the furthest. In its chronic form, *le cafard* could lead to suicide, the number of instances of which remains unknown due to their having been counted in with deaths by drowning and through illness.[16] The feeling of certainty that your lover back home was being unfaithful, a long-term state of depression caused by the stress of combat or the sight of comrades getting killed or the desire to make amends for having shot a mate were all causes that sometimes lay behind suicides that were made easy to carry out due to the possession of a weapon, or behind a particular form of suicide accomplished through repeated drinking binges. It was only a minority, such as the Saharan troops who became followers of outlandish groups like 'the Order of the Wild Locust' or 'the Order of the Tarantula of Tidikelt', that were able to defeat *le cafard* through an attitude of scornful defiance.[17]

In the evening, on their return to quarters, all troops that had suffered losses would be infected by *le cafard*. It was a fundamental difference between the national service soldiers at war in Algeria and their predecessors from other wartime generations that they never got used to witnessing the deaths of their comrades. Though far fewer soldiers died than in the First World War or in Indochina, the losses suffered were never accepted.[18] This state of permanent revolt could lead to excessive acts of on-the-spot vengeance being carried out against prisoners or injured enemy soldiers, acts that became part of the obscure reality of this guerrilla war. In particular, torture, forced population movements and actions bordering on the transgression of normal acceptable wartime conduct took place in restricted areas where anything was permitted (the use of napalm, the destruction of villages, the burning of crops, livestock rustling, etc.); it has to be admitted that those involved became well accustomed to a level of violence that became the norm because it was inherent in the strong-arm tactics used in the pacification process. Some of those involved still retain a sense of shame, a feeling that remains the most difficult for them to express.

Whether omnipresent or sporadic, according to the different units, fear is a feeling common to all wartime generations. In Algeria, this took on particular forms in a land where the enemy was everywhere and nowhere. Stoked up to a certain degree by the nocturnal harassment directed at military outposts, the fear of the sentry, who had the impression that he was a constant target, was shared by those who regularly carried out night patrols. Fear of an FLN ambush was a constant. On leaving the camp, mines were a particular concern. It was a sign of the modernity of the Algerian War that the territory for mines was no longer just the front-line. The first mines used by the 'fells' were home-made contraptions using butane gas bottles or booby-trapped shells, the insurgents being every bit as inventive as their French opponents with their undetectable 'inkwell mines' on the East and West frontier barriers. Mines could be swept away by rainstorms and could become dangerous to everyone. When in a convoy, soldiers would always be anticipating the possibility of the enemy attacking to take advantage of the tiredness of men who formed a sitting target trapped behind the awnings and slatted sides of GMC lorries. Our sources from the Languedoc region expressed this fear with a particularly colourful phrase: 'we were producing some oil!' One great fear in particular, however, stood out from all the others, and it was a fear that was carefully stoked up by the officers as the best possible defence against desertion; that fear was the fear of being taken prisoner. Many recalled murderous ambushes in which mutilated bodies were found.

Military festivities

One of the best means of exorcising anxiety while giving proof of morale and combativeness is to parade or to give oneself over to the rituals of the military celebration. In Algeria, in its public form, this had a triple purpose: it was supposed to reassure the European population, worry the enemy and show him that the streets were not his domain, and reinforce the belief of the troops in their own strength and cohesion. The idea on 17 June 1955, when the 7th Division of Mechanized Infantry under General André Beaufre paraded with its tanks in Algiers, was to convey impressions of protection and dissuasion.

The national holiday on Bastille Day regularly affirmed the French presence in Algeria. The psychological importance of parades on 14 July led onto a political challenge that could then lead to terrorism. In 1960, for example, that day's celebrations in Sétif ended in mourning when a grenade thrown into the crowd left three people dead and 72 injured.

Military celebrations were associated with, or added to, the scenes of brotherly solidarity in May 1958, principally in the focal centre of Algiers. They gave added potency to the most intense moment of patriotic emotion on 4 June when, before a tightly packed crowd, General de Gaulle lit the flame on the war memorial. At the time for the minute of silence, eight *Mistral* planes flew over the town and, just before a passionate and hope-filled rendering of the *Marseillaise*, the guns of the cruiser *De Grasse* rang forth.[19] The euphoria of Algiers was not universally shared, however. In Batna, on 18 June 1958, the authorities wanted to give a particular lustre to the commemoration of mobilization. Despite the presence of a significant array of official representatives, the garrison parade left a bitter taste for those involved, the Muslims discreetly leaving in small groups while the *Marseillaise*, followed by 'Song of the Africans', rang out.

As part of the process of pacification, the Psychological Action service of the 5th Bureau (intelligence bureau) encouraged the participation of the

Muslim population in military celebrations such as that of 11 November. Another aspect of military celebrations linked to the pacification process was that associated with the ceremonial handing over of arms (shotguns or outdated weapons) to self-defence groups, offering proof that army command had re-established peace. Based upon the traditions of the spahi (native North African cavalry corps of the French army) and Algerian infantry regiments, the *Aid es Seghir* festivities marking the end of Ramadan concluded with the barbecue of a whole roast sheep (a *méchoui*).

Military celebrations could take on a more intimate nature involving demonstrations of *esprit de corps*. On 29 or 30 September, the parachute regiments would carry out a sacrifice in honour of their patron saint, Saint Michael. While lacking the decorum of the *Camerone* commemorations of the Foreign Legion (a celebration that took place every 30 April), these festivities would sometimes involve mass in the morning, a copious meal at midday and a 'massive beano' in the afternoon. These rituals were not rigid in nature, given the relatively short history of this section of the forces. Military reviews to mark the handover to a new corps commander of a general reserve unit, events at which attendance was habitually limited to members of that regiment, often had a hint of the exotic about them.

For largely static sectoral troops, military celebrations were either lack-lustre or non-existent. A small community of twenty or so men stuck on top of some peak of the Ouarsenis massif would not have the means for such festivities, and nor would their hearts be in it, especially at Christmas. If it were a grey day, that day would seem even more interminable, thinking of families back at home. The dull everyday life would be spiced up; live turkeys were even parachuted in.

Ragging was another essential aspect of military festivities. If barrack-room jokes about the days of training classes are excluded, a vague feeling of melancholy clearly reigned in the small military posts where 'blueys' (rookies) were welcomed in a simple manner. In response to our survey, many veterans remembered their arrival with their corps being marked simply by a few drinks with the more experienced of their new comrades and long conversations late into the night with 'un pays' (an area), that is to say someone from a different training class but from the same village. In garrisons based in towns, ragging lasted only for a very short time, being something along the lines of a false alert and an inspection of the kit belonging to the 'blue-dicks', undertaken by a phoney captain. One tradition respected in the officer corps was the welcome given to reserve officer cadets. The inversion of ranks and mixing of duties were practised. The first impression the 'caddie' received would be decidedly apocalyptic: a phoney battalion commander, pretending to be drunk and wearing a tatty, dishevelled uniform, would set out the detail of some surreal and grotesque supposed regulation in force in the unit. A variant on this consisted in setting up a fake ambush prior to the young officer's arrival with the troop, leaving him with a weapon containing only blanks. The air and naval service and the air force were characterized by the variety of their ragging japes. Second Lieutenant Gérard Paris, a T6 observer in Batna 3/10 squadron, recalled his first visual reconnaissance outing, near Biskra, in a chott (saline lake) below sea level; the altimeter started to show 100 feet below while a giant marabout (Muslim shrine) (in fact a mirage) appeared on the horizon towards which the plane seemed to be heading.[20]

As for the conscript soldiers, they had a ritual that had been around as long as conscription itself, but which achieved cult status in Algeria: the festival of *Père Cent*, which was to celebrate there being a hundred days left until the end of the period of military service. The future *quillards* would ceremoniously bury or destroy a small coffin representing *Père Cent*. A sort of ritual of temporary release, akin to the Roman Saturnalia festival, where you would say everything that was on your mind, it would be accompanied by heavy drinking and bawdy songs. This was one of the few occasions on which group singing would take place.

It was a sign of the modernity of the war culture of Algerian War combatants that it was marked by less chanting and more songs. Radio and the growth of the record turned the musical universe of the armed forces upside down. The traditional chants of troop solidarity, such as the zouaves' 'Pan, Pan l'Arbi', the chasseurs' 'Sidi Brahim' and the paras' 'La Prière' were restricted to their official functions, even if Bigeard's paras did chant when returning from operations.[21] As this war without a recognized enemy did not encourage the jingoistic singing of songs like 'Madelon', at their posts or yomping across difficult terrain soldiers would hum the latest Platters slow number or Sacha Distel's 'Scoubidou', the big hit of 1958. Sometimes, even in paratroop units, they'd play at provocation by striking up with songs that were banned, such as Boris Vian's 'Le Déserteur' ('The Deserter') or Francis Lemarque's 'Quand un soldat' ('When a soldier').

One final aspect of military ceremonials in Algeria should be mentioned, which is that, at the end of April 1961, in the regiments involved in the putsch, they took on a decidedly political character. In his personal diary, Jean-Pierre Haro provides an exceptional account in which panache, defiance and a sense of honour mark the final hours of the rebel soldiers of the 18th Regiment of Paratroop Chasseurs, the only conscript regiment to remain more or less unified right up to its disbandment. On 26 April, with Algiers in a state of complete anarchy, lieutenant-colonel Masselot told his men that the shedding of French blood by Frenchmen should be avoided. *Esprit de corps*, then, triumphed one last time. On 27 April, at Philippeville, one last parade took place on the beach, near the Jeanne d'Arc Centre. Then, with their feet in the water and 'our guns in our hands, we went to fire a salvo towards France, towards those who had abandoned us without understanding the reason for our rebellion. "Fire at will", was the cry and all guns were discharged simultaneously, the volley of gunfire lasting for five minutes.'

Conclusion

This brief overview of the military culture of French combatants in the Algerian War, strongly marked by the rituals of the temporary troops, that is to say those recalled to active service, the reservists and the conscripts of a mass army, shows, first and foremost, a degree of continuity with previous wartime generations. The veterans' associations are adamant about this. One of the most recent of these associations, founded in 1955, has an interesting name: the Union nationale des Anciens Combattants d'Indochine, des TOE, d'Afrique du Nord, et de toutes les générations du feu (National Union of Veterans of Indochina, Overseas Theatres of Operations, North Africa and All War-Generations). At its first national conference, at Montélimar on 1 June 1996, the members of this association proclaimed their pride in their wartime service on the same basis as those who served in the two world wars. A common thread unites them around the same expressions and, above all, the same feelings in the face of danger and solitude, not at the front but in some isolated military post or in a general reserve unit pursuing an enemy who was, for the most part, invisible.

Nonetheless, a specificity of the Algerian conflict surfaces when it comes to the meanings of military festivities and demonstrations of *esprit de corps*. Perhaps rather more than for previous generations, the culture of war in Algeria was marked by very technical, coded language. It is a sign of recognition among initiates, veterans of a war not like other wars. A war that was lost in political and diplomatic terms, the Algerian conflict, while won on the ground, remained a 'dirty war'. This nuance comes across, for example, in the euphemisms used to refer to ways of killing or of obtaining information. In the absence of a national declaration of war and in the name of the violent methods of counter-revolutionary combat and its corollary, psychological warfare, combatants in Algeria were induced to carry out or to witness acts that ran completely counter to the professional code of ethics that was the republican inheritance of a French soldier. For this reason, the war culture of Algerian combatants was based less on glorified memories of battles, more on silences sometimes associated with a desire to forget. That culture finally leads to a demand for recognition of the sacrifices accepted by the men of a conscript army who gave two years of their youth for a lost cause. In this, no doubt, we can find the only feeling shared by the paratroop chasseur with Front National sympathies and the soldier recalled to active service in 1956 who has remained a communist activist: that the French nation should recognize that these citizen-soldiers suffered physically, spiritually and emotionally.

Notes

1. As distinct from the overall combination of factors making up a way of thinking and its environment in terms of media, religious and political influences ... defined by Franco Cardini for the period prior to 1918 in *Culture de guerre* (Gallimard, 1992).
2. 3/1 H 1261, Service Historique de l'Armée de Terre (French Army Historical Service).
3. The spelling represents a play on words as, in the days of sailing ships, a *cap de mouton* (sheep cape) was a pulley designed to tighten the shrouds.
4. The 'Bouteillon', originally 'Bouthéon' (1887), was an inseparable companion of the French First World War soldier and of the Algerian War soldier who followed in his footsteps. This camping pot was also used to transport water, soup, etc.
5. As examples of this historical point, which is an important one as it is often denied, see: 11/12/1955, 1/7 U 3015, Marching & Operations Journal of the 2nd Colonial Parachute Regiment and 3/7 U 750, Marching & Operations Journal of the 18th Shock Paratroop Infantry Regiment, 14/1/1955, Service historique de l'armée de terre (French Army Historical Service). The term 'wood duty' principally appeared in personal diaries.
6. Seven great collections of very cheap paperback books offered the works of Georges Simenon, Agatha Christie, Boiteau-Naujac, Auguste Le Breton, San Antonio, etc. In 1960 the Gallimard, 'Black Series' alone published 71 books: Pierre Lebedec, *Polar: dix livres après* (Catalogue for the 'France in the Algerian War' exhibition, held at *Les Invalides* between 6 and 22 June 1992 (BDIC, 1992), pp. 240–4.
7. Georges Mattéi, one of those soldiers recalled to active service in 1956, also uses 'gusse' in the singular in his autobiographical account *La Guerre des gusses* (Balland, 1982).
8. Groups of young people were called up at the age of 20; in these abbreviations, the figure indicates the semester (1 or 2) and then a letter was given in order to each even-numbered month. From 1957 onwards, this was changed to odd-numbered months. Thus, N.Giraud, in the class of 1958 (born in 1938) was included in the 1st semester, in July (the fourth odd-numbered month).
9. The figure placed before the number of the regiment indicates the battalion.
10. In his Marching Journal, Marcel Barbeau, corporal in the 9th Regiment of Marine Infantry, describes how, on 4 January 1961 and in the absence of the Base Commander, his comrades at Abbo... 'took down the flag and replaced it with a superb skittle stained with red wine': cf. *Ils avaient vingt ans dans les djebels. Témoignages, 1952–1962, la guerre d'Algérie, les combats du Maroc et de la Tunisie* (FNACA (National Federation of Algerian War Veterans), 1989), p. 365.
11. *3/1 H 2470, Service historique de l'armée de terre (French Army Historical Service).
12. *La Guerre d'Algérie vue par un appelé du contingent* (Le Seuil, 1984). Collection of photos with preface by Henri Jeanson.
13. See, *inter alia*, Thérèse Blondet-Bisch, *La photo-déclic des appelés* (BDIC Catalogue, op. cit.), pp. 232–6.
14. Marc Flament, *Les Hélicos du djebel* (Presses de la Cité, 1982), p. 128.
15. As an example, on 6 January 1958, Colonel Guillermaz, commander of the 9th Regiment of Colonial Infantry, notified the regiment that Sergeant C. André

had been transferred to another unit due to 'a serious breach of discipline' (1/7 U 2639, French Army Historical Service). Any transfer to another unit on disciplinary grounds generally also involved demotion.

16. Armed Forces Ministry statistics of 19 November 1968 show that between 1 November 1954 and 19 March 1968 there were 1,038 cases of death due to illness, suicide or drowning (French Army Historical Service, and Jean-Pierre Vittori, *Nous les appelés d'Algérie* (Temps Actuels, 1977), p. 196).
17. Formed in 1882, the first Saharan Order, that of *La Sauterelle délirante* (the Wild Locust), still had followers in 1954–62, as did those of *le Cafard de Médenine* (the Cockroach (the other meaning of *Le Cafard*) of Médenine) and *Le grand ordre du Scorpion noir* (the Grand Order of the Black Scorpion): cf.: *Historia Magazine*, Algerian War series, no. 291, p. 2102.
18. Out of 2,300,000 young Frenchmen who crossed the Mediterranean between 1 November 1954 and the Evian Accords, 5,583 died in action, 7,817 died in accidents, 200,000 were injured and 1,000 were declared missing or were taken prisoner.
19. General R. Salan, *Mémoires*, vol. 3: *Algérie française* (Presses de la Cité, 1972), p. 372.
20. Interview no. 799, 25 June 1996, Service Historique de l'Armée de l'Air (French Air Force Historical Service).
21. As Commander of the 3rd Colonial Paratroop Regiment from 1 November 1955 onwards, Lieutenant-Colonel Bigeard produced a succession of 'Guidance Notes' for officers in which he moulded the style of his regiment. The Guidance Note of 4 January 1956, relating to chanting while returning to base, ended with the following statement: 'Life is better and weighs less heavily upon one if its everyday rhythm is broken up' (2/7 U 3027, French Army Historical Service).

7

The *Harkis*: the Experience and Memory of France's Muslim Auxiliaries

Martin Evans

> 'To shake the hand of a *harki* would be like asking a Frenchman to shake the hand of a World War Two collaborator.' (President A. Bouteflika, interview on French radio, June 2000)

On 14 June 2000 President Abdelaziz Bouteflika began an official visit to France. The bitter legacy of colonization meant such an invitation was bound to stir up tension, especially given that Bouteflika was a former ALN maquis leader.[1] But when this is added to the fact that he was only the third Algerian head of state since independence to be accorded this welcome, at a time when his country was plunged in violence, this controversy was magnified still further. Nevertheless during the following four days Bouteflika called for a new beginning in Franco-Algerian relations. Recrimination, the President explained in a speech to the National Assembly, must be replaced by cooperation and mutual aid.[2] Yet, for all the talk of reconciliation, on the issue of the *harkis,* those Muslims who took a pro-French position during the war of independence, his stance was unforgiving. In Bouteflika's eyes the *harkis* were traitors to the Algerian nation, no different than pro-Nazi French collaborators during the Occupation. Why, therefore, should Algerians show sympathy or understanding?[3]

In equating the *harkis* with Nazi collaboration Bouteflika was reasserting an article of faith for Algerian nationalism. Ever since independence successive leaders have cast the 1954–62 war as a world of rigid absolutes where Algerians could only be for or against the FLN. There was no room for hesitation or error, no place for compromise or ambiguous behaviour. The choices were simple and the *harkis* chose the wrong side. For this reason they must remain the pariahs of the Algerian people.

While recognizing the responsibility of many *harkis* for atrocities and torture, which in turn explains why they were singled out for pitiless retribution, this chapter will take the line that their experience is much more complex than the official Algerian perspective suggests. In doing so it will be mindful of the limitations of the collaborationist example as a framework of understanding. To amalgamate the Milice, the Vichy police force used to repress the Resistance, with the *harkis* is misguided. In effect such a conclusion hides a reality which was often messy, awkward and complicated.

Who were the *harkis*?

Harka is the arabic word for movement. It is also the term used to describe militia units raised by a political authority, a strategy with a long tradition in Algeria stretching back to the eighteenth century. In this strict sense *harkis* should only refer to those Muslim auxiliaries raised by the French army between 1954 and 1962, but in reality it has become a catch-all phrase for all Muslims who took a pro-French position. Who, therefore, were the pro-French Muslims?

In the first place there were those categories whose pro-French allegiance long pre-dated November 1954. In concrete terms this meant the assimilated elite as well as Muslims who worked in the administration or were members of the police or armed forces. The assimilated elite was composed of the small minority who had taken up French citizenship. Until the 1947 reforms Muslims were automatically categorized as subjects rather than citizens whereby they came under the umbrella of Islamic, as opposed to French, law. Ostensibly this arrangement was designed to protect local religion and culture but in practice it acted as a barrier against assimilation. It made the route to citizenship difficult and controversial because the price of French nationality was the signing away of the right to be governed, in non-criminal jurisdiction, by Muslim law. In the eyes of the Muslim majority this represented a betrayal of Islam and the handful who did, a mere 2,500 by 1936, were viewed with enormous suspicion.

Next to the assimilated elite were those Muslims who worked in the administration. In the remote mountains of the Aurès and Kabylia, where even as late as the early 1950s some Algerians had never seen a French official, these intermediaries functioned as a bridgehead between rulers and ruled, dispensing justice and collecting taxes.[4] Some were ex-servicemen, whose war record marked them out as loyal servants; some were local leaders who wished to carve out a privileged relationship with the colonial authorities; others, as the titles *bachaga* (tribal leader), *cadi* (judge) and *caid* (tax collector) suggested, were remnants from the Ottoman administration. If many felt that they were genuinely working on behalf of the population, many too were appalling cheats and swindlers. Given the scale of illiteracy the scope for corruption was vast with the result that the cheating *caid*, exploiting their position in the colonial system to live off the fat of the peasantry, became a standard hate figure in popular folklore. For this reason it is not surprising that the first casualty of the war was the premeditated execution of a loyal *caid*, Hadj Sadok, and thereafter the number of

Muslims in the administration became a test of strength between the national liberation struggle and the colonial authorities.[5] For the French their expansion in public life was a demonstration of equality; for the ALN such Muslims were a dangerous intermediary force who threatened the polarization of settlers and natives into two warring factions. Inevitably those who did not heed nationalist calls to resign became targets of assassination.

Another area with a strong custom of native recruitment was the police. Although in a minority in Algiers and Oran, in the outlying areas away from the Mediterranean littoral the Muslim numbers in the police rose dramatically. In the cases of Biskra and Batna, for example, they made up 59 per cent and 71 per cent of the total force respectively. Jean Vaujour, appointed head of security in Algeria in June 1953, was determined to increase this level of native recruitment still further and his efforts led to the creation of the Groupes Mobiles de Police Rurale (GMPR) in November 1954.[6] Modelled on the mainland Compagnies Républicaines de Sécurité (CRS), with priority given to ex-servicemen, these units were well armed and highly mobile. Their task was to give colonialism a visible presence, covering areas where French authority was under-administered. Each of the initial 34 GMPR units totalled 85 people (one-third from the immediate locality, one-third from nearby and one-third non-local) and in 1957 they were renamed Groupes Mobiles de Sécurité (GMS). Recruitment rose from 3,400 in 1954 to 10,000 at the end of the war, evidence of the way in which Muslim auxiliaries came to play a key part in the French counter-terrorist strategy. Indeed during his time as a Special Inspector-General in Constantine between 1956 and 1958 and later as Prefect of Police in Paris Maurice Papon deployed these units to deadly effect. Under him the auxiliaries were given a free rein to break the national liberation struggle by any means necessary, a strategy which reached a grisly climax during the winter of 1961–2 when Papon let loose his *harkis métropolitains* on FLN supporters in Paris.[7] Mass round-ups, torture, arbitrary arrest, these methods became the norm as Papon's auxiliaries operated outside the judicial system. Mounting acrimony from the left-wing press eventually led Papon to be cross examined by the Paris Municipal Council on 18 March 1961 and in the face of his accusers Papon was unrepentant:

> I was Special Inspector-General in Constantine for two years...There I learned that the main characteristic of subversive warfare is its secrecy. Clandestine warfare being impossible in a country like ours, where everything ends by being brought to court, I felt that our operations must be shrouded in at least some degree of secrecy.[8]

If colonial administration was one pole of attraction for the native population, followed closely by the police, the final and most important one was the army. Indeed just one month after the landing at Sidi Ferruch in 1830 the Zouaouas Berber tribe, which had always raised troops for the Turkish dey, supplied 500 *zouaves* for the invasion force. By 1841 the number of native soldiers fighting with the French had risen to 8,704 during which time many became notorious for brutality, in large part because they knew that if France was to lose they would be subjected to terrible retribution. On 1 January 1856 it was decided to formally channel this pro-French sentiment with the creation of three Algerian infantry regiments and henceforth Muslim troops were to distinguish themselves on the battlefields as far afield as the Crimea, Mexico and Madagascar. The year 1912 witnessed the introduction of conscription for Muslims, and during the First World War 170,000 Algerian natives fought in the French army. Likewise in the Second World War they formed the backbone of the army of Africa, supplying 250,000 troops for the Italian campaign including Ahmed Ben Bella, Mohamed Boudiaf, Mostfa Ben Boulaid and Belkacem Krim, all future FLN leaders.[9] At the time of the March 1962 ceasefire the number of Algerians in the French army amounted to 20,000 career soldiers in addition to 40,000 conscripts.

The administration, police and army: by November 1954 all of these institutions had well-established patterns of Muslim recruitment. However, the battle for hearts and minds led the army to search for new ways to win over the native populace and one of the first innovations was the creation of the *mokhaznis*. These were locally raised militiamen who worked with the new Sections Administratives Spécialisées, a corps of administrators drawn from the French army but assigned a whole series of civilian duties. The SAS were the brainchild of Jacques Soustelle who was Governor-General in Algeria from January 1955 to February 1956 and their role was to counter chronic under-administration in the remoter parts of the country. Nicknamed the blue caps because of their distinctive headgear the purpose of the SAS officer was to reach out to the Muslim masses, teaching them about construction work and agriculture, as well as clothing, health and justice. From the beginning, therefore, the SAS officer skilfully cultivated the language of protection and education. Part administrator, part teacher, part soldier, his role was not only to shield the population from ALN terrorism but also to win them over to the French cause and in this precise sense he was the very personification of the civilizing mission. The SAS officer represented the assertion of a daily presence among the natives, a fact that was underlined by the way in which each detachment went well beyond any strict military remit to include a book-keeper, a wireless operator and a nurse. Significantly too in 1958, in a concerted effort to win over Muslim women, a female orderly was added to each detachment with a view to promoting women's health care issues. Each SAS unit was placed under orders, not from the military, but the local Prefect and their effectiveness was demonstrated by the rapid expansion of SAS detachments from 30 in September 1955 to 641 by

December 1959. Usually each unit was housed in a *bordj* (fort) and the commanding officer would be charged with the training of local militiamen, commonly referred to as *mokhaznis* from the Ottoman word *maghzen*. Normally 25 *mokhaznis* were attached to each SAS unit and they would live with their families in close proximity to the *bordj*. In principle they had a dual role – to provide armed protection and to act as the eyes and ears of French authority. But in practice the level of commitment could vary enormously. Nicolas d'Andoque, as SAS officer in Ain Chedra in March 1960, routinely took his men out on night patrols and at regular intervals they became involved in skirmishes with the ALN.[10] In contrast, Alain Maillard de la Morandais, SAS second-in-command at Oum Djerane, paints a portrait of local villagers happy to be housed and to receive regular food but not terribly enthusiastic about military operations because they did not wish to compromise themselves in the eyes of the ALN.[11] Overall the number of *mokhaznis* rose from 17,000 in 1957 to 19,000 in 1959, peaking at 20,000 in 1961.

A second innovation introduced by the army were the *groupes d'autodéfense* (GAD) where villagers and farmers were organised into self-defence units. Each person received a weapon and their village and farm was made secure through the construction of sentry boxes and the erection of barbed wire fencing. In this way the army set out not only to protect the population from attack but also to starve out Algerian resistance by depriving the ALN of food and shelter. For these reasons they deliberately targeted villages of strategic importance, dramatically expanding the number of villages organized into GADS from 18 in January 1957 to 385 three years later. This expansion was an integral part of the 1959 offensive because the GADs were seen to be a statement about the reassertion of French control and the widespread claims of military victory in 1960 were in large part based upon the winning over of villages to the anti-ALN cause. Now photographs of politicians and officers handing out weapons to loyal Algerians became a standard trope of anti-ALN propaganda. Yet, how much these were genuine expressions of fidelity was open to question. For some Algerians it was a question of survival, a way of saving their village from repression and torture.[12] For others it was part of a complex double game whereupon the image of a GAD provided the cover for the ALN. On top of this some army officers were cynical about the real meaning of any rallying to the French cause. Too often it was obvious that psychological intimidation had been the key factor.

The final and most important military innovation was the *harkis* themselves. The first units of Muslim auxiliaries were raised in Arris in the Aurès mountains in November 1954 in the wake of the ALN revolt. Here Jean Servier, an ethnologist with a specialist knowledge of Berber customs, assumed command and he immediately exploited the traditional hostility between the Ouled Abdi and Touabas tribes.[13] Having convinced Ouled

Abdi leaders that the Touabas were behind the rebellion the former supplied Servier with 50 recruits whom he immediately organized into a militia. But after this initial spurt of recruitment there was considerable reticence among the *colons* about arming the native population. Fundamentally their misgivings stemmed from the belief that the Algerians could not be trusted, a line of argument which was reinforced by the spectacular defection of 50 Algerian *tirailleurs* to the ALN on 18 February 1956.[14] Nevertheless the army was convinced of the need to raise and train auxiliaries. General Lorillot in particular was the impetus behind recruitment during spring 1956 and by July 1957 the first units were judged to be ready for combat.[15]

Initially *harki* units were used in secretive counter-insurgency operations and here the French were to experience a number of embarrassing reversals. One disastrous experiment was 'Force K', an anti-ALN guerrilla force made up of Kabyle separatists, which was immediately infiltrated by Belkacem Krim's fighters from Wilaya 4.[16] Likewise the hope that Bellounis, the leader of the private army of MNA dissidents operating just north of the Sahara, could form the basis of another anti-ALN *maquis* eventually dissipated through his brutal treatment of the local population. By July 1958 it was clear that his actions were doing damage to the French cause at which point Colonel Trinquier's paratroopers were dispatched to wind up the operation and liquidate Bellounis.

'Force K' and Bellounis left a taint of suspicion which was to linger until the end of the war. However, these setbacks were balanced out by the successes of Captain Paul Léger who deployed the first urban *harki* units to deadly effect during the Battle of Algiers. Many of Léger's 800 *harkis* were ex-FLN prisoners and he skilfully exploited this inside knowledge to infiltrate and ultimately destroy the FLN command structure in the capital. Léger's example was one of the factors which fuelled the massive expansion of numbers in 1957 under the new commander in chief, Raoul Salan who insisted that they be properly integrated into the existing military structure lest they lead to the creation of an embryonic Algerian army. The second wave of expansion then took place under General Challe between 1958 and 1960.[17] In planning the grand offensive to eradicate the ALN Challe came to see the *harkis* as central to victory. Logistically they would overcome the problem of the 'hollow classes' since conscription was now drawing upon the young men who should have been born during the Second World War. Financially the *harkis* would reduce the cost of the war because they would be paid at a lower rate than either conscripts or professional soldiers. Finally *harki* participation had enormous political significance because it would mean that the native population would see victory over the FLN as their victory too. For all these reasons Challe pushed for the expansion of harki numbers from 26,000 to 60,000, threatening resignation unless de Gaulle gave into his demands.

The *harkis* were also central to Challe's military tactics. He knew that the ALN's greatest asset was knowledge of the terrain allied with tacit support of the local populace. This allowed them to pursue a strategy based on limited actions and the avoidance of pitched encounters. Small packets of guerrillas would derail a train, ambush a convoy or attack an SAS outpost then melt back into the night. In Challe's eyes this meant that the key to victory was the relentless pursuit of the ALN maquis. Refining the hunt, tightening the net, isolating the prey: these became the guiding principles of the Challe offensive. Henceforth there would be no safe havens, neither the mountains (*djebel*) nor the night would be left to the rebel forces, and here the *harkis*, many of whom were ex-FLN prisoners, were to play a pivotal role in tracking down the guerrilla bands.[18] In this way the army in general and the *harkis* in particular became involved in a dialectical relationship with the ALN, learning from the ALN tactics to use those self-same tactics against them. Thus like the ALN the *harkis* would use ruse, guile and continuous movement. Like the ALN they would draw upon their intimate knowledge of the terrain to live nomadically and like the ALN they would mount commando raids and ambushes. However, as the eyes and ears of the hunt, the purpose of the *harkis* was to locate and pin down the ALN unit. Once this had been done the paratroopers would be immediately helicoptered in to finish off the job, hitting the rebels again and again until they had finally been broken.

When women and children are added to the numbers of auxiliaries recruited Michel Roux puts the total of pro-French Muslims at 1.5 million out of a native population of 9 million.[19] Undoubtedly their existence is uncomfortable for Algerian nationalism. It opens out the complex reality of the colonial period, immediately undermining the image of an Algerian people resisting as one against French occupation. Right from the beginning various tribes and clans sided with the French in order to further their own interests. Significantly too the *harkis* demonstrate that French culture did have a deep impact upon Algerian society. In fact by 1961 there were more Algerians fighting in the French army than in the ALN.[20]

Motivations

What motivated Muslims to side with the French was diverse. The assimilated elite was in the main drawn from the professional classes, plus remnants of the Ottoman empire. Teachers, doctors, lawyers and landowners: they were Muslims who had received a French education and explained their allegiance in terms of patriotism. They saw themselves as French and found it impossible to identify with the Algerian nation. This is not to say that they were all servile creatures of the colonial system. On the contrary, many had been subjected to racism and were painfully aware of the extent to which the settlers were resistant to political change. But they believed that reform would come from the mainland through an extension of citizenship rights to Algerians. Popular rebellion coupled with FLN violence filled them with horror and although some, such as Ferhat Abbas, did come to support the liberation struggle many sided with the forces of law and order. The most famous example of this last political trajectory was Bachaga Said Boualam. A prominent landowner whose local fiefdom was the Orléansville region, by 1962 he had risen to become the vice-president of the National Assembly. Writing after the war, when he became the leading spokesman for the *harki* community in France, Bachaga Boualam emphasized his family's allegiance had been forged on the battlefield.[21] A Boualam, he proudly asserted, had fought in every major campaign since the Crimean War. This patriotism was blended with a strong sense of anti-communism. In Boualam's eyes FLN victory would mean Soviet-style socialism and the expropriation of traditional landowners like himself. The *harkis*, therefore, were an anti-communist third force and the true meaning of the 1958 referendum, in which the *harkis* played a key role in organizing the Muslim vote, was a rejection of one party totalitarianism and a vote in favour of integration.[22]

For the Muslim administrators their day-to-day role inevitably instilled a close identification with the colonial status quo. In many cases it was a question of a family tradition stretching back to the Ottoman period and this too served to reinforce still further the gulf between them and the rest of the indigenous population. Significantly most *caids* remained loyal and sought sanctuary in France in 1962. In a similar fashion the army inculcated a close identification with France. Historically speaking many Muslims saw military service as a way out of grinding poverty. The upshot was that many Muslim ex-servicemen came to see the army as their home, equating the loyalty to a particular regiment with loyalty to the French nation.

Perhaps the most significance motivation for *harki* recruitment was revenge against FLN violence. The national liberation movement might have projected the image of mass struggle but the cornerstone of ALN strategy was control of the population. The ALN survival hinged upon silence and complicity and to achieve this it had to create a climate of mystery and force. People had to know that betrayal would lead to immediate retribution. To underline this the ALN struck out in two directions – at pro-colonial Muslims, dismissed contemptuously as *béni-oui-oui*, and at any possible third force alternative to the FLN. Consequently Algerian administrators, politicians, MNA members, anybody disobeying Muslim rules of conduct: all ran the risk of throat cutting, mutilation or assassination as the ALN imposed iron discipline.

The Algerian historian and former FLN activist Mohamed Harbi notes that the number of *harki* recruits is striking and he interprets this as a reaction against the excesses of the ALN.[23] Many Muslims, Harbi admits, came to resent ALN justice as unfair and arbitrary, especially when local leaders were accused of exploiting their power to settle clan and family disputes. In his diaries the writer Mouloud Feraoun conjures up an atmosphere of wanton ALN violence which, in a society with such a strong code of honour, inevitably fuelled a cycle of revenge and counter-revenge.[24] This aspect is also underlined by Michel Roux in his seminal study *Les harkis ou les oubliés de l'histoire*. For him ALN ruthlessness, best exemplified by the Mélouza massacre in 1957 when a whole village was wiped out because it was suspected of being pro-MNA, pushed much of the native population towards the French camp. Yet, Roux emphasizes, anti-Muslim ALN violence has been ignored in post-colonial Algeria. It has been ignored because such brutality muddies the image of a heroic ALN maquis. It has been ignored because it points towards the civil war dimension of 1954–62. And finally it has been ignored because the violence begs many questions about the transition to independence, in particular how far ALN intransigence instilled a set of attitudes which paved the way to the army dictatorship.

If ALN violence was a major factor in *harki* recruitment so too was money. Under colonialism the Algerian peasantry was impoverished. For the head of a family, therefore, joining up became attractive because it held out the promise of food and regular income. It was a way of feeding hungry mouths. In equal measure enrolment in a *harki* unit gave recruits a feeling of status. At last they had tasted a small measure of power, something they had never previously been accorded under colonialism. The historian Mohand Hamoumou, in his exhaustive study *Et ils sont devenus harkis*, points to a further dimension which has been underestimated – the difficulty of joining the ALN maquis.[25] The ALN was not a club which recruits could join. It was dependent on the say of a local leader who wielded enormous power. Often this leader was strongly identified with a particular tribe or family and from 1959 onwards, as the international situation began to shift inexorably towards the FLN, many began to look ahead to post-independence. Mouloud Feraoun notes leaders began to reject volunteers because they no longer wished to divide the spoils of victory and in Hamoumou's view this created a sense of exclusion and forced large numbers of Muslims, even many who supported independence, to look toward the army.

Conversely there was the issue of French army tactics. On the one hand there was a genuine attempt to win over the population. Unlike the ALN, routinely represented as crazed animals and criminals, the army argued that it was building a new society based on equality and here May 1958 and the subsequent referendum were central to this claim. For the likes of Salan May 1958 was the colonial equivalent of 4 August 1789 when the nobles abolished feudalism. On the other hand the army regularly employed psychological manipulation and entrapment. Said Ferdi's autobiography, *Un enfant dans la guerre* published in 1981, is a powerful portrayal of a teenage boy who is caught in a terrible dilemma.[26] Initially he works for the ALN but when he is taken prisoner the army offers him a stark alternative – either change sides or his father will be tortured. Ferdi was typical of the manner in which the army ensnared many ALN prisoners, locking them into a brutal logic whereby they had the most to fear from independence. And finally there was the relocation policy which aimed to isolate the ALN guerrillas by moving two million Algerians away from their villages into temporary camps. Undoubtedly this created a culture of dependency which the army ruthlessly exploited to enlist *harki* volunteers.

How effective were the *harkis*? General Buis remembers that at the time he was suspicious of the *harkis*.[27] He made limited use of them in his sector because he suspected that they had a foot in the nationalist camp and this belief, he feels, explains why the *harkis* were left open to ALN retribution. Buis's comments provoked Abd-El-Aziz Méliani, himself a former lieutenant in the Algerian war, to write a book refuting the double game accusation. In *Le drame des harkis*, published in 1993, he set out to put the record straight, proving beyond doubt that the *harkis* were loyal and highly effective.[28] Yet whatever the military balance sheet what is not in doubt is the role the *harki* question played in the April 1961 revolt. For Challe it was a question of honour. He had to lead the rebellion because he had given his word that the *harkis* would not be sold out to the FLN.

The massacres

The demobilization of the *harki* units at the end of 1961 produced a collapse of morale among pro-French Muslims. Now, as the contours of independence began to emerge, they knew that they would be left to face pitiless reprisals. Yet initially it was unclear what would happen. Admittedly there was no specific clause dealing with their plight under the Evian agreement but arguably their status was safeguarded by the general commitment to protect human rights. Similarly some conciliatory noises were made at local level by ALN leaders with talk of the *harkis* forming part of a transitional police force. But after such a bitter and protracted war only the most hopelessly naive could have imagined that the *harkis* would be integrated into the new Algeria. They were particularly vulnerable to *les marsiens*, Algerians who were so-called because they joined the FLN after the Evian ceasefire in 19 March 1962 when FLN victory was clearly unstoppable. Some were opportunists who had waited on events but many were *harkis* deserters. Organizing *harki* purges now became a way of effacing their past and immediately proving their loyalty to the incoming regime.

At the same time it is vital to remember the climate of hatred and violence which reigned in summer 1962. In the wake of the OAS scorched earth policy few Algerian nationalists felt in the mood for reconciliation.

Euphoria at independence was mixed with a basic desire for revenge and with the FLN leadership exercising little control over the grassroots it was local leaders who made the running, their pent-up fury eventually exploding into a full-scale quest to root out the enemies of the people. Now, in an explicit inversion of colonial power, the hunters became the hunted as the *harkis* were subjected to every conceivable form of torment. Angry onlookers hurled abuse while men, women and children were beaten, tortured and killed and this bestial maltreatment had a strong ritualistic element. Some men were castrated, some were buried alive, others were dressed up as women and paraded in the streets – in each case the intention was to insult their manhood and underline their separation from the nation.

In the Akbou arrondissement situated in the Sétif department the massacres went through a number of stages between March and November 1962. After an initial stand-off the *harki* purges started in earnest in late July. By mid-September the bloodletting had petered out leading to a period of calm. However, the arrival of the Algerian army from Tunisia, impatient to assert its authority in an emphatic manner, led to a renewed wave of violence which lasted into December. By this time approximately 2,000 had been killed out of a total Muslim population of 100,000. How far Akbou was typical of the course of events in the rest of country is difficult to gauge and this in turn has fuelled an ongoing controversy about the scale of the purges. At the time the *Le Monde* journalist Jean Lacouture put the numbers killed at 10,000, but this has since been attacked as a gross underestimation. Mohand Hamoumou argues that the figure must be 150,000, while Guy Pervillé feels that it is more accurate to talk about 70,000.[29]

In the face of this human suffering de Gaulle was adamant that the *harkis* could not be repatriated. According to de Gaulle's cold calculus the *harkis* had to be sacrificed because, unlike the settlers, they belonged to a separate culture and religion. Thus those *harkis* who tried to escape to France were sent back. Likewise the army was given explicit orders not to intervene over the massacres. Many former SAS officers, notably Nicolas d'Andoque, were disgusted by de Gaulle's policy and organized clandestine networks to save the *harkis*. How many *harkis* escaped is difficult to calculate. Abd-El-Aziz Méliani puts the number at 270,000 to which must be added 10,000 who were FLN prisoners freed through the Red Cross between 1962 and 1972.

In France the *harkis'* fate met with a muted response. To a large extent this was because the specificity of the *harkis* massacres was subsumed into a general impression of uncontrolled bloodletting. But it was also indicative of a hardening of attitudes; by autumn 1962 the vast majority of French people did not care, they were thoroughly sick of Algeria and wanted to turn the page as quickly as possible. Ironically then the fiercest denunciation of Gaullist policy came from the intellectual Pierre Vidal-Naquet, one of the most outspoken supporters of Algerian independence. Writing in *Le Monde* in November 1962 he berated de Gaulle's cynical abdication of responsibility. Having enlisted them as an instrument of repression France had a duty to save them. In this sense, Vidal-Naquet argued, the *harkis* were themselves victims of the colonial mentality.[30]

The triple silence

Since 1962 the *harki* experience has been subjected to a triple silence.[31] In Algeria this silence was linked to the fact that for the new regime these massacres were a statement about Algerian sovereignty. They were seen as an act of psychological self-liberation which marked the purification of the nation and the end of colonial control. Put simply the purges were the foundation stone of the new Algeria and could not be questioned. Henceforth the *harki* was forever fixed as a traitor and within the Algerian political lexicon it has come to stand as the worst term of political abuse. Thus within the contemporary Algerian crisis the government has regularly stigmatized the Islamist movement as being comprised of sons of former *harkis*. In this sense, it is claimed, the present counter-insurgency war must be understood as a new battle between the *harkis* and 1954–62 ALN veterans. On the opposing side political Islamists have spread the notion that the *harkis* successfully infiltrated the national liberation movement at independence, exploiting their power to impose an alien Francophone culture. This means that the purpose of the Islamist movement is to cleanse the nation of *harki* influence and thereby reassert the true Arabo-Islamic identity. Given the fierceness of these polemics and the way they are hopelessly enmeshed within contemporary politics it is not surprising that the reality of the *harkis* has been ignored.

The second aspect of this silence has been within France where the *harkis* have suffered from official marginalization. For de Gaulle post-1962 the phenomenon of decolonization was reconfigured as a victory for modernization. The *harkis* became untidy reminders of a colonial past which had to be forgotten and what intensified this amnesia still further was the extent to which their sacrifice punctured de Gaulle's myth of infallibility. The massacres became a taboo because they raised the issue of Gaullist culpability and sullied his image as a great leader.

For the French army too it is a shameful episode. In 1991 General Buis expressed regret.[32] Selling out the *harkis*, he admits, underlined the most basic failure of the army's mission, namely the protection of the population from attack. Indeed, as Bachaga Boualam recounts, some French units, by knowingly duping the *harkis* into handing over their weapons, colluded with the massacres.[33] On another level the abandonment of the *harkis* demonstrated that equality under *Algérie française* was a fiction. The *harkis* were not considered to be French and that is why de Gaulle did everything to block their escape. For the Left the *harki* experience was interpreted in terms of the Second World War. The *harkis* did not warrant any sympathy because they acted like pro-Nazi collaborators. The Third Worldist Left in particular, heavily influenced by Frantz Fanon's vision of FLN violence as an act of liberation freeing Algerians from a colonial psychology, understood the *harkis* as a throwback to subservience. The *harkis* were Algerians who had internalized colonial values and this made the massacres a necessary, if regrettable, stage in decolonization.

Finally there was the silence of the *harkis* themselves. The majority of those who escaped to France were illiterate peasantry and for them the experience of loss, exile and separation was psychologically devastating. Despised by their country of origin, disowned in large part by the French authorities, many male veterans found it difficult to contemplate the consequences of their choices for them and their families. In fact the more that they came to feel that they had made the wrong choice the more they retreated into a guilty silence. According to Laurent Muller, in his study of the transmission of memory within *harki* families in Alsace and the Vaucluse, this silence, symbolizing their inability to communicate their war experience, is a defining trait.[34] *Harki* sons and daughters explained to him that within the family the Algerian War was a taboo subject. Nobody was allowed to talk about it and inevitably this amnesia eventually stimulated their own search for the historical truth. Beyond the family, at school and within the media, the second generation sought to piece together the past, connecting what happened to their parents in Algeria with their own sense of place and identity. Through this slow process many were able to come to terms with the past, understanding the way in which their own experience had been determined by their parent's painful personal history.

Treatment in France since 1962

As the most prominent pro-French Muslim, the army provided Bachaga Boualam and his entourage with a safe passage out of Algeria. However, such treatment was the exception rather than the rule. For those *harkis* fortunate enough to escape the massacres their arrival in France was a humiliating experience. Housed in camps surrounded by barbed wire they were made to reapply for French nationality. Facilities at Rivesaltes in the Pyrenees, already notorious because of its usage by the Vichy regime to intern Spanish Republican refugees and Jews, were squalid and the fact that the winter of 1962–3 was very hard left an enduring memory of betrayal and deprivation. Thereafter the government followed a policy of segregation deliberately separating the *harkis* from the rest of the French population. For example, large numbers were relocated to makeshift villages and employed in forest clearance.

The failure of successive governments to break away from a paternalist mentality fuelled a feeling of injustice within the *harki* community. By 1975 two-thirds of the *harki* population were under twenty. Of these many were unemployed, many had no qualifications and many had been subjected to racism creating a sense of exclusion which eventually ignited a wave of protests in the summer of 1975. Through direct action, including the kidnapping of an Algerian official in France, a new more militant generation aimed to bring their plight to the attention of the French public. Above all they now demanded practical measures which would bring about genuine political and economic integration.

During the 1980s there was a plethora of *harki* organizations which made it difficult to develop a common platform.[35] Some *harkis* were attracted to anti-racist organizations like *SOS Racisme* and *France-Plus* while others, notably Mourad Kaouah, made common cause with the National Front arguing that Algerian immigrants were giving Muslims a bad image and thereby threatening *harki* integration. Nonetheless 1991 witnessed a renewal of direct action across France. Toll roads were blocked and hunger strikes launched while Narbonne in the south of France experienced six weeks of rioting. A common thread to these protests was the need for justice and recognition, and for the *Le Monde* journalist Alain Rollat this was enormously significant.[36] By proudly asserting their identity as the children and grandchildren of the *harki* community they had once and for all broken the conspiracy of silence and reclaimed the singularity of their experience.

Rollat's remarks were indicative of a new climate of understanding. In part this climate had been fostered by the research of Michel Roux and Mohand Hamoumou who had approached the *harki* experience in a more compassionate light. In part too it was also the product of a new context for remembering within France. October 1988 saw the gunning down of 500 unarmed civilians on the streets of Algiers by the Algerian army. In the light of these killings some *harkis* drew a line between October 1988 and the 1962 massacres, arguing that the *harkis* now had to be understood as the first victims of the army regime. Equally parallels were made with atrocities in the Balkans leading to the claim that the *harki* massacres were a form of ethnic cleansing. On top of this the way in which France at last came to terms with Vichy's role in the Holocaust during the 1990s provided a powerful impetus for the *harki* community. As with the Jews, it was argued, France now had a duty to come to terms with the *harkis*. And finally there were the terrible events in contemporary Algeria. In 1962 it was difficult not to project the *harkis* as the losers in history. Now in the face of new bloodshed the *harki* memories could be reconfigured, the apparent failure of Algerian independence finally vindicating their pro-French stance during the 1954–62 conflict.

During the 1990s truth, dignity and justice were the watchwords of the *harki* community. In 1993 Abd-El-Aziz Méliani called on the government

to integrate the *harkis* into the collective memory through the erection of a specific memorial.[37] He also demanded greater efforts in the fight against anti-Muslim racism, above all the need to recognize the place of Islam within French society. This new assertiveness was also reflected in the website for the association *Justice pour les harkis et leurs familles*.[38] Formed in 1997 and bringing together fifty *harki* groups, the association is campaigning for the recognition of responsibility by the French state for the massacres, as well as the erection of a monument and the establishment of a special day of commemoration. Added to this there are practical demands such as free circulation between France and Algeria and the need for financial aid, including reparations for property lost during the war. Significantly for the first time these demands have found an echo within the political mainstream. Writing in the left-wing *Nouvel Observateur* at the conclusion of Bouteflika's visit in June 2000, the leading political commentator Jean Daniel castigated the Algerian President for his remarks about the *harkis*.[39] Often, Daniel reminded readers, the *harkis* had rallied to France because they were being persecuted by uncontrollable elements within the ALN. In Daniel's opinion the *harkis* are the most painful symptom of the colonial syndrome. Now what is needed is a common gesture whereby both countries recognize their responsibilites and offer reconciliation.[40]

Notes

1. Bouteflika was elected president on 15 April 1999.
2. The speech, given on 14 June, was boycotted by half of the Démocratie libérale deputies. Defending their action the Démocratie libérale spokesperson, Claude Goasguen, invoked the memory of the *harkis* as the primary consideration.
3. The *harki* associations were calling for *harkis* to be allowed free circulation between France and Algeria. Bouteflika deliberately ignored demands to meet with *harki* representatives.
4. At Arris in the Aurès mountains in November 1954 one administrator and two assistants were responsible for 60,000 people.
5. Returning from Biskra to Arris to warn of impending revolt Hadj Sadok was on the bus which at 7 a.m. on 1 November 1954 ran into an ALN ambush near the Tighanimine gorges. Sadok had already dismissed the rebellion as the work of criminals and when he made to reach for his pistol he was caught in a burst of gunfire which also wounded a French teacher, Guy Monnerot. That the killing of a prominent local Muslim was a premeditated execution there can be no doubt. The bus driver was told to drive to Arris with Sadok's body, whilst Monnerot was left to bleed to death.
6. Jean Vaujour, *De la révolte à la révolution. Aux premiers jours de la guerre d'Algérie* (Paris: Albin Michel, 1985).
7. On the role of the *harkis* in Paris see Paulette Péju, *Les harkis à Paris* (Paris: Maspero, 1961).
8. Pierre Vidal-Naquet, *Torture: Cancer of Democracy* (London: Penguin, 1963), p. 114.

9. This explains why so much of the ALN was based upon the French army model.
10. Nicolas D'Andoque, *1955–1962, guerre et paix en Algérie* (Paris: SPL, 1977).
11. Alain Maillard de la Morandais, *L'honneur est sauf* (Paris: Seuil, 1990).
12. For example the procuring of food which was tightly controlled by the army who used this as an 'incentive' for the recruitment of loyal villages.
13. Thereafter the army drew upon Servier's expertise to advise on the recruitment of natives. On his role in November 1954 see Jean Servier, *Dans l'Aurès sur les pas des rebelles* (Paris: France Empire, 1955).
14. The deserters killed eleven including a lieutenant and took a large stock of weapons.
15. The raising of *harki* units was officially established in February 1956.
16. The French did not pick up on the double game for months with the result that hundreds of automatic weapons were lost to the rebels,
17. Maurice Challe, *Notre révolte* (Paris: Presses de la cité, 1968).
18. For an eyewitness account of the role of *harki* commando units see Marcel Bigeard, *Pour une parcelle de gloire* (Paris: Plon, 1975).
19. Michel Roux, *Les harkis ou les oubliés de l'histoire 1954–1991* (Paris: La Découverte, 1991).
20. Guy Pervillé, 'La guerre d'Algérie sans mystification ni tabou', *L'Histoire*, 1986, no.93.
21. Bachaga Boualam, *Mon pays la France* (Paris: France Empire, 1962).
22. On this point see Bachaga Boualam, *Les harkis au service de la France* (Paris: France Empire, 1964).
23. Mohammed Harbi, *Le FLN, mirage et réalité* (Paris: Jeune Afrique, 1980), pp. 310–313.
24. Mouloud Feraoun, *Journal, 1955–1962* (Paris: Seuil, 1962).
25. Mohand Hamoumou, *Et ils sont devenus harkis* (Paris: Fayard, 1993).
26. Said Ferdi, *Un enfant dans la guerre* (Paris: Seuil, 1981). Apart from two books by Boualam the only other *harki* eyewitness account is Brahim Sadouni, *Français sans patrie* (Rouen: Copie plus, 1985). The complexity of the *harki* experience is also dealt with in novel form by Medhi Charef, *Le harki de Meriem* (Paris: Mercure de France, 1989).
27. 'Entretien avec General Buis', *L'Histoire*, January 1991.
28. Abd-El-Aziz Méliani, *Le drame des harkis* (Paris: Perrin, 1993). Maurice Faivre brings together a whole series of documents on the *harkis* to demonstrate their effectiveness in *Les combattants musulmans de la guerre d'Algérie – des soldats sacrifiés* (Paris: Harmattan, 1994). This image of sacrifice is also repeated in Bernard Moinet *Ahmed connais pas – le calvaires des harkis* (Paris: Godefroy de Bouillon, 1997).
29. Guy Pervillé, 'Guerre d'Algérie: l'abandon des harkis', *L'Histoire*, July 1987.
30. Pierre Vidal-Naquet, 'La guerre révolutionnaire et la tragédie des harkis', *Le Monde*, 11 November 1962, reproduced in *Face à la raison d'état: un historien dans la guerre d'Algérie* (Paris: La Découverte, 1989).
31. On the *harki* memory see Mohand Hamoumou 'Les harkis, un trou de mémoire franco-algérien', *Esprit*, May 1990 and Jean-Jacques Jordi and Mohand Hamoumou, *Les harkis, une mémoire enfouie* (Paris: Editions Autrement, 1999). To understand the violent terms in which many ALN veterans still denounce the *harkis* see the interview with Mohammedi Said, leader of Wilaya 3, reproduced in Benjamin Stora, *La gangréne et l'oubli* (Paris: La Découverte, 1991). The interview, in which Said says that the *harkis* deserved to be massacred, was

originally broadcast as part of Benjamin Stora's documentary series *Les Années algériennes* on Antenne 2 in autumn 1991.

32. 'Entretien avec General Buis'. See also General Buis, *Les fanfares perdus* (Paris: Seuil, 1975). This view was not limited to the military leadership. By 1962 the *harkis* were also viewed suspiciously by many ordinary conscripts. On this point see M Lemallet, *Lettres d'Algérie, la guerre des appelés* (Paris: Jean-Claude Lattes, 1992).
33. Boualam, *Les harkis au service de la France.*
34. Laurent Muller, *Le Silence des harkis* (Paris: Harmattan, 1999). Within the book Muller produces twenty biographies of *harki* children.
35. On this point see Catherine Withol de Wenden, 'La vie associative des harkis', *Migrations Société*, October–December 1989.
36. Alain Rollat, 'L'histoire refoulée des harkis', *Le Monde*, 7 August 1991.
37. Abd-El-Aziz Méliani, *Le drame des harkis.*
38. 'Collectif Justice Pour Les Harkis', http://www.chez.com/justiceharkis.
39. Jean Daniel, 'Entretien avec le président algérien', *Le Nouvel Observateur*, June 2000, pp. 22–8.
40. In 1999 the French government denied the *harkis* permission to place a memorial wreath to their dead comrades at the Arc de Triomphe. However, in 2001 the government established 25 September as France's first national Harki remembrance day.

Part II
Images

8
Anglo-Saxon Literary and Filmic Representations of the French Army in Algeria

Philip Dine

Introduction

The point of departure for the present chapter is the desire to plug a perceived gap in the critical analysis of the processes of individual and collective memory as they relate to the history of the Algerian War, 1954–62. For if much has been written about the impact of the war, and especially its psychological legacy, on the societies of the principal protagonists, France and Algeria, then very little has been said about its impact on the wider world.[1] This is doubly ironic in that the Algerian revolution, precisely as an example of decolonization, was by definition part of a global phenomenon, namely the European retreat from overseas empire in the postwar period, and was, moreover, a conflict in which the very processes of internationalization constituted a strategic consideration of central importance.

On the one hand, the French authorities were consistent in their determination to affirm the 'Frenchness' of Algeria, and thus the essentially domestic nature of the 'disorder' which occurred during the eight long years of the undeclared, and logically undeclarable, war in and over the territory. This, of course, is the core of the myth of *Algérie française*, that is to say the legal and administrative fiction that Algeria was nothing more nor less than three French *départements*, and as such an integral part of the one and indivisible Republic. On the other hand, and as a direct consequence of this systematic negation of Algerian national identity, not only was the Front de Libération Nationale (FLN) pushed into launching its armed challenge to continued colonial rule on 1 November 1954, but also Algerian nationalist politicians, exiled in Tunis or at the microphone of the United Nations, were led constantly to proclaim the international character of the conflict between France and its North African 'province'.

The political, and to a lesser extent military, internationalization of the war was clearly accelerated by events such as the bombing by the French air force of the Tunisian frontier village of Sakhiet-Sidi-Youssef in February

1958, a 'blunder' which required the intervention of an Anglo-American 'good offices' team in order to restore normal relations between the France of Félix Gaillard and the Tunisia of Habib Bourguiba. Similarly, the revelations made from 1957 onwards regarding the use of torture and other internationally outlawed 'pacification' methods in Algeria, and particularly during the Battle of Algiers, undoubtedly made a major contribution to the critical awakening of international opinion, together, of course, with that of the metropolitan French public.

It should come as no surprise, therefore, to discover that a number of Anglo-Saxon (i.e. British and American) authors and film-directors should, throughout the 1960s and into the 1970s, have taken a keen interest in the Franco-Algerian dispute. Indeed, the attention shown by these producers of literary and filmic fictions may even be said to have parallels with what is a well-established Anglo-Saxon tradition of critically examining France's Algerian war – from Dorothy Pickles to David Schalk – in part directly as a response to the lack, until comparatively recently, of anything like a consensual and scholarly French history of this troubled and troubling period. However, the proclivity of British commentators in particular for picking at our nearest neighbour's colonial sore spots is not always the high-minded exercise it would wish to appear, and may on occasion have its roots in the history, both during and after the age of empire, of regularly strained relations between the foremost imperial rivals. By the same token, the avowed anti-colonialism of the United States of America may be seen in a number of these works to be motivated by less than wholly altruistic considerations. In spite of this, or perhaps precisely because of it, the relevant literary and filmic productions constitute remarkable historical documents, for reasons which I shall seek to contextualize by means of some preliminary observations regarding the nature of the corpus.

Reflections on the corpus

My own research on the French – as opposed to the Algerian French-expression – literature and cinema of the Algerian War has convinced me of the significance, both artistic and sociological, of the mass of fictional narratives generated in response to developments in France and Algeria in the period 1954–62. In particular, I have argued that the substantial body of creative writing, and the inevitably much smaller number of feature films, produced in response to the relevant historical events offers a privileged route into the political, ideological and, perhaps most intriguingly, psychological complexities of this specifically French reaction to the end of empire: together they constitute a literary and filmic *lieu de mémoire* in the absence of a physical one of the kind associated with earlier French conflicts.[2]

In the course of my research, I came across a number of English-language novels and films dealing with the Algerian War, while colleagues and friends have been kind enough to bring others to my attention. The total number of such narratives is hard to estimate, and what follows is based purely upon the nine novels and two films which I have been able both to identify and, crucially, to obtain.[3] This sample, although essentially arbitrary as regards the manner of its selection, does, nevertheless, display a formal and thematic commonality which leads me to believe that it may well be both representative and genuinely significant. Moreover, the reading which I propose of these texts, which all date from the period 1961–71 (or 1973 if the film version of one of the novels is included) is borne out by a recent discussion of elements of this corpus as part of a much wider ranging survey of the image of Algeria in Anglo-American writings.[4] Unfortunately, the obvious chronological coherence provided by the 1961–71 time-frame – that is to say, the decade which included the final years of the war and its immediate aftermath – means that I shall not be able to focus here on the very small number of Anglo-American works of fiction devoted to the Franco-Algerian conflict which have appeared since this time. Perhaps most notable of these is Robert Irwin's *The Mysteries of Algiers* (1988), a work which the author himself has been conspicuously keen to promote. However, Osman Benchérif's characterization of this work as being 'in the tradition of the James Bond series ... [and] an altogether absurd story' may be taken as a reassurance that Irwin's novel is essentially a revisiting of thematic territory extensively explored in the texts presently under discussion, rather than a significant departure from or addition to them and their collective mind-set.[5] The texts in chronological order of publication or release are as follows:

Novels:

Harry Whittington, *Guerrilla Girls* (Originally published in the United States of America by Pyramid Books in 1961; London: New English Library, 1970).

Maurice Edelman, *The Fratricides* (London: Hamish Hamilton, 1963; London: Panther, 1966).

Alan Williams, *Barbouze* (London: Anthony Blond, 1963; London: Panther, 1965).

Alan Sillitoe, *The Death of William Posters* (London: W.H. Allen, 1965; London: Star Books, 1979).

Alan Sillitoe, *A Tree on Fire* (London: Macmillan, 1967; London: Grafton, 1986).

Alan Sillitoe, *The Flame of Life* (London: W.H. Allen, 1974).

Francis Fytton, *The Nation Within* (London: Ambit Books, 1967; London: Panther, 1969; first published in *Stand* magazine).

Con Sellers, *The Algerian Incident* (Reseda, CA: Powell Publications, 1970).

Frederick Forsyth, *The Day of the Jackal* (London: Hutchinson, 1971; London: Book Club Asociates, 1972).

Films:

Lost Command (US: Mark Robson, 1966).
The Day of the Jackal (GB/France: Fred Zinnemann, 1973).

Why should these novels and films exist at all? Part of the answer lies in the period covered by these productions. Neatly spanning the decade 1961–71, they are, at one level, products of their time and their perceived market. The novels were all made available in inexpensive paperback editions, and in several cases (Whittington, Williams, Sellers and even Forsyth) look to the Algerian War as a topical, and conveniently exotic, backdrop for the sensational treatment of sex and violence, as, in their different ways, do both of the films. A number of the books consequently have lurid cover designs, accompanied by jacket blurbs which seek straightforwardly to titillate a 'popular', and undoubtedly male, audience. Whittington's title, *Guerrilla Girls,* is a particularly obvious appeal to the dubious attractions of the Algerian War as a source of 'cheap thrills', while the subtitle 'The Female Legion of the Damned' and the cover photographs remove any possible doubt as to the likely nature of the volume's contents. Of course, the peculiar literary appeal of sexuality in the colonial context is a regular theme of critical commentators on western culture – especially the literary and artistic tradition of Orientalism[6] – and the supposed charms of the harem and the slave-market are never far away from the thinking of some of these writers and film-makers. Further, while several works take up an overtly anti-colonialist stance, Fytton's novel is the only one genuinely to challenge traditional gender roles in its depiction of FLN militancy, a fact which is, perhaps, to be understood in the light of feminist critiques of the structural linkage between patriarchy and colonialism. It is also worth noting that the supposedly glamorous world of the foreign correspondent is variously evoked by Williams and Sellers, while Forsyth's professional assassin similarly moves in a world of fast cars, beautiful women and ready cash.

If Whittington and Sellers are the most 'downmarket' of the works represented here, then Alan Sillitoe would, by general agreement, be considered the most 'highbrow' of the authors under consideration. Fytton's work also makes a strong claim to be taken seriously as literature, as, for that matter, do the other novels published by Panther (by Edelman and Williams), which would thus seem to have become established as a regular publisher – or, more accurately, re-publisher – of some of the better Anglo-Saxon material inspired by the Algerian War. In a class of its own as a publishing phenomenon, however, is Frederick Forsyth's *The Day of the Jackal*. A huge international best-seller, it was first published in French, under the title *Chacal*, by Mercure de France in 1971. Nowadays available in Gallimard's 'Folio' paperback series, it is undoubtedly the only one of the works under consideration here to have had a significant, and durable, impact on the French publishing market. However, it is not the only work to have been translated into French, as Maurice Edelman's *Les Fratricides* was itself published by Presses de la Cité in 1964.

How do these texts compare with the French literature and cinema of the Algerian War? In particular, do we find a consensus as regards the representation of the French army in Algeria, or do we find a politically grounded polarization of opinion as we demonstrably do in France itself? Further, do we find the same sort of stereotypes put forward concerning such other actors in the Algerian drama as the 'indigenous' population of the territory and the *pieds-noirs*? And finally, how is the French nation as a whole depicted in the light of its Algerian experiences? In order to begin to formulate answers to these questions, we must now consider the representation of the Algerian war in our selected texts.

The representation of the Algerian War

The single most striking feature of the French literature of the Algerian war is the enormous range of personal accounts of the French army's campaign, as experienced in their very different ways by the elite troops of the parachute regiments, senior army commanders and the extremely heterogeneous mass of *appelés* and *rappelés*. Indeed, such is the dominance of this type of literature that it might be said to be *the* characteristic mode of French literary reflection on the Algerian war (although the same could emphatically not be said of the French cinema of the conflict, in which the hostilities in Algeria are primarily conspicuous by their absence from the screen, being evoked indirectly for the most part). However, in contrast, the Anglo-Saxon corpus is primarily notable for the almost total absence of accounts of the war 'on the ground' in Algeria, at least as experienced by the French troops sent to fight there. The only exception, in the dozen or so English-language works considered here, is the American Mark Robson's *Lost Command* (1966). However, this film, the only conventionally heroic 'war film' to have been inspired by the Algerian conflict, is very much a special case in that it is merely a Hollywood screen version of Jean Lartéguy's best-selling novel *Les Centurions* (1960).

The film is generally a faithful adaptation of Lartéguy's book, and has a cast which notably includes Alain Delon (Captain Esclavier), Maurice Ronet (Captain Boisfeuras) and Anthony Quinn (Colonel Raspéguy). As the director of such well-known box-office hits as *Von Ryan's Express* and *The Inn of the Sixth Happiness*, Robson could hardly have been expected to make anything other than a Hollwood blockbuster out of Lartéguy's very pro-military novel, and the film's lack of any perceived threat to the French national memory of the Algerian War meant that it was widely distributed in its dubbed French version.[7] With George Segal and Claudia Cardinale cast as FLN militants, the film conformed to the familiar Hollywood (mis-)representation of the non-European 'Other', while its Algerian landscape (filmed in Spain) is essentially stereotypical and serves to constitute a neutral backdrop for the military heroics and sexual antics of a hard-bitten group of professional *baroudeurs*, who could be of any nationality and any political persuasion.

Nevertheless, the film does provide images of the Algerian War which were at this time still absent from French screens: ambushes, the murder of a family of *pieds-noirs*, the mutilation of captured French soldiers, bloody reprisals by their comrades, *ratonnades* and even the barbed-wire, searches, raids and *interrogatoires renforcés* of the Battle of Algiers. However, the fundamentally unthreatening and even reassuring image of the war communicated by Robson's film, although historically significant in helping to break the French cinematic taboo on the direct representation of the Algerian conflict, is straightforwardly to be contrasted with another, much more troubling, depiction of the paratroopers' 1957 campaign against the FLN's Algiers bomb networks. The Italian director Gillo Pontecorvo's *La Bataille d'Alger*, released just one year earlier in 1965, may have won the prestigious 'Golden Lion' at the 1966 Venice film festival – which the French delegation walked out of in protest – but was not to be granted certification in France until 1970. When it was eventually shown on a few French screens, the film met with considerable hostility from groups of *anciens combattants* and repatriated *pieds-noirs*, with a number of violent incidents being recorded. Part of the significance of Pontecorvo's uncomfortable vision of France's war in Algeria can be gauged from the intensity of this reaction alone. In comparison, Robson's film appears altogether more lightweight both technically and politically.

What then of the representation of the war in the eight novels under consideration? Three distinct perspectives are, in fact, represented: the war as seen from the FLN side; the war as a clandestine conflict fought out primarily in Algeria; and the war as a clandestine conflict fought out primarily in France. Each of these points of view may usefully be illustrated and examined.

Harry Whittington's *Guerrilla Girls* (1961) is a strange tale which, as its title suggests, focuses on a group of mixed 'European' and 'Muslim' female volunteers based in an FLN camp in the Aurès mountains. The narrative pays scant regard either to historical plausibility or to the mechanics of female participation in the insurrection as it combines regular sexual titillation and rather juvenile military heroics in what is a distinctly odd mixture. However, the text does, here and there, address the politics of the Algerian War, thereby providing scope for the statement of what is effectively a liberal American anti-colonialism, albeit given voice by Whittington's very contrived French and Algerian characters. So, for instance, we find a ringing declaration by an FLN commander of his belief, whatever the odds, in the nationalists' ability ultimately to overthrow the colonial order (1970: 43). Such claims inevitably ring rather hollow nowadays, given the nature of political and military developments in Algeria since independence, and, for that matter, coming as it does from an American commentator just prior to the embroilment of 'the land of the free' in the Vietnam tragedy. However, the FLN's political case is made in a sympathetic fashion, with emphasis being placed on the military valour of an adversary all too frequently dismissed by French writers, of official declarations and literary fictions alike, as merely 'une poignée d'irréductibles'. Interestingly, Whittington's FLN commander goes on to argue that the blood of the Roman Legions very likely runs in his veins rather than in those of his colonial adversaries, in what is a fascinating inversion of the familiar theme of North Africa's Latin heritage, a constant of French colonialist writing from Louis Bertrand to Jean Lartéguy.

Altogether more serious both as a political critique and as a piece of creative writing, however, is Alan Sillitoe's representation of the war in Algeria. Well known for such works as *Saturday Night and Sunday Morning* (1958) and *The Loneliness of the Long Distance Runner* (1959), Sillitoe will require little by way of introduction here. In the three volumes of his William Posters trilogy – *The Death of William Posters* (1965), *A Tree on Fire* (1967) and *The Flame of Life* (1974) – the Algerian conflict is the object of sustained attention by Sillitoe, himself a veteran of active service in Malaya and also a long-term resident in France. Through the character of Frank Dawley – an English working-class anti-hero who drifts from his home in the Midlands to London, Paris, Tangier and, eventually, Algeria – Sillitoe is able to cast light on major transformations affecting both British and French society in the postwar period. A fierce critic of capitalism and colonialism alike, Sillitoe analyses the French role in the Algerian tragedy in terms which are, perhaps, broadly predictable. So, at the most basic level, Algeria is presented as 'a country labouring under barbarous torments and oppression' (1986: 133). It is this which justifies what Sillitoe refers to euphemistically as the 'crude simplicity' of the FLN's organization of the Algerian struggle against continued colonial rule, deeming its methods 'necessary if the wretched of the earth are to become collectively strong and not be defeated by genocidal maniacs' (1986: 167–8). The Fanonist rhetoric on display here is an accurate indicator of Sillitoe's political sympathies, as are the favourable references which he makes to Mao Tse Tung's treatise on protracted warfare (1986: 165–6) and a selection of extracts from *El Moudjahid* (1986: 301–5). For Sillitoe, as for Fanon, revolutionary violence has a cleansing effect on the oppressed Algerian population. Indeed, even the retaliatory violence of the French oppressor can serve this function. So, in the case of the 'tree on fire' which provides both a title and a leitmotiv for Frank Dawley's experiences of the anti-colonialist struggle, an image of technologically 'superior' French oppression – specifically, an air force jet's destruction with napalm of the tree in question, together with the Algerian 'suspect' who sought to hide in it – may become a symbol of continued struggle and ultimate victory: 'The tree had burned off its foliage, but the tree was even hardier, and ready to grow again' (1986: 202).

In contrast to Whittington and Sillitoe, the remainder of the writers considered here prefer to focus not on the guerrilla war fought out in the Algerian hinterland between the FLN and the French army, but rather on the various clandestine campaigns conducted in the European cities of the littoral and/or in metropolitan France. So, for instance, the two British novels published in 1963, Maurice Edelman's *The Fratricides* and Alan Williams's *Barbouze*, while both historically well informed and technically accomplished pieces of writing, shift the emphasis firmly away from Franco-Algerian hostilities and towards the depiction of the conflict as essentially a French civil war. Whether depicted positively, as in Edelman, or ambivalently, as in Williams, the Gaullist secret agents or *barbouzes* employed in the French authorities' bitter struggle against the European terrorists of the Organisation Armée Secrète (OAS) thus become established as the focus for the novels' respective treatments of the Algerian War.

Such a perspective is inherently reductive in at least five main respects. First, the indigenous Algerian (i.e. 'Muslim') population is relegated to a very minor role, if it is considered at all: Algerians are essentially depicted as the innocent victims of forces wholly beyond both their comprehension and their control, with women and children regularly foregrounded as particularly helpless figures, rather than being shown as political and/or military actors in the unfolding of events. Second, the significance of the rural heartland of Algeria is effectively denied as attention is focused exclusively on the urban centres, and above all Algiers. Third, events in Algeria prior to mid-1961 are only treated as being of significance in so far as they account for the emergence of the OAS. Fourth, and following on from the previous point, the historical significance of the OAS is systematically exaggerated. Fifth, the conflict as a whole ceases to be a problem of decolonization and becomes just part of a much longer running *guerre franco-française* or permanent, if generally low-intensity, French civil war. It is such a racially defused perspective which gives Edelman his title, and which leads Neil Ingleby, the quintessentially 'decent' English journalist at the centre of Williams's tale of intrigue and mutual betrayal, to be fatally caught up in what he perceives as 'this ugly game of fratricidal strife' (1965: 119).

This said, both Williams and Edelman make important comments about the nature of the war in Algeria in the course of their novels. More specifically, both draw attention to the real suffering of the European population of Algeria in the final days of the war, and particularly the often forgotten violence associated with the army's reduction of the OAS stronghold of Bab-el-Oued.[8] By the same token, although both evoke the European 'exodus' as independence approaches, it is the attention given by Edelman to what is one of the most frequently forgotten episodes of the war, the French army's massacre of European demonstrators in the Rue d'Isly on 26 March 1962, which is worthy of note, particularly in its drawing of critical attention to the gloss put on the relevant events by the French authorities (1965: 201).

Where Edelman's *barbouze* hero significantly underestimates the spiteful durability of the OAS, Williams's hapless protagonist does considerable harm and ultimately dies because of his naive wish to 'try to help' in a situation which he does not understand. In this, he might fruitfully be compared with Pyle, the eponymous hero of Graham Greene's novel of the French war in Indochina, *The Quiet American* (1955). In complete contrast, American journalist Lee Croix, the dashing hero of Con Sellers's *The Algerian Incident* (1970), bestrides the clandestine war between the French state, the OAS and the FLN – or what the jacket blurb revealingly describes as 'the Algerian government, the French colonials, and the Bedouin tribesmen' – like a colossus. This sex-and-violence potboiler is without doubt the most unintentionally comic of all the texts represented here, with the very limited interest of its American author in the Algerian War accurately summed up by the title's reference to the eight-year-long conflict as an 'incident'. Predictably, the introduction of the leading character sets the tone of the novel, and thereby establishes its resolutely sexist, racist and, above all, 'Amerocentric' perspective (1970: 6).

Given the narrative's unswerving belief in the combined power of the mighty dollar, good tailoring and Hollywood-inflected masculinity, Lee can surely have little to fear from his personal exposure to the Algerian War. Yet, even this masterful representative of the world's most powerful nation must admit to a certain difficulty in finding a straightforward solution to the territory's problems. However, when all else fails, he resorts to the trusty stand-by of 1960s American foreign policy, namely a visceral anti-communism combined with a paranoid fear of the Soviet Union's 'evil empire':

> But for now the Reds were playing their familiar game, supplying guns and ammunition, pushing one side against the other while the Kremlin smirked and schemed, while good men died on both sides. And as women and children were blown into bloody shreds in cafes. (1970: 121–2)

Ironically, for all Lee's expressed sympathy for de Gaulle's predicament, the Cold War world-view represented here is much closer to the *guerre révolutionnaire* theorizing of the 'activist' members of the French officer corps, and thus the OAS, than it is to that of the then President of the French Republic. The representation by other Anglo-Saxon commentators of this particular mind-set, and of those French soldiers who were historically led by it into open revolt against republican legitimacy, will be returned to shortly. Before that, however, we must briefly consider the two cited novels in which the Algerian War is represented as a clandestine conflict fought out essentially in France. We are here confonted by two radically different texts: Francis Fytton's *The Nation Within* (1967) and Frederick Forsyth's *The Day of the Jackal* (1972). Paradoxically, the interest of these two works is inversely proportional to their celebrity.

To begin with, Fytton's text is undoubtedly the more technically complex of the two novels, and is, indeed, the most formally innovative of the works considered here, a fact which led one critic to describe it as 'A new type of fiction – documentary fiction', when its three overlapping narratives were first published in *Stand* magazine.[9] Moreover, it puts forward the most challenging image of French society yet encountered, in that it depicts a society morally and politically contaminated by the Algerian War. This is a familiar enough theme in the French literature of the conflict, and one often summed up by means of the notion of 'gangrene'. Fytton's three starkly depicted episodes – 'Manifestation', 'Assassination' and 'Interrogation' – together make for uncomfortable reading and reveal a Paris where conventional standards of civilized behaviour have collapsed under the pressures of the nation's belated and unwilling withdrawal from its last and most important colonial territory. The assassination in question is that of a Paris-based *harki* by an FLN militant, while the interrogation involves the torture and murder of an Algerian woman by the police. Both of these graphic accounts would merit closer examination, but it is his account of the brutal suppression by the Paris police of the peaceful Algerian demonstration of 17 October 1961 against the curfew recently introduced on North Africans residing in the city that will be considered here.[10] Effectively denied by the French authorities at the time and since, and largely forgotten by French novelists until 'rediscovered' by Georges Mattéi in 1982 and, perhaps more effectively, Didier Daeninckx in 1984,[11] the British literary commemoration of this awful occurrence as early as 1967 is particularly to be noted.

Fytton's account of the massacre (1969: 9–47) provides an interesting parallel with Edelman's depiction of the Rue d'Isly shootings, and in its concluding focus on the minutiae of state-sanctioned violence is reminiscent of Daeninckx's moving portrayal of the same events:

> There was little to be seen: the broken windows of the Café de la Gare had been boarded up; the shattered scooter had been propped against a

> tree; the glass had been swept into the gutter; the shoes had been crushed to leather-pulp by the passage of wheels; the rain had washed away the blood. (1969: 47)[12]

In complete contrast, we have Frederick Forsyth's tightly plotted, minutely detailed, but also curiously unfeeling and, consequently, ultimately unsatisfactory narrative. The real focus of attention here, indeed, is not France in the wake of its Algerian experience, still less Algeria's emergence from a century and a quarter of colonial rule. Rather, it is the icy, amoral and, above all, apolitical professionalism of the hired gunman: an aristocratic English outsider, who provides one more reassuring Anglo-Saxon self-image to go with those already evoked of the decent Englishman, the tough American, the foreign correspondent and the working-class anti-hero. Played to perfection by Edward Fox in Fred Zinnemann's film version of Forsyth's novel, the anonymous killer provides no channel for sympathy, with the end result that the narrative is 'an incisive, observant and professional piece of work', but no more than that.[13]

The representation of the French army

As might be expected given the observations made above as regards the Anglo-Saxon depiction of the nature of the Algerian conflict, the representation of the French army in the texts under consideration is – with the obvious exception of *Lost Command*, Mark Robson's 1966 film version of Jean Lartéguy's *Les Centurions* – at best critical and at worst thoroughly damning. So, for instance, where Williams maintains that 'France is obsessed with phantoms of military glory' (1965: 45), Sillitoe depicts a French army which is unsure of itself and its reasons for being in Algeria, and is all the more dangerous in consequence. For Sillitoe, indeed, the French army in Algeria combines technological and numerical superiority with moral bankruptcy, pointless brutality and tactical ineptitude. His FLN guerrillas, in comparison, are 'harder, craftier, and more subtle' (1979: 266), and as such are constantly able to exploit the gaps in the colonial power's formidable armour. Unsurprisingly, Sillitoe attaches particular significance to the role of the Foreign Legion in Algeria, and particularly to those former Nazi troops who have sought refuge in its ranks. So, for instance, we read that 'German Nazis from the Foreign Legion had set up torture-houses in Algiers, trained others in the same game' (1979: 324), while the protagonist reflects in the following terms on the identity of his opponents:

> Frank emptied a magazine at encroaching figures who, he thought, might be Germans from the Foreign Legion, so sent off another clip for Stalingrad. (1979: 197)

This is, to say the least, a strange image of Franco-Algerian hostilies, as Sillitoe's English working-class anti-hero lines up on the side of Stalin's Russia against the representatives of Hitler's Germany. However, what it does usefully do is to highlight the extent to which memories of previous conflicts colour the treatment accorded to the Algerian War, and this is as true of Anglo-Saxon texts as it is of French ones.[14] Moreover, there is an apparent consensus on the part of these British and American commentators that responsibility for many of the most abhorrent features of the French army's campaign of *pacification* – such as the massacre of civilians and, of course, the torture and summary execution of Algerian 'suspects' – can ultimately be laid at the door of Hitler's Germany rather than de Gaulle's France. Even such a thoughtful writer as Fytton describes the men who kidnap his Algerian heroine prior to her torture and murder as speaking 'guttural French: Teutonic French' (1969: 148), while, at the other end of the literary scale, Sellers is at his most appalling in the relish which he brings to the depiction of Foreign Legion Captain Carl Junger, a veteran of Auschwitz as well as Dien Bien Phu (1969: 139–47 and *passim*).

For all the prurience of his writing, Sellers is also typical of a broader determination on the part of these authors to seek to find explanations for present military outrages in the past experiences of the French army. In particular, those ex-soldiers responsible for the European terrorist outrages of the OAS are old *Indo* hands to a man, with Williams's opium-smoking theorist of *guerre révolutionnaire*, Colonel Pierre Broussard (1965: 39–41 and 193–8) being a typical representative of the species. Where Broussard is 'a little insane' (1965: 41), Frederick Forsyth's Colonel Marc Rodin – the man responsible for hiring 'the Jackal' in a last-ditch attempt to assassinate the hated de Gaulle – is represented as fatally blinkered in his ruthless determination to keep Algeria French: 'The escalating costs of the war, the tottering economy of France under the burden of a war becoming increasingly unwinnable, the demoralisation of the conscripts, were a bagatelle' (1972: 24).

However, while such disgruntled professional soldiers as Broussard and Rodin may be depicted as dangerously obsessive and, like their real-life counterparts, wholly ruthless in their devotion to the cause of *Algérie française*, they are nevertheless perceived by the majority of these Anglo-Saxon commentators to be motivated by laudable considerations, such as patriotism, anti-communism and a strict code of military honour. In this, they achieve something very like the nobility that French literary defenders of the *paras* such as Jean Lartéguy have identified and celebrated in their writing. In contrast, Maurice Edelman puts forward an alternative, and rather less flattering image of French military involvement in the OAS. The scene is a 'kangaroo' court at which a liberal Jewish doctor will be tried and sentenced to death by the OAS for giving medical treatment indiscriminately to both sides in the Algerian conflict.[15] The relevant passage is worthy of quotation at some length:

> 'Hassid!' said the President, and leaning forward Hassid could see the earnest, rather scholarly face of the Colonel. It was a face which he had known, although he and Chatelain had not met for many years. It had become familiar in connection with the Resistance, since Chatelain in Equatorial Africa had been one of the first to rally as a young lieutenant with de Larminat to de Gaulle. He had fought a gallant but despairing campaign in Indo-China. And when he had been posted to Algiers, he had arrived with the reputation of a liberal who had made a special study of psychology. It was he who had 'regularized' as he put it the conduct of the paratroopers after the Battle of Algiers. If now he was an OAS leader, it was almost an accident, a lack of flexibility in a proud mind which regarded it as ignoble to abandon a moral and intellectual position as it would have been to surrender a physical stronghold. His fellow-officers, some who had been most violent in their hostility to de Gaulle after the Colonels' Revolt, had come to feel like chastened hounds. Chatelain had been isolated, too slow to conform, too arrogant to submit, smarting above all from a personal rebuke which the head of the State had given him in front of some junior officers during his quick visit to Algiers. Hassid looked from him to the ex-legionary with the clipped red hair and the battered mouth who stood guard, wearing a zip-up jacket, at his side, and thought that Chatelain no longer seemed a fallen proconsul; he had the air of an absconding college bursar who has fallen into bad company. (1966: 228)

This is an unusually shrewd analysis of the many and varied motives for a given individual's participation in the French military's revolt against the head of state: they inevitably include what Rousso calls 'the complex posterity of resistance participation',[16] the experience of defeat in Indochina and the subversive officers' patent theory of 'revolutionary war', but also less easily admitted factors, such as inertia, arrogance and pettiness. This, I would suggest, hints at a sophisticated reading of military *activisme* which is not generally available in either the Anglo-Saxon or the French literature and cinema of the Algerian War.

Conclusion

Two features stand out from this rapid overview of Anglo-Saxon literary and filmic representations of the French army in Algeria. First, a tendency to resort to stereotypes of the Other, whether French or Algerian, together with reassuring images of the Self: it is too often a case of 'decent English journalists' and 'rugged American reporters' coming to terms with the warring tribes of a doubly dark African continent, at once French and Algerian. In this, the texts considered here undoubtedly add another dimension to the more or less familiar processes of mythification and mystification associated with the remembering (and/or forgetting) of the Algerian War, but they do not generally distance themselves from those same processes, still less reflect critically upon them.

Second, and this too mirrors the French literature and cinema generated by the conflict, we find a systematic under-representation of the non-European Other. Sillitoe's novel cycle is at least a partial exception in this respect, and may be regarded as of importance in consequence. It is this desire to 'write out' and to 'white out' the Algerians, and particularly the male FLN combatant – the most durably troubling image of anti-colonialist violence for French and Anglo-Saxon readers alike – that explains the almost overwhelming interest in the thematic of the 'fratricidal' war between the OAS and the *barbouzes*. By focusing on these European antagonists, it is possible to avoid the abiding challenge of the Algerian War and, come to that, of every other war of national liberation from colonial rule in the postwar period: that is to say, 'Third World' rejection not only of colonialism, but also of 'the West' in its entirety, together with its political, economic, and cultural models. Few of these texts make any real contribution to furthering our understanding of this disturbing historical truth.

Notes

1. An obvious exception to this general pattern is the essays contained in Part 4 of Jean-Pierre Rioux (ed.), *La Guerre d'Algérie et les Français* (Paris: Fayard, 1990): 'La guerre d'Algérie et la France dans le monde', pp. 369–493.
2. See Philip Dine, *Images of the Algerian War: French Fiction and Film, 1954–1992* (Oxford: Clarendon Press, 1994). See also the same author's 'Reading and remembering *la guerre des mythes*: French literary representations of the Algerian war', *Modern and Contemporary France*, NS2 (2), 1994, pp. 141–50. For an introduction to the Algerian French-expression literature of the war see Christiane Achour, 'La guerre de libération nationale dans les fictions algériennes' in the collection *Trente ans après: Nouvelles de la guerre d'Algérie* (Paris: Le Monde Editions/Nouvelles-Nouvelles, 1992).
3. Also of interest is the French film version of *pied-noir* author Jean Pélégi's *Les Oliviers de la justice* (1959) directed by the American, James Blue (France, 1962).
4. Osman Benchérif, *The Image of Algeria in Anglo-American Writings, 1785–1962* (Lanham, MD and Oxford: University Press of America, 1997), pp. 229–60. Among the significant writers usefully discussed by Benchérif who do not figure in my own analysis are Paul Bowles, Mary Motley and Norman Lewis.
5. Robert Irwin, *The Mysteries of Algiers* (New York: Viking, 1988 and Langsford Lodge, Cambs: Dedalus, 1993); Robert Irwin, 'A war without a name', *Times Literary Supplement*, 19 January 1996, p. 22; Benchérif, op. cit., pp. 258–9.
6. See, among others, Edward W. Said, *Orientalism* (London: Routledge & Kegan

Paul, 1978) and Rana Kabbani, *Europe's Myths of Orient: Devise and Rule* (London: Macmillan – now Palgrave Macmillan, 1986).

7. However, according to Pascal Ory, the film was not a great commercial success: 'malgré la présence à son générique d'Alain Delon, Maurice Ronet et Anthony Quinn, [le film] ne passionne pas les foules', 'L'Algérie fait écran', in Rioux, op. cit., pp. 572–81; p. 578 for the quotation.
8. See Edelman (1966), pp. 194–201; cf. Williams (1965), pp. 176–9 and 193–4.
9. Jon Silkin, cited in the preface to this edition, p. 7.
10. The bloody repression perpetrated in Paris on 17 October 1961 is painstakingly and harrowingly reconstructed by Jean-Luc Einaudi in *La Bataille de Paris* (Paris: Seuil, 1991). This incident was brought to wider public attention during the 1997 trial for crimes against humanity of Maurice Papon, a key administrator under the wartime Vichy regime who went on to become Prefect of Police for Paris in the postwar period, as well as by the subsequent libel action brought by Papon against Einaudi in 1999.
11. Georges Mattéi, *La Guerre des gusses* (Paris: Balland, 1982), pp. 212–14; Didier Daeninckx, *Meurtres pour mémoire* (Paris: Gallimard, 'Folio', 1984), pp. 11–38.
12. Compare Daeninckx's account, op. cit., p. 37: 'Au petit matin il ne restait plus sur les boulevards que des milliers de chaussures, d'objets, de débris divers qui témoignaient de la violence des affrontements. Le silence s'était établi, enfin.'
13. Leslie Halliwell, *Halliwell's Film Guide*, ed. John Walker, 8th edn (London: Grafton, 1992), p. 276.
14. See Philip Dine, 'The Inescapable Allusion: the Occupation and the Resistance in French Fiction and Film of the Algerian War', in H. R. Kedward and N. Wood (eds), *The Liberation of France: Image and Event* (Oxford: Berg, 1995), pp. 269–82.
15. Benchérif, op. cit., p. 247, points out that 'Dr. Hassid is based on Dr. Henri Aboulker, a distinguished Jewish doctor who had organized the resistance in the city and helped the Allied Landing in 1943'.
16. Henri Rousso, *The Vichy Syndrome: History and Memory in France since 1944* (London: Harvard University Press, 1991; originally published as *Le Syndrome de Vichy*, Paris: Seuil, 1990), p. 79.

9

The Image of the French Army in the Cinematic Representation of the Algerian War: the Revolutionary Politics of *The Battle of Algiers*

Hugh Roberts

Algerian films about the national liberation war generally conform to the rule that war films are implicitly or explicitly propagandist in nature. But the most celebrated film about the Algerian War, Pontecorvo's *The Battle of Algiers*, is a striking exception. Not only does it depict both sides of the war with objectivity and detachment, and both its Algerian and French victims with equal sympathy, it also refuses to moralize about the methods used by the French in suppressing the terrorism of the FLN. Given the particular circumstances in which the film was made, and the degree of Algerian involvement in its production, this aspect of the film is remarkable. The explanation suggested is that the political content of the film reflects the real outlook of the wartime FLN, which was not liberal but revolutionary in character.[1]

In his discussion of the way in which the painful experience of the Algerian war has been handled in literary and artistic production in both independent Algeria and post-1962 France,[2] the historian Benjamin Stora considers how the protagonists of this war have been depicted in the various French and Algerian films which have been produced, and expresses considerable dissatisfaction with this. Writing of the image of the French army in the Algerian War promoted by various French films – notably René Vautier's *Avoir Vingt Ans Dans l'Aurès* (1971), Yves Boisset's *R.A.S.* (1973) and Laurent Heynemann's *La Question* (1977) – and one American production – Mark Robson's *Les Centurions* (1966) – he remarks that:

> Until the 80s, in all films, the soldier was an 'anti-hero', incapable of living out complex and contradictory situations. The Algerian was absent, or his presence only served to draw out the 'passions' of the French soldier.[3]

Of the Algerian films produced in the 1960s and 1970s, notably *Les Fusils de la Liberté, Djazaïrouna* and *Patrouille à l'Est,* he comments that their very names are

> ... so many 'sign-posted' titles which, on the image front depict the relationship that the Algerian authorities wanted to cultivate between the cinema and the people 'on the road to freedom'. These often Manichaean films (the heroic freedom-fighter squaring up to the wicked colonialist) are usually branded with the stamp of 'propaganda'.[4]

Now it cannot be denied that Algerian films about the war have had a propagandist dimension. It would be surprising were this *not* the case. One cannot help being struck by the inclination of French (or French-based) commentators on Algerian affairs to be scandalized by the discovery that the Algerian state behaves in many spheres...just like other states, including the French state. Were it the case that French war films did not represent the French resistance fighters as heroic and the German occupiers as villains, one might well concede Stora's point. But it is not the case, any more than it is the case that British and American films about the Second World War have refrained from caricaturing the German and the Japanese enemy. 'Our' heroes and 'their' villains are the staple *dramatis personae* of war films everywhere, and as a rule it is only when the issues at stake in the conflict have long been transcended and the scars have healed that it becomes possible for non-propagandist scenarios for war films to find commercial sponsors and a more realistic and sympathetic treatment of both sides of the conflict to reach the cinema screens.

However, it is not the case that all the films about the Algerian war have had the faults which Stora notes, nor did we have to wait until the 1980s for a film which is not vulnerable to these strictures. While I do not for a moment disagree with Stora in respect of the empirical accuracy of the generalization he is advancing as a general rule, it so happens that there is an exception to this rule, and one which he appears to have overlooked. This is Gillo Pontecorvo's *The Battle of Algiers*. In this film, the colonialists are by no means presented as villains, and the French soldier is by no means presented as 'incapable of confronting complex or contradictory situations'. On the contrary, the film presents a very different, and extremely interesting, image of the French army which merits fuller consideration.

Stora refers to Pontecorvo's film in passing, and notes that:

> The film is based on actual events, the assault launched by Colonel Bigeard in the winter of 1957 on the Algiers Casbah. The colonial officers are described as 'professionals' turned cold by the anti-guerilla struggle, torture included.[5]

This is more or less true as far as it goes, but it does not begin to do justice to the film. Of course, Stora is not undertaking to provide detailed treatments of the numerous films he discusses, and cannot be faulted for not doing so. But a reader unfamiliar with Pontecorvo's film could be forgiven for inferring from Stora's comment that the film is unsympathetic to the position of the French army and tends to caricature it, and that it includes a denunciation of the French army's resort to torture in particular. In fact, *The Battle of Algiers* is (and does) nothing of the kind, and the image it presents of the French army is exceptionally complex and exceptionally interesting, from numerous different points of view.

Portraying revolutionary warfare

The Battle of Algiers is an intensely and profoundly political film. But to say this is not to say that it is a film with a 'message', let alone an overtly propagandist one. It does not grind a political axe in any obvious way at all. What it does is portray the reality of a revolutionary war.

The film is neither fiction nor documentary, but a dramatization of real events, the historic Battle of Algiers from its beginnings in mid-1956 to its conclusion with the defeat of the FLN organization in Algiers (the famous Zone Autonome d'Alger – ZAA) in the autumn of 1957, to which is appended a coda in the shape of a brief but powerful depiction of the popular rising of December 1960 in which the people of Algiers, with apparently little in the way of political leadership or organization, demonstrated their support for the independence struggle in the most emphatic and unanswerable way.

The substance of the film deals with the events of 1956–7, however, and depicts the reality of urban guerrilla warfare from the point of view of both its protagonists, the clandestine FLN on the one hand and the French authorities and military commanders on the other. It shows how the FLN engaged in carefully targeted, discriminating, terrorism at first, with attacks on gendarmes and other members of the colonial security forces. It also shows how this prompted an unofficial recourse by the French police to indiscriminate counter-terrorism by placing a massive bomb in the Casbah, the official resort to executing FLN prisoners, and the subsequent turn by the FLN to indiscriminate bomb attacks in order to 'harness' the anger of the Muslim community and thereby continue to control it politically. And it finally shows the French authorities' turn to the French army in place of the normal police forces to deal with the problem, and this army's systematic use of torture as the key method of destroying the problem's source, the FLN organization in Algiers.

It thus shows both the spiral of violence and its logic, how one thing led to another in an infernal chain of cause and effect, and does so in a way which is both faithful to historical fact and devoid of any political propaganda or moralizing. While the film unquestionably presents a sympathetic vision of the Algerian national revolution, and enlists the unprejudiced spectator's sympathy for this without difficulty, very little of the film's politics is explicit. In particular, there are only eight or nine scenes where the actual political character and outlook of the FLN are portrayed:

- the scene early in the film where the petty criminal Ali la Pointe is approached by the FLN represented by the urchin Petit Omar, who overcomes Ali la Pointe's prejudice against a mere boy and simultaneously conveys to him his (Petit Omar's) true representative standing in his opening phrase: 'men have two faces' – the nature of the FLN as a clandestine movement that is omnipresent but invisible is conveyed in a few words, which are immediately understood by Ali la Pointe;
- the scene where Djaafar, the head of the FLN's organization in the Casbah, explains the strategy and tactics of the FLN's revolutionary war to Ali la Pointe;
- the scene where the FLN, represented by Ali la Pointe, establishes its monopoly control over the Casbah of Algiers by physically eliminating the Muslim gangster, Hacène el Blidi, who had previously controlled a part of it;
- the scene showing a group of children mercilessly attacking a drunkard after the FLN had announced a ban on alcohol;
- the scene where a representative of the FLN conducts a Muslim marriage service in the Casbah (clearly, if unemphatically, portraying the Islamic dimension of the FLN's nationalism);
- the scene where Ali la Pointe leads a march of angry Muslims, beside themselves after the European bombing of the Casbah, only to halt the march at Petit Omar's pleadings and enable Djaafar to reassert the FLN's control over the Muslim population by sending everyone home with the promise that 'the FLN will avenge you';
- the scene where the most senior FLN leader shown in the film, Larbi Ben M'Hidi, reflects on the revolution in a brief conversation held on a Casbah roof-top and insists that the war is only the beginning of the revolution and, in fact, the easy part of it;
- the scene where Ben M'Hidi, after his arrest, is paraded at a press conference and is taxed by a French journalist with the 'cowardice' involved in sending out women with bombs in their shopping baskets, to which he replies by asking whether it is not also cowardly for the French to send aeroplanes to bomb defenceless villages, adding memorably 'give us your planes and we shall readily give you our shopping baskets'.

These brief scenes convey something of the particular character of the FLN as a revolutionary nationalist movement, and in doing so express an aspect of the politics of the film. But as such they are spare, elliptical, austere in the extreme. There are no diatribes against French colonialism, no explicit, let alone emotive, statement of the nationalist case, at all. We need to look deeper if we are to see the real politics of this film.

Algerian attitudes

While *The Battle of Algiers* was directed by the Italian Gillo Pontecorvo, and is justly held to his personal credit, it was in fact an Italian–Algerian co-production. The production company involved on the Algerian side was Casbah Films. The managing director of Casbah Films was a certain Yacef Saadi. Yacef Saadi's name appears on the credits of the film, but not as co-producer; it appears among those of the actors. It is Yacef Saadi who plays the role of Djaafar. But 'Djaafar' is the *nom-de-guerre* of the leader of the FLN in the Casbah who, in historical reality, was none other than...Yacef Saadi. Yacef Saadi plays himself. This needs to be borne in mind when considering other aspects of the film.

The film was shot on location in Algiers, in the Casbah itself and in other parts of the city, in the summer of 1965.[6] The project was begun and carried out in the last months of the presidency of Ahmed Ben Bella. It clearly had the permission and consent of the Algerian authorities. Given the central involvement of Yacef Saadi (who had supported the Ben Bella–Boumédienne alliance in the factional struggle within the FLN in July–September 1962), it is virtually certain that there was a consensus within the Algerian government of the day in favour of the making of the film. And it is improbable, to say the least, that the Algerian authorities allowed the film to be made without having a clear idea of its political content.

In the light of these considerations, it is striking that the portrayal of the Algerian protagonists is an entirely objective one. The depiction of the French security forces is not merely objective, it is even sympathetic. While the brutality of the French soldiers breaking the FLN strike in January 1957 is shown very fully, we are also shown a remarkable scene of decency and moral as well as physical courage when, at the Hippodrome the following month, a French gendarme intervenes to rescue a Muslim youth from a lynch mob of Europeans maddened by the bomb attack which has just occurred. Moreover, far from glorifying the FLN's *fidaïyyin*, the film shows them, among other things, shooting French gendarmes in the back at an early stage in the drama and firing indiscriminately at Europeans from a speeding van at a later point.

Even more striking is the even-handedness of the film's depiction of indiscriminate terrorism and its human consequences.

The film contains two major episodes portraying bomb attacks, the first being the European terrorist bomb in the Casbah, which caused massive destruction and scores of Muslim victims, the second being the FLN's terrorist reprisals in bomb attacks on two European cafés and the office of an airline company. The first is longer, but the shorter duration of the second episode is compensated for by the fact that the victims are individualized. The numerous Algerian victims of the European bomb are not shown at all prior to the explosion; they are thus entirely anonymous: all we see are bodies, distraught relatives and grim-faced men carrying stretchers or digging desperately in the rubble. In contrast, the (considerably fewer) European victims of the FLN's bombs are shown at length before the bombs go off, and as ordinary people, not as cardboard cut-outs or caricatures, but as human beings, flesh and blood:

- a middle-aged man having a drink at the bar of the café chosen as the target for the woman terrorist Hassiba Ben Bouali who, mistaking her for a European, tries to chat her up in a perfectly courteous manner and, when she leaves (having deposited her lethal handbag beneath her bar stool), remarks wistfully 'Are you leaving, Mademoiselle? Pity';
- young people having normal youthful fun dancing to pop music from a juke-box in the second café, whom we observe at length because the camera shows us the second woman terrorist (Zohra Drif) observing them at length, with a wistful expression on her face suggestive perhaps of her own wish to be able to join them – a wish made impossible by the racial barrier between Europeans and 'Arabes';
- even a baby, in one of the two cafés, the quintessence of human innocence.

In this context, I disagree with Paul Schulte's claim that 'it seems impossible to find a single favourable depiction of *pied-noir* civilians in the film'.[7] Perhaps it depends on precisely what one means by 'favourable'. But there can be no doubt that the depiction of European civilians instanced above is at least *sympathetic*, and that this ensures that the human consequences of the FLN's terrorism are brought to the attention of the spectator in a way which is almost unbearable but which makes evasion of the issue impossible: these people do not deserve to be blown to bits, but they are about to be. The same elegiac and extremely moving music is heard on the soundtrack after the explosions on both occasions. The European victims are shown as no less innocent than the Muslim victims, the spectator identifies with them more, and they are mourned as the Muslim victims are mourned. In a film which is unmistakably supportive of the FLN's cause, and which was made with active Algerian involvement and official Algerian approval, this treatment of the FLN's terrorism is remarkable.

This brings us to the film's treatment of the French army.

The honour of Lt-Colonel Mathieu

Although *The Battle of Algiers* is a dramatization of a real event, it does not pretend to be pedantically faithful to historical fact in every point of detail, and certain scenes are clearly invented, while nonetheless defensible as being faithful in spirit to the reality of what happened. Nonetheless, it is a remarkably realistic film in many respects. In particular, the personages of Djaafar/Yacef Saadi, Ali la Pointe, Petit Omar, Hassiba Ben Bouali and Larbi Ben M'Hidi are all real historical figures accurately portrayed. This realism has one major exception, however, on the French side. The commander of the paratroopers called in to take on the FLN, Lt Colonel Mathieu, is not a real person at all, but a composite.

Mathieu is certainly shown to be a professional, but there is nothing particularly 'cold' about him and he certainly is not a bogey man or a monster at all. On the contrary, he is given some very good lines, and no bad lines, and is arguably the most complex and rounded character in the entire film. At the very outset, when he is first seen leading his men as they march into Algiers to the relief and applause of European onlookers, a voice-over gives his biography in which his heroic role in the French resistance to Nazism is emphasized. Thereafter, he is presented as a crisp, efficient, no-nonsense professional soldier, sure of himself but not arrogant, highly intelligent, with a sound appreciation of his FLN adversary and a measure of respect for it, an attractively dry, laconic, way of speaking and a nice line in irony, and a total absence of hypocrisy.

This comes out very clearly in his remark that, if he were the FLN, he too would use bombs. But it comes out above all in the crucial scene of a press conference at which a journalist raises the question of the methods used by Mathieu's men to obtain information from FLN prisoners. Observing that, for as long as the press employs circumlocutions, Mathieu can only respond allusively, the journalist suggests that people stop beating about the bush and that 'we are talking about *torture*.' Mathieu immediately replies 'Understood' – without any evasion, any squirming, any shiftiness, without moving a muscle in his face. He takes responsibility.

What then follows is the most extraordinary statement of the justification for the use of torture. Mathieu explains that, in the FLN (which, as he has previously told his hearers, is structured in such a way that no FLN activist knows more than three other activists, the man he takes orders from and the two men he gives orders to) each activist is instructed to hold his tongue, if arrested, for 24 hours – the time needed to enable his comrades to give the alert – after which he is free to sing like a canary. Mathieu points out that the information obtained after a lapse of 24 hours would accordingly be quite useless, and that if the army is to get anywhere in stopping the bombing, it has to get FLN prisoners to talk before they are willing to do so. Acknowledging that the methods involved are repugnant, he then insists that the question of torture is not the real question; the question is, *should France be in Algeria or not?* Decoded, this is a clear challenge to his (French) audience: '*messieurs*, if you will the end, will the necessary means.'

Two things are remarkable about this discourse. First, Mathieu is shown as being entirely rational and entirely coherent, morally sure of himself. He has thought about what he is doing, and is quite clear where the ultimate responsibility lies. What he is saying is that, if the French press, French public opinion, French democracy, etc. do not like the fact that the French army is torturing FLN suspects, they must realize that the FLN cannot be defeated by other methods and must reconsider their commitment to *l'Algérie française*. If this outlook can be described as 'cold', its coldness is the coldness of political lucidity.

Second, at no point in the film is any attempt made by any character to refute Mathieu's argument. Its coherence and moral force go unchallenged, *which means that they are allowed to stand*. This in turn has two implications.

The first is that, when we link Mathieu's behaviour to that of the FLN in its resort to indiscriminate bombing of civilians, we are shown that both protagonists are committed to the struggle they are waging and are equally prepared to be ruthless, but that this ruthlessness is rationally calculated and each side is morally sure of itself. To employ the vocabulary of existentialist philosophy, neither the FLN nor Mathieu are guilty of 'bad faith'.[8] Second, and in consequence, the film demonstrates a total and consistent refusal to demonize or moralize about this character, who is virtually the star of the drama. This is all the more remarkable when we realize who Mathieu really is.

Stora rightly mentions the name of Bigeard in his reference to *The Battle of Algiers*. Colonel Marcel Bigeard was indeed the commander of the regiment of paratroopers to which General Jacques Massu entrusted the dirty job of destroying the FLN in Algiers. Since Bigeard had already won a solid reputation as a fine soldier, and was still alive in 1965 (indeed, he was still alive in 2002, aged 86), it is perhaps understandable that the makers of the film should have hesitated to paint him black. Nonetheless, the device of a fictional character (Colonel Mathieu) enabled them to do so if they chose. That they chose not to is all the more interesting for the fact that the personage of Mathieu combines aspects of Bigeard's role with aspects of the role of a very different character, Colonel Yves Godard, a former French Resistance hero[9] who by 1957 was directing military intelligence during the Battle of Algiers and actually performed some of the functions which the film shows Mathieu as performing, in analysing information obtained and plotting it on an organigram of the FLN on blackboards in operations rooms and so forth.[10]

Now, whereas Bigeard stayed out of the subsequent die-hard politics of the French army in Algeria, and by adhering strictly to the code of the professional soldier was able to end his career triumphantly as Minister of Defence under President Giscard d'Estaing in the 1970s (a point the makers of the film could not have anticipated, of course), Godard went the other way, taking an active part in the army's putsch against de Gaulle's Algeria policy in April 1961 and then acting as the principal guiding spirit of the murderous OAS.[11]

All this is bound to have been known to the makers of *The Battle of Algiers,* and its Algerian backers and participants in particular, many of whom had been actively involved in the FLN's efforts to control the Muslim population of Algiers in the summer of 1962 and in particular to restrain it from responding to the provocations of Godard's OAS. And yet, while resorting to the device of a fictional paratroop commander, the makers of *The Battle of Algiers* refused to avail themselves of the opportunity to assault the moral credibility of the chief of the torturers that they had contrived to give themselves. There is not a shred of moralizing about torture in the film, and not a stain on the honour of Mathieu at the end of it. This refusal to moralize about torture or demonize the torturers even extends, as we have seen, to attributing to them a comparable philosophical attitude towards the FLN; the moral coherence of the outlook expressed in Mathieu's frank statement of the true rationale of what he is up to is attested to by his corresponding refusal to demonize *his* adversary and, in particular, by the tribute he pays to the *moral* qualities of the dead Ben M'Hidi.

It seems to me that all this is quite extraordinary. The film was made in 1965, when the scars of the war had barely begun to heal, when the most bitter and painful memories were still extremely fresh. This alone makes the film's objectivity remarkable, and a credit – along with its numerous other virtues as cinema – to its director, Pontecorvo. But while Pontecorvo's own political background and itinerary[12] no doubt furnish a satisfactory explanation of his own sophistication, this hardly explains what needs to be explained. To account for the film's political content essentially, let alone uniquely, in terms of Pontecorvo's own personal vision is to elide – indeed, deny – altogether the Algerian element of its nature.[13] Yet, as Schulte himself admits, the Algerian contribution to the film was of the first order. Not only did Yacef Saadi co-produce the film and play himself in it, not only did other former active members of the wartime FLN participate in it, playing themselves or the parts of dead comrades (one of them notably played the dead Hassiba Ben Bouali), but Yacef himself was also involved in the writing and rewriting of the screenplay.[14]

Given this degree of implication of the Algerians and, specifically, members of the wartime FLN, in the making of the film, the radical absence of any moralizing about the French army's resort to torture, this willingness to present the French paratroop commander precisely as someone psychologically, intellectually and morally capable of confronting a complex and contradictory situation, calls for explanation, to put it mildly.

Conclusion

It is not clear what the explanation is. But a hypothesis can be advanced. This consists of two main points.

The first is that the film actually represents in this respect the true outlook of the wartime FLN. While happy to enlist the support of French liberals during the war, and willing to make the most of their opposition to the torture resorted to by the French army, the FLN did not actually share their outlook in the least,[15] and, with victory gained, felt no need to pretend to do so thereafter. For the historic FLN, the ruthlessness of the French army was not the problem; the problem was exactly as Mathieu stated it: should France stay in Algeria or not? That was it.

The second is that the film was made in the early years of independence, before the Algerian state had got its act together (as it was to do under Boumédienne), and at a time when cinematic production, like artistic production in general, was yet to come under strict state supervision. To my knowledge, there have been no sequels to *The Battle of Algiers* in the sense of co-productions involving non-Algerian partners dealing cinematically with the Algerian War. When the film was made, there was no ministry of culture in the Algerian government. This may have meant first that the film-makers could enjoy a degree of freedom denied to later, purely Algerian productions; second, that in these circumstances the outlook of the Algerian protagonists of the war could inform the representation of their French adversary (as distinct from a representation drawn by government ministers from the intelligentsia with no experience of the fighting but militantly Zhdanovist conceptions of cultural policy).

That outlook, on the evidence of this film, was a revolutionary and politically sophisticated one, at ease with the moral complexities of the life-and-death struggle that had been fought, and saw a purpose in depicting these complexities honestly. And that is why the politics of *The Battle of Algiers* may be considered to be revolutionary, and worthy of the historic FLN, which did not need to misrepresent its French adversary, just to defeat it.

Notes

1. This chapter is a revised and slightly extended version of an article published under the same title in the *Journal of Algerian Studies*, Vol. 2 (1997), pp. 90–9. It originated in a paper which I presented to a Conference on *The Algerian War and the French Army: Experience, Image, Memory, 1954–1962* held at the University of

Salford, 11–13 October 1996 before I had learned of P. G. Schulte's essay, 'Interrogating Pontecorvo: the continuing significance and evolving meanings of *The Battle of Algiers*' (Royal College of Defence Studies, 1996 Course, 82 pp., plus Appendix; unpublished). While I by no means share all of Mr Schulte's judgements and opinions and instance two of my disagreements in the text, there is evidently much common ground between our respective views of the film, and a number of the revisions which I have made to this article have been prompted by his paper.

2. Benjamin Stora, *La Gangrène et l'Oubli: la mémoire de la guerre d'Algérie* (Paris: Éditions La Découverte, 1992).
3. Ibid., p. 252.
4. Ibid.
5. Ibid., p. 250.
6. Bruno Etienne remarks (in his book *L'Algérie, Cultures et Révolution*, Paris, Éditions du Seuil, 1977, p. 24) that when Boumédienne's tanks moved into the city in the coup of 19 June 1965, some people may have thought that this was simply part of the filming of *The Battle of Algiers*!
7. P. G. Schulte, 'Interrogating Pontecorvo: The Continuing Significance and Evolving Meanings of *The Battle of Algiers*', Royal College of Defence Studies, unpublished paper, 1996, p. 34.
8. In this context, it is interesting that the makers of *The Battle of Algiers* chose to call the composite figure of the French paratroop commander Mathieu, the name of the central protagonist of Sartre's *The Age of Reason* in *The Roads to Freedom* trilogy. At one point in the film, Sartre's pro-FLN stance is mentioned, provoking Mathieu's mildly irritated (or wistful?) retort: 'why is it that the Sartres are always on the other side?' Since Sartre's Mathieu is full of bad faith, there would be a delicious irony – and the implication of remarkable sophistication – in this choice if it was a conscious one.
9. Alistair Horne, *A Savage War of Peace: Algeria 1954–1962* (London: Macmillan, 1977), p. 189.
10. Ibid., p. 194. Arguably the figure of Mathieu combines the roles of at least four different people: not only Bigeard and Godard, but also, if in a lesser degree, those of Colonel Roger Trinquier, who organized the policing of Algiers through his Dispositif de Protection Urbaine, and Colonel Pierre Jeanpierre, the commander of the 1st Foreign Legion Parachute Regiment (the famous 1er REP) whose men took over from Bigeard's 3rd Colonial Parachute Regiment (3e RPC) in the last phase of the battle in autumn 1957; see Schulte, op. cit., p. 17 and Appendix, pp. A3–5.
11. In Fred Zinnemann's film *The Day of the Jackal* (1972), Jean Martin plays an OAS member, Victor Wolenski, a former paratrooper, who is abducted by the French police and dies after being tortured for information about the OAS's latest plans to kill de Gaulle. This was presumably a conscious in-joke on Zinnemann's part; in the same film, Philippe Léotard, who in *Avoir Vingt Ans Dans l'Aurès* had played the young officer who supports the 1961 generals' putsch against de Gaulle, plays the gendarme whom the Jackal kills with his last shot before he too is killed.
12. Pontecorvo was of Italian Jewish extraction and a Marxist; he fought with the Partisans during the Second World War and commanded a Partisan brigade in 1944–5; he left the Communist Party over Hungary in 1956; see Schulte, op. cit., p. 13.

13. It is thus, among other things, to reproduce the classical French colonial vision of the Algerians as at best mere executors of enterprises in which the work of conception and direction must forever remain a European preserve.
14. Schulte, op. cit., pp. 13–14.
15. That the FLN commanders did not have an absolute moral objection to torture in itself is evident from the fact that they themselves resorted to it on occasion, notably in the notorious *bleuite* affair, when perhaps several thousand FLN cadres were tortured and many executed on suspicion of treason following the ingenious planting by French counter-insurgent experts of falsely incriminating evidence intended to get the FLN to chase its own tail; see Mohamed Benyahia, *La Conjuration au Pouvoir* (Paris: Éditions Arcantère, 1988), p. 62 *et seq.* According to the Algerian historian Mohammed Harbi, a number of FLN cadres involved in a plot against the provisional government based in Tunisia were also the victims of torture; see Harbi, *Le FLN, Mirage et Réalité* (Paris: Éditions J.A., 1980), p. 228.

10

The Algerian War through the Prism of Anglo-Saxon Literature, 1954–66

Michael Brett

The Anglo-Saxons, to use the term employed by the French in the 1950s for the Americans and British, had passed in force through Algeria in 1943 without taking much interest in the country and its problems. The two-volume handbook on Algeria published by the Naval Intelligence Division of the British Admiralty in 1942–4 was based on prewar, mainly French information which gave little cause for political concern. The chapters on 'history' and 'peoples' referred only briefly to the movements led by Ben Badis, Ferhat Abbas and Messali Hadj, and to the influence of Arab nationalism and French Communism, dwelling if anything on the loyalty of the Muslim population to France in 1939 and its hostility to Axis propaganda. From November 1942 until the end of the Second World War, first-hand American and British perceptions of the country's real political, social and economic problems were confined to official correspondence. They went no further, since from the outset the need to win the war with French cooperation overrode the need to win the peace on the basis of the Atlantic Charter and the four freedoms. While the hopes of the Muslim population may have been raised by the Anglo-American presence, the country was left firmly in French hands. Faced with the repression by the French authorities of the rising at Setif on VE Day 1945, which drew an ineffectual protest from the United States, American anti-colonialism could only look to de Gaulle and the constitution-makers of the Fourth Republic to introduce a new regime in Algeria in accordance with the General's speech at Constantine in December 1943.[1]

For the next ten years, Algeria lay for the most part below the horizon of the English-language press. In the early 1950s it was contrasted with Tunisia and Morocco as a country in which, despite its problems, the French achievement was so great as to preclude the political troubles of the two Protectorates. That was the view from Paris, where the BBC correspondent Thomas Cadett was stationed, prompting his initial description of 1 November 1954 as an outbreak to be speedily brought under control by firm military action. Only as the revolt escalated did he concede that the social and economic problems of a rapidly growing Muslim population exceeded the French achievement and placed a solution almost beyond reach.[2] The attention of the British and American public, however, was caught by a more immediate issue with the publication in translation of Jean-Jacques Servan-Schreiber's *Lieutenant in Algeria*, and of Henri Alleg's *The Question*. *Lieutenant in Algeria*, published by Alfred A. Knopf in New York in 1957 and by Hutchinson in London in 1958, condemned the brutality of the repression. *The Question*, prefaced by Sartre and translated as well as published by John Calder in London early in 1958, exposed the use of torture by the police and army. Drawing the comparison with the Second World War, they cast the Fourth Republic in the image of Vichy and Nazi Germany, and the idealism of the officers represented by Servan-Schreiber in that of Free France. Thereby they struck a loud chord in British thinking about postwar France.

That chord was represented by Ronald Matthews, Paris correspondent of the *Daily Herald* and *The Birmingham Post*. In *The Death of the Fourth Republic*, published in London in 1954, he described 'the Liberation betrayed' by short-sighted politicians. The same conclusion was reached by the Swiss writer Herbert Luthy in *The State of France*, published in translation in London in 1955. To his general indictment of the state of the nation, Luthy added a denunciation of the way in which the liberal principles of the proposed new Statut de l'Algerie had been subverted by electoral dishonesty. In a postscript dated December 1954, he regarded the past year as a possible turning-point, but noted that the troubles in Morocco and Tunisia had now reached Algeria. Matthews' own postscript was none other than the translation of Servan-Schreiber for which he was responsible. There, the prophetic words put into the mouth of Colonel 'Galland', that France was at last about to rise to the challenge of de Gaulle in 1940,[3] were an affirmation of the national spirit whose demise Matthews had lamented in *The Death*. In this way the Algerian War came to be represented in the English-language literature as what indeed it was, a crux in the history of France. At stake were the principles for which de Gaulle and the Resistance had fought during the Second World War.

The sequel to *The Death of the Fourth Republic* was written not by Matthews, but by a second British journalist, Edward Behr, Paris and North African correspondent of Reuters and *Time* magazine. *The Algerian Problem* was published in London in 1961, after the assumption of power by de Gaulle through the action of those most criticized by Servan-Schreiber. It followed Matthews in ascribing the actual death of the Fourth Republic to the feebleness of its politicians, who in the face of *colon* intransigence had resigned the government of Algeria to the army. De Gaulle, by contrast, had restored the authority of the state in France itself; he had defied the military and civilian extremists in Algeria; he had opened the eyes of the nation to the Algerian problem; and he had won the country over to his side for a settlement on the basis of Algerian self-determination, in effect for Algerian independence.

With the prospect of peace, attention thus turned away from the predicament of France to that of Algeria. Behr, whose introduction traced the root of the Algerian problem to discrimination against the native Muslim population and the campaign for civil rights to which this gave rise in the early twentieth century, thereby subscribed to the conventional view that Algeria was, in effect, the creation of France. Nevill Barbour, on the other hand, an Arabist recently retired from the Eastern Services of the BBC, was close enough to the subject to express the contrary view of the Algerian nationalist historian Mostefa Lacheraf,[4] that an original Algerian nation was reviving after a long period of silence under French rule. In his authoritative *A Survey of North West Africa (the Maghrib)*, first published in 1959 by the Royal Institute of International Affairs,[5] Barbour nevertheless shared with Behr the opinion of the French historian Charles-André Julien, that the French had thrown away opportunity after opportunity to make concessions on civil rights, most recently in the declaration of a State of Emergency in 1955 instead of a serious commitment to reform. Such a programme had at long last been announced by de Gaulle at Constantine in October 1958, but Barbour remained sceptical of its effect, having drawn the melancholy conclusion that the famous 'moat of blood' dug between the two communities by the massacres at Philippeville in 1955 was too wide to bridge with such formulae. Algerian independence was the only solution.

Behind these conclusions lay the question of the relationship of the Muslim majority to the FLN on the one hand, the European community on the other. The short answer to the first was provided by Behr, who quoted Soustelle's warning of 1955 that the political discontent of a small Muslim elite was joining the social and economic discontent of the masses to create an explosive force. More specifically he relied upon the distinguished French anthropologist and member of the Resistance, Germaine Tillion, who argued in *France and Algeria: Complementary Enemies*, published in translation by Knopf in New York in 1961, that the nationalist organization had taken control of the Muslim population in 1956; the war itself had done the rest. Tillion's answer to the second question stemmed from the original hope of integration which she had expressed in *Algeria: The Realities*, a previous essay translated once again by Ronald Matthews and published by Knopf in 1959: the 'complementary enemies' who had rejected such integration would nevertheless have to reach a negotiated settlement, if only because they were economically inseparable. The official answer of the FLN was given by Barbour, to the effect that all inhabitants of the country would be entitled to become the citizens of an independent Algeria, forming a nation to which both communities would belong on equal terms. That was the basis on which the Evian negotiations were in fact conducted and the final agreement reached in 1962. The peaceful cooperation which it envisaged was anticipated by M'hammed Yazid, Minister of Information in the GPRA or Provisional Government of the Algerian Republic, in his preface to Tanya Matthews, *Algerian A.B.C.*, published in London at the end of 1961.

Published in America as *War in Algeria, Algerian A.B.C.* effectively concluded the series of British publications which treated the Algerian War as the final act of a French revolution beginning in 1940 and ending with Algerian independence. In the relative optimism engendered by the prospect of a settlement, the question of atrocities on both sides, and the use of torture by the French, were treated by Behr with regret rather than indignation in conclusion to *The Algerian Problem*, while Tanya Matthews, wife of Ronald and correspondent of *The Birmingham Post* at Tunis, did not sustain her comparison of French Algeria to Stalin's Russia.[6] She did indeed contemplate the likelihood that independent Algeria would itself become a one-party state on socialist principles, but whether it would thus fall into the clutches of the Communist bloc was treated by Behr as a problem for the future. Both agreed that de Gaulle had successfully overcome the challenge of the European diehards. It was left to C. L. Sulzberger, correspondent of *The New York Times* in Paris, to predict in the final article of *The Test: De Gaulle and Algeria*, a collection of his pieces published in London in mid-1962, that the counter-terrorism of those diehards in the OAS might nevertheless lead to the expulsion of the European community by the Muslim majority.

The Test belongs more to the literature of French redemption than Algerian independence; but its pessimism was shared from the opposite point of view by *Algeria in Turmoil*, the first American publication on the war, in New York in 1959. For Michael Clark, a former correspondent of the *New York Times* who had lived in Algeria since the end of the Second World War, the villains were not the *colons* and the army, but the FLN. Americans should beware of dogmatic anti-colonialism. French repression in Algeria was justified by the character of the rebellion, the work of ruthless terrorists backed by the Egyptian dictator Nasser. These had always been a small minority; the situation had got out of hand because of the failure of successive governments to make it clear that the French were in Algeria to stay. That required the suppression of the rebellion followed by the complete integration of Algeria into France, which in Clark's opinion was the wish of the great majority of the Muslim population. It would be achieved not by immediate political emancipation, but by raising the Muslim standard of living to that of the French. That would naturally overcome the cultural barriers between the two communities by entailing the social and legal integration of the Muslim population into the European system.[7]

In its plea for economic development, *Algeria in Turmoil* thus echoed the argument of Tillion in *Algeria: the Realities*. In its plea for the prior suppression of the rebellion, it echoed the call of Albert Camus in his writings on the conflict in the first years of the war.[8] In 1959, the year of Clark's publication, with the army winning the guerrilla war and the implementation of the Constantine plan, it was still possible to believe in such a solution. But not only did such thinking run counter to the trend of liberal opinion; Clark's proposals for integration stood in contrast to his own diagnosis of a country racially and therefore radically divided between two communities, one of which was a backward Arab Muslim mass. The nationalists, including the small minority who had masterminded the rebellion, formed a westernized elite of malcontents belonging to neither. By their actions they had inflamed racial prejudice on both sides to the point at which the future might well lie with South African style apartheid, certainly not majority Muslim rule.

Such a thesis of civilization under attack failed to convince what Clark called 'the unbending liberal mind', when in the preface to the second edition of 1961 he replied to his reviewers on the subject of torture used by the French forces. To condemn such torture, said Clark, was to approve terrorism, which was far worse: terrorism attacked the innocent, whereas torture was almost always applied to the guilty. But the cause was virtually lost, and the epilogue to the edition, written for Clark by Samuel J. Blumenfeld, was almost an epitaph. De Gaulle, far from carrying out his mandate to win both the war and the peace by clear and decisive action, had played straight into the hands of the FLN by his pusillanimous elections and his referenda, which had opened the way to French withdrawal. Unlike Israel, which had stood up to Arab nationalism, Algeria now faced the prospect of a tyrannous dictatorship on a par with all those that had recently sprouted in the Third World.

The American critics of Clark's point of view, who went to print in 1960, certainly felt, in the words of Lorna Hahn, that 'along with the propaganda went perhaps more than a necessary amount of intimidation and terrorism' on the part of the FLN.[9] They were, on the other hand, all convinced that right was fundamentally on the nationalist side; independence was now the will of the people. In *Ordeal in Algeria*, published in New York in late 1960, therefore, Richard and Joan Brace were as sceptical about de Gaulle as Clark, for the very different reason that he had allowed the repression to continue. His was the final episode in a sorry story which would only end with Algerian self-determination. The longer the story lasted, the more difficult it would be to keep the new nation in the democratic western camp, under 'the benevolent influence of Morocco and Tunisia', and out of the totalitarian clutches of the East. That was the principal question addressed by Hahn in *North Africa: Nationalism to Nationhood*, a book published in 1960 in Washington DC with an endorsement by John F. Kennedy as a work of public importance for America. In the circumstances of the Cold War, it was in the interests of the United States to support the cause of Algerian independence from France, to prevent the country falling to the Soviet Union, and turn it instead into a bridgehead of American influence in Africa. Developing the line of thought represented by Barbour, Hahn maintained that Algerian nationalism itself was both natural and legitimate; the rebellion had been the work of a younger generation impatient for results. The leaders of the FLN had shown great skill in winning the support of a politically apathetic Muslim population, and converting it into a self-conscious nation. They were 'men with whom we can still work out a mutually profitable relationship'.[10]

Hahn's thesis was reiterated in the same year by Joan Gillespie, *Algeria: Rebellion and Revolution*, written in Washington on the basis of her doctoral research, but published in London, again in 1960. Like Clark, Gillespie saw the conflict in terms of two disparate ethnic groups; like Barbour, she saw the history of nationalism in terms of initial resistance, subsequent silence and eventual awakening; unlike Hahn, she emphasized the role of the people: 'The success of the Revolution seems due not primarily to its leaders, but to the vast reservoir of the Algerian people, to whom it has given a new sense of dignity and participation.'[11] But her enthusiasm for the revolution chimed with the same concern for American interests. American support for France and its silence on French atrocities was wrong in principle and foolish in practice: 'the Communists on the Atlantic would be serious indeed!'[12]

In this way, American anti-colonialism blended into the strategic considerations of the Cold War to present American observers with a dilemma. As an exercise in colonial repression that played straight into the hands of the Soviet Union, the war required the United States to distance itself from France. But as in the war against Germany in 1943, any American commitment to the cause of Algerian nationalism was calculated to alienate a vital partner in the Atlantic alliance against the Eastern bloc. 'How absurd it would be', said David Schoenbrun, writing the introduction to the translation of Jules Roy, *The War in Algeria*, published at Westport, Connecticut in 1961, 'to save North Africa and lose the North Atlantic!' America, however, could only act in partnership with its European ally. It followed that 'the success or failure of France in bringing an honourable peace to Algeria will be the success or failure of the United States'.[13] The hope that de Gaulle would get Washington off this particular hook was expressed more explicitly by H. C. Allen, Commonwealth Fund Professor of American History in the University of London. Writing *The Anglo-American Predicament* in Princeton in 1959 for publication by Macmillan in London and New York in 1960, he looked to the policies of de Gaulle, for whose success 'almost all observers abroad most ardently pray', to solve the Algerian problem for the benefit of France and the free world.[14]

The stage was thus set for the postwar reckoning – the verdict on the war in the light of its aftermath, from the flight of the European population predicted by Sulzberger to the deposition of Ben Bella by Boumédienne. Pierre Bourdieu's *Sociologie de l'Algerie* was published in translation at Boston in 1962 under the title *The Algerians*, with a new last chapter on 'The revolution within the revolution'. Three years before the works of Fanon and Memmi began to appear in English, this expounded the now familiar theme of the colonial situation as an objective evil, locking the colonizer and the colonized into an antithetical relationship which could only be resolved by revolution. The revolution in Algeria had completed the destruction of the original society of the colonized; on the other hand it had freed them from their cultural inhibitions to make the future of their choice. But since so much had been destroyed, a revolutionary solution was required to build a harmonious social order and develop a modern economy. The choice was likely to be between chaos and 'an original form of socialism that will have been carefully designed to meet the needs of the actual situation'.[15]

The American academic David C. Gordon meanwhile brought out his *North Africa's French Legacy 1954–1962* under the auspices of the Center for Middle Eastern Studies at Harvard, taking as his starting point the second of Fanon's contentions in *Les damnés de la terre*, published in French in 1961, that the westernized elites who had come to power in the Third World had betrayed the cause of the people in the anti-colonial revolution. Dealing with Morocco and Tunisia as well as Algeria, he therefore reviewed the literature on the westernized *evolués* of North Africa to see how they compared with Fanon's unflattering portrait. As far as Algeria was concerned, he tended to Tillion's opinion that the war had raised a nation in support of the largely westernized leaders of the FLN. As for their political philosophy, he quoted with approval a wartime statement in the FLN newspaper *El-Moudjahid* to the effect that Algerians were the most Muslim of peoples and at the same time the most imbued with the spirit of the modern West; the challenge they now faced was to turn this revolutionary rhetoric into reality.[16] But writing a few months after independence, he was aware not only of the 'staggering economic problems' of the country, but also of the political 'maneuvering for purely personal popularity and power'. The choice seemed to be between civilian democracy and military dictatorship at home, cooperation with France and alignment with Cairo or the Eastern bloc abroad. In this way he gave a very guarded reply to Fanon, which revived the whole question of what the war had been about.

For Dorothy Pickles in *Algeria and France: from Colonialism to Cooperation*, London, 1963, it had been about the birth of the Fifth Republic, and an end to the crisis that had begun in 1940. As far as Algeria was concerned, it had been about the birth of a nation, and the establishment of a new relationship with the new France. Picking up the argument that the French connection was economically indispensable, she set out to evaluate the prospects for collaboration now that the worst had happened and the European population had fled. I. William Zartmann, in his *Government and Politics in Northern Africa*, published in New York in 1963, was pessimistic. The war had indeed 'forged a spirit of national consciousness in the heat of combat', but its destruction of society had been capped by the mass emigration of Europeans over the previous year, leaving the Evian Accords a dead letter and Algeria a 'headless social body' without upper and middle classes. Thoroughly unsettled by the war, the masses had become a revolutionary force that pressed for revolutionary change. But the collective leadership during the war had bred as much competition as cooperation between its members. To avoid an irresponsible struggle for power, these needed a doctrine, which they did not have, and a party organization for government, not war. Socialism, and the single-party political system proposed by Ben Bella, might be the only way to control factionalism on the one hand, revolutionary aspirations on the other; but it was likely to be authoritarian, with few liberties.

Anxiety at the turn of events since independence clouded the last entries in Richard and Joan Brace's second book, *Algerian Voices*, published in New York in 1965. Intended to celebrate the emancipation of the Muslim population from all the constraints of the past, its preface compared the leaders of the revolution to those of the United States: Washington, Jefferson, Franklin and Adams, but ended with 'the hope, now a little tarnished, that [these] leaders will not forget to let all voices speak'. Positive disillusion dominated Arslan Humbaraci's *Algeria: a Revolution that Failed. A Political History since 1954*, published in London in 1966. A journalist who had followed the rebellion sympathetically, he traced the degeneration of its cause to the adherence of the 'old guard' of nationalist politicians, which had converted the FLN from a body of closely knit conspirators into a rambling political movement of activists, opportunists and ideologues. By 1962 its fragmentation was only disguised by the common desire for independence; but independence had released the fissiparous forces which prevented the conversion of the FLN into an effective party of government. The struggle for political survival had ensured that power came to rest with the strongest. The brothers whom Humbaraci had seen during the war as 'a race apart', heroes dedicated to the cause, had begun in 1962 murderously to pursue the feuds which had long divided them. Idealism vanished, lip-service alone was paid to socialism, and by 1966 Boumédienne's Algeria was a police state as before.

It was for Gordon in his second book, *The Passing of French Algeria*, published by Oxford University Press again in 1966, to offer a more sympathetic evaluation of the outcome. Discussing the conflict of Marxist and Muslim ideals in the struggle for power, he repeated his conclusion that the revolution to come would be 'a struggle both for entry into the modern world and for a revitalization of Islamic values',[17] in which the question of

Arabization would play a central role. Whatever the war might have been for at the time, these were the issues which it had thrown up, and those which would provide the politics of the new nation with a lively agenda.

In retrospect, Gordon seems remarkably prescient.[18] By comparison, Leon Carl Brown's opinion that Islam in North Africa had powerfully reinforced movements for national liberation, but that independence had paradoxically led to a decline in interest in religion and its relevance to society and state, seems dated.[19] At the time, however, it was the strong impression of many observers. Mary Motley (Margaret Sheridan), who had lived on and off at Biskra most of her life in great intimacy with her Muslim neighbours, concluded her *Home to Numidia*, London, 1964, by noting the hopes of her own generation for a modest new prosperity, and the expectancy of a modern, Western lifestyle by the young. Old-fashioned as she may have been on the subject of Arabs and Berbers, convinced as she was that in 1961 the majority of the Muslim population was still on the side of the French against 'the extremists of the FLN', she saw, in effect, a people for whom seven years was indeed enough, who wanted a return to law and order, who distrusted 'the extremist Ben Bella party', but who looked for a measure of personal freedom hitherto denied by custom. From such a society, it was the turn of a nostalgic fifty-year-old to feel alienated.

Notes

1. J. J. Dougherty, *The Politics of Wartime Aid* (Westport, CT and London, 1978); M. Khenouf and M. Brett, 'Algerian nationalism and the Allied military strategy and propaganda during the Second World War', in D. Killingray and R. Rathbone (eds), *Africa and the Second World War* (Houndmills and London, 1986), pp. 258–74.
2. *The Listener*, LII (July–December 1954), 837–8; LIII (January–June 1955), 1059; LIX (January–June 1958), 387ff.
3. *Lieutenant in Algeria*, p. 162.
4. Collected essays: *L'Algérie: nation et société* (Paris, 1965).
5. Oxford, 1959; 2nd edn, 1961.
6. *Algerian A.B.C.*, p. xiii.
7. *Algeria in Turmoil*, pp. 438–40.
8. Albert Camus, *Actuelles III Chroniques algériennes 1939–1958*, in Camus, *Essais* (Paris, 1965), pp. 887–1018; see my article, M. Brett, 'Dad's Algeria. Jacques Berque and Albert Camus on the land of their fathers', *J. Algerian Studies*, I (1996), pp. 84–102.
9. Lorna Hahn, *North Africa. Nationalism to Nationhood* (Washington, DC, 1960), p. 158.
10. Ibid., p. 252.
11. *Algeria: Rebellion and Revolution*, p. 174.
12. Ibid., p. 176.
13. *The War in Algeria*, pp. 7–10.
14. *The Anglo-American Predicament*, p. 72.
15. *The Algerians*, p. 192.

16. *North Africa's French Legacy*, p. 84.
17. *The Passing of French Algeria*, p. 50.
18. For the subsequent English-language literature, see M. Brett, 'Anglo-Saxon attitudes: the Algerian war of independence in retrospect', *J. African History*, XXXV (1994), pp. 217–35.
19. L.C. Brown, 'The role of Islam in modern North Africa', in L. C. Brown (ed.), *State and Society in Independent North Africa* (Washington, DC, 1966), pp. 97–122.

11

Le Monde's Coverage of the Army and Civil Liberties during the Algerian War, 1954–58

Mohammed Khane

Introduction

From time to time in French colonial history, traditional republican values of democracy and the rule of law have given way, under particular circumstances, to military rule and exceptional powers. In Algeria, however, military rule was the norm throughout the history of the colony. Despite the administrative inclusion of the territory into France after the Second World War and the introduction of the 1947 Statutes when it passed to civilian rule, large areas were made up of *communes mixtes* (districts with a majority of indigenous inhabitants) and were under the control of the military administration.[1]

Following the start of the uprising in 1954, successive governments claimed that their police powers were insufficient and that, under the pressure of events, they increasingly needed to adopt emergency powers. The job of policing Algeria (including areas under civilian control) was handed over to the military under the control of area commanders.[2] This change was facilitated by the adoption of legislation permitting the use of these exceptional powers. The governments of the Fourth Republic, and even those of the Fifth (after 1958), always claimed that they were trying to steer a middle course between two priorities: protecting life and property on the one hand and maintaining civil liberties on the other. What in fact happened was very different. They progressively implemented a repressive regime whose victims included a large number of innocent people and which resulted in a loss of civil liberties for all Algerians (referred to by their religious denomination as 'Muslims') and for most of the Europeans (non-Muslims) who espoused their cause.[3]

The coverage of the Algerian War, a very important historical period in French history, by *Le Monde*, one of the most prestigious papers in France, is altogether revealing. It is particularly significant in that the paper claims to give space to all shades of opinion and is looked to as a source of authority in almost every field.[4] Although there is inevitably a degree of media bias, and 'objectivity' itself is a deeply problematic notion, indeed something of a myth, this is not admitted by many of the readers of *Le Monde*, nor by journalists and editors whose accounts are extremely partial.[5]

This chapter argues that *Le Monde*'s coverage of the Algerian War was in many respects shaped by information from the army and official sources. These set the parameters of the newspaper's discourse on the Algerian War. Any alternative discourse was seen as a minority voice or as 'illegitimate'. *Le Monde*'s discourse and construction of events described the French army in a more positive way than one would expect from this paper. It even justified what frequently amounted to the abolition of civil liberties through the use of special powers and the recourse to the army to put down the 'terrorists' and the FLN 'criminals'.[6]

This argument will be illustrated by considering the newspaper's discourse on the army itself, and on civil liberties, under two headings. First, we will assess the army's role in the Algerian context and its activities, which can be seen within a legal/legalistic context and outside it (as some of the army's actions had no legal/legalistic justification). Second, we will examine the description of the army itself throughout the pages of the paper.

The French army's role and activities

Inside the legal framework

The introduction of the State of Emergency (31 March 1955) was seen by *Le Monde* as a moderate and, indeed, necessary measure. The newspaper was generally supportive of this 'better legal arrangement', which was seen as an intermediate measure.[7] One of *Le Monde*'s leading journalists, André Chenebenoit, seemed unsure whether the means were disproportionate.[8] However, a thorough reading of his text indicates, nevertheless, that his concerns about the excessive nature of the measures were only expressed in respect to unforeseen circumstances that had not then materialized. Chenebenoit seemed reassured by the fact that the French National Assembly would retain its sovereignty and, indeed, even appeared pleased that democracies were prepared to take this type of measure:

> One should be thankful that democracies can rely on legal texts as a framework for this kind of measure, all the more so because citizens may be assured that guarantees offered by the Republican system can be maintained.[9]

The measures enabled the army to do away with any right of appeal by resorting to the use of military tribunals, and to issue residence orders restricting the movements of any persons under suspicion. It was hardly surprising to find out, through reports of a leaflet being distributed a couple of months later by an Algerian students' union, that there had been atrocities as this leaflet contained revelations about the real nature of the measures adopted.[10] It indicated that there had been forced transfers of population, the setting up of 'resettlement centres' or camps, euphemistically termed 'shelters' (*centres d'hébergement*), and an extension of the legislation's implementation to include Algerians found in mainland France. The last was a striking departure: metropolitan France normally provided sanctuary from the special legislation applied to Algeria, and this step consequently facilitated the transfer to Algeria of suspects arrested in metropolitan France who would normally have enjoyed far better protection in terms of civil rights.

In any case, it became evident that the extraordinary measures introduced had failed to quell the rebellion. Within a year of the introduction of the emergency powers, the Fourth Republic resorted to a new set of repressive measures under the Special Powers specifically designed to deal with the Algerian uprising. These were adopted on 12 March 1956. This time, also, the same reaction of *Le Monde* could be seen through the presentation of the new measures which were seen, as before, as both necessary and justified.

Even though the repressive nature of the measures dominate, with the recall of the reservists, new army deployments and increased military activities, a great stress was put on the economic and social measures to be implemented (but which in the end failed to materialize), and on official statements alleging the success of the methods adopted.

The Emergency Law and the Special Powers provided a legal framework for many of the repressive measures adopted in Algeria.[11] These measures were not clearly spelled out in the newspaper's coverage of the legal texts being tabled, which then became an everyday modus operandi in dealing with local inhabitants, who themselves became, rightly or wrongly, increasingly suspect in the eyes of the security forces, and who became the victims of the now generalized implementation of measures that were supposed to be selective. These exceptional powers were, nevertheless, justified by *Le Monde*. So, too, were the collective sanctions that ensued. These included the establishment of 'interdiction zones' or *zones interdites* ('free-fire areas' where French troops' rules of engagement permitted them to shoot at will, much like the zones similarly designated by US forces operating in South Vietnam in the late 1960s), and the subsequent enforced population movements from these areas.

Arrests were routinely made on the slightest suspicion and picked up Algerians right across the social spectrum. Other publications were at times able to discuss these questions and comment on them. It is scarcely conceivable in light of the sheer number and nature of arrests – which included doctors, intellectuals, professors, lawyers, communists and even former army officers – that *Le Monde*, through its journalists, did not seek to question what was really happening in Algeria and to raise serious problems about the situation there.[12] But this did not happen. Furthermore, from the newspaper's position, there seemed to be no need for alarm, notwithstanding the serious erosion of civil liberties in Algeria.

The coverage of trials was often very biased, whether these were of Algerian 'terrorists' or European sympathizers (at times labelled 'communists' and at others 'progressive Christians', according to their politico-religious leanings). Reports and views expressed did not criticize trial irregularities or the executions that ensued.[13] As 'national security' was said to be involved, activists convicted of minor actions and even innocent people convicted of crimes they never committed were inevitably sent down in these trials.[14] One such example was the case of Badèche, the alleged assassin of Amédée Froger – whose conviction was secured on very shaky grounds and despite the protests of eminent lawyers such as the Batonnier Thorp.[15] In other instances, lawyers for the defence had been prevented from ensuring their case was adequately presented before the courts.

There seemed to be an acceptance of the dubious new rules and of the various consequences that followed their adoption. But a measure of double standards was clearly indicated when extending the same set of rules to mainland France came under consideration. At this juncture there was very strong opposition, and this extended to detention camps and to the death penalty, expressed by the paper's journalists as well as outside contributors such as members of the *Académie française* including the eminent Maurice Garçon.[16]

What were the basic motivations behind this silence on the civil liberties of Algerians which, at crucial times, amounted to complicity in disregarding the most fundamental principles on which the French Republic was built? Perhaps a 'higher principle' engaging uncritical nationalist discourse, in the sense that the uncritical attitude of the newspaper could be justified out of a sense of patriotic duty to the country? Or a desire not to 'voice dissent' at the time when international opinion and decisions could be unfavourable, indeed detrimental to France and her policy of retaining Algeria?[17]

Outside the legal framework

The paper's broad approach to reporting, which consisted of playing down the repressive factors and placing a very positive gloss on the repressive action of the army, was even clearer when military actions fell outside the scope of the legal framework. This occurred during the massive repression that took place in 1955 (ten years after the massacre of Algerians in May 1945), which became known as the events of 20 August 1955 – the 'massacre at Philippeville' (present-day Skikda). In one instance, after accurately reporting the slaughter of the innocent population of a village in *Le Monde*, one of the paper's full-time journalists, Georges Penchenier, found himself fighting his own corner against the state without the support of the paper. The latter, far from backing its own journalist's report, allocated him a small column to reiterate the atrocities he had witnessed at Carrières Romaines, about 5 km outside Philippeville on the eastern coast between Algiers and Constantine. This stood in marked contrast to the masses of official reports flatly denying the incidents.[18]

There were also reports of many incidents of repression on a smaller scale throughout the country. However, these often came from official or military sources, where the security forces were always said to have been provoked, even when newsreel footage showed executions in cold blood. Any version given would invariably grant the army the benefit of the doubt, at the very least. Scenes of lynching where civilians were involved were framed in the same way. This lack of information or its deformed, distorted representation remains a mystery as far as *Le Monde* is concerned from 1955 onwards when, plainly, other contemporary media reports and sources other than *Le Monde* itself were more complete, more candid and more informative.

A worrying aspect of the newspaper's coverage was to be found in the absence of reports of torture, indeed their occultation, even at a time when the use of torture was not in doubt. It had, after all, been reported and, at times, publicly denounced, in *L'Express*, *Franc-Tireur* and *France-Observateur*.[19] There was, hence, a very limited coverage indeed of the well-known cases of Henri Alleg and Maurice Audin.[20] It is difficult to understand the moderation of the language used by *Le Monde*, its reserve and its reticence, at a time when it might have been difficult but, nevertheless, quite possible to take a stand against the use of 'uncivilized means' in the pursuit of what was considered a 'noble civilizing aim'. The more conventional ideals of journalism 'to inform the public' did not seem to outweigh the responsibility the paper felt in the need to observe silence, most of the time on a voluntary, self-censoring basis.

A very feeble interpretation of the duty to inform public opinion

An analysis of the paper's reports throughout the Fourth Republic shows that even when civil liberties had been suppressed, there was at best a very feeble attempt, if any, by the paper to inform public opinion. At the same time, there was a very lukewarm defence, if any, of those who tried at the time, despite all odds, to inform public opinion.[21]

When there was not outright opposition to them, there was no more than a very mild defence of the few most enlightened intellectuals, such as Jean Amrouche, Memmi, Jean-Paul Sartre, André Malraux, André

Mandouze, Henri Marrou and others, who saw it as incumbent upon them, alongside journalists of other publications, to inform public opinion and to express their disapproval of France's position and views as reflected in government policy.[22] Another dominant feature of *Le Monde*'s reports at the time was the non-existent defence against press seizure and the arrests of journalists, even when the newspaper itself was affected.[23]

The lack of desire to ascertain the situation quickly and make these findings public was also evident in the very tepid support for freedom of investigation and inquiry, following the repeated calls for public inquiries. This can be seen in a number of episodes surrounding the publication of various reports.

In its reportage on the Provo *Commission de sauvegarde des droits et libertés individuelles* (with its very meagre findings) and the *Commission internationale contre le régime concentrationnaire*, the Radicals' Commission and that of the Red Cross, *Le Monde* offered only feeble objections to the sanctions imposed on, and the persecution of, the intellectuals and the journalists who dared challenge the colonial world or the methods used to preserve it.[24] It expressed little sympathy towards their opponents. Although, ironically, it deplored the readers of *The Times*, the *New York Times* and the *Herald Tribune* being better informed than French readers, the paper seemed unwilling or unable to remedy this state of affairs.[25]

Coverage of the army and the predominance of the army's discourse

An in-depth study of the characteristics of the coverage of the French army in the pages of the newspaper suggests that it was dominant, influential and authoritative. Through the prominence and the frequency of the army's views publicized in *Le Monde*, framing any interpretation of measures and events and giving added credence to ideas developed in various other outlets, a reader could conclude that, far from being mute, *La Grande Muette* was extremely vocal.[26]

Additional space was also given to the coverage of books and memoirs published by high-ranking officers such as Marshal Alphonse Juin and General Paul Ely, advocating severe repression while simultaneously preaching a 'discourse of love and charity'. Quite in favour of election-rigging, since the 'other side would do it anyway', these generals also called for the introduction of conscription as it would 'keep people busy and would prevent the Muslim youngsters from being forcibly enrolled by the rebels'.[27]

Although their causes were always put forward as being multiple and varied, including internal and external dimensions, the 'troubles' were said to be predominantly due to 'poverty, high birth rate and lack of administration'. In *Le Monde*'s reports of army publications, it becomes fairly evident that the 'emancipating mission of France' is very easily forgotten when more immediate concerns come to the fore, such as the fear of seeing the French democratic process being 'swamped by numbers in a Single Electoral College'. Moreover, it was stated quite clearly, at times, that 'democracy was not for export' but for internal French consumption only, and that tough measures should be adopted against those who thought otherwise among this 'strange mixture of people of good faith, conscientious objectors, defeatists and professional traitors'.

The neighbouring countries, Tunisia and Morocco, were advised to keep out, as the minimum request expected from the 'presumptuous neighbours, prematurely promoted to independence' was to stop 'believing in extravagant dreams' and to suspend their help to the 'terrorists' and 'rebels'.[28]

Though it was clear that the concept of revolutionary warfare seemed inappropriate to describe the activities of a peasant-based, illiterate and profoundly Islamic movement, there was no hesitation in the use of the concept, and in recommending 'methods' to deal with it. The paper echoed reports published by the official army sources such as the *Revue militaire d'Information* and the advice of army leaders, such as Ely, given to high-ranking officers and military leaders, to assume their historical role, to resolve any problems of conscience for their subordinates by taking responsibility for their actions, and asking them to carry out orders without allowing any discussions that would weaken the resolve of the army in this task, as history would be unforgiving.

> The implacable judgment of History may forgive the army for having some scruples, for wavering and experiencing some sort of malaise before adjusting to the situation. It would not absolve it of its guilt if it tried to run away from its mission when the fate of civilisation was at stake.[29]

Although the army was not entirely as one in its thinking, voices and actions of a different kind had difficulty in finding favourable coverage in the paper. 'Spectacular' moves were to be avoided, according to these reports.[30] When these 'spectacular moves' took place, one found that there was some delay in the time taken by *Le Monde* in providing the real explanations for these actions. Such was the case, for instance, when providing the real reasons behind General Paris de Bollardière's resignation in 1957.[31]

When, occasionally, views were expressed and attitudes adopted by army leaders unwilling to 'toe the line' in implementing severe repression, these got short shrift. Colonel Roger Barberot, one of those officers voicing their opposition to mainstream attitudes, was presented as a loner, the sole dissenting voice, when *Ceux d'Algérie* was published. This gave the impression that the French army was 'doing a good job' (in a census of over 3,000 respondents on Algerian war experiences commented upon by *Le Monde*),[32] and that the positive description of the state of affairs in Algeria by French officials was more accurate and credible.[33]

The paper possessed in-house expertise in the military field. One of its staff reporters, Jean Planchais, who later became an important army observer and historian, was able to report on the needs of the corps and its dissatisfaction with its lack of adaptation to the conflict,[34] and its view that this could be remedied by an urgent technological and psychological revolution and the provision of American aid. The reluctance of the army to take over the destiny of the country from civilian authority is clearly highlighted by another of *Le Monde*'s journalists who was also able to give the clearest sign of the army's manifest intention not to let the French government follow a path that did not meet with its approval.[35]

News of the army and the ambivalence of *Le Monde*'s discourse

Le Monde presented a glut of information concerning the army, official communiqués, troop movements,[36] funds available to the military and decisions affecting it. These news items found in the paper often came directly from the chief of staff of General Headquarters. They restated the legitimacy of the fight and the peaceful nature of its purpose ('pacification'). The guarantee of victory was never placed in doubt.[37] An examination of the coverage by the paper also reveals a discursive overlap between the views of journalists and those of the military strategists. Both argued, for instance, that a larger deployment of the troops would be very useful in terms of acquiring intelligence and information-gathering.[38]

There was also a significant degree of care taken in avoiding any use of the language of 'war' in the terminology employed – even when authentic instances of combat were being described. As epitomized in a number of titles published,[39] one can only find reference to 'the troubles' (*les événements*), even when the description of the fighting left the impression that real battles were taking place. Readers cannot have found it easy to understand why all this was being done if the aim, as was often claimed, was merely to rid the country of 250 'pieces of dirt'.[40] The nature of the operations were in fact much more ferocious and ruthless – villages at times being bombed and napalm used against a population that, as even army reports at times acknowledged, was not involved in the fighting.

Some questions still elude a definitive answer: did *Le Monde* fall victim to the shrewd propaganda tactics of the government machine? Did it not see fit to oppose the official view?

It would have been difficult for the paper to form an independent view if its perception of the 'troubles' was conditioned by the official authorities or unless its perspectives were distant from the official views. Among the latter, the dominant opinion was more in tune with Jacques Soustelle's view of his 'beloved, suffering Algeria'[41] (although this, ironically, perceived the assimilation policy, understood as giving similar rights and duties to Muslims, as a part-cause of the problems encountered). The travels with the army by *Le Monde*'s Eugène Mannoni could not but influence his understanding of the causes when he reported on the role of the so-called 'pieces of dirt', the indifference of the settlers and the abuse of their positions by members of the Muslim community who had assumed positions of power and responsibility.[42]

The sources of information used by the paper were not varied, but were very often one-sided and conformed to the official line. This meant that the comments made and news provided were shaped by the army as one of the main sources, if not the exclusive source, of information. Hence the way particular issues were framed, and the agenda set, ensured that the paper could only perceive the causes of the conflict as being: '*crime* rather than *nationalism*'.[43]

The positive image given of the army, which had 210,000 men in Algeria in February 1956, increasing to 250,000 by 1 May 1956, outlining its fears and praising its discipline and organization – yet which could not get rid of 15,000 or 20,000 rebels – posed no difficulty for a sympathetic André Blanchet, a journalist and professor at the Institut d'Etudes Politiques. He explained that the army job was not an easy one.[44] One of the more complex issues that arose was the fact that revolutionary warfare was stated to have been used by the rebels. As a result, it was argued, counter-revolutionary methods needed to be adopted to deal with them. Nevertheless, there was an outright rejection of the fact that there was any impending major colonial disaster, or that there was any likeness with the actions undertaken by the French army in the Indochina conflict a few years earlier, in terms of considering that the army had carried out an intensive psychological warfare there, or in terms of perceiving the likely outcome of the conflict as being similar to the earlier one in Asia. Despite the many similarities,[45] there was a clumsy denial of any analogy with the Indochinese situation and an utter dismissal that there might be any meaningful parallel between the war in Indochina and the pacification undertaken in Algeria.[46]

Because of their uncritical reporting,[47] the journalists of *Le Monde* did not cover the operations from various angles, as was achieved by other journalists such as Serge Bromberger, Jean-Jacques Servan-Schreiber and Robert Barrat, who ensured a far more critical coverage for other publications: *France-Observateur*, *L'Express*, *Témoignage Chrétien* and others.

The blind acceptance of the official line meant that there was a lack of use of inverted commas and quotation marks when (Muslim) suspects were literally described as being bombers as soon as they were arrested (for example, Taleb Abderahmane), and before any evidence had been laid before their tribunals.[48]

It would be very difficult to argue that *Le Monde* fell victim to the official propaganda, as it is plain that the paper intended to give a very 'soft image' of the army at the time when other media were reporting excesses and brutalities.[49] *Le Monde* described the military as discerning and restrained in its use of force and very protective of the population. The paper reported that French soldiers did not really want to harm 'these people' whom they considered as friends. In his stories, Mannoni tried to emphasize that there were many affinities between the Muslims and the army.[50] When brutalities were eventually conceded by the paper they were described as having occurred 'elsewhere', or the reader would learn that they had been perpetrated by army personnel other than those interviewed by the journalist for the paper.[51]

This style and manner of reporting gave a very simplified and sanitized view of the work of the army in Algeria during the 'pacification phase'. Apart from the 'peaceful' connotation of the word, many aspects of the work of the army were played down in the newspaper's reports. They included the use of force, torture and summary executions,[52] the progressive establishment of forced resettlement camps, euphemistically called 'shelter camps' (*camps d'hébergement*) – plainly a 'soft' yet disingenuous term, like the removals under Apartheid in South Africa which were also a form of human rights abuse. Only the flimsiest explanations – if any – were provided by *Le Monde* as to why these people had been moved or resettled, such as that 'they had been deceived by their brothers in faith' who had taken advantage of them. It could be easily observed that these deeds and actions were not shown in their true light to the paper's readers, even when journalists were sent to Algeria to report on the activities of the army. At the very least, it is extremely surprising that a paper which claimed to be well-informed and knowledgeable about revolutionary warfare was unable to draw any parallel between the psychological warfare explanation of the theory of 'fish in water' and the removal of the population from particular areas.[53]

The paper went on, superficially reporting the 'desolate aspect' of the fields left empty behind the relocated populations – which in reality meant everything for these peasants and to which they could not return for fear of their lives (as orders had been issued to shoot on sight anyone found in areas evacuated which had become 'prohibited zones' (*zones interdites*) – and which had been replaced by the enjoyment of the relative security of a village 'that will become prosperous'.[54] This was, in a sense, the sanitized image of pacification with its dual aspect of destroying only the 'bad' and building only what is 'good'.

> Other soldiers who have destroyed bad hamlets (rotten because they had been used as stopovers by the rebels) elsewhere are building clean, attractive houses for the Muslims, and a school of which only the foundations are visible.

As if this were not enough, there were 'added benefits' to this 'pacification process' which was followed by the gift of water brought to these old Muslims ('incredulous Muslims who had never even seen the principle of communicating water vessels at work'), to whom small enclaves of land 'will be given' after they had been prepared by the army.[55] The reader cannot but be drawn up short, to wonder about the multi-talented skills of these soldiers who had plainly swapped their swords for ploughs so soon after downing their trowels and plumbing tools.

It might still be argued that the paper had simply fallen into the propaganda trap, and was confused about the true meaning and consequences of 'pacification'. But this interpretation becomes unsustainable after reading in the paper about the advocacy of the same 'pacification' by one of the better-known columnists of *Le Monde*, Robert Escarpit. This was a writer who had, in all probability, not even set foot on Algerian soil but was able to reveal his awareness of the true meaning of the concept when he recommended its methods:

> methods which had been successfully tested in the pacification of France and in ridding her of a few rowdy characters who were poisoning its political atmosphere.[56]

The evidence available suggests that, throughout the pages of the paper, no comprehension of the army's role from the perspective of the local population filtered through. Instead there were images of the 'Boy Scout' and the 'Good Samaritan' roles played by a very small group of officers of the Special Administrative Sections (SAS or Sections Administratives Spécialisées), whose numbers were often exaggerated in reports:

> There are many former officers; those who were in charge of indigenous affairs, young SAS officers who discharged their mission with enthusiasm and a selflessness which leaves us in awe.

The series of articles published in the summer of 1957 reflected these very ideas and gave the same general picture of the troops involved in Algeria, whose main objectives were said to be the 'winning of hearts and minds' (*le ralliement des coeurs*).[57]

The officer as tutor, doctor, administrator...

Far from being mainly the military hardware, the army's three principal instruments of pacification were described as the 'town hall, the health dispensary and the school (three major tools of pacification)', as well as the construction of roads and the building of houses and villages. The propaganda campaign was rife and optimism radiated from these articles outlining the role of the SAS officer as the tutor, the teacher, the doctor, the superhero who took charge of the village unit. No doubt there were about 200 SAS stations, but very often the whole outfit was a one-man band.[58] Yet even *Le Monde* stated that the ministry of defence was so impressed with their work that it intended increasing the size of the corps to a battalion.[59]

Although there is no doubting that some of these SAS officers went to the far-flung corners of Algeria, what they were doing was not primarily aimed at fulfilling the basic needs of the local inhabitants. Usually the indigenous population had been removed from their dwellings which, however, modest, were functional and appropriate for their needs. They now needed housing, food and general care as they could no longer fend for themselves once they had been uprooted from their way of life and removed from their natural environment.

Nor must one overlook that the building of schools, though beneficial to the children, was designed to facilitate their assimilation of French colonial values and their acceptance of the established order. The building of roads, as elsewhere in Africa, though useful for the population, was more instrumental in providing access for the foreign invader and had a key part in making remote parts accessible and controllable by the authorities. Even the continued presence of the officers in the midst of the population was intended to ensure constant contact with the locals and to prevent their socialization into the values of the rebels. In any case, given the limited number of those involved and the finite means at their disposal, the health care and the social welfare provided, despite being heralded as being important in *Le Monde*, would have been comparatively modest overall.[60]

The positive description of the troops and their role still prevailed. This was so even when there was clearly more than a malaise in the army, with high-ranking officers becoming restless from all quarters as *La Grande Muette* headed for a takeover in 1958 and a fully fledged *coup d'état* in 1961.[61] Opposing and critical voices were bound to come from the Right. They received an impetus from Faure who was arrested for his links with a plot being organized to overthrow the authority of the French state in Algeria.[62] Despite all that, *Le Monde* did not see fit to consider writing of the existence of a serious plot of any kind.

In his articles, Jean Planchais had gauged the right measure of the army's discontent and its potential for rebellion and revolt when he wrote just over a year before the 13 May 1958 crisis that:

> soldiers are not there to break strikes or to empty dustbins, the Army is not a 'jack of all trades' and one has only to recall the old adage, 'jack of all trades, master of none'. Without doubt it is to be feared that although our army in its lassitude has no desire to overthrow the regime

> itself, it might do nothing to prevent the latter's brutal demise should it be attacked.[63]

Given the means employed, problems of conscience appeared and opposing and critical voices were also bound to emerge from the Left as well as from indigenous members of the army officer corps.

On the Left the most serious form of protest was by a senior officer, General Paris de Bollardière.[64] Deeply troubled by a request from his superiors 'to intensify the struggle against the terrorists' – whose meaning has to be understood in the repressive context of the time and which obviously had nothing to do with applying due judicial process to punish these 'terrorists' – Bollardière resigned and returned to France. This was a dramatic gesture by a man holding the Legion of Honour medal, a Companion of the Liberation, one of the most decorated serving officers at that time.[65]

The problems which shook the French army at this time also hit one of its component fractions very hard indeed. This was the small community of officers of Algerian extraction, who numbered between 250 and 300 out of a total of 3,500 present in the theatre of operations. The protests of these officers were against the methods used in the conduct of the war for the two previous years, but also against having to fight their own kin when, for instance, even in the Foreign Legion, Vietnamese soldiers had been freed of the obligation to fight their own kind. A letter written by some of them to René Coty, the President of the French Fourth Republic (1954–8), expressing their grievances at the highest level, led to the arrest of 52 officers for 'demoralization of the army'.[66] *Le Monde*'s treatment of this sorry episode in the war was as partial as other aspects of its reportage on the conflict. On 18 May 1957 the paper even published an article stating that the leader of these indigenous Algerian officers, Lieutenant Rahmani, had been bailed, a report which Rahmani read while still in fact in prison. More importantly, even when the newspaper started to express some concern, its criticism of the state seemed to be limited to the psychological mistake being committed in tempting the Algerian soldiers to take leave while in possession of their arms and ammunition.[67]

It could also be argued that there was further opposition to the war effort and to the conflict in general by conscientious objectors, communists, pacifists, students in general, and even real cases of mutiny from within the troops and draftees, followed by subsequent trial and condemnations. However, a more complete picture could not be provided if *Le Monde*'s pages were trusted as the main source.[68] There was a continued refusal by *Le Monde*, following the official line, to recognize explicitly or implicitly the fact that a war was indeed going on in Algeria, despite the despatch of an entire army to the other side of the Mediterranean.

Conclusions

The image of the conflict that readers of *Le Monde* were invited to construct deviated very little from the official line. The constructive activities of the army were highlighted at the expense of the army's most immediate and most manifest role which entailed crushing a popular uprising. Hence the army appeared under a very pacific light, offering the readers of the paper an extremely simplified, sanitized view of a pitiless effort to crush the Algerian uprising.

What predominated in the paper's reportage was a representation of the army as a very discerning body, active only against criminals and terrorists, playing down or occulting all reports of the unacceptable behaviour used in 'pacification' (which did not have any peaceful connotation and was a euphemism employed to cloak the most severe forms of repression of nationalist dissent). Perhaps this style of depiction and discourse was, however, to be expected at a time of nationalist pride in the army in France. After all, the conflict in Algeria followed on not long after the debacle of the Second World War for France and the failure to hold onto Indochina. The construction placed on the military's conduct by *Le Monde* might have been a subconscious attempt to foster an image that would rehabilitate the army and increase French pride in it, in the aftermath of the previous humiliating conflicts (including the Suez debacle of November 1956, even more fresh in the minds of readers of the paper).[69]

As far as the Algerian War in the period of the Fourth Republic is concerned, analysis of the pages of the paper reveals a definite lack of support, if not a blatant opposition, to the pro-independence stance in Algeria. There was not even an attempt to provide a balanced representation of the opinions expressed and attitudes taken with regard to this conflict. Though *Le Monde* was often accused of being one of the four major proponents of the 'anti-French propaganda', and was reportedly often read voraciously by the FLN fighters themselves – who were most probably not surprised to find the paper's antipathy to their cause – the evidence uncovered does not support the progressive outlook which is assigned to the paper by historians and journalists alike,[70] and least of all any endorsement of the independentist cause. Quite the contrary: in its reports, comments and editorials, *Le Monde* behaved in the same way as any other establishment paper, providing support to the army in the context of decolonization, by adopting a very soft stand on abuses of civil liberties, and by failing to embrace probing standards of investigative journalism when covering 'incidents'.

Given the surfeit of information in some cases and the paucity of details and comments in others, *Le Monde*'s coverage could be perceived as confusing. Since information not found in the paper could be read in other contemporaneous publications, *Le Monde* at the time must be judged both misinformed and disinforming. One might ask whether the shifting of responsibility as far as the various developments were concerned, and the tendency to publish 'sanitized' information, demonstrates that in much of its reports the paper was being deceived by events and itself became an involuntary dupe of psychological warfare. It appears more likely, however, that the paper was a willing and witting victim. For it chose to impose on itself a one-eyed policy, engaging in self-censorship either out of fear of authority, or fearing loss of income if it were abandoned by pro-army and pro-*Algérie française* readers. Perhaps it was influenced, too, by a conscious desire not to 'rock the boat' and harm the interest of France. At any rate it pursued a deliberate policy which consisted of not publishing, even of opposing the publication by others, of reports and commentaries perceived to be detrimental to what was regarded as French 'national interest'. In doing so, *Le Monde* did itself major damage by massively compromising its adherence to the values of critical journalistic integrity.

Finally, this examination of *Le Monde*'s reportage of the Algerian War's most contentious aspects reveals the problematic use of the paper as a source of historical reference. One may conclude that, by contrast with an earlier period of French history, the Algerian episode failed to become a mid-1950s Dreyfus Affair for the paper, as was the case with Emile Zola's article in *L'Aurore* at the beginning of the twentieth century. Because of its obfuscation, sophistry and want of political/journalistic courage, *Le Monde* made no contribution to highlighting the real causes and parameters of the conflict. As far as being a true reflection of the problems of society, or helping make known the truth about the decolonization of Algeria, the role of the *Le Monde* was quite modest, if not indeed decidedly controversial.

Acknowledgement

The writing and publication of this chapter would not have been possible without the support of the Hong Kong University Grants Committee, for which the author is greatly indebted. Warmest thanks are also due to both the Baptist and the Chinese universities of Hong Kong.

Notes

1. See Pierre Montagnon, *La Guerre d'Algérie. Genèse d'un engrenage* (Paris: Pygmalion, 1984), esp. chs VI and VII.
2. See Pierre Miquel, *La Guerre d'Algérie* (Paris: Fayard, 1993).
3. See Alistair Horne, *A Savage War of Peace: Algeria, 1954–1962* (London: Macmillan, 1977).
4. See C. Julien, 'Les problèmes du Monde', in *Débats*, no. 24 (March 1993), p. 19, and many others who claim that *Le Monde* is *the* French newspaper of reference.
5. See P. Albert, *La Presse* (Paris: Presses Universitaires de France, 1982), and a number of books written about the newspaper, including E. Sablier, *La création du Monde* (Paris: Plon, 1984).

6. For a more thorough study of the theme, see M. Khane, '*Le Monde* on the Algerian War under the Fourth Republic: a study of the newspaper's coverage (1954–1958)', PhD thesis, University of Kent, 1993.
7. Using the official terminology, one of the main journalists of the newspaper commented: 'an intermediary/intermediate legislation between Common Law and a State of Siege, suitable for an intermediary state of affairs between peace, on the one end of the continuum, and outright insurrection, on the other, keeping the exercise of traditional powers with the civilian authorities, concentrating and reinforcing them in such a way as to make them more adapted to events more akin to a public calamity likely to endanger public order or to undermine national sovereignty.' See *Le Monde*, 2 April 1955.
8. The journalist commented that: 'Here we have, one would admit, a really enormous measure if the aim is only to put an end to the petty actions by the bandits of the Aurès Mountains.' Thinking that these measures were 'excessive', he expressly asked: 'One would wonder, in this respect if we are not using a sledgehammer to crack a nut?' *Le Monde*, 24 March 1955.
9. Ibid.
10. *Le Monde*, 15 June 1955.
11. Most of the repressive powers were quite extensive and included the powers to suspend local councillors, to delegate all necessary powers to the military, to create military zones, to detain people without trial, to assign them to particular areas, restrict their movements, etc. See Arlette Haymann, *Les Libertés publiques et la Guerre d'Algérie* (Paris: LGDJ, 1972).
12. Throughout spring 1957. See, for examples, *Le Monde*, 24–5 March 1957, 26 March 1957, 5 April, 17 April, 19 April, 23 April, 24 April 1957.
13. Under the general motive of 'threat to national security', innocent people ended up being executed. Fernand Yveton was the first European to be sentenced to death and executed for a minor attempt to blow up the small gas factory where he worked when only material damage would have occurred. See Jean-Luc Einaudi, *Pour l'exemple: L'affaire Fernand Yveton* (Paris: L'Harmattan, 1986).
14. This is the time when lawyers such as Gisèle Halimi and Jacques Vergès were beginning to break new ground and establish their controversial reputations during the Algerian War and afterwards.
15. See *Le Monde*, 28 February 1957.
16. See his article on 'De l'Arbitraire', *Le Monde*, 15 March 1957, pp. 1–6.
17. This seems to be the stock answer one obtains from most journalists of the time.
18. Penchenier, a full-time reporter for the paper, left it in 1956 after going undefended in the face of government denials and accusations of treason and causing the demoralization of the army. See M. Khane, op. cit., p. 291ff; also *Le Monde*, 24, 25 and 30 August 1955 and 13 October 1955.
19. See M. Khane, p. 302ff. What is most amazing is the justification of torture by an army priest which was echoed by the paper while there was a very timid discussion, if any, of the use of torture through the ambivalent support of the article written by former army officer Pierre-Henri Simon, 'Contre la Torture', in the form of the article by *Le Monde* editor Hubert Beuve-Méry: 'Sommes-nous les vaincus d'Hitler' (to which he replied in the negative), when the paper possessed incontrovertible evidence from the Rapport des Jeunes Scouts, from Paul Teitgen (a senior civil servant, secretary-general of the Prefecture of Algiers, 1956–7) and from victims such as Evelyne Lavalette, which it began to reveal very cautiously.

20. See H. Alleg, *La Question* (Lausanne: Les Editions de Minuit, 1958 and 1961); Pierre Vidal-Naquet, *Mémoires. II: Le trouble et la lumière, 1955–1998* (Paris: Seuil/La Découverte, 1998), pp. 52–71; Vidal-Naquet, *L'Affaire Audin* (Lausanne: Les Editions de Minuit, 1957, reissued 1989); Vidal-Naquet, *La Raison d'Etat* (Paris: Maspéro, 1977).
21. There was a very limited coverage of the reports by Robert Barrat and Jean-Jacques Servan-Schreiber and a lack of support for, and indeed a very poor defence of, these journalists' own conception of their duty to inform, and of the meaning of press freedom.
22. See M. Khane, 'Perceptions of Algerian identity in the 1950s: *Le Monde*'s treatment of intellectuals' views', in *Bulletin of Francophone Africa*, no. 4 (Autumn 1993), pp. 47–75.
23. See *Le Monde,* 6–7 January 1957 and the reports of a little girl killed by stray bullets.
24. Provo was the Socialist Party *rapporteur* for the report of a seven-member parliamentary commission entrusted on 28 October 1956 with reporting urgently on allegations of mistreatment in Algeria. The report appeared in March 1957. One member of the Commission (M. Hovnanian, a member of the Radical Party), dissented from the Report's conclusions and called it a whitewash.
25. See M. Khane, op. cit., ch. 13.
26. This section draws heavily on M. Khane, ch. 5, esp. pp. 115–19.
27. Marshal A. Juin, *Le Maghreb en Feu* (Paris: Plon, 1957).
28. See the review of Juin's book, *Le Maghreb en Feu* in *Le Monde,* 15 March 1957.
29. In 'General Ely définit le rôle du chef dans la guerre révolutionnaire', *Le Monde,* 20 June 1957.
30. A reference to General Paris de Bollardière's refusal to carry out an intensification of the repression, followed by his resignation and departure for France. See *Le Monde,* 20 June 1957.
31. See *Le Monde,* 7–8 July 1957.
32. *Le Monde,* 25 December 1957.
33. Although *Le Monde* did not share Edmond Michelet's gloomy and pessimistic conclusions, the paper was quite complimentary about the former Defence Minister's work whose scope was judged to be applicable far beyond Algeria. E. Michelet, *Contre la Guerre civile* (Paris: Plon, 1957). See *Le Monde*'s review of this book, 25 December 1957.
34. The reporter was told: 'We are a sledgehammer sent to crack a nut and of course we cannot manage to flatten it; it always manages to jump away every time we hit the anvil.' In Jean Planchais, 'Le Malaise de l'Armée', *Le Monde,* 29 October 1955. It is noteworthy that Planchais subsequently widened his investigations into this theme of army disaffection, publishing a book entitled *Où en est l'armée* (Paris: Correa, 1959).
35. See Herreman in *Le Monde,* 11 July 1957.
36. Especially, reinforcements from 50,000 to 450,000 on each side of the Mediterranean – over 2 million soldiers ending up serving in Algeria.
37. See M. Khane, op. cit., ch. 5.
38. See *Le Monde,* 21 May 1955.
39. For instance, the title of John Talbott's book, *The War without a Name: France and Algeria, 1954–1962* (New York: Alfred A. Knopf, 1980), and the absolutely contrasting title adopted by Alistair Horne for his book *A Savage War of Peace* (London: Macmillan, 1977).

40. Who were said to be terrorizing 700,000 inhabitants. See Jean Planchais, *Le Monde*, 29 October 1955.
41. J. Soustelle, Governor-General of Algeria to 1956, published a book entitled *Aimée et souffrante Algérie* (Paris: Plon, 1956).
42. E. Mannoni in *Le Monde*, 14 December 1956 and 12 December 1956.
43. '... which was difficult to find amongst these quarrelsome clans', even after a full year of conflict. See *Le Monde*, 27 and 29 October 1956. Essentially the main causes were seen as '*banditisme*', fanaticism, the poverty of the masses and external interference. The abundant literature on the subject denies this narrow conception of the conflict.
44. See A. Blanchet, *Le Monde*, 5–6 February 1956.
45. See the work of George Armstrong Kelly, *Lost Soldiers: The French Army and Empire in Crisis, 1947–1962* (Cambridge, MA: MIT Press, 1965), for a thorough study of the issues involved. Clearly, as far as *Le Monde* is concerned here, although the Algerian conflict was put into the Cold War context, the psychological nature of some of the French army's duties admitted, and lessons learnt from the Indochina War acknowledged, there was throughout the pages of the paper a clumsy denial of any similarity between the Algerian and Indochinese contexts, and between the pacification process in Algeria and the war a few years earlier in Indochina.
46. See *Le Monde*, 15 December 1956.
47. Because of its heavy reliance on military sources, the operations of the French army were reported as being invariably successful in 'ridding the area of outlaws' and leading to normal life resuming in the countryside and the villages where, it was stressed, 'children were playing outside ... and the Muslims were drinking and smoking ... in defiance of the FLN ban'. See *Le Monde*, 13 December 1956.
48. See *Le Monde*, 30 April 1957, for instance. Suspects executed with or without trial were also labelled as being guilty without that guilt ever being established.
49. For instance, *L'Express* and *France-Observateur*, as well as editors such as Les Editions de Minuit, and most publications of the Left.
50. *Le Monde*, 14 December 1956.
51. *Le Monde*, 19 March 1957.
52. See H. Keramane, *La Pacification* (Lausanne: La Cité, 1960). A shrewd and critical reading of various articles written on Algeria by *Le Monde* at the end of 1956, for example that of 13 December 1956.
53. In psychological warfare jargon, this equated to depriving the fish (terrorists) of their natural environment (water), that ensured their existence and reproduction by providing material and logistical support through the local population. Notable expositions of the doctrine by leading French partisans in Algeria occur in Michel Deon, *L'Armée d'Algérie et la pacification* (Paris: Plon, 1959) and Colonel Roger Trinquier, *La Guerre moderne* (Paris: la Table Ronde, 1961). Cf. Peter Paret, *French Revolutionary Warfare from Indochina to Algeria* (London: Pall Mall Press, 1964), and a later memoir by another 'revolutionary war' enthusiast in Algeria, Colonel Antoine Argoud: *La décadence, l'imposture et la tragédie* (Paris: Fayard, 1974).
54. *Le Monde*, 11 and 13 December 1956.
55. *Le Monde*, 11 December 1956.
56. *Le Monde*, 13–14 January 1957, p. 1.
57. In a series of articles entitled 'Contre la propagande et les pressions du FLN', *Le Monde*, 23 and 24 July 1957. These followed other articles following similar lines (e.g. *Le Monde*, 14 December 1956).

58. See Nicolas Andoque, *1956–1962, Guerre et Paix en Algérie: l'Epopée silencieuse des SAS* (Paris: SPL Editions, 1977).
59. *Le Monde*, 21 January 1957.
60. The kind of contradictions about the role of these special troops such as the SAS and the *commandos noirs* can be illustrated by the reports of Jean-Jacques Servan-Schreiber described by *Le Monde* (26 January 1957) as being optimistic of the outcome when a few months later he was able to contradict this view by publishing a very different story in *L'Express* and in his *Lieutenant in Algeria* (London: Hutchinson, 1958).
61. Very useful in looking at this crucial episode of French military history are Kelly, *Lost Soldiers*, and Jean Planchais, *Une Histoire politique de l'armée. II: de De Gaulle à De Gaulle (1942–1967)* (Paris: Seuil, 1967).
62. He had told Paul Teitgen of a possible coup being organized by right-wing officers and the Fédération des maires d'Algérie.
63. J. Planchais in his 'L'Armee s'inquiète' of January 1957. See M. Khane, ch. 5, and *Le Monde*, 18 January 1957.
64. See *Le Monde*, 29 March 1957 and 2 April 1957.
65. Subsequently he wrote a letter of support to Servan-Schreiber who had served under him in Algeria and was persecuted by the French authorities over the publication of his letters in *L'Express*, followed by his book recounting his Algerian service, *Lieutenant en Algérie* (Paris: Julliard, 1957), which a year later appeared in English as *Lieutenant in Algeria*, trans. Ronald Matthews (London: Hutchinson, 1958). Cf. *Le Monde*, 29 March 1957; Roger Barberot, *Malaventure en Algérie avec le Général Paris de Bollardière* (Paris: Plon, 1957); J.-J. Servan-Schreiber, *Passions* (Paris: Fixot, 1991), pp. 323–72.
66. See *Le Monde*, March, April, July 1957.
67. The paper was concerned to avoid temptation as far as these soldiers were concerned, but the reader is not told why these soldiers should be tempted to leave and join the rebels when the latter were always portrayed as terrorizing everybody.
68. See, for instance, *Le Monde*, 9 February 1957, which could not be relied on to provide the reader with a full picture.
69. A contrast can be clearly drawn, nevertheless, between *Le Monde* and the representation of the conflict found elsewhere in the coverage of the Algerian War in other media.
70. See Patrick Eveno and Jean Planchais, *La Guerre d'Algérie* (Paris: La Découverte/*Le Monde*, 1989).

12
Psychological Propaganda during the Algerian War – Based on a Study of French Army Pamphlets

Nacéra Aggoun

Of the significant historical antecedents, two particular influences were to have a bearing on the approach of the French army to the Algerian War. The first of these was the recent colonial war in South-East Asia, which had been going on since 1946 and which came to an end with the Dien Bien Phu surrender of 1954, after the discovery of the revolutionary guerrilla presence among the native Asian population. The second dated back to the epic of the 1830 conquest when the army had conquered the region by force of arms. The early years of the colony were marked firstly by military occupation and then by military administration. Is it not the case, after all, that officers of the SAS (Section Administrative Spécialisée) were assimilated into the Bureaux Arabes, while the very vocabulary of the military present in the region during the Algerian War makes reference to the task of 'pacification'.

From these two experiences, one recent and one linked to tradition, and based upon a theoretical ideology of psychological warfare, came the institution of a precise and sophisticated system. This system was built around the control of space and the supervision of population groupings on a local scale. A propaganda and information service was created in 1956, and every military staff was provided with a Fifth Bureau.

In addition to the violence of police methods and the use of torture, the development of propaganda and the classic tools offered by pamphlets, posters and handouts were at the forefront of army action on the ground. This documentation provides the historian with a far from insignificant source of material from which to build up a picture of the Algerian War between 1956 and 1959, the dates between which the service was in operation.[1] The leaflets and posters produced were targeted at members of the army itself, French soldiers, and at the Muslim population and what official terminology described as 'rebel troops'.

The orders of the 5e Bureau were clearly defined from the end of 1956 or beginning of 1957 onwards: '... a leaflet will only produce the effect anticipated if it is talked about ... it must be designed to stigmatise, to poison, to demoralise and to rally support ...' The means of distribution varied according to the target audience. Propaganda might be distributed by soldiers and patrols or through the postal system, or it might be left in public places, posters might be put up if a meeting was due to take place or, finally, material might be dropped by plane or by helicopter.

The history of leafleting certainly raises questions as regards methodology and, of course, as regards the treatment of information. The leaflet has its roots in both written and visual propaganda, and even, where it is the subject of debate beforehand, in oral propaganda. In the area of methodology, attention must be paid not only to the written content but also to the texts' visual elements. This is because it is important that attention be paid to typography (the choice of letters and characters, given further prominence through the bold use of size and colour), and to the drawings and pictures used for propaganda ends.[2]

From the body of work studied, one can schematically divide the period into two. The first period, lasting from the end of 1956 until 1958, was characterized by the production of a great quantity of leaflets and brochures while the second period, between 1958 and 1959, corresponded to a strengthening of military control (the Challe Plan) and to an ideology based upon integration. Photographic poster hoardings became dominant and were to be seen on walls everywhere.

This mass psychological propaganda was based on a campaign of awareness and explanation whose central theme was one of reconciliation between France and Algeria. 'The army has a mission and a vision for the future' ... the message being sent in one tract is self-evident: 'A soldier's return from Algeria to France is a gift for the future.' This did not constitute an exaltation of the warrior class, but we are not too far away here from the earlier colonial imagery of the *worker-soldier* or the ceaselessly propagated image of the smiling SAS officer surrounded by children.

Material targeted at the troops shows an increased awareness of their lack of comprehension of Algeria, a gap in their knowledge that needed to be filled. In 1956, therefore, the use of propaganda leaflets was not the most important task, the goal being rather to provide information through a series of brochures. Going beyond offering advice concerning logistics and the 'Military Code' (the good soldier's manual), such as how to look after weapons and the importance of discretion, the army seemed to be keen to increase knowledge about Algeria through informative pamphlets which explained the economic, social and cultural context. Material addressed to the leaders of *communes mixtes* and to administrative managers followed the same line: how to attain a better understanding of Algerians, the development of a guide to everyday living (what to do when you meet a Muslim, religious restrictions, etc.).[3]

From 1956 onwards, the main theme was the fight against terrorism and rebellion. A series of bilingual pamphlets entitled 'The voice of truth'

(French on one side, Arabic on the other) was directed at rural communities and douars (Muslim villages) as the most important task was to cut the Algerian resistance movement off from those communities that were lending it their support. The call to these people to have confidence in France was explicit, the pamphlets summoning the people of the douars not to give in to the rebels, nor to 'the lies of bandits whose actions sowed only the seeds of ruin and terror'. The old colonial vocabulary reappeared, juxtaposing 'French Peace' to the barbarism of the outlaws ... 'the choice is yours!' Here the text itself, brief and powerful, is the order of the day. Pictures were not neglected, however, and pamphlets could also feature a dramatic structure almost cinematic in nature. For example, the following description represents more than one viewpoint and hints at several different interpretations. 'Terrorism hinders the good work of doctors', reads the prominent slogan. The picture, meanwhile, is divided into three sections: in the top left-hand section a father holding his child in his arms is trying to make a phone call; in the bottom right-hand section the doctor is on the phone; and, in the diagonal section cutting in between the other two images, the telegraph pole is being sawn down by a 'rebel'.

The leitmotif 'French-made in Algeria' is represented by the doctor and the telegraph pole, one of the most important achievements of colonial dominance. The theme chosen here illustrates the seriousness of the text, the threat to life; the *maquis* is equated with death. The choice of the child who cannot be saved involves an appeal to the deepest of parental feelings.

Between 1956 and 1957, the goal was to discredit the guerrillas of the *maquis* and to incite Algerians to inform on them, the *Renseignez-nous* ('Let us know!') campaign was launched from spring 1957 onwards. Its slogan was *La confiance mène à la confidence* ('Feeling secure makes you share your secrets') and it was targeted principally at women and ex-servicemen.

Propaganda in the form in which it was practised during the Algerian War was only an improved version of the endeavours and the experiments carried out from 1946 onwards to counteract the nationalist efforts that followed the Sétif bloodbath of 1945. The GGA (General Government of Algeria) organized a cinema-based tour which laid emphasis on reaching the douars in order better to get into areas criss-crossed by lorries. In parallel, an enormous campaign was directed towards ex-servicemen, each population centre being given its own Maison du Soldat or Dar el Askri (Soldiers' Centre), while Franco-Muslim friendship was promoted through commemorations and parades (complete with the rituals of military saluting and the wearing of medals).[4]

In 1957 a scheme based on comradely pep-talks was aimed at Moslem ex-servicemen, who were expected to become 'good soldiers' again and continue to serve France by telling what they knew, spreading the word and encouraging others to talk. The role of the army veteran was also to convince others of the need for talk. The theme of brotherhood and solidarity between the two bodies was omnipresent: the ex-serviceman would find himself explaining the mutual assistance and mutual benefit, how 'support had been given to mainland France during past wars' and 'now, the sons of the homeland were coming to help ensure victory for Algeria'. The *maquis* guerrilla, on the other hand, was turned into a complete hate-figure. The *fellagha* Arab guerrilla, used to symbolize the enemy, was depicted either as a faceless dark bulk with a human outline or as some sort of vermin, a locust or a poisonous scorpion. FLN corruption was another central theme, and they were portrayed as being riven with internal rivalries and disputes, their members being referred to as 'the sons of Cairo' and shown as living a life of incredible luxury. Furthermore, they went around killing one another ('jackals eat one another', as the saying goes). One leaflet even showed the nationalist leaders in prison.

Along with calls on people to inform were appeals for those with the guerrilla movement to desert. A great play was made of the example set by defectors, such as the announcement of the surrender, on 1 November 1956, of Adjou-adjou, the leader of the *maquis* in the Aurès mountain region: 'He's shown the way ahead, he's understood that the uprising is doomed; Follow his example and the army of pacification will welcome you with open arms'.

Another strategy here was to portray the nationalists living outside Algeria as living a life of depravity. 'You're living a life of misery, bloodshed and mourning. In Tunis, in Morocco and in Cairo, they're living a life of wealth and debauchery'. The visual imagery representing this is high in colour, with shades of red and gold. The leader is shown in western clothing and *chèche* turban, surrounded by buxom women, often dancing (western-style), in a casino. Bottles of vodka, large banknotes and purses filled with gold accentuate this vision of sheer debauchery. These leaflets portray the *maquis* guerrillas as not being good Muslims and attempt to demonstrate their association with embezzlement and their involvement in financing armed groups.

Around the end of 1957 or beginning of 1958, this humorous style of propaganda faded away, to be replaced by a hardening in the language used. The balance of power between the armed groups on the one hand and the French military forces on the other was becoming more even and the people found themselves caught between the two. A study of ALN propaganda would certainly have shone further light on this. The pressure exerted is clear from the threat: 'Accomplices of the rebels will be punished too'. Population groups forced to change location and regroup also attracted the attentions of the propagandists: 'The French army is there to provide protection to citizens forced to move to new centres'.

The year 1958 was a watershed, particularly as regards leaflets, the style of which was modernized. Out went satirical cartoons based on caricatures and high in colour, to be replaced by a completely new tone of sobriety.

The change in politics was obvious. The attempt to achieve national integration was also to use the channel of mass propaganda, but was to feature, in addition, the introduction of photography. 'All children of France' was the fashionable slogan doing the rounds. With the change in political strategy, the broad 'France-Africa' community, encompassing mainland French, Algerians and Africans was to be fêted as a forerunner of 'Eurafrica'.

Presentation was considerably more dynamic and propagated the image of a creative, modern France and glorified technology and progress. From 1958 onwards, with de Gaulle becoming President and the establishment of the Fifth Republic, the Algérie Nouvelle concept came into use. National integration was the goal now (the *Algérie, c'est la France* theme) and this was to be achieved through modernization of the territory, hence the launch of economic and social reforms such as the Plan de Constantine. The role of the army was seen as being to protect the French nation, with Algeria seen as an integral part of that nation.

It was based on displays of large panel-photographs, divided into different sectors of activity and with a title in the centre to indicate the theme they represented: for example, laboratories, agricultural equipment, industry (power stations, refineries), armaments (air, sea and land). They were displayed for between eight and ten days.

This vision of the future came accompanied with a new and heightened emphasis on the value of youth, an emphasis not previously evident in this era. Physical education and sport, team spirit and the enjoyment of physical endeavour were themes which were conveyed by the photos. In one, a group of children carrying the French tricolour are to be seen smiling at Youth, the future of France.

Other series of posters were directed also towards women and, a new development, towards workers. 'Women are the cornerstone in the construction of the new Algeria', declared one hoarding, 1.2 metres by 2 metres in size, devoted to the theme and proclaiming Algerian women's desire to achieve emancipation and integration. The role of Algerian women was perceived by the proponents of colonial ideology to be a vital part of the modernization process in Algeria. In this regard, one has only to mention the political initiatives introduced by the French to discourage Algerian women from wearing the veil (a phenomenon referred to as *le dévoilement*). Other photographs were designed for the July 1958 presidential election, such as the one that proclaimed: 'De Gaulle, Renewal and Brotherhood. You'll get all our votes.'

While the armed conflict continued, the key theme of the year 1959 was that of peace and the restoration of order: 'It is through us that peace will be reborn and peace is the traditional and sacred vocation of women'. Peace is personified and identified with women. Two images are superimposed, one on the other, on leaflets: in the foreground are a mother and child, in the background is a school. This choice of theme was because teaching and education remained the principal means of meeting others and of achieving personal contact between communities.

Conclusion

As has already been emphasized, the army seemed to return to its past role as colonial administrator. Military writings from the period of the conquest contributed to the development of myths (for ethnographic purposes, they look at the native in a particular way and tie him down to one everlasting stereotype).

This old colonial source shows up a series of representations from which the army was to be able to draw during the period of the war of Algerian decolonization. Further proof of this is provided by the leaflet that promoted emigration to France through the slogan 'Kabyle common sense'.

The French army in Algeria felt itself to be invested with a mission, a mission sustained by its experience of guerrilla warfare in South-East Asia. The confrontation was one on the ground between an organized army and clandestine armed groups which launched surprise attacks and held their own thanks to the 'support' of the Algerian people. The tactical approach was aimed at turning this 'support' around as part of an overall strategy based on controlling territory and controlling minds. The use of institutionalized psychological propaganda by the Fifth Bureau was an effort to obtain the consent of the Algerian people.

This technique of mass psychological propaganda had shown its value during the Second World War, but in Algeria its message did not really attain the results hoped for due to its target audience not being very open to influence. The verdict on the effectiveness of this propaganda and on the issue of whether or not the Algerian people were receptive to this approach remains open. In fact wider research needs to be carried out with regard to the French integrationist doctrine. Rapid, large-scale pamphleteering was just one element in the French armoury and fitted in alongside the logistics of warfare on the ground and the distinction that the armed forces made between rebel areas and areas in which peace had been reimposed. If we are to talk of the failure of this propaganda (and Algeria did end up winning independence in 1962) then more extensive research must be undertaken and analysis carried out covering the whole range of literature that sets out the theories behind psychological warfare.

Nonetheless, this does not detract from the fact that French propaganda had a significant effect on individuals at a psychological level. It played an important role in creating an atmosphere of terror (torture, the rape of women, making children give up information, publicly stringing up the bodies of those killed). The objective in creating new settlements for those displaced from their homes was also to cut people off from their roots and their home areas in order more conveniently to 're-educate' them to a new structure and way of life. In this regard, the involvement of the sociologist Jean Servier is revealing. It indicates the desire to acquire a detailed grasp of the way Algerian society functioned so as to maximize the degree to which people's attitudes could be manipulated and steered in the desired direction. This strategy was not without success for the French. This was illustrated by the research in the field by two other sociologists, Pierre Bourdieu and Abdelmalek Sayad, who, in their work *Le Déracinement* (published in 1964) write of the emergence of new types of social relationships in the villages they investigated. One might also ask how much influence the counter-propaganda initiatives of the Algerian freedom-fighters had in combating the measures taken by the Fifth Bureau.

In conclusion, the study of the use of propaganda in the Algerian War is significant on a number of levels and contributes a major dimension to the historiography of that war. That study does, however, come up against certain problems as regards source materials: firstly, relevant archives are not readily accessible and secondly the use of personal accounts may lead only to recollections of war that are fed, misled and falsified by ideological imagery, writing and discussions relating to that war.[5]

Notes

1. This source may be consulted at the Bibliothèque Nationale (Paris) and originates from the Bureau Psychologique of the 10th Military Region (Algiers). The collection encompasses 2,060 items obtained from a variety of sources and then compiled into a number of volumes.
2. Bibliographic notes on methodology: on political propaganda, see Jacques Ellul, *Histoire de la propagande* (Paris: PUF, 1990) and Jean-Marie Domenach, *La propagande politique* (Paris: PUF, 1973); on visual imagery and propaganda, see Fabrice d'Almeida, *Images et propagande* (Paris: Casterman, 1995), p. 191, and Laurent Gervereau, *La propagande par l'affiche* (Paris: Syros, 1991), p. 605.
3. Cf. Robert Lacoste's special instructions of 1 May 1957 on interpersonal relations between the citizens of the various communities.
4. Various reports from administrators of mixed communities with regard to propaganda directed at ex-servicemen associated with the creation of the Association des Amitiés Africaines (African Friendship Association) and the tour of duty (1952) of General Montsabert.
5. Particular mention should be made of the valuable resources relating to the period of the Algerian War held at the Centre des Archives d'Outre-Mer (CAOM in Aix-en-Provence) and the Service Historique de l'Armée de Terre (SHAT, Paris-Vincennes) where a large amount of material is either subject to strict codes of secrecy or is still not on file.

13

Remembering the Algerian War: Memory/ies and Identity/ies in Téchiné's *Les Roseaux Sauvages*

Brigitte Rollet

The 30th anniversary commemoration of the Evian agreements (March 1962) which officially put an end to the Algerian war 'marked the conflict's entry into the mainstream of French historiography'.[1] Thirty years later, has the 'need for a literary and/or cinematic replacement for the physically absent *lieux de mémoires* disappeared'?[2] Regarding cinema, both André Téchiné and Bertrand Tavernier's recent films suggest that the need is still very strong. Tavernier filmed his major documentary *La Guerre sans nom* (1992) in which 30 conscripts were asked to share – most of them for the first time – their experiences of the Algerian War. In his film portrait of French conscripts who fought in Algeria, personal and collective amnesia was a central theme. André Téchiné's *Les Roseaux sauvages* (Wild Reeds) (1994) was extremely successful and received four French Césars (out of eight nominations) and the prestigious Louis Delluc award. It was part of the project 'Tous les garçons et les filles' launched by the cultural Franco-German channel Arte. Producer Chantal Poupaud's idea was to ask French film directors to make a film about their adolescence. The only rules given to the directors were that the film should be set within a teenager environment and that a party had to take place within the narrative. Téchiné's film, initially broadcast on French television under the title *Le Chêne et le roseau*, was later distributed in French cinemas.[3]

Téchiné, now in his fifties, chose the 1960s which corresponds to his own youth. His film is set in his region of origin, the south-west of France where many of his previous films were already located. *Les Roseaux sauvages* takes place in 1962, at the end of the Algerian War in Villeneuve sur Lot, a small provincial town of Lot et Garonne. Téchiné declared that he had always wished to make a film about this period, and that none of his previous projects worked.[4] More than 20 years ago, his previous plan to adapt Marie Cardinal's bestseller *Les Mots pour le dire* (1975) and 'a primary source of French literature of the Algerian war',[5] collapsed after the commissioner of the project forbade him to mention the conflict which according to him 'was still a taboo at the time'.[6]

The Algerian War has always been a very sensitive subject in French society and history as well as in French culture. Despite recent attempts to identify a corpus of films representing the 1954–62 conflict,[7] Dine is correct in his view that 'given the French record on censorship as regards colonial issues, [it is not] surprising that mainstream commercial studios should have continued to avoid the subject when it became clear that things were going badly wrong on both sides of the Mediterranean'.[8] By choosing to set his film at the end of the conflict, Téchiné took the opportunity of finally realizing an old and cherished project. It is hard to say whether he has achieved his initial project in *Les Roseaux sauvages*. The fact that his film is supposed to be autobiographical gives it the value of a testimony of a period still vividly sensitive in the French national psyche. Thirty years after the war, the emphasis is very much on personal testimony, not only for *La Guerre sans nom* but in Stora's *Les Années Algériennes* as well.[9] Beyond the personal memories of the director, the film can be seen as expressing not only most of the ambiguities of France in the late 1950s and early 1960s, but also of more recent accounts of the period. Although the conflict is never directly shown, I shall argue that the war is a key element of the film as it pervades the narrative and the characters. Téchiné addresses issues related to both national and sexual identities which are entwined within the context of the conflict itself. War therefore can be read as a symbolical element which blurs all boundaries and destroys beliefs and identities.

Unlike other conflicts, it has often been stated that the Algerian war has never generated 'war films' in French cinema. For Pierre Guibbert, 'tout se passe comme si, pour de multiples raisons, les "événements" d'Algérie avaient du mal à se couler dans le moule du "film de guerre"'.[10] The only film he identified as such was the cinematographic adaptation of Lartéguy's *Les Centurions* by the American Mark Robson in 1965. Pascal Ory distinguishes different 'categories' of films related to the Algerian War. He finally mentions: 'un temps d'écho, où les jeunes générations s'en servent pour parler de ce qui les préoccupe désormais: la quête d'identité'.[11] Téchiné, like other directors identified by Ory, belongs to a generation which was too young to fight in Algeria. Ory wrote that: 'Pour eux [these directors], malgré l'intensité des liens sentimentaux qui peuvent les unir au sujet, la guerre d'Algérie n'est plus l'interrogation centrale mais un simple révélateur'.[12] In French cinema from the 1980s onwards, the war has been used either as a trigger, a backdrop which does not address the issue contained within the Algerian War, or as a mean of expression of an individual identity. It has become a 'pretext' to talk about something else ... although the conflict within these narratives is an important fact in itself.

In *Wild Reeds*, Téchiné chose to show the repercussions of the war on a small group of teenagers, miles away from the battleground. François is one of the protagonists, a character who may be the alter-ego of the young

Téchiné. He is a pupil at the local boarding school with Serge, the son of Italian-born farmers, and Henri, an older *pied-noir* pupil. François' best friend and confident is Maïté, the daughter of his French teacher, an activist in the local Communist Party. The war – although invisible – distorts every aspect of life, as things are rarely what they may be at first sight.

The end of certainties

The film starts with what seems to be on the surface a happy event. Pierre, Serge's brother, is getting married. The shots of the wedding offer a mixture of close-ups of smiling faces or medium-shots of groups of happy people, eating, drinking, singing and dancing in an idyllic setting, the sunny countryside of southern France. Everything seems peaceful until Pierre reveals to his former teacher Madame Alvarez (Maïté's mother and the current French teacher of Henri, François and Serge) that he only got married to have a few days leave and that to do so, he had previously written to three women he knew, hoping that one at least would accept. The reason for his uniform is made clear. He is a conscript fighting in Algeria and trying everything he can to avoid going back there. He wants Madame Alvarez to help him to desert, having heard that communist activists had done this in the past. She refuses and abruptly leaves the wedding with her daughter and François.

Madame Alvarez seems initially to be the only adult (there are actually very few grown-ups in the film) who knows what to believe in and to stand up for. She is the only politicized character and follows the Party's lines regarding the conflict. A few shots of posters from the Communist Party (PC) towards the end of the film work as a reminder of the PC opposition to the conflict and more especially its strong condemnation of the OAS activities.[13] However, they only appear on the screen after the death of Pierre has shattered her initial strong beliefs. Like the youngsters, her former convictions are put in question by the absurd death of the young conscript who – like thousands of others – wanted neither to fight nor to be a hero, and who was killed by OAS troops. From the opening sequence of the wedding to the lunch-meeting with her substitute at the end of the film, Madame Alvarez goes through different phases which could be summarized as the end of certainties. Two key events (the arrival of Henri and the death of Pierre) have major consequences for her. Initially seen as a strong and independent character both in her class and during the wedding, she completely collapses after the death of Pierre. She starts suffering from a serious nervous breakdown and holds herself responsible for completely different ordeals, from the departure of her husband to the death of Pierre. All her beliefs are being shattered by this dramatic event to such an extent that while at the hospital where she is shown as a ghost painfully trying to get on with her life, she has visual hallucinations of the dead soldier appearing in her bedroom like a ghastly reminder of what she sees as her own fault. This apparition is like an echo of the last scene in her classroom, where, struggling to control herself, she declaims with a broken voice, Mallarmé's poem *Azur*: 'je suis hanté, azur, azur, azur', before breaking into tears.

Mr Morelli, who replaces Madame Alvarez in the middle of the film, brings another insight into the war. A former teacher in Algiers where he taught for 15 years and where he got married, he knows the Algerian issue better than anyone else (except maybe Henri). Far from taking sides in the conflict, he expresses doubts, unable to choose between what is right and wrong, black or white. The audience never learns his real convictions and feelings, even when Henri asks him what he thinks of Salan's being sentenced to life imprisonment. The reason for his refusal to take sides is partly explained at the end of the film when he introduces his Algerian wife, Aïcha, to his colleague Madame Alvarez. By his mixed marriage, Morelli seems to be between the two sides.

While having lunch with Morelli at the end of the film, Madame Alvarez seems to be back to her former self, assertive and secure, an attitude which provokes Morelli's ironical comment: 'Vous avez de la chance. Vous pouvez dire: "il a tort, il a raison, c'est bien, c'est mal, je suis pour, je suis contre". Moi je ne peux pas'. This irony is even more acute when after lunch, he introduces Aïcha who had been staying in the car. Left alone in the restaurant's car park, Madame Alvarez seems to realize the extent of her own prejudices, and her narrow-mindedness regarding not only her colleague's obviously painful experience of the war, but more generally other people's ordeals whatever side they supported during the conflict. Her face expresses a terrible sense of loss and perhaps of regrets. She has learnt a difficult lesson and one cannot help feeling that she will not be the same or think the same ever again.

A short sequence between Maïté and her mother is interesting when dealing with gender and more especially gender and the war. Wartime has often been perceived as a moment where gender roles can be reversed and women are presented as stronger characters than men although some of them are directly affected by the war. This 'reversal' of gender is expressed as well through a 'feminization' of the male characters who are all weakened in one way or the other. Either physically (François has a weak heart condition) or psychologically (both Serge and Henri have to get over the difficult mourning of their relatives), they could be seen as symbolizing 'emasculated' or 'devirilized' heros. Both widows, however, (soldier) Pierre's wife and (*pied-noir*) Henri's mother, have to get on with their life without necessarily understanding the issues at stake in the conflict. They are left alone with their suffering, unlike Madame Alvarez and her daughter, the former an independent divorcee, the latter a feminist *avant la lettre,* both communist activists and with a strong ideological 'framework' to refer to and solid convictions. Another type of pain and anguish is also visible in the highly symbolic character of Aïcha, Mr Morelli's Algerian wife. She anticipates in a way the commencement of a changing French society, but her mutism (a critic even refers to her 'autism') and withdrawal in the car while her husband is having lunch with his colleague could illustrate as well her status as an 'outsider'.

Mise en abyme? The youngsters and the war

Like the other characters, François is too young to be directly involved in the conflict. Living in the boarding school of a small town, their lives change with the arrival of a young *pied-noir* Henri. He literally brings the war with him inside the school. His entrance in the narrative coincides with the death of Pierre, the newly wed conscript. From this moment and from these two apparently unrelated events, the pupils' lives are altered in many ways by what is happening on the other side of the Mediterranean. From the opening sequence of the film which takes place before the Evian agreements, to the final scene which is set just after the end of *l'Algérie française* and after the exodus of the *pieds-noirs*, the war directly affects their identities, beliefs and perceptions of the outside world be it real or fictional (as their reading and understanding of literary texts will show).

The group of teenagers can be seen as reproducing some attitudes and beliefs of French people at the time of the conflict. Maïté shares her mother's ideas to a greater or lesser degree, and like the teacher, she only sees Henri – who supports the OAS's actions – as the enemy, at least until the very end of the film. She is as 'pro FLN' as he is 'pro OAS'. Serge, without the same kind of ideological background, refuses the absurdity of the war, without ever questioning the reasons of the conflict. He experiences the war on a very personal level (his brother dies in Algeria), but unlike Henri who becomes pro-OAS because of his father's death in an FLN bombing, Serge will not go beyond his grief and mourning, nor channel his anger into any political action.

François is probably the least involved or 'committed' character of the group. More educated and literate than his schoolmates, he has another conflict to sort out. His own 'war' relates to his secret awareness of his latent homosexuality. An aesthete very much more interested in arts than in politics he is the only one who never mentions the war. François' behaviour is quite different from his friends'. Far from taking sides in the conflict, he completely ignores it. He seems unable to discuss the consequences, even when they directly concern his friends (as for example Serge's difficult mourning after his brother's death, or Maïté's personal trauma when her mother is temporally confined in a psychiatric hospital after her nervous breakdown). What makes his character interesting is the fact that he is supposed to be the director's alter ego. He illustrates here the contrast between individual and collective memory. There is, I would argue, an obvious link between the 'war with no name' and the 'love with no name' or 'which does not dare to speak its name'. In a sense, his painful experience in fighting the hypocrisy surrounding his sexual orientation could be associated with the general hypocrisy of the time regarding the conflict and the failure to call it what it was, i.e. a war.

In this regard, François' painful self-confession alone in front of a mirror that he is a 'pédé', a word he repeats endlessly and louder and louder, is even more significant. When trying to get some advice from a known gay middle-aged man from the village, he comes out to him in a desperate attempt to speak out and to find out about homosexuality. He only receives in return the sad look of an old man, unable to speak, and embarrassed in a way which recalls Mr Morelli when confronted with Henri's questions and doubts. The reaction of his schoolmates is amazingly tolerant from a realistic point of view (as the sexual revolution has not really started yet!). Could their acceptance be because it is a minor event when compared to the 'real' war? François' obsession with his own war is as strong as his indifference for other people's war. He is neutral, as, unlike the other characters, it is never known what he actually thinks of the war, and he is an outsider as he is the only one not to be directly or indirectly affected by it.

A sequence illustrates this aspect of François, and shows that he is completely the opposite of Henri. Both had studied Rimbaud for an essay. Their choice can be explained by the strong 'tradition' of social and sexual rebellion that the symbolist poet epitomizes which has made him rated highly among French teenagers of all time. François' choice of Rimbaud might have been influenced by the poet's sexual orientation. Or, as her teacher notices, because of the difficulty of Rimbaud's work. She criticizes what she calls her pupil's 'infatuation' (her actual word is *narcissisme*), although she recognizes the intellectual quality of the content. Beyond their different approach towards the poet (see below), this sequence reveals a lot about the pupils and their teacher. Far from dealing just with literature and the various readings of literary texts, it illustrates two visions of the world and of the relationship between Art and Life. François – and this goes far beyond literature – seems to be fascinated by highbrow culture (his choice of films and directors like Bergman and Demy emphasizes this aspect) more than by social and political issues.

A parallel could be drawn here by his physical attraction for Serge first and then Henri, or in other words from the 'victim' to the 'executioner'. What he sees in them has nothing to do with what they believe in and stand for. His attraction is purely sexual. Despite Maïté's warning that Henri by supporting the OAS is a 'fascist', François cannot help being fascinated by the young *pied-noir*. Could his indifference for everything which is not him, and his individualism and/or narcissism be just another cliché about gays? Or has it more to do with the need, within a narrative dealing a lot with tragic events, to introduce a character who epitomizes life and love, despite death, hatred and destruction. In this regard, François could express the eternity of love and desire, and the blind power of desire and love going far beyond morals and historical upheavals, a view shared by Henri who often calls sex the only good thing in life.

This is somehow summarized in the final sequence. The river could therefore be seen as a symbolic reminder of Serge's comment: 'tout passe'. François has appropriated Ronsard's main idea in his poem, 'Mignonne allons voir si la rose', a text which Morelli gives to Henri unable at the time to think further than Salan's sentence. 'Carpe diem' (seize the day) could be François' motto.

The relationship among the four youngsters is influenced as much by the war as by their personal feelings and attraction for each other. The quartet offers another form of 'Racinian' love/desire chain but with a happy ending: François loves/desires Serge who does not love/desire him, who loves/desires Maïté who does not love/desire him, who eventually loves/desires Henri who loves/desires her back. Before this providential epilogue, the pro-OAS *pied-noir* Henri epitomizes for the others, individually or collectively, a hated group. He is perceived by the others as the most negative and frightening character. Serge sees in him his brother's murderer/s (he tells François that: 'les gars comme lui c'est tous les mêmes'), while François feels a sort of attraction/repulsion for him ('des fois je te vois comme un ennemi et des fois je voudrais qu'on soit amis,' he declares). Maïté goes even further when she confesses that: 'je croyais que les mecs comme toi, j'étais capable de les tuer'. Her mother is as critical of her pupil as her daughter. The only one who tries to defend Henri is Madame Alvarez' substitute Mr Morelli. Henri's 'status' as the 'black sheep' is reinforced in a way by the recurrent TV and radio reports which repeatedly mention the OAS as the war enemy.

Almost no mention is made of the Algerian fighters. In this regard, the film is Francocentric by the way no attention is given to the Algerian perspective. The conflict, as it appears in the film, seems to be more a civil war than a colonial one. This choice could be explained by the fact that the OAS period is in a sense an easier one for the French left-wingers to deal with. Indeed the fight became for the left a more familiar one as the OAS and its members were seen as fascist, and 'fits' therefore more in the 'traditional' mould of the PC habitual enemy. This could also explain why so many French memories of the Algerian war tend to focus on the end of the war.

Another indirect effect of the war within the school, is the way literature becomes a symbol and Madame Alvarez' class a space where conflicting ideas and opinions are expressed. Like François, Henri has chosen

Rimbaud, although for a very different reason and from a completely different perspective. Henri uses the poet's opposition to the bourgeois of Charleville whom Rimbaud hated and despised, and compares them with the *Français de métropole*. His reading of literature is so biased and against his teacher's beliefs that she refuses to give him a grade while recognizing the quality of his work as far as structure and clarity are concerned. When Henri asks her the grade he would get at his finals with his essay, should she mark it, he is told that she would fail him. Despite the wish she expresses to her pupils not to transform her literature class into a political forum, Madame Alvarez lets her personal convictions take over her professional duties. This scene reinforces the specificity of the character presented from the very beginning of the film as someone who knows and restricts the truth. She does not want to help Pierre because for her the war is over. In the same way, she thinks she holds the truth for literature and refuses interpretations of literary texts which are not hers and which go against her own political convictions.

One 'lesson' or the moral of the film comes from a somehow unexpected character: Serge, Pierre's brother and François' first 'lover' (although this homoerotic pleasure was more a physical experience for him than anything else). Serge repeatedly expresses a denial of heroism, the same heroism which often characterizes fiction and representations of wars. He repeats Pierre: 'la grandeur ça me dégoûte' and reacts at his brother's funeral when an army officer qualifies the dead soldier of an 'example' and a 'hero' by stating that: 'Pierre, c'est pas un héros.' He adds: 'Je trouve ça dégueulasse qu'ils aient besoin de héros.' This implies that the war seems to be the last place where traditional heroic soldiers can be found. Nothing about what is known about Pierre contributes to the construction of a heroic individual. In this regard, he resembles the previous soldiers in French films made before the 1980s who were, according to Stora, '"anti-heros", incapable de vivre des situations complexes et contradictoires'.[14] Pierre just is a conscript at the wrong time and far from being an important experience in what is often seen as a significant aspect in the construction of a national identity, his military service becomes a nightmare as he is killed by other Frenchmen. His desire to desert has nothing to do with a reaction against colonialism. His motivations to do so are much more individualistic. Benjamin Stora commented on the so-called 'passivity' of the French *contingent*, by quoting Jean-Louis Hurst, a deserter during the conflict for whom, 'cette grande colère des soldats rappelés en 1955 ne s'explique pas par une prise de conscience anti-coloniale; plutôt par un: "Je veux me marier, j'en ai rien à foutre de vos colonies"'.[15] Interestingly enough, the image of the deserter, or here of the 'deserter-to-be', is a recurrent one in French fictions of the Algerian war although there were very few desertions during the conflict.

Pierre's murderers are not heroic either. As Serge sadly declares: 'C'est personne qu'a tué mon frère, c'est n'importe qui'. Like the other characters, the war changes Serge's life and vision of the world. At the end of the film, his comments on memory and forgetting, and his conclusion that: 'Il y a quelque chose de plus violent que la guerre: c'est que tout passe', summarize in a sense the whole film. Once the war is over and the dead are buried, life has to continue.

The evolution of Henri follows a similar pattern. After the exodus of the *pieds-noirs* which he watches on TV, his fight seems senseless. Disappointed by Morelli's refusal to take part, he leaves the school at night, and in a desperate attempt to do something, he sets fire to communist posters calling for an end to OAS terrorist attacks. Later, he goes to the Party's headquarters, having decided to blow up the place. This is when and where he meets Maïté who is working in the meeting room. After a difficult start, she agrees to lodge him for the night despite the fear she confesses he inspires in her. Her strong feelings against Henri are altered when he insists she reads a letter his mother had sent him, which he never had the courage to open. The discovery of Henri's mother's tragedy after her husband's death and her departure from Algeria, expressed in a very matter-of-fact way, makes Maïté see the war from the other side and recognize her own intolerance. It is only when Henri, tormented by the guilt of his failed second terrorist act, confesses it that her previous rejection of fascism she feels he epitomizes takes over and she throws him out.

The attraction of extremes is at work here. These extremes find a meeting point when in the last, and probably the most beautiful sequence of the film, the four teenagers go to the river, a place where Pierre used to go with his girlfriends. Here, in this symbolic place, Henri and Maïté make love for the first time. Between their two encounters, both have questioned their own feelings and views. This attraction of extremes could be explained by the fact that once the war is over, the convictions they defended are no longer rightful. Therefore, both teenagers, having previously taken sides in an adult conflict, come back to a reality closer to their age, i.e. the discovery of the first love. In doing so, they forget their differences, and desire and love each other for the sake of love/desire only, an attitude which François has had during the whole film.

The title refers directly to La Fontaine's 'Le chêne et le roseau', a text given by Mr Morelli during an in-class test. Different associations could be made of this allegory of the weak surviving while the strong collapse. While the two countries at war (France and Algeria) could easily take a part each, the main characters of the film are often presented either as an oak or a reed: Madame Alvarez, whose strength is underlined often at the beginning of the film, was an oak before she broke down. Her substitute warns Henri not to be like the oak of the fable.

Téchiné has it seems successfully tackled two main taboos in French society: the Algerian War and homosexuality. Far from the official debates on both subjects, he portrayed in a very sensitive and personal way dilemmas of a sexual and political nature. From a political point of view, one could wonder what it means to make such a film more than 30 years after the end of the war. Téchiné has not achieved in his film the impossible consensus France has vainly tried to attain since the end of *l'Algérie française*. On the contrary, all his characters' views about the conflict are presented as acceptable and understandable, and none of them is portrayed in a negative light. As in Tavernier's *La Guerre sans nom*, the perspective is French-only and no Algerian voice nor viewpoint can be heard. This aspect of the film might seem a bit ambiguous. The audience is put in the position of Mr Morelli, sharing his uncertainties and wonders.[16] As the director declared: 'I don't make politically militant films. I don't make films with a message. I make films which deal with ethical and moral questions.'[17] By choosing non-professional actors, has Téchiné expressed in a different way the denial of heroism suggested above by refusing the identification with known stars? Or has he tried to symbolize/suggest the 'anonymity' and in the same time the 'credibility' of his young characters?

The historian Lucien Febvre once wrote that 'we only ask in a past tense, questions about the present time'. The questions Téchiné addressed in a film dealing with a (recent) past are concerned by the issue of conflicting sexual identities as well as with national identity/ies. Simultaneously, Téchiné is also dealing with the problem of ideology and/or sensibility, morals and/or politics. In this regard, he expresses recurrent concerns from the late 1980s onwards.

Despite the autobiographical component of his film, the director has opted for the fable more than for a realist account of the period. One cannot help wondering what the 'moral' of the film is regarding homosexuality. If we keep in mind a possible reading of La Fontaine's *Le Chêne et le roseau*, i.e. that the weak and/or the oppressed and/or the minority survive the strong, what does it say about being gay and/or 'beur' in France today? While François the reed, unlike the other oaks of the film, has maybe won his own war, it is unclear what the future of Aïcha is.

Notes and references

1. P. Dine, *Images of the Algerian War. French Fiction and Films, 1954–1962*, (Oxford: Clarendon Press 1994), p. 234.
2. Ibid.
3. Interestingly, none of the films of the series made by women directors (such as Claire Denis and Patricia Mazuy among others) were distributed in cinemas, while all the men's were (see those by Cedric Kahn and Olivier Assayas).
4. Interview with A. Téchiné, *Les Cahiers du Cinéma*, no. 481, June 1994, p. 15.
5. Dine, op. cit., pp. 238–41.

6. *Les Cahiers du Cinéma*, op. cit., p. 15.
7. Two recent publications are devoted to the subject: Guy Hennebelle (ed.), *La guerre d'Algérie a l'écran, CinémAction* No. 85 (Corlet, 1997) and Benjamin Stora, *Imaginaires de guerre: Algérie – Viêt-nam, en France et aux États-Unis* (Paris: La Découverte, 1997).
8. Dine, op. cit, p. 218.
9. Similar comment can be made about the Second World War. See Malle's autobiographical film *Au revoir les enfants* (1987) when compared to *Lacombe Lucien* (1974).
10. P. Guibbert, 'La guerre d'Algérie sur les écrans français', in L. Gervereau, J.-P. Rioux and Benjamin Stora (eds), *La France en guerre d'Algérie*, Musée d'histoire contemporaine, BIDC, Nanterre, 1992, pp. 247–55.
11. P. Ory, 'L'Algérie fait écran', in J.-P. Rioux (ed.), *La guerre d'Algérie et les Français* (Paris: Fayard, 1990), pp. 573–81.
12. Ibid, p. 580.
13. The attitude of the Communist Party during the Algerian War was quite ambivalent as it has not always campaigned in favour of an independent Algeria. Let us remember here that it was a left-wing government (with both communist and socialist ministers) led by Guy Mollet which voted the 'pouvoirs spéciaux' in March and April 1956.
14. B. Stora, *La Gangrène et l'oubli. La mémoire de la guerre d'Algérie* (Paris: La Découverte, 1992), p. 252.
15. Jean-Louis Hurst quoted by Stora, op. cit., p. 52.
16. More than François, Morelli could be the alter-ego of the older Téchiné, a tempting suggestion as the actor Jacques Nolot is a very close and old friend of the director. He played several times in Téchiné's films (including several gay characters), and like the director, he is a native of the south-west of France.
17. Interview with André Téchiné, by Peter Lennon, *The Guardian*, 23 February 1995, G2T, p. 14.

14
Children of the Occupation and Colonial Ideology

Bernard W. Sigg

The first international conference of historians on the subject of the Algerian War took place in Paris in December 1988, a conference subsequently followed only by the great commemoration of the ceasefire at the Sorbonne, which took place in March 1992, and then the conference on the French cinema and the wars in South-East Asia and Algeria, at Hérouville in April 1996. Four occasions in four decades for us to consider together a conflagration whose effects are still being powerfully felt is very few indeed. Of these conferences, two were organized by specialists from outside France, one of them by Patrick Leboutte, the Belgian historian of the cinema, the other by British historians in Salford in 1996. There's food for thought! Even more so if one considers the scant quantity of French academic publications on the period. This gap, or blank space, is all the more striking in the field of psychology when one is aware of the number of citizens who were psychologically destabilized by the war. Almost two and a half million young conscripts effectively found themselves plunged into a war due to the volte-face of a government which, having been voted into office by an electorate the majority of whom were in favour of peace, decided to perpetuate French domination in Algeria. What is even more intriguing, however, is that very few people indeed refused to submit to this unpopular policy. If one sets apart recalled soldiers, who constitute a special case, one would have had to wait until 1961 before any opposition worthy of the name made its presence felt, either in France or in Algeria. The overall picture, then, bears the mark of a widespread and long-lasting abstention, or even inhibition, from reaction. Faced with this the psychoanalyst, like the historian, comes to a dead halt.

I would therefore like to attempt to consider with you the factors that weighed so heavily upon the recruits that they should have remained so submissive vis-à-vis the army and should have become so exposed to war neurosis, when the armed combat never reached the degree of horror of the two World Wars, of Korea, or of Vietnam. May it not be that there were other factors, further back in history or more deeply ingrained, which affected the conscripts? Since, furthermore, they have said nothing about it and show themselves still scarcely capable of talking about it, one is forced to hypothesize that the factors in question are unconscious factors. Could it be, then, that all or almost all of these young people shared the same psychological make-up? I do not believe this can be true, each subject being a distinctive individual. On the other hand, I do believe that the association of similar relationships to the historical moment with a powerful ideological influence may lead to a convergence in the attitudes and sensibilities of the great majority of a group, going beyond the types of psychological structures and reactions that are individual to each person. In making this assertion, I am venturing my opinions somewhat and look forward, therefore, to further research in this field.

An initial commentary that others have made relates to the period in which those who were subsequently to become involuntary participants in the war had their roots. Starting from the earliest call-ups of demobilized troops in 1955 and going up to the final pre-call-up enlistment in 1962, one can see that they were born between 1932 and 1944, a historical bracket of dates which is probably significant given that it correlates exactly with the period when Nazism was a force in Europe. Would the parents of the conscripts not have been affected by the threat of Nazism and then the oppression that followed? It is an inquest that remains to be carried out, but I cannot avoid noting that, besides the political upheavals of 1936, which were largely directed towards domestic and social policy reform, the French people as a whole, for the most part, showed a dismaying placidity in the face of fascist and Nazi aggression, the Spanish Civil War and, then, even the German occupation of French soil. On this theme, I can remember that among the people I knew, the Republicans in Spain were referred to only by the derogatory phrase 'the routed army', and as soon as the Germans were on the advance, we were urged to keep quiet, to never pick up leaflets dropped by British planes and, above all, never to express an opinion in front of the Germans. As for the Resistance, they were seen as 'terrorists'. That my father should listen to Radio Londres used to be enough to scare my mother who, as she couldn't prevent him from doing so, used to carefully close all the doors and windows. Is that, then, how young people are to be trained to grow up with bold and critical minds? Certainly not, and this reality lay heavy upon us. Looking again at some of the personal accounts collected for *Le Silence et la Honte,*[1] then, I quote from one of them, telling of his involvement in the 'pacification' of Algeria:

> Every morning an hour stuck in front of the flag where the *Marseillaise* would be followed by *La terre de France*! In my unformed political unconscious of the time, that reminded me of Nazis on the parade ground.

The impact of this common childhood experience remained limited, however, since, in contrast and in very large numbers, those soldiers recalled for a further period of service in Algeria reacted strongly against their remobilization. It is true that after 18 months of active service, the aura of the army and the attraction of overseas journeys with the battalion had pretty much lost their charm and, moreover, they might already have acquired serious commitments in terms of careers, marriage and even parenthood. It is this that explains their anger, for the most part, as they were not really opposed to colonial wars any more than those who had simply been called up.

We need, therefore, to search for another influence, introduced into the thinking of these young men at an earlier stage, which might have rendered them docile or even compliant, without forgetting the role played in this by the pervading behaviour of the time. This influence, while not the only factor, was the colonial ideology that, to varying degrees and in various ways, inflamed French passions during the first half of the twentieth century. That is why I shall attempt to locate manifestations of such ideology, firstly in the general population, then in the army and, finally, among the conscripts themselves.

It is important, at the outset, that I should demonstrate schematically what I understand by the term 'ideology', given the extent to which this concept is surrounded by vagueness and confusion. Ideology is first and foremost, in my view, discourse without a subject, which grows up in a class or category of people having a strong desire for power; it is transmitted unwittingly without limits and without coherence. It was in this way, bit by bit, that colonial ideology came into being in the nineteenth century in the circles of the expansionist bourgeoisie. It subsequently spread rapidly to other social strata, at the time through the accounts of travellers and popular ballads, through newspapers and literature, through clichéd simplistic images and even painting. However, I do not believe that one could find either a structured account or a theoretical explanation of this ideological development, while economic and demographic evidence is available only in a scattered form. Ideological discourse is comprised of images and signifiers which are the product of the past – such as the spectres of what Derrida calls 'hauntology';[2] this discourse normally escapes all subjective criticism or censure through being organized at a subconscious level, in the manner of the 'phantom' described by Nicolas Abraham.[3] It is this that has allowed there to be discussion of 'ideological fantasies'. We should mention here a few of the old clichés that serve as examples of colonial ideology: the explorer, the greatness of France, the Empire, the mission to civilize. All these ideological clichés emit, without the knowledge of their consumers, a conviction of supremacy, that has its roots in Ancient Rome, together with those desires for self-enrichment, adventure and boundless luxury that everyone tends to deny. The unfortunate ventures in Mexico and Panama can be seen, thus, as the modern – and unacceptable – caricature of the stampede of the conquistadors. The ideological capture of the subject is achieved, it seems to me, by means of the superego; the ideological schemas combine there with personal ideals, thus enhancing the strength of their drives, starting with the death drive. In this way, we can understand that all, or nearly all, ideology involves an antagonist who fulfils the role of a bogeyman. This antagonist, to continue the application of my theoretical framework to colonial ideology, is none other than the 'savage', whether Arab, Negro or Annamite, who is at the same time the object of and the detestable obstacle to the colonizing enterprise. Slavery may, it is true, have been abolished. Yet desires for conquest and 'pacification' retreat in the face of nothing and one may note that the old adage 'the only good nigger's a dead nigger' has more often been used as the angry expression of an emotional desire than as a witty remark. The overall effect of this ideological subjugation of a subject is to cast on them, without their knowledge, a lens through which events, situations and texts may be seen, and this process works all the more easily when such a lens has previously been lacking. The mechanism for this is the coincidence of forms and signifiers that have already become familiar. Is it not likely that such metonymic entwinement, looking at the record of violence linked to colonization, conveyed the meaning of delinquency, pathological impulsiveness and 'primitiveness' both to Carothers and to the French neuro-psychiatrists in Algiers?

Colonial ideology and the French general public

Notwithstanding these assertions, during the interwar period, the French did not see themselves as colonialists or as racists. However, if I go back to the years of my childhood, I remember hearing North Africans referred to as 'bicots' ('wogs') and blacks as 'niggers'. I can also still see the special Christmas display in the shop window of the Grands Magasins du Louvre with its exhibition of the deep dark jungle of Africa filled with monkeys and cannibals. I can remember singing 'Have you seen Père Bugeaud's cap?' and it reminds me of avidly reading albums glorifying the exploits of the good Dr Livingstone and the brave Savorgnan de Brazza, even before I was able to move on to adventure books eulogizing the colonial conquest, such as *L'escadron blanc*. 'What a strange family', you may reply. Maybe, but while it may have been my parents who fed me such material, they were only making it available to me: they were not the ones who had created it. It was the national spirit of the times that created it. One only needs to cast an eye over the playground rhymes that were popular at the time:

A black woman was drinking some milk,
'Oh!', she said, 'if only I'd the chance
to dip my face into that bowl of milk,
I'd be as white as any person in France!'

That rhyme is well known, but we are less familiar with this one:

Saracen, Saracen,
We're coming to complain,
That your son, Saracen,
Is taking all our girls,
From our sheets he takes those pearls,
He's taking them away.

This next one is even less well known:

Little Chinaman from
Indochina,
if on me you start,
You I'll murder,
With a knife in the heart.

Contempt and fear are mixed together here in an outwardly perky format in which virile protest and hatred of the colonial subject are already clear. The process by which such clichés are repeated to the point of banality cannot take place without leaving its mark on the eager mind of the child, especially when it is combined with latent hostility towards North African Arabs, as exemplified by the 'dangerous' figure of the Maugrabin or the Moor in stories and legends.

However, the influence of colonial ideology spreads well beyond childhood and, something which confirms its unconscious mechanism, not only among professional categories seen as particularly vulnerable to its influence, such as settlers or the police. This is the case with the racist psychiatric school in Algiers, as was demonstrated by the publications of professors Porot and Sutter. 'The native', wrote the former in 1935, 'a severe mental defective, whose intellectual and cortical activity is very underdeveloped, is principally a primitive being whose life, mainly vegetative and instinctive, is predominantly organised through his Diencephalon', while, writing together in 1939, the two of them stated that: 'It seems that the native cannot, without risk, escape from the primitivism to which he is predestined by his race, his inheritance and his psychological constitution ...'[4] This school of teaching, whose propagation of the famous 'our ancestors the Gauls' we are already familiar with, in Africa offers us some more amusing examples. For example, the celebrated *Syllabaire de Mamadou et Bineta*, published by Davesne in 1931 and written for a readership in the colonies, was reissued numerous times with the same highly symbolic illustration. On the page for the letter 'P', which is decorated with a picture of an African peasant kneeling down near his little girl, a grand piano is used to exemplify the syllable 'pi'! It is difficult to see any rational choice in this and one should not forget that in 1927 the Ministry of Public Education was encouraging teachers to create 'a truly colonial point of view' in schoolchildren. Between these two dates, the great Colonial Exhibition had taken place in Paris, at which living 'natives' were exhibited who had been taken from among those same populations which had provided a large contingent of cannon fodder during the First World War and were to do so again during the Second World War: turcos (Algerian riflemen), zouaves, and Algerian, Moroccan and Senegalese infantrymen. All this took place in complete ignorance of African civilizations and languages, to mention but a few!

These peoples who were to be 'Frenchified' were not granted French citizenship, and were given even less in the way of rights. Meanwhile, in contrast, the project to build up a sort of colonial aristocracy, along the lines of the *pieds-noirs* or Algerian French, went ahead, even if this aristocracy was largely composed of Spanish and Italian émigrés, together with some Maltese and indigenous Jews. The slogan 'Algérie française!' ('Algeria is French!) had its origins in this, leading on to the juridical fiction that was 'the French *départements* of Algeria', and then to the belief that Algeria was actually part of France...

Colonial ideology and the French army

The hold exerted by colonial ideology did not spare the armed forces. On the contrary, the military displayed an almost megalomaniac insistence upon the belief in French techno-cultural supremacy. This superiority complex assumed a compensatory value due to the humiliations suffered by the forces in 1940, 1954 and 1956. This humiliation was not greatly assuaged by the successes of 1944, which had been permitted by a hasty re-amalgamation of three bodies that were not easily integrated: the Free French forces, troops formed out of the Resistance and the Armistice, or so-called 'Vichy army'. How can one ignore, either, the continued existence in *la Royale* (the habitual name used for the navy) and in its colonial infantry of an ideology soaked in intolerant Catholicism, rekindled by the memory it guarded of battles against British fleets and Barbary Coast pirates? This atmosphere was known about and was designed to attract exactly those people who had a yearning for expeditions to faraway parts and who, no doubt, had already been unknowingly influenced by the global expansion of the French empire. This can be juxtaposed, in the other branches of the forces, with the old unspoken dream of being the heirs of the Roman legions, as is shown by the Foreign Legion and the title of Jean Lartéguy's novel, *Les Centurions*.

Aside from these inflated aspirations, of a specifically ideological nature, it is important to underline another characteristic of the French army at this time: the tendency of some of its officers to see themselves as above the laws of the Republic. Furthermore, the civil administration, far from counteracting this, made numerous concessions, authorizing compulsory population movements, the seizure of police powers and, finally, the violation of international law (the hijacking of the Moroccan plane carrying Ben Bella, the bombing of Sakiet-sidi-Youssef, etc.). How can one then be surprised at the growing disorientation among conscripts who saw the military hierarchy breaking the law with greater and greater facility?

As far as I can recall, this combination of circumstances had resulted in the formation of very mixed impressions of the army among young people. These impressions were not improved by the efforts made to restore the reputation of the army: for example, the upgrading of popular generals to the Marshalcy. This did not erase the fingerprints of Pétain, the officer corps, indeed, having seen very little in the way of any clear-out after the liberation of France, as is recalled by Maître[5] Nordmann, who held a legal post at the Ministry of Justice at this time.[6] The aura of the citizen-soldier had been lost and military service often seemed close to penal servitude, given the extent to which the Colonel Blimps had taken the place of the citizens' army. The tragi-comedies of the 'Day of the Barricades' (24 January 1960) and then the generals' putsch (21–24 April 1961) only confirmed that, at the same time awakening some awareness of civic duty among the troops. The amnesty and rehabilitation of the mutineers, on the initiative of François Mitterrand, would unfortunately bring a belated confirmation of the unseen hold of colonial ideology.

Colonial ideology and the conscripts

The conscripts were overtaken by surprise and, even more, disorientation when they disembarked in Algeria. While they believed themselves to be serving in their own country and to have simply come to maintain order, now here they found themselves in a foreign land. It was a land with whose customs and languages they were unfamiliar, in a climate of hostility or of war, requiring the same precautions that they had seen the Nazi occupiers take in France. The shock was often severe, therefore, and the loosening of ties with the family entourage (a lack of leave and sometimes of mail) was to accentuate this further. The acceleration of the assignment to active service, often serving under NCOs made bitter by their experiences in South East Asia, generally destroyed their last defences. Identification with other privates, whether submissive or zealous, would allow military-colonial ideology to subjugate the majority. Only a few progressive Christians and communist activists preserved their critical faculties, thanks no doubt to their access to alternative or counterbalancing influences.

My own arrival on an Oran aerodrome covered with combat aircraft and helicopters[7] had surprised me less than the barbed wire, watchtowers and various weapons I encountered offering protection to military establishments. What revolted me the most, however, were the racist attitudes and language used there towards the Algerian population. I had been brought up to have respect for other human beings, and I was discovering that this no longer applied here. I did not know the half of it, either; for others, who were not so fortunate as to be doctors, the disappointment was even more severe. A paratroop officer told me of his 'shame ... at having become an occupier'. Another wrote to me at length, emphasizing that

> a lot of conscripts had experienced another war before that one, that is to say the Nazi occupation of France between 1940 and 1944. Everyone knows that the Nazis did not pussyfoot around, and that violence was a permanent aggression against my sensibilities as a child. It also involved ... seeing farms burning in the distance and men suddenly disappearing ..., it was also the petrified silences that followed the torture of members of the Resistance captured after someone had been careless or had denounced them ... that was our 'kindergarten', as Yevtushenko puts it. During a war of defeat, the child is humiliated as much as the adult, because through the adult the child feels the humiliation, as well as the fear or the hope ... Naturally, such an experience during the first ten years of your existence does not leave you particularly predisposed to go and participate in colonial wars, especially if you know them to be a lost cause from the word 'go' ...[8]

The reaction of the majority was to deaden their sensibilities, often with alcohol, to shut themselves away in silence and, above all, not to think. While obeying orders, and frequently the toughest of orders, they often used to drag their feet. This led Daniel Zimmerman to write:

> This war is not always spectacular, it is not only a matter of hunting down Arabs, of concentration camps and of torture ... it's also like a sort of creeping mould which has sullied the conscripts to their very core.
>
> *Chronique du rien* (*A Chronicle of Nothingness*)

How could these men make sense of the profound confusion they felt when the traces of colonial ideology influencing their outlook collided with their impression of having rapidly acquired a split personality, suddenly taking on this second identity as the detested occupying soldier and yet feeling disgust at the horror in which they were forced to become involved, whether at close quarters or not.

This is even more so given that, at the same time, their governments persisted in denying that there was a war taking place, and that they were covering up war crimes, taking legal action against those who dissented, and sometimes even against the victims themselves. As for the soldiers' families, they put up barriers so as to refuse to listen to them altogether. Public opinion, finally, still appeared to be oblivious to what was happening, only its feminist element engaging in political struggle ... in order to obtain the right to contraception. It is quite astounding, indeed, to note the historical synchronicity between the various stages of these two (respectively, political and military) campaigns:

	Birth control	*Algeria*
1955	Start of the controversy	Anti-war campaign
1956	*Maternité heureuse* set up	Victory of the Republican Front
1958	Transformation into Family Planning	13 May *coup de force*; arrival of De Gaulle
1960	First centre in Grenoble	First negotiations at Melun
1961	Condemnation by the Church	Generals' putsch in Algiers
1962	L'Ordre des Médecins says no	OAS opposes the ceasefire

These parallels, which I offer to stimulate debate, stop there. The explosion of male assertiveness was forced to come to an end in Algeria with the declaration of independence on 5 July 1962, while the demands of the feminists were not to be satisfied until five years later, with the Neuwirth legislation of 28 December 1967. Nevertheless, one might wonder as to whether there was a deepening of the ideological gulf between the sexes at this period in history, one which might have contributed to the intense sexualization of the war.

It is still true, however, that among the forces in Algeria, the great majority were submissive, withdrawing into themselves, something which one might attribute to what Michel Vovelle, writing about 'the history of Resistance', described as 'the force of inertia in mental structures'.[9] Others among the forces, though relatively few in number no doubt, relinquished all control over their drives and participated in illegal or inhumane activities. Roughly a quarter, however, judging by our own impressions and by making comparisons with the results of American research undertaken into the psychological condition of Vietnam War veterans, saw the cohesion of their self-regard fracture before shattering altogether, whether in the long or the short term. Nor were those who suffered such problems simply those who were the most fragile in the first place.

The picture today

There are thousands of men, many known to me and now close to retirement age, who for nearly forty years have been living a life of anguish and instability, suffering from nightmares and mood swings. Others (perhaps 10 per cent of the total group), when unexpectedly confronted with images or facts which bring back to them their experiences of war, suddenly lose their composure and fall into depression, suffer mental disorders or commit suicide. In all likelihood, the remaining traces of colonial ideology, cracked but not destroyed by the victory of the Algerians, do make some contribution to these instances of repressed feelings resurfacing or to the sudden resurgence of the death drive. What is quite certain is that they have contributed to the rise in intolerance and hostility towards North Africans in France. To psychoanalysts, who are familiar with people's propensity to put into action latent feelings which can neither be symbolized nor sublimated, this does not come as a surprise.

As regards the end of the French invasion of Algeria, in fact the things that have not yet been said, or even the things that people have been forbidden from saying, remain important. I was myself a victim of this phenomenon, as 23 years went by before I wrote about this subject. What is the most symbolically important factor, however, is that French governments since the war, so indulgent of the crimes committed by the OAS, until 1999 always refused to speak openly of the conflict as a 'war', perhaps so as better to be able to ignore the debts they owe. This is clearly the case with the war veterans, already treated unfavourably in comparison to veterans of other conflicts, who find that the psychological problems they suffer as a result of their immersion in the bloody unravelling of the colonial project are not even recognized. These psychological problems, furthermore, are either ignored or given scant attention in certain works of military psychiatry. Not a single legal or practical measure, then, has been implemented to support these veterans. It is scandalous – when one is aware of the fact that it is shame, even more than guilt, that deters them from asking for practical care or a war pension – to hear ministers use these inhibitions to refuse the veterans what was granted to US Vietnam War veterans more than twenty years ago. On 11 December 1995, the Chef de Cabinet (Principal Private Secretary) of the Ministry of Former Combatants made the following declaration: 'What emerges from the analysis undertaken is that demands for such war pensions [i.e. those in respect of psychological problems attributable to active combat in Algeria] are, in fact, few in number, which tends to give a reassuring indication as to the good state of health of veterans of the North African conflict.' This contrasts with the unequivocal response to the needs of the (fortunately far less numerous) victims of terrorism, in whose interests legislation was enacted, a national research commission was established, consultations were undertaken and a compensation fund was established.

Everything, or almost everything, then, remains to be done. This means making a start on the preliminary investigations and production of statistics (this latter requirement being one which a psychoanalyst and leading military psychiatry official attempted in vain to have the authorities act upon) to the definition of a new juridical approach that would allow victims of psychological trauma caused by war to have their problems taken into account and to receive free care. The most important thing for us still remains to exorcise the ghosts that continue to haunt the minds of those who served in Algeria, rendering them almost mute. To achieve this it is still necessary for the insidious grip very much maintained by colonial ideology to be broken sufficiently to allow us the necessary freedom (a freedom scarcely granted by the press and by television, with its propensity for cutting or postponing relevant programmes) and to allow men whose ranks are thinned every day through suicide or old age the time to do so.

Notes

1. B. Sigg, *Le Silence et la Honte – névroses de la guerre d'Algérie* (Paris: Messidor, 1989).
2. J. Derrida, *Spectres de Marx* (Paris: Galilée, 1993), p. 31.
3. N. Abraham, *L'écorce et le noyau* (Paris: Flammarion, 1987).
4. Quoted in R. Berthelier, *L'homme maghrébin dans la littérature psychiatrique* (Paris: L'Harmattan, 1994).
5. Maître is the title given to a qualified barrister.
6. M. Nordmann, *Aux vents de l'Histoire* (Paris: Actes Sud, 1996), p. 163.
7. Cf. 'Nouvelles Nouvelles: Trente ans après, nouvelles de la guerre d'Algérie', *Le Monde* (éd. 1992), p. 139.
8. Sigg, op. cit., p. 61.
9. M. Vovelle, *Idéologies et Mentalités* (Paris: Flammarion, 1982).

Part III

Witness Testimonies

15
Officer Corps Veterans

Isolating the Algerian rebellion and destroying armed bands by General Alain Bizard[1]

As a personal introduction, I would like to tell you that from an elementary stage of my education I was taught that Algeria consisted of three French *départements* and that these *départements* formed part of France before the Alpes Maritimes and Savoie regions that had only become part of France in 1860. I had suffered the humiliation of military defeat in 1940 and had spent seven years in Indochina, where I had again suffered the humiliation of French defeat. I had then been in Tunisia when I was again called to leave and arrived in Algeria, an integral part of France.

That being as it may, I shall avoid all political debate in order to content myself with military matters, completing the strategic framework outlined by Colonel Coustaux. As you have already acquired an understanding of the strategic background, it is my role to speak to you briefly about the way we isolated the uprising and then destroyed the politico-administrative infrastructure of the insurgents.

The departure of French troops from Tunisia and Morocco in 1956 and 1957 allowed rebel support bases and training camps to be set up in these two countries and, from summer 1957 onwards, armed groups which had been equipped in Tunisia started to come across into Algeria. French military command decided to construct a continuous barrier along the length of the borders of Algeria so as to prevent the infiltration of armed groups. These barriers consisted of two electrified fences, 10 metres or so apart, about 30 metres in front of which were sections of barbed wire. Mines were laid between the barbed wire and the electric fences (3,200,000 mines of various types were laid) and inside the barricade was a 10-metre wide strip of ground which the army ploughed up every day, alongside which ran a track allowing use on a nightly basis by armoured patrols. Five regiments of the Armoured Light Cavalry were allotted this role on the eastern frontier. Company posts were set up along the length of the barricades, about 15 km apart, providing power for the electric fencing and allowing any breach in that fencing to be detected. There were two such barriers, one along the Tunisian frontier and one along the Moroccan border. I will discuss mainly the barrier along the Tunisian border.

Along the Tunisian border, the barrier ran for 290 km and the railway line between Bône and Tébessa ran between the electric fencing. It was completed at the end of 1957. Subsequently, a second border barricade, about 30 km in length, which you can see on the map, was to be constructed in front of the first barricade in order to control no man's land. It started at Lakal and met up with the other barricade at Tébessa. In the flat region to the south of Tébessa, six 'radar gun' posts had been set up. It was anticipated that these would provide the finishing touch to the system, but this solution very quickly proved to be inadequate as it became clear that people were getting across during the night and, in 1958, the barricade was extended as far as Négrine.

These barriers were not of course watertight, particularly in the early days, when they had not reached the full level of sophistication I have just described. Nonetheless, they allowed the time and location of any breach in frontier security to become known very rapidly as every 10 to 15 km there were operational posts that provided a 5,000-volt electric current to the fence and allowed the time of any cut in the power supply to be known. An armoured patrol would go straightaway to check the location at which the fence had been crossed. In this manner, once it became known that the barricade had been crossed, a military operation would be launched at daybreak. A military unit would make its way to the point at which the crossing had taken place where, thanks to the many clues left at the scene, it would make an approximate assessment of the size of the group that had crossed over. This unit, known as 'la tête chercheuse' (homing device), would set off in pursuit of the rebels. Simultaneously, taking into account the time at which the crossing had been made, sector units would cordon off the zone in which the infiltrated group was to be found. Once the group had been located, one of the parachute regiment parts of the reserve behind the barrier was transported by helicopter or even by lorries, if the weather were bad, in order to destroy it. Artillery and air support supported these operations.

Between January and May of 1958, 3,320 rebels were put out of action in the vicinity of the border barriers, although, all the same, 2,700 managed to get into Algeria, carrying with them modern weapons, in particular 200 German light machine guns. Two-thirds of these insurgents got round to the southern side of the border barrier without being detected. By the end of 1958, the barriers were becoming ever more effective. In early 1959, Boumédienne, then commanding ALN forces from Tunisia, attempted several crossings. Faced with losses that he judged to be unacceptable, he gave up on the idea of trying to get his *faileks* (battalions) across the border barriers. The 8,000 fighters stationed in Tunisia were to await the ceasefire before crossing over into Algeria where, at the time of the ceasefire, furthermore, their ranks were to swell to 15,000. By 1959, the French had won the battle of the frontiers and the task remaining now was to defeat the rebels within Algeria.

'Opération Jumelles'

Colonel Coustaux has explained the nature of the Plan Challe. I shall describe for you one of the phases of this plan, Opération Jumelles. Its objective was to mop up in depth the Grande Kabylie and the western part of the Petite Kabylie, which was one of the strongholds of the rebellion. As it lay close to Algiers, this region was very important. It was also the area through which was to be constructed the pipeline that was to carry oil from the Sahara to Bougie via the Soummam valley, a well-known site as it was the setting for the famous 'Soummam conference'.

The operation started on 22 July 1959. A considerable volume of general reserve troops were deployed to supplement sectorial troops: three Foreign Legion regiments, three Tiralleurs battalions, a battalion of Fusilliers Marins, Commandos de l'Air, three regiments of the 25th Parachute Division and the entire 10th Parachute Division. General Challe took personal command of the operation from a headquarters located on one of the highest peaks of the Kabylie (Poste de Commandement (PC)Artois).

For a fortnight, a series of major operations were carried out, but with few results as the *fellaghas* avoided combat, disappearing into the bush and the holm oak forests which cover the rough terrain of the region. General Challe then decided to leave his troops in place in a more static phase so that they could pursue the mopping up of the region, each regiment being allocated a dedicated zone to deal with in liaison with sector units. Ambushes then started being set up by day and by night on all tracks and paths and in the bottom of the *oueds* across Kabylie, while the population had been moved and securely placed with SAS (Section Administrative Spécialisée).

After a few days, the *fellaghas* started coming out of hiding to get information, to stock up on provisions and water. Each night, a large number of prisoners were taken, these prisoners then being immediately moved by helicopter to the interrogation centre at the Artois HQ. A certain number of leaders and political commissars who had defected were waiting there and they found it easy to obtain information from the prisoners, information that was immediately acted upon. There was no question of any torture. I often attended interrogation sessions myself and can assure you that the whole process was very amicable. One of the rebel leaders from the locality who was familiar with the unit to which the rebel prisoner belonged would always be found and very quickly the prisoner would tell everything he knew. Then, straightaway that same day, the prisoner would be taken back to the unit so that the intelligence obtained could be acted upon that very same night. Moreover, many of these prisoners subsequently enlisted in my own company. This approach created a snowball effect. Plenty of information was obtained, rebels started to defect and members of the OPA (Politico-Administrative Organization) were arrested. Villages started to set up their own self-defence systems.

Even by 15 October, the figures already spoke volumes about the operation: 2,245 rebels had been killed, 1,073 had been taken prisoner, 149 had come over to the French side and 1,127 members of the OPA had been arrested.

The Wilaya 3 (Kabylie) was starting to suffocate. General Challe decided to continue with the mopping up and extended the area further to the east by deploying the entire 11th Infantry and 25th Paratroop Divisions in the Collo and Philippeville sectors (this was 'Opération Pierres Précieuses').

This troop deployment was to be maintained for the whole winter. The cold, the isolation and the hunger put an end to the last insurgents and the OPA was broken. The pipeline was constructed without hindrance and its security assured by auxiliary troops, of which a significant proportion had been recruited from among those who had defected or been taken prisoner during 'Opération Jumelles'.

The psychological effects of the Constantine Plan and of the destruction of the insurgents' organization were such that, in March 1960, the leaders of the Wilaya 4 asked to do a deal. They were confident of obtaining the approval of the new leader of the Wilaya 3 (who had replaced the bloodthirsty Amirouche), of the Wilaya 6, which had been under the control of the Wilaya 4 since the death of Si Houès, who had been killed near Djelfa together with Amirouche, and, finally, of the Wilaya 4, which had been greatly weakened and was now commanded from Morocco.

These rebel leaders were brought to the Elysée Palace itself, where the President received them but did not enter into negotiations with them as he had already started bargaining with the GPRA (Provisional Government of Algeria), based in Tunis. Nonetheless, this meant that three-quarters of the rebel forces remaining were seriously considering giving up the fight. Be that as it may, the Wilaya 2 and the Aurès-Némentscha Mountains still had to be cleaned up and on 4 October 1960 two parachute divisions were deployed in the Arris and Kenchela sectors.

The clean-up operation in this difficult region was still underway when the events of 22 April 1961 intervened. All operations stopped – it was now to be politics alone that would determine the fate of Algeria.

I shall add only that, in June 1960, Ferhat Abbas gave an interesting speech to the GPRA in which he described how catastrophic the state of play was, as the rebellion within Algeria and that beyond her boundaries had been completely cut off from one another. He also described how the rebels within Algeria resented the fact that their comrades outside the country did not come to their assistance.

The Algerian War: personal account of Colonel Henri Coustaux[2]

For five years I was a witness to events in Algeria; and I was a participant in those events, too. It is that which justifies my presence among you today.

As a veteran of the Indochina conflict, having graduated from the Ecole de Guerre in 1956, I chose to serve in Algeria, on the basis of which I am able to give the following account of my experiences.

At the time of the battle of Algiers, in 1956–7, I was in charge of the 3eme Bureau of the Algiers Army Corps. On 13 May 1958, and throughout the days that followed, in my role as Commanding Officer of the 1st RCP (Regiment de Chasseurs Parachutiste), I welcomed General de Gaulle and was responsible for guarding the Forum. In 1959, more particularly in July and August of that year, as officer in charge of the 1st RCP, I took part in Opérations Jumelles and Etincelles. I had the opportunity of informing General de Gaulle, when he visited, of my certainty that militarily we had won and that the French government now had the time to ensure that the outcome for Algeria involved the strongest possible role for France.

In January 1960, during the 'the week of the barricades' in Algiers, I was commanding officer of the 3rd Bureau at the staff HQ of the Commander-in-Chief, General Challe. I went to the Maison Blanche airport to collect Monsieur Debré, the Prime Minister, and Monsieur Guillaumat, the Minister of Defence, who had come as representatives of General de Gaulle. I took part in their enquiry into the situation at the headquarters of the Commander-in-Chief. In 1959, at the time of the 16 September speech, I was in command of the 1st RCP in Kabylie.

Between 1959 and 1961, after General Challe's departure, I served under two other commanders-in-chief: General Crespin and General Gambiez. I was then second-in-command at the Operations Headquarters. General Crespin, who had researched and introduced the barricades on the Moroccan border, in the Mecheria region, then greatly improved those on the Tunisian border. He took personal control over their efficient functioning and improvement. I dined at General Crespin's residence with Monsieur Tricot, General de Gaulle's representative, in order to look into the Si Salah affair.

In December 1960, while still at General HQ, I witnessed crowds of people streaming into Algiers, brandishing green and white flags. That was a day when quite a number of hopes, and even illusions, vanished. Finally, in April 1961, during the putsch, I had the office adjoining those of the four generals: Generals Challe, Salan, Jouhaud and Zeller.

Having been a witness to all these events, which often went beyond the strictly military, if I can phrase it that way, I am here to speak to you about the strategy of the army in Algeria. Obviously that is what I shall do, but my purpose in citing all these major events is that they may serve to justify the following warning to you: while outcomes in the field in Algeria may have constituted a great success, I do not consider that the military activity and success of the army was the main factor in the outcome of the conflict. Too many other considerations, desires and pressures, both national and international in scale, exerted an influence for this to be the case. Be the nature of these factors political, partisan, human or other, from 1958 onwards they competed for the attention of the dominant figure of de Gaulle making it impossible to view the activities and achievements of the army in the field as decisive.

That does not mean that the struggle of the army in the field was of no significance. For our purposes, I shall limit my account of that struggle as much as possible to its strategic aspects (the theme of army tactics will then be addressed by General Bizard of the Army Corps, who was the most outstanding captain at my disposal in the 1st RCP). Furthermore, in order not to exceed the limitations of the time that has been allocated to me, I shall schematize and simplify my account.

I shall start with the mission of the army. Despite the different attitudes and various uncertainties under French governments from Guy Mollet to de Gaulle, this mission never changed throughout the years of the Algerian conflict.

The mission was:

1. To pacify Algeria. This would be achieved by firstly protecting the civilian population (both *pieds-noirs* and Muslims) against the rebels and gradually facilitating their active involvement in the fight against the rebels, using the means at their disposal of contributing to that struggle, that is to say the *harkis*, self-defence groups and *moghaznis*). Secondly by re-establishing confidence in France through the introduction of political and economic reforms, and thirdly by using psychological tactics supported by assurances that the French presence in Algeria was a permanent one and that the colonial system would undergo fundamental reform based upon political, social, cultural and economic integration and equality.
2. To crush the uprising and, in particular, to destroy or at least neutralize the principal units (*faileks*, *katibas*) that the units responsible for pacification were unable to deal with, either because they were too large and were concentrated in areas to which it was difficult to obtain access or because they made use of sanctuaries across the borders of friendly neighbours.

The enemy

The rebel military organization employed in succession by the FLN, the ALN and the GPRA always remained the same.

Within Algeria itself, five *wilayas* plus a sixth, less active, such zone in the Sahara sustained small local groups of *djounouds*. These groups were mobile, possessed few weapons and did not stray far from tightly restricted local areas. They also sustained larger units that progressively took on the combat and mobility potential of well-organized, well-armed regular units and operated across wide areas and from hideouts, generally in mountainous areas.

On the whole, the Algerians, like the Moroccans, were tough fighters. When armed with guns, they liked to use them.

Outside Algeria, in Morocco and, particularly, in Tunisia, where the Bourguiba government was welcoming and sympathetic to them, the rebel forces consisted of armed units that were of a significant size and well-equipped. Boumédienne's switch from Morocco to Tunisia made the Tunis-based ALN the more important force.

The sea offered the rebels their most convenient route for supplying arms to their units inside Algeria.

In France, which was divided up into *wilayas*, the uprising benefited from every possible sort of connivance. The role here was to collect and send to Algeria the money needed to finance the war.

The leaders were of prime importance in the Algerian uprising: for example, Krim Belkhacem and then Amirouche in Kabylie, and Boumédienne in Morocco and then Tunisia, and Ben Bella in Oran occupied a pivotal role. Eliminating them was very important; it led to disorganization and had serious consequences when it took place.

Geography

There are two aspects to the geography of the conflict. Firstly the terrain was extremely varied. It included major cities, such as Algiers, Constantine and Oran, that were well suited to spectacular and murderous bombings. It also featured fertile plains (the Mitidja region), that provided food and were the source of fresh supplies, high plateaux that were cultivated, fertile and heavily populated (the Hodna region) and mountains covered in forest and boulders and cut through by deep canyons. This latter terrain constituted the ideal setting for conducting guerrilla warfare.

Secondly there was the impact of demographics. The population was the real battleground in the midst of which military activity took place. From the war in Indochina we knew that the real battleground of the war would be the civilian population. People were concentrated in towns or grouped in villages (the scarcity of water sources meant there were few isolated dwellings). They were not hostile to us, but were generally afraid both of the rebels and of ourselves.

We had to make use of this population, or at least to prevent it from helping the FLN, in particular to prevent it from providing the FLN with supplies. The next step would be to pacify it and win it over to our cause.

Resources

In the case of military resources, I shall be referring principally to those available to General Challe, as it is of his period of command that I can offer personal testimony. The French army had 380,000 men at its disposal, the majority of whom were conscripts.

These were the only resources available to Challe and, in his view, they were not enough to meet the task. From the first, this war was not going to be a war based upon equipment, but was to be a great consumer of manpower.

Challe had received authorization to recruit 60,000 *harkis* locally. He had only 28,000 *harkis* in 1958, though this figure was to be exceeded in 1959. To increase the dynamism of the sectorial forces, Challe made increasing use of *commando de chasse* groups (74 by April 1959) that indicated the position of the *katibas*, fed back information and could call on the assistance of the ALAT (Army Aviation) if they engaged a rebel group in combat. Twenty thousand *moghaznis* (soldiers from Algerian units) were taken on and put at the disposal of 661 SAS (Special Administrative Sections) sections and 27 SAU sections so as to defend villages and the civilian population.

Challe needed a lot of personnel both to 'occupy the terrain by night and by day', as he always advocated should be done, and to make up his general reserve troops, with which he planned to destroy the big battalions of the ALN. Above all, he wanted young active officers of high quality. For the pacification phase, in particular, he wanted offensive-minded officers. He asked for them, but wasn't allocated as many as he wanted.

To make up his troop mass, he was obliged to relieve certain large units of their *quadrillage* roles, so as to integrate them either into the reserves or into the mobile troop units on the frontier barriers. It was in this way that the 7th DMR came to be removed from the Mitidja region and transferred onto the Tunisian border barriers.

Finally, there were the parachute divisions, including the 10th Parachute Division, which had returned from Suez and had been freed from its duties in Algiers. These divisions were to make up the hard core of Challe's strike force.

The navy was to maintain control of the whole coastline, in liaison with the air force, guarding in particular against the importation of arms. Navy and air force were to provide fire support to the army. They were also to set up commando groups, which were to prove particularly effective.

Commander's intent and its application

There were three elements to the operational strategy: pacification, the frontier barriers and large offensive operations.

I will put at the core of this operational strategy the constant gathering, analysing and use of intelligence. One of the principal lessons from the war in Indochina was the vital need for intelligence. This is true of all wars, but it is particularly so in the new forms of warfare fought in the midst of the population. Furthermore, intelligence was not just the prerogative of the specialized services, or of the 2 Bureaux. It was everyone's primary mission, all the way to the bottom of the military hierarchy, where one was in contact with the population, the major source of information. It was also the mission of those who captured prisoners, of those who engineered or took advantage from the defections of rebels and of the infiltrated elements. (Major Léger will be able to give you a better account than I can.)

Another major feature of intelligence is that it must be used in a timely fashion as the enemy was particularly mobile.

That said, the plan of action and manoeuvre consisted of, first, putting the appropriate territorial infrastructure (sectors, quarters, military posts, screens, etc.) in place across the whole area where we wished to maintain a permanent presence, using assets that Challe wanted to be more and more mobile, based around fixed positions that were to be maintained. In these areas, pacification was the objective.

I can vouch for the fact that it would be an error to think of the Plan Challe as simply having been the famous 'steamroller', as the media called it. Challe wanted to pacify, protect, convince and win people over to the French cause, and gradually move from protection provided by the army to self-defence. In the time available, it is impossible to describe all the military, psychological and human elements of pacification. To complement the orders he had already given, Challe tasked his HQ to prepare 'Pacification Directives' covering its objectives and methods. I was part of the writing up of these directives. I must state that this substantial undertaking, which was supervised by the General himself, was not a simple one. The obstacle we came up against was that we were constantly imprecise as to the future we were offering. In this regard, we inevitably remained in a state of political flux. In Algeria a lot of things were said that could not be written down.

When it came out at the end of 1959, the document did not include the phrase ('Algérie française') that the majority of combatants were still using. In contrast to our difficulties in writing the document, General Challe himself drafted the long introduction in one go (and he wrote only rarely), in his magnificent handwriting and using green ink, without a single hesitation or crossing out.

The second aspect of the plan of action was the barriers built along the frontiers. These had two major goals: firstly to prevent the ALN within Algeria from receiving reinforcements in men and weapons; secondly to undermine the morale of the rebels in Algeria by isolating them. The guarding of the frontiers was completed along the coast by the navy and from the air. In the Sahara this was done by reconnaissance patrols.

The third aspect of the plan comprised the major operations to search and destroy the main rebel units. Challe, who had considered the problem in some depth and had drawn certain conclusions, appreciated the extent to which these operations, if they achieved their principal goal, could have a negative effect on the ground, due to their obvious morale and material after-effects the population had suffered. In effect the population suffered as the fighting could occur among it, or at best after they had left the area. One avoids such difficulties by instructing the troops to make every effort so that the population would be spared. I can attest to the fact that this order was taken seriously. My regiment never fought in a village. Furthermore, two methods were found and put into practice to offset the disadvantages resulting from these operations.

The first method was to move the populations and relocate them to controlled and protected areas. The ALN found refuge in the mountainous regions, where one can find both substantial numbers of people and significant food supplies. Here it lived off the population, exploiting it and holding it to ransom. By relocating the local inhabitants, the ALN was deprived of a source of supplies and of all sorts of assistance and there would be no need for civilians to become caught up in the fighting.

Was this a judicious response? With the 1st Regiment of Parachute Chasseurs, I had the opportunity to organize and lead the evacuation of the Jebel Hodna and the relocation of the local population to Sétif. After 20 days of military engagement on this high plateau, we had either eliminated or chased from the area all rebel groups located there. The commanding officer for the area then decided to relocate the local civilian population. The Hodna, a plateau and breadbasket for cereal crops, was inhabited by a contented and hardworking people, people I would even describe as rich. Their relocation, which was perhaps justified in itself, brought with it many disadvantages: the bad living conditions in the camps, due to the lack of financial resources for their facilities, the detrimental material and psychological consequences suffered by the people moved and the fact that they then became propaganda targets for the rebels. In fact, a few months after the Hodna was cleared of its population, the 1st Regiment of Parachute Chasseurs took part in Opération Etincelles (Operation Sparks) there, and there was nobody to be found. However, I think that in general the outcomes of these population relocations were of debatable merit.

Secondly from 1958 to the end of 1959, the focus for the deployment of the general reserves shifted from the west to the east. Challe started from

Oranie where pacification was showing clear signs of success (Dahra, Saida, Ouarsenis). As a matter of priority, this achievement needed to be bolstered and protected against the actions of rebel groups, particularly those in the Saharan Atlas. This was to be the operation in the ZOAS (Zone Operationalle de l'Atlas Saharien), in which I took part and during which, on 19 November 1958, we were involved in a very difficult clash with the enemy.

Challe had decided to give up on small-scale operations, which provided an ineffective response unless based upon up to date and reliable intelligence. If the latter was not the case, the rebels would simply scatter or flee the area. Challe also wanted to avoid the detrimental impact of such operations upon the *quadrillage*. So as to avoid this he applied two methods.

- Firstly, he put the reserves under the command of local commanding officers (zones, sectors). Challe personally took charge only of Jumelles, due to the importance of this operation.
- Secondly, jointly with local troops, he organized long operations that would leave a given area, definitely free of large rebel units, but also where pacification had been continuous, and could restart and progress.

In 1959, after the operations in the ZOAC, the following operations took place:

- initial operations in Oranie from 10 February to 3 March;
- from 18 April to 19 June, Opération Courroie in the Atlas Tellien in the north of Cheliff. At the same time, under the command of the sector commanders, the 10th Parachute Division, operating on a regiment level and acting upon intelligence, dealt with part of Kabylie and the western Constantine region of Les Portes de Fer, to the east of Bou Saada. It was there that my regiment and the 6th RPC took part in operations, under the orders of the General commanding Kabylie, or sectorial commanders such as those of Borj Bou Arrerich and Aumale. It was during these operations that Amirouche, the commander of the 3rd Wilaya, and Si Haouez, the commander of the 6th Wilaya, were killed;
- from 8 to 20 July, Opération Etincelles in the Hodna region;
- from 24 July onwards, Opération Jumelles in Kabyle;
- from 6 September onwards, Opération Rubis;
- from 2 November onwards, Opération Turquoise;
- from 6 November onwards, Opération Emeraude;
- from 9 November onwards, Opération Topaze.

The latter four operations took place in the northern part of the Constantine region, between Bougie and Bône. They were extended in 1960 with the major operations in the Aurès Mountains.

Was the Plan Challe a military success? My answer is yes.

I had the opportunity to express this opinion to General de Gaulle in Kabylie. The ALN within Algeria was largely destroyed. It was undermined by internal arguments and purges; seeing the ALN in Tunis as too passive, it blamed it for its lack of arms.

In Tunisia, Boumedienne was aware of his inability to intervene as the frontier barriers became more and more efficient. From the end of Opération Courroie onwards, the British and American press, which had previously been quite negative, wrote about our successes. In the *Sunday Times*, Richard Neville wrote: 'for the first time, military victory is within the reach of the French Army'. Following his visit to Kabylie, de Gaulle himself sent a message to Challe expressing his satisfaction and noting the significant progress in the pacification campaign, particularly in those areas where Challe concentrated his principal effort.

However, I am aware of the historical slant I have given to my account thus far. Given that I was invited here as a witness and participant to these events, my conclusion will adopt a more personal tone.

On 20 March 1959, I had been injured during bitter fighting in the Bibans mountains, in which the 1st RCP wiped out a powerful, well-armed *katiba*. During my short convalescence, General Challe visited me in Algiers and suggested that I join him at his HQ. In October 1959, as my time as commanding officer was drawing to a close, I accepted his invitation. In Algiers, I was able to get a broader view of the situation than that which I had been able to obtain from the *djebels* where, with my morale bolstered by the fighting, the bravery and extraordinary self-sacrifice of my men, I had obtained an impression of things that was more optimistic, but also incomplete. When I pinned the Croix de la Valeur Militaire on the coffins of my soldiers, I couldn't imagine that they had died for nothing. To boost my own morale and to hide my emotions, I would raise my voice to say to them: 'Thanks to your sacrifice, Algeria will remain French.'

During 1960, I was sent to Paris as Deputy Chief of Staff by General Crépin, to report back on the situation, where I met General Ely (Ministry of Defence Chief of Staff), General Olie (Chief of Staff attached to the President) and M. Guillaumat (Minister of Defence) on numerous occasions. I made a point of describing and emphasizing to all of them the poor state of morale of the army as a whole. It was probably due to the recollection of these objective but nevertheless alarming reports that General Olie generously and courageously came to my defence when I was imprisoned at La Santé in Paris after the putsch.

My position, which I explained to my officers in Kabylie as early as 17 September 1959, was that the army, because, of the affection it was held in by the French and Muslim populations, as well as the *anciens combattants,* its successes, its presence and especially its cohesion, would influence the direction taken in future decision-making and would even, once the decisions were taken, have a say in how they were put into practice.

My mistake was to be unaware of, or to underestimate, so many other factors: different international and national opinions, priorities and pressures; the incomprehension, disapproval, weariness, hostility or, at best, indifference, felt by the French people, as with the Indochina conflict; and the disquiet of the conscripts, who were anxious to return home. I shall end this rather incomplete list by the evocation of de Gaulle's personality. He remained a justification and a reference point for the troops and the different populations, and especially vis-à-vis himself.

My conclusion, then, brings me back to my introduction, which is how it should be, and my conclusions have not changed in 35 years. The army was, especially at the end of General Challe's period in command, the author of indisputable military successes. Were they sufficient? Was sufficient advantage taken of them?

Personal account of Chef de Batallion Paul-Alain Léger[3]

Having listened to the elevated contributions on politics, tactics, strategy and even psychoanalysis that have been presented to you, I now ask this worthy company to put itself at the level of a young paratroop captain, the man I was in early 1957. In other words, I am asking you to return to a more basic level: to what, in French, we refer to as 'the level of the daisies'. Only too often, alas, the destiny of Algeria and her peoples has been forged on the fields of battle and the daisies that have grown there have often been stained with blood.

Initially, I would like to take you back a little bit, though not too far as the period I mean is the second half of the 1950s. Firstly, however, I should give one warning, which is that I shall be obliged to speak in the first person. I appreciate that this may be a bit strange and may grate somewhat, but it is unavoidable, given that I was a participant in the events that I am going to describe. I am sure you will appreciate that I accept full responsibility for this.

Let us go back, then, to the second half of the 1950s. In August 1956, the Soummam Conference took place, out of which the CNRA (National Council of the Algerian Revolution) was set up. The Council consisted of 17 members and 17 deputy members, although the majority of the deputy members were not actually to be nominated. The CCE (Coordinating and Executive Committee), whose members were Krim Belkacem, Benkhedda, Benhamdane, Benali and Dahlab, who did not attend the conference, was chosen from among members of the CNRA. The CCE took a decision to take to the *maquis*, but they definitely preferred to be based at Alger which they considered as an urban *maquis*. Furthermore, Yacef Saadi was already based at the Algiers Casbah. From the age of 29, in 1950, Yacef Saadi, the son of the owner of a bakery and a public bathhouse and, incidentally, a very good footballer, had put himself at the disposal of the FLN, which had given him the responsibility for numerous assignments in France and in Switzerland, where he had met Boudiaf. It was on this latter occasion that he had been arrested by the Swiss police, who handed him over to the French authorities.

According to the history of the affair, he had offered to help the French police but, in any case, had been released and, on his return to Algiers, had been forgiven by Abane Ramdane. It seems that Abane demanded that he prove himself in the company of his associate and subordinate Amar Ali, known as 'Ali la Pointe', who was a petty pimp at Pointe Pescade, hence his nickname Ali la Pointe. Furthermore, the latter had hastened to take in hand the Muslim underworld of the Casbah, whose members were mostly armed due to their 'activities', and were well connected to the European underworld of Pescade. This assignment had been given to one Mohamed Ben Ali, known as 'Ali les yeux bleus', who, by the way, got arrested.

On my arrival in Algiers in February 1957, then, I could no longer recognize at all the city I had known a few years previously. Like a metaphor for the prevailing insecurity, the inhabitants – the Europeans as well as the Muslims, I should add – bore in their faces the signs of their fear and also of the suspicion that they felt towards one another. The fear of violence hung in the air as the women, both Muslim and European, would push their children onto trams or into shops. As they knew, the explosion of bombs was not unheard of.

Completely isolated from the European parts of the city, the Casbah had become the impenetrable hideout of the FLN. The gulf between the two communities grew ever wider and deeper. This gulf was further exacerbated by rebel attacks, but also, I have to say, by the unpredictable and irrational 'ratonnades'[4] of the Europeans. The police were powerless to halt the insidious undermining process that resulted from the FLN leadership using terrorism for propaganda purposes. Despite the setback suffered by the rebels in January 1957, with the outbreak of the great strike, apart from a few *zouave* patrols, the old town was out of the control of the authorities.

It was clear that some means needed to be found to fight back against such an opponent. Myself, I heard them referred to by some as terrorists and by others as rebels and people would talk about urban guerrillas, saying that it was just like in France. They were all terrorists. I don't think so. That's not how we saw it. I can accept those who fought openly in the djebels as real active combatants, but personally I must say that I have never approved of just placing a bomb somewhere or sticking a bullet in the back of someone's head while they're looking at a shop window. I feel able to say this quite openly as I had no time at all for the incidents of a similar nature that took place in France, down in the Metro or wherever.

At Algiers I met again with Colonel Trinquier, under whose command I had served in Indochina. With the agreement of the political authorities,

Trinquier had set up an urban protection system, the organization of which was very simple: the city was divided into a number of zones, comprising buildings and blocks of houses. These buildings or blocks had each been allocated letters and/or numbers and the police had been given the task of marking these figures on them with white paint, all the data being recorded on a plan of the city. The various individual elements of this system were supervised by volunteers or appointees, whose principal task was to indicate the arrival or departure of residents of a building etc. This system was put into place very quickly in the European part of the city but, obviously, a lot more difficulty was encountered in the Casbah. The problems were not so much to do with putting letters or numbers on houses, but above all in appointing people to take on the responsibility and in getting them to understand the nature of their role. This was a problem we, and those on the other side, feared as well. In the European part of the city, then, things went very well.

So without wishing to underestimate the achievements of this system, I immediately took the view that we needed to set up a tailor-made and organized structure for collecting and analysing intelligence so as to get hold of information from the very heart of the enemy organization. As I was convinced that tangible results could only be obtained with the support and involvement of members of the Muslim community, my preference was that they should form an essential part of the recruitment process. There were three principal structures to the organizational system. The first, which was one of Trinquier's ideas, consisted of recruiting a certain number of unemployed veterans and, after having put them through an intelligence course, offering them employed positions with firms. The idea then was that they would work within the firm, listening and reporting back. I barely need to say that this method did not provide the intelligence that had been anticipated, and this was to be expected, once these brave chaps had their position with the firm, they'd be wary about saying anything at all and if I happened to call them in they'd tell me that everything was going well, everything was fine and there was nothing to worry about. I thought that it was better to recruit action men, rather than dithering individuals. So I decided, instead, to approach the enemy directly, in this case people we knew about whose names appeared in important positions in the enemy organization charts and who had been arrested. The method had already been tried in Indochina. The idea was to have a chat, as we had assessed that we could not use any information provided under duress or after brutality had been used, because we automatically found ourselves dealing with false information that was seriously misleading.

In the beginning, I had a European officer under me, a fine blond-haired, blue-eyed lad, together with an NCO who was a 'colossus', and despite his name, was a French Muslim, who had served in Indochina. These were the two officers at my command. However, little by little, I then managed to assemble a small group, following the arrest of a number of leaders, in particular Amara Ali, known as Alilou and one of the subordinates of Yacef, and Faas Said who had been a subordinate of Mourad, respectively the political and military leaders in the autonomous area of Algiers, then under the command of Yacef Saadi. I had quite candid discussions with them as I was certain of my mission. I told them that this was a civil war and that we were all Frenchmen. I also told them that I had spent a large part of my youth in Sétif in Algeria, on the high plateaux, and that in that town there was a chemist's shop run by a man named Ferhat Abbas, who was a friend of my father's. Ferhat Abbas often used to come to our house. I was 14 at the time, but I remember perfectly well how, when he spoke with my father, he used to ask him: 'Well now, when is the French government going to get round to giving us French nationality, just like the French citizenship that you gave to the Algerian Jews?' That was the question I always remember hearing and I draw your attention to it now. In the course of some long discussions, I explained to them that I saw them as Frenchmen. Whether their names were Mohammed, Djamel or Said, to me it was just the same as if they were called Paul, Pierre or Jean.

Having recruited some leaders, then, the next task was to go in search of intelligence where that intelligence was to be obtained, namely among the people themselves. I asked for authorization from Colonel Godard to go into the Casbah with a few men, 'a few' being four or five as these were all we had at our disposal. We would go armed, of course, and dressed according to the fashion of the time, for young people particularly, that is in 'Chauf' blue. This, moreover, was the system used by the FLN people, allowing them to carry a submachine gun under their jackets. When I explained this to Colonel Godard, he asked me if I was mad. 'If you want to get yourself killed, that's your business, but what I won't accept is for you to allow the rebels to get their hands on more submachine guns'. He categorically refused my request. Fortunately, he was due to go on leave the following day and I took advantage of his absence to carry out my intention of infiltrating the very centre of FLN power, namely the Casbah, and impose the contrary to what the FLN had ordered. The FLN had, for example, forbidden smoking, the punishment for those that did not obey this order was to cut one's lips and nose with a razor. It was similarly forbidden to listen to the radio and anyone caught listening to Radio Alger, even if it was Arab music, had their ears cut. So when we got in the Casbah, we went into the first bistrot that we saw. Of course, we passed round cigarettes and it so happened that the people there thought that we were FLN brothers, especially when we passed round the cigarettes and asked for the radio to be put on as loudly as possible. Then Alilou told them that the orders of the Front were no longer valid and we were now in command. So that's how we did it. There we were in the evening, we had set off for the

Casbah in the morning, listening to music, the radio was on, everyone smoking and playing dominoes.

It is quite clear that the operation was a success, but only, it has to be emphasized, a relative success. We needed to go much farther. We needed to go much farther in that the discipline of the FLN, imposed by the FLN itself, was enforced, in particular, by groups of young men, the self-proclaimed shock troops, that were not very dangerous. In general, these were young men aged between 17 and 22 or 23, but who were clearly unemployed and who had been given the responsibility for enforcing orders that were given. So I won these people over and proceeded with them in the same way as I had with the more high-profile rebels. I left them exactly as they were, under the control of their own leaders, asking only that they should do precisely the opposite of what they had been asked to do previously. I have to say that they fulfilled this role perfectly, all the more so since these young people were flattered just to be given duties to carry out and a little card to be kept more or less in secret – and which, furthermore, had no real value whatsoever. They were very happy indeed with this situation.

This meant that the people of the Casbah started to get involved, but of course what remained was to arrest the principal FLN leaders, particularly Mourad, Hamel and the military and political subordinates of Yacef, or to ensure that they were no longer in any position to do any harm. Through intelligence obtained in this way, Mourad and Hamel were eliminated in the Place St Vincent Paul in the Casbah and, a little later, Yacef was arrested using the same means. Obviously, as I only have five minutes left, I cannot explain the whole story to you, but I shall give my explanation when you ask me questions at the end. All that I can say is that the arrest of Yacef, the death of 'Ali la Pointe' and the arrest of the final political agent in the Casbah came about precisely as a result of the use of these same methods, namely as a result of our having taken the place and the appeal of the rebels themselves. We established contacts and messengers with Yacef and his band. After the arrests, these contacts continued in the 3rd Wilaya, that is to say all the insurgents in Amirouche's command. In fact, I sent representatives to the Yahout meeting and my representative came back with a piece of paper, which declared him to be the political and military leader of the new autonomous area of Algiers. That is to say that, in reality, I myself was in command of the autonomous area of Algiers!

I spent three days out in guerrilla country, collecting arms – submachine guns, handguns, grenades, etc. Exchanges were kept up for a period of six months and, obviously, during that time, there were no rebel attacks. The only attacks that took place were phoney attacks that I organized myself in order to make Amirouche believe that a rebel organization truly existed in the Algiers area. All this had to end someday. He had promised me what he called 'fishes', that is to say large bombs to plant in Algiers. As, on the other hand, I had no desire at all to set off a device like this, I went myself to get hold of these 'fishes' from the insurgents as part of an operation in which the paratroopers from the 1st RCP came looking for me as I occupied the HQ of the 3rd Wilaya rebel area and, of course, I was in regular contact with them.

Some time after this, they realized that they were surrounded by traitors, something which was false, and, of course, among the insurgents there was a certain Captain Mayouf who started to torture a good number of his subordinates. While I am talking about torture, I'll give you an example: the 'helicopter' is what he called torture, the form of torture that he practised. The unfortunate victim would be hung from a pulley above a 'kanoun', that is to say a brazier, naked, of course, and with their feet attached to their back. Then they would be lowered above the burning embers until they talked. I don't want to go into that any further. You will see shortly how accounts can be given about all sorts of events from this period and all sorts and numbers of names can be denounced for the part they played in it. So that is what happened and then purges took place on a large scale, both in the 3rd Wilaya, in the first instance, then, later, in the 4th Wilaya. Then, finally, the sequel to all this was the Si Salah affair, but that is quite another matter. I thank you for your time and attention.

Notes

1. Translation of the conference speech by General Alain Bizard edited by Alexander J. Zervoudakis.
2. Direct translation by Alexander J. Zervoudakis of the original text; the style of Colonel Coustaux's text has been preserved.
3. Direct translation by Alexander J. Zervoudakis of the conference speech by Chef de Batallion Léger. A full and comprehensible account of the activities of Paul-Alain Léger during the conflict can be found in his memoirs, *Aux carrefours de la guerre* (Paris: Plon, 1983).
4. Translator's note: *ratonnade* – rat-hunt or Arab-bashing, derivative from *raton,* the derogatory *pied-noir* slang word for an Arab; not to be confused with the military term *ratissage* which means 'search of an area'.

16
Anti-War Activists

Testimony of André Mandouze

Our English friends from Salford and Portsmouth should be congratulated on their decision to meddle in matters of internal conflict in French history, of internal conflict in Algerian history and of conflict between French and Algerians. There are times when it is important for matters to be looked at afresh from a different viewpoint. From my own experience working in universities, I know that a university needs someone to come from outside to offer a dispassionate assessment of the institution so I congratulate the English historians who have facilitated this debate about the Algerian War.

Indeed the conference organizers were audacious enough to invite me to speak on the topic of the Algerian 'War', as opposed to the Algerian 'Affair' (*les événements*). That was the term that was employed for so long and put the armed forces, and particularly the armed forces facing combat situations, in such an impossible position. That really was idiocy in the extreme. On that theme, I should like to pass on an amusing anecdote. It came about when I was testifying at the trial of Francis Jeanson, this being the very same time that de Gaulle himself had just used the phrase for the first time. On the day before I was due to take the stand, Paul Teitgen had uttered the word 'war', which had made the presiding judge start and Teitgen had said to me 'So, you're going to dare to criticize de Gaulle, are you?' So, having witnessed that, the next day I spoke of the Algerian 'War' and the response of the presiding judge certainly merits repetition: 'Yes, that's alright, Monsieur le Professeur, you can use that description now, but, I beg you, please use it as little as possible.' So a whole façade came into existence, one that our English friends are helping to fracture. I am grateful for their contribution.

I made my contribution to the Algerian War Conference only as a modest replacement for my friend Pierre Vidal-Naquet who was unable to attend. He is well qualified to speak about this matter and about the issue of torture in particular. He is a man who is prepared to give a lot but who is often very tired so I know that his absence was due only to necessity. It so happens that there is a distinction between my position with regard to the Algerian War and that of the French intellectual class as a whole, even where the individuals concerned were people with whom I stood shoulder to shoulder at the barricades. Obviously, I had a certain feeling of superiority, or at least of being different, as I was conscious of having lived in Algeria for a total of 16 years, the ten years from 1946 to 1956 and then the six years between 1963 and 1968. This means that, having been deeply immersed in the problems of the Algerian people, I have perspectives on the matter that maybe even the best among my friends and colleagues do not have. It is for this reason that my views should not be seen as representative, rather they will stand out as somewhat different for precisely the reasons I have outlined. I sometimes argued with Fernand Braudel, a man I am proud to have been able to call a good friend, about this very matter. On returning from Algeria, I told Fernand Braudel that I had just written an article about what I had just seen there that was to be titled 'Witness, Participant, Historian'.[1] He told me that I could not do this, but I insisted that I could and that is what you will see in my contribution here: my experiences as a witness of events, my personal involvement as a participant and my account as a historian. The reader may justifiably feel that there is a lack of clarity and distinction between these three elements of my contribution, but often we do not have complete control over how we live our lives. My work, my personal experiences and my active contribution all took place in Algeria during this period of history and at times it is beyond my powers to separate them.

On this subject, I would claim that we start with the witnesses who are going to follow us. It is a tricky exercise because we ourselves are not there, I do not have my academic hat on, of course. I have ceased to be my normal self and am present only as a witness and that is a difficult issue to tackle. It is us that carry the can at the end of the day.

In my view, the theme on which I was invited to make my contribution, 'The widening of the war in practice on French society', is a very good one. By 'widening' I understand, firstly, the spread of the rebellion. Previously people did not know much about it but after this they will know a little bit more. Furthermore, this opportunity to put some things on the record came at an opportune moment as I was writing my memoirs and had just finished chapter fifteen, the very title of which was '1956' and which, as you would expect, covered everything that happened during that year. The focus on that year is entirely justified because, as I wrote myself in the relevant chapter, that was precisely when all the problems concerning Algeria really came to a head. The influence that an individual can have is limited but those who have read my work or to whom I have spoken will be aware of the importance of that period.[2] I should remind you, indeed, that it was only in early 1956 that, for the first time, full-scale demonstrations in favour of independence took place.

Secondly, by 'widening' I mean the internationalization of the Algerian question. The UN became involved and it ceased to be a matter concerning only France and Algeria. Throughout the course of the year there were advances and retreats but by the end of the year the issue had become more clear-cut. The image of the subservient yes-men was exposed as a myth and we had the 61 deputies who called for the National Assembly to be dissolved, which heralded a new phase in proceedings. On 22 April it was not only Tewfik el Madani that we saw leave for Cairo but also Ferhat Abbas, and Ahmed Francis too. Then not long afterwards Abderrahmane Farès adopted a stance in favour of negotiations. As a result, I believe that it must be plain to all that this year represented a turning point, not least as it was the year of the Soummam Conference. On the subject of the Soummam Conference I should like to retell another amusing little anecdote linking me to that conference in a way that I only learnt about myself after the event. I am passing on this personal anecdote only to show how deeply ingrained, when it came to the Algerians, was the suspicion in the minds of French politicians and civil servants. This was how it came about that, when officials at the French Ministry of Defence got hold of a copy of a document produced by the famous FLN 'platform', none of these top strategists could believe that the Algerians were capable of having drawn up such a considered and well-structured document. Furthermore, one of them felt himself in a position to announce that he recognized the handwriting of the author of the document (though where he could have recognized it from is another matter) and that this provided the cast-iron proof of my involvement in the uprising. A colleague and associate of mine was present at the commission and later told me about the incident and the great difficulty that he had had to persuade his colleagues, on the basis of his own extensive experience of the Resistance, of the plausibility of the idea that the document had been produced by the Algerians. If he had not been there, then I would have been able neither to share these recollections nor to have attended any conference on the Algerian War for the very good reason that I would have been quickly done away with as a westerner guilty of collaboration with the enemy. This was a scenario both logical to their minds and imaginatively fabricated.

Now that I have recounted that episode, I should specify my position, or how I see my role vis-à-vis the intellectual class in general as regards the nature of this 'widening'. In particular, I should like to take on the same role as a man who was greatly feared, and was a very close friend of mine, namely Henri Marrou, a great historian. It was in 1956 that he wrote his famous paper, 'France ma patrie' (France, my homeland), which I have never seen in newspaper article form but which was published in *Le Monde* on 5 April. In that article he wrote some things that were just as fresh as they had been when he had been in the Resistance. There was something he wrote that was absolutely true: 'Who are they trying to fool when they say that the *fellaghas* are just a disparate and disorganized bunch of known criminals, religious fanatics and agents of Egyptian imperialism? In any case, it certainly cannot be us, the veterans of the Resistance Movement, who know how a guerrilla movement operates and that they cannot sustain their struggle without the deep-rooted sympathy of at least a large proportion of the civilian population.' If we move on to the matter of torture, I am unable to avoid comparisons with the Gestapo and so on. It is a matter of general knowledge where this all led for the politicians and the powers that be. In any case, he had a little visit and they threw his papers around and mocked him to his face, talking about 'our lovely little lecturers'.

There was Henry Marrou, Claude Bourdet, my friend Robert Barrat, the priests from the Mission de France (French Mission) and Monsieur Robert Lacoste, a Minister who disagreed with the policy and was kept at arm's length, and the involvement of these people should not be forgotten. The thing that really annoyed them, they said, was to be outflanked on the left by the clerics. Then that little article entitled 'L'Espoir Algérien' ('The Hope for Algeria') was published and distributed for a short period of time before being banned for three years. Without going into too much detail, it is necessary to situate ourselves with regard to the historical background and we can then move on to get a broader view of things.

My disagreement with Camus, which came about in the December, resulted from his opinion that it would be possible for a truce to be negotiated, something I completely disagreed with. He had left Algeria by this stage and we were no longer in agreement about the way forward. Then there was Ferhat Abbas. I was seen in two very different fashions. At one meeting, it really was the last straw and, for good reasons that I shall explain, I deliberately did not hold back. I said that as of that very morning the terror campaign and the national resistance movement were present in Algiers; what I said, specifically, was that they were everywhere, even in Algiers itself. 'There are still those', I added, 'who will not believe that they are walking past members of the ALN in the street on an everyday basis'. I then moved onto the matter that was really the key point. 'If you want to put pen to paper, negotiations could begin tomorrow. The combatants could enter into dialogue with the French government and reconciliation between the two peoples could be achieved by tomorrow.' This was all a front, though what I was saying was true, but I was really in Paris for quite another reason. That very day I had been summoned to see Mendès France, who was a member of the Front Républicain coalition. He knew that I knew the Algerians well and was in contact with them and had asked me to come and let him know what was going on, to fill him in on the details before I left. He spent an hour and a half scribbling down what I was telling him, expressing surprise and saying that they did not know anything about the things that I was telling him. In effect, what I was giving him were the negotiating proposals of the FLN, which I had been given in the name of Ramdane Abane and Ben Khedda, who were the two leaders at that time. I am confident that if Mendès France had been Prime Minister then peace could have been agreed within a year. He told me to come and see him again if there was anything else that bothered me.

When I went ashore in Algeria, I learned that Frantz Fanon had called saying that it was imperative that he see me straightaway, so I headed off to Blida, where he informed me that for the first time ever he intended to breach the medical code of ethics by which he was bound as a doctor. He revealed to me some information about one of his patients, the wife of an individual who had played a terrible role in the 1945 events in Sétif and who had just taken charge again of a training camp where some commandos were based. This woman had let him know that her husband was busy seeking to recruit some common or garden gangsters with the intention of turning the first anniversary of 6 February 1956 into a scene of complete carnage. So I made sure that I caught the first plane I could and met Mendès straightaway to discuss the matter of the resistance and so on and, somehow or other, we managed to defuse the situation. In the end the only incident involved the throwing of a few tomatoes and the tomatoes there were something else, I can assure you. The follow-on from this, I should like to say, was that Mollet adopted a shameful strategy from here on. So that is what the end of January of that year involved for me. As a result of all this I had to remain in Paris throughout the whole of the following month because, as can be imagined, people in Algiers were told immediately about what I had said in order not to be seen as a negotiator. The following day I was called everything under the sun in the '*Echo d'Alger*'; I was threatened; my children were threatened; my wife was threatened. As a result of all this, my classes could not start up again. The Minister kept me there as long as he could but, despite this, towards the end of the month I ended up returning to see the rector, who was a friend of mine and who did not want to see me getting killed during one of my lectures. I told him that backing down was not an option. This just was not something I could consider and so, on 6 March, I took my class and an attack was launched against it. Those who launched the attack stopped at nothing to try to lynch me and my loyal supporters defended me. Quite a few were French, Jews or Christians but there were also a lot of Algerian students whom I met later in life as ministers or ambassadors. There were about forty people against three hundred but I managed to come out of it unscathed.

The reason for giving an account of these events is that they brought to a close the first period I spent in Algeria. The same week, after my home had already been attacked and my car wrecked, I was going to mass when

I came across a line of people who were also on their way there. They told me that I should not go to mass but should go to the mosque since I was such an Arab-lover. Normally they would not have spoken to me using the 'tu' form but now they did so and that they did so then was very much intended to convey their hostility. The priest was upset at this. Then, when we were leaving the church, the last straw was that those people threw blows at me. It was then that I decided to leave but vowed to return. It was then that I realized that these people, whose parting shot was to rain blows on a friend, were no longer friends of mine. Those were not the actions of friends. We then returned to France and the Minister gave me a new academic posting in Strasbourg.

This account of my personal involvement shows how events proceeded in a very ad hoc manner and tended to have a momentum of their own. That momentum subsequently increased with the resignation of Mendès, which left me completely exposed to all sorts of attacks. Leaflets were published in which I was accused of being a murderer and so on, of carrying out undercover raids and of undermining national security. We published information, of course, to let people know the truth about the existence of the FLN and what we were up against. Mendès knew all about this and he was to use those texts as the basis for his account of the Algerian revolution. The thinking of Soustelle was that there should be an expansion of the franchise in Algeria and I see no reason why I should not have gone to the French people to let them know the reality of the situation, without being partisan about the matter.

At that time, I had just taken up my appointment in Strasbourg and we still did not have a house there. Then, on 22 October, the kidnapping of the 'celebrated five' took place. On 9 November, three cops came and picked me up in Strasbourg. They said that it was just because I had some information that would assist them in their enquiries, but I certainly knew what they meant by that. I was taken back on the train that evening and the following day I was arrested by the DST (Direction de la Surveillance du Territoire)[3] and the military judge accused me of no more nor less a crime than treason. Maybe there was some truth in that, by which I mean that I was betraying people who were betraying France as I knew it; these people were betraying France as the cradle of human rights, they were betraying all my most cherished ideals. In any case, the charges piled up under the provisions of articles 76 and 80 and I found myself facing 40 years in the nick. In fact, I served 40 days, exactly the same length of time as the period of Lent, so it was an ideal opportunity for me to read the works of Saint Augustine in order to research my thesis on the Augustinian Orders. My wife was an exceptional woman, of course, to put up with the escapades of such an adventurer. To add a little colour to my account of those 40 days, I should like to say that I had a prison guard who was very respectful towards me and would bring me the newspapers every morning, since I had the constitutional right to receive information about political developments. The 'celebrated five' were there too, but whereas they were all together, I was kept on my own except that at shower-time we were allowed to have a coffee together. Then the morning came when the guard said to me: 'Monsieur le Professeur, you are being released' and I could not believe it. 'You may not be aware of this', he said to me, 'but those of us who are living today are indeed fortunate as God has created woman in the form of Brigitte Bardot.' As you can imagine, with Brigitte Bardot appearing in posters in skin tight, scanty clothing, it felt as if the very birds in the trees had been calling for my release.

A whole range of people, coordinated by François Mauriac and including Henri Marrou, Louis Massignon, André Malraux, André Philip and Georges Suffert had been due to testify in my defence; it certainly was not just anybody. Then that very day, I was released. They were hoping to shoot my public position down in flames but the result was simply that I found myself in the position of a man who was supposed to be dead but finds himself, instead, listening to his own funeral oration. My 40 days were up and, once it was all over, my thoughts were that perhaps that prison time was not completely wasted.

Testimony of Georges Mattéi

What I should like to do here is to give a summarized account of the rebellion of the conscripts recalled to military service. There had been elections in January 1956, but the views expressed by the voters were ignored. That, of course, was due to the Algerian War. In my opinion there were a number of different wars in Algeria, including the period from 1954 to the end of 1955. I myself arrived there in 1956 as a result of the decision to recall all available troops to active service, a decision taken by a National Assembly elected to make peace which is something that it is very important to remember. It should be remembered, too, that in that parliamentary vote even the Communists voted to give special powers to Guy Mollet's coalition government of Socialists and Radicals. That episode also gave us the opportunity, once again, to hear from the Minister of Police in the Mendès France government, one François Mitterrand, that Algeria was part of France. For those of us who were conscripted or recalled to military service, I think that this idea that Algeria was part of France lay at the heart of much of the controversy on the French side. The role of the French armed forces, or at least of those comprising National Service conscripts, was to defend French national frontiers. Those conscripted or recalled to military service only needed to step ashore in Algeria to see with their own eyes that the French *départements* of Algeria were not really part of France and it was from that realization that a great part of the discontent stemmed, in my view. To give a little colour to my account I should say that there is still a rural peasant class in France and I saw country people from the Savoie region who had never taken a train or a plane or, indeed, a boat, as the conscripts sent to Algeria went by boat just as the volunteers taken to Indochina had done, and there they were in a foreign land.

I was one of those who was recalled to military service. When I received my recall papers I was unsure what to do, whether to comply or not, as I was fundamentally opposed to militarism, but then I accepted the idea, reminding myself that my father had undertaken active service, besides which I told myself that I should go and see what it was all about. So I was motivated, too, by a degree of curiosity as to what war was like. Then the next thing was that I found myself, together with others who had been recalled, in a barracks in the Paris area. Some extraordinary things went on in that barracks and that is a subject to which historians, in my view, have yet to give a due degree of attention.

This phenomenon, which I refer to as the 'recall revolt', was one of the most important aspects of the war, in my view. I was merely a soldier in the ranks, but we had NCOs, and officers too, who were school teachers. There was no respect for hierarchy. There were basic grade troops who came from a higher social class than their NCO. Nobody obeyed orders. This army was a complete and utter shambles; this was not anarchy, this was chaos and it was an extraordinary thing to experience. I absolutely adored this situation, the contact with others and the feeling of brotherhood. Of course, I should add that I am only giving my personal account, which is as it should be, and that I only witnessed one small part of the story. Nothing really evil went on, after all. We went off as men in uniform with a brand new helmet to pick, or rather pilfer, cherries; the decision was taken to leave and some extraordinary things went on. We were about to leave when an officer arrived on the scene and he was mistreated somewhat and lost a lot of his dignity, though nothing too vicious took place. We did not obey the officers any more, they did not exist for us, and this excuse for a company or detachment, I should say, became known as the 'daisy detachment' afterwards. So the detachment left and arrived at the gates of the barracks, where there were some conscripts who were performing their duties in a more serious manner. They spoke to the sergeant who was in command of the post, he told them to let us through and we went through and off home, shouting as we went. We just did not want to go. So then we took a train back to Paris, where we rejoined our families, parents and friends.

After that escapade, though, something very sad happened which was that we went back and, obviously, the authorities had learned a few lessons from the episode and we boarded the trains to go to Algeria from locations a long distance from the main stations. There were demonstrations against the recall to military service right across the country – in Marseilles, in Rouen (and there were certain events that took place in 1955 as well) and in Toulouse, as I recall. So, specifically to avoid us having any contact with the civilian population, we were put onto trains at goods stations. In order to appreciate the reasons for the reaction of those who were recalled, I think that it is necessary to consider our situation prior to the recall. We had all done our national service and were 'reservists' to use the term that was most widely used. We had all completed our period of national service and, in France at any rate, this was a man's responsibility and as we were men, quite a number were married. That was a fact of life and so for those blokes with responsibilities the idea of being recalled for a further stint of national service went down like a lead balloon, to coin a phrase. Particularly as this was the time when the consumer society was just starting to take off so people were starting to buy fridges on HP and so on, all on the assumption that they would have a job after they had finished their military service. So they had debt commitments. Then they found themselves being recalled, in some cases less than a year after having finished their first stint of national service, so the idea of having to go off to Algeria held very little appeal and, furthermore, they could see no worthwhile purpose to the venture.

I would like to make brief mention of the journey to Marseilles, which was like something out of another world. There were still a few carriages that had alarm bells and we set these off repeatedly, so the train would stop and people would get out and then get back on again, so the journey seemed to last forever. Then we finally arrived in Marseilles, which was practically a foreign land for the Parisians. We were in a camp and I can recall this wonderful expression that one guy had, a guy who was punished for demonstrating, which was '*Barbaque*, here we come!'; 'barbaque' was meat that had gone off, really gone rotten. Then we took the boat across and, once we had arrived in Algiers, I was sent to the 1st Company of the 27th BCA (Bataillon de Chasseurs Alpins) in the region of Azazga. Those who had been selected were taken and attached to units that had already been fighting for a number of months and, in the case of the 27th BCA at least, had already suffered losses. They were used to plug the gaps in those units. There had already been 17 killed and 35 wounded in the 27th BCA. The young soldiers who were there were still not retained troops but they had already spent more than a year, certainly, out in the djebels.

During the first night I spent with my company I heard someone crying aloud which alarmed me, but my comrades reassured me that it was nothing to worry about. Then we moved to set up base at a military post where things became clearer. There was a senior NCO at the post who was a veteran of the war in Indochina and he was acting as intelligence officer which meant, not to mince words, that he was the torturer-in-chief. The company had a shack where systematically, and I do not use that word lightly, all or nearly all enemy prisoners were tortured and interrogated.

This took place on the orders of this warrant officer and professional NCO but three young conscripts also took part. That went on throughout the six months that I was stationed there. We were taking part in mundane military operations and among the things I recall was that there was one man there who was waiting for something. It turned out that he had been brought to the camp and, because he came from a particular village, he was interrogated and then, early in the morning, together with a number of other prisoners, was summarily shot. I am giving a witness account here and I could even take you to the place where those men were buried. At breakfast time they said to me: 'Well, Mattéi, do you want to come and see how to clear the cobwebs off your rifle? I have a guard's rifle, do you want to come and see how to get the rust off that rifle?' I did not take them up on that offer, but I heard a few gunshots from under the olive trees opposite the post.

Eventually I returned to France and at that time my state of mind was such that I had a feeling of outrage. This was not the vision of France that I had cherished. I had not found the France that I was looking for; rather I had gone through this experience out of loyalty to my family and fuelled by idealistic ideas about the resistance movement and now found that what I had seen in Algeria left me unable to view myself as on a par with the resistance heroes in the *maquis*. Even if they formed a minority, the *maquis* of the French Resistance movement were heroes. It is always the minority who are heroes. In contrast, I could not help but see myself in the role of the occupying Nazi troops, for that is how I felt about it. Fortunately, as chance would have it, I found myself face to face with one of the great thinkers of the day, Sartre, prior to leaving for Algeria. Three weeks after my return to Paris, I had a meeting with Sartre and for an hour and a half I explained my deepest feelings to this great and generous man. Among other things, I was able to explain to him all the weaknesses that one may have when witnessing these scenes for the first time. That was something very important, after all.

To research and do justice to the 'recall revolt' would require a lot of work, in my view. The first witness accounts of the Algerian War to be published were those written by men recalled to military service. There is 'Le Dossier Jean Muller in *Cahiers de Témoignage Chrétien*, 'Des Rappelés Témoignent' in *Comité de Résistance Spirituelle*, the first article signed by Robert Bonnaud in *Esprit* in 1957 and then my offering, 'Jours Kabyles' in *Les Temps Modernes*. That issue of *Les Temps Modernes* was impounded on the orders of Mollet's Socialist government and later the article was republished in *Témoignage Chrétien*. You would have needed to have been there to be able to appreciate the sort of atmosphere there was at that time, though. The editor, Jean-Paul Sartre and I were summoned before a military judge. What I said to the judge was: 'My name has not been given in my article. Nobody's name has been given, so go ahead and try us if you wish. Names would need to be named. There are none given in the article, it is as simple as that!' Those are the main aspects of my personal experiences in the Algerian War.

Testimony of François Sirkidji

Bringing to public attention the diverse experiences and painful memories of Algerian War conscripts has been a difficult business. One of the most important breakthroughs was the making of Bertrand Tavernier's film *La Guerre sans Nom* at the beginning of the 1990s. This consists of four hours of personal accounts. Nothing substitutes for seeing the film. However, I should like to address the theme of the Algerian War as 'the Conscripts' War'. Before discussing the testimonies we recorded, I should like to provide some idea of my own involvement in the preparation of the film, some idea about my outlook on the Algerian War, too, as I was involved to some extent both as an active participant and in the preparation of the film with my friend Georges Mattéi. In addition, I should like to discuss the shooting and editing of the film.

The film lasts for four hours and the question as to whether that is too long or not is open to debate. It consists of a collection of 28 personal accounts provided by conscripts and men recalled to active service for the Algerian War, nearly all of whom came from the town of Grenoble. Our choice of young men called up for their military service as conscripts and serving in the general ranks allowed us to get a better understanding of what we call 'La France profonde', the broad mass of French people. Grenoble was chosen initially because for a town of that size it attracted a fair amount of publicity when men were recalled to active service in May 1956 as violent demonstrations took place, expressing the opposition of young conscripts and their friends to the call-up. One must remember, of course that an election campaign had taken place at the end of which the vote had been in favour of peace negotiations but that this mandate had not been put into effect. The level of anger was rising, therefore.

So the decision to obtain personal accounts solely from conscripts who came from one particular town was a conscious decision that gave the film a greater degree of cohesion and accentuated its dramatic qualities. We had unity of place, then, together with unity of time, namely the eight years of the Algerian War, and unity of action in the way in which that war developed. So we made contact with those who had served in the war. I got in touch with 120 people myself and, liaising with Georges, who was up in Paris, we employed a particular methodology to contact people. I would have a dozen people to audition per day, sometimes over two days. I decided which people to use and we were gradually able to see more and more people until the total reached about eighty, if my arithmetic is correct.

For the filming a second selection process took place in Paris, involving about 45 or 46 men who had been chosen to have their accounts recorded on film. The criteria applied during this shortlisting were based entirely upon the desire to get the fullest possible understanding and the most complete overview of the war. So according to these criteria we sought to obtain accounts covering the whole period from the outbreak of war in 1954 until its end in 1962 using men who had served right across Algeria from the Tunisian frontier in the east to the Moroccan front in the west and from the north to the south of Algeria as well. The experiences of the men differed according to the geographical locations in which they had served, but also according to the phase of the war. The experiences of someone serving on the Tunisian frontier blockade at the outbreak of war were not at all the same as those of soldiers based in other regions and nor did those serving on that same front at the end of the war have comparable experiences. So we took a deliberate decision to take a cross-section of men with different experiences in order to get a more balanced picture and we sought to do the same with regard to the ranks of the people interviewed. A mere private would not have the same view of the war as a corporal, a sergeant or an officer. I myself had a lot of contact with officers who held the rank of captain, major or regimental commander at the time. The importance of this war, though, lay in the experiences of the rank-and-file squaddies, rather than the second lieutenants, lieutenants and captains, because people's experiences on the ground left a powerful impression upon them and had an importance all of their own. The types of active service that the men were involved in also varied widely. As the personal accounts in the film show, there were marked differences between military campaigns or between serving in different branches of the forces or serving in the djebels. We have accounts from members of parachute regiments, of the naval infantry, motorized units, the social action services and the medical services, indeed, as I myself had personal experience in the latter field. We see a whole spectrum of different opinions on the war. For example, there was one man who was chosen because he had refused to go, saying 'I'll go to Germany, but I don't want to go to Algeria' and he spent two years in prison. He gives an account of that. At the end of those two years in prison, they said to him: 'Right! What are you going to do? Do you still refuse to go?' and if he had refused to go, he would have been faced with another two years in prison. Nor was he exempt from military service, so he served for four years, including two years to acquit himself of his obligations with regard to the war.

The great majority of those who gave their accounts automatically found themselves on the side of those who, on the whole, were against the war. They went to Algeria but, at the end of the day, were not very enthusiastic about doing so; or there were others who supported the war when they went to Algeria but then often changed their minds, sometimes while they were out there, sometimes on their return, sometimes a long time afterwards. There is a whole spectrum of different viewpoints that is interesting to compare.

While working with Georges on the auditions, we also took care to question people and to listen to them with as much tact as possible so as not to upset their feelings and so as to reserve the real substance for the filming. As soon as we felt that someone had something interesting to say, we would cut the discussion short there. We would stop so as to ensure the filmed interviews were not staged performances as we wanted to avoid that. We wanted the interviews to be spontaneous and that meant they conveyed an exceptional degree of sincerity, they conveyed sensitivity and openness with all the quality of freshness that one finds when something is being said for the first time. This meant we avoided manipulation as far as was possible. It was to achieve this goal that the whole film was based upon one-take interviews with no retakes, something that is very much the exception for this type of film-making.

The director also had a role in the choice of material. He didn't want to use any filmed news footage, any documentation, whether written or otherwise, or any specially designed posters. We just used a few photographs taken by the conscripts themselves to provide some visual expression of what they were saying plus letters or drawings that they did and which we showed on screen to accompany their personal accounts. So this question and answer process allowed us access to their most hidden memories, which were often being opened up for the first time. The filming was a mysterious process, always very moving and full of sincerity, during which we saw what a magical thing the memory can be. That was the nature of these interviews, interviews that took place over a long period of time as the research lasted for six months and the filming for a further month.

When the filming took place, I would hear certain phrases time and again. I noted them down and shall repeat them here: 'This is the first time that I've talked about that' or 'My family, my wife and my children don't know anything about what I have just told you, no one does' or, again, 'I'll ask my family to come and see the film. I am still not able to talk to them about my experiences in the Algerian War'. Participants would often thank us for allowing them the opportunity to express themselves at last, some thirty years or more after the event. So we have to ask the simple question as to why, then, they had so stubbornly kept their experiences to themselves? I know that there are people who have undertaken research into the phenomenon of people remaining silent about their wartime experiences. There were a range of responses among those who had served in the Algerian War. On returning to France some had chosen to talk about it but had found that no one was ready or willing to listen to them, so they retreated into silence. Other individuals chose that silence straightaway, turning the page once and for all upon their experiences in the Algerian War.

What we also often heard about in the explanations offered for that silence was the 'pointlessness', to use a much repeated term, 'the pointlessness, the cruelty and the stupidity' of that war. For people expressing that emotion, then, remorse would seem to be the principal cause of their silence. The question has often been put to me, regarding this film: 'How did you manage to obtain dozens upon dozens of personal accounts, in particular how did you manage to persuade these people to speak in front of a camera and into a microphone for the making of a film?' Obviously, in my opinion, we benefited from an awareness on the part of the interviewees of our common history as veterans of the war. These Algerian War veterans placed a certain amount of confidence in me and I believe that if I had not been an Algerian War veteran then the majority of those people would not have been prepared to talk about their experiences.

On the other hand, I occupied quite a privileged position in Grenoble as a doctor, gynaecologist and obstetrician who had spent 30 years in the town and was a friend of the family, if you like. Together with my brother, I have brought thousands of Grenoble children into the world and we are now approaching retirement, so we have a whole network of friends and acquaintances who had taken part in the Algerian War and who agreed to give their personal accounts, but they agreed only on condition that I be present at the filming. Obviously, in the case of a good number among them, we see one another regularly. Some of them call me to ask how I am and, maybe, come to see me. This sort of atmosphere had been created and paved the way for the making of this film. So once we had filmed all the interviews we had about sixty hours of footage, which was absolutely phenomenal. The editing process took nearly a year, which was an extraordinary amount of time, a world record as far as documentaries are concerned. I should say that the reduction from 46 to 28 accounts was not based on political or ideological criteria or any such thing. Those decisions were purely taken on technical grounds. So filming took place over a period of a little over a month, during the winter of 1990–1, and the film première, of course, as a symbolic gesture, took place in Grenoble in February 1992.

I would like to mention one particular interview that we were to do, the one with Serge Puygrenier who had been injured, having lost a leg in combat. I choose to discuss the case of Puygrenier because he was an invalid, but his disability did not simply affect him at the physical level, it had a terrible effect upon him on the emotional level. Just when we were about to start filming, he said to me: 'François, I can't go ahead with the filming; I don't want to; it's all completely hopeless.' I am repeating this in the hope that it may promote some reflection upon the isolation and the silence that some people have to go through and upon the idea of national solidarity, or whatever term one may prefer to use, a phenomenon which can help people to overcome obstacles like that.

With Puygrenier it was not a matter of money. It is true that he had an income of around 3,000 francs a month and had been unemployed for years. No one would give him a job because there was nothing that he could do. They would say to him: 'You're fifty years old and only have one leg, there's nothing we can do for you.' In my opinion there are problems of a social nature that can become psychological or psycho-affective problems and that is something, in my view, that one should be aware of and should not forget. Some people have been very seriously afflicted in this way. Anyway, Puygrenier told me that he could not go through with it and we talked about it. We had locked ourselves away in his bathroom, because we were filming in his flat and, sitting on his bath, we talked about it at great length and, in the end, he agreed to go ahead on condition that his wife took part in the filming with him. This went against what we had previously agreed, namely that we were not going to allow wives to be involved, but we went ahead and filmed the interview with his wife present too. That was important because she had been the only person who had shared the suffering he had been through as a result of his injury. When he spoke about his experiences, he needed this woman he loved, and had loved, indeed, since the time of the Algerian War, to be with him. The letters that he had written to her were read out in the film. Those letters made an extraordinary impression. That whole episode was highly symbolic of suffering that had been shared and that process of sharing is something that is vitally important. We are not machines and, even if we were, it would seem that machines work better if you talk to them.

The personal account given by Bernard Loiseau, in my view, represents one of the most sublime explorations of fear. He is still scared to death. He is frightened. Simply to admit to being afraid is a brave thing in itself but, in addition, he talks about his fear with great simplicity. He was scared in combat situations. He was scared all the time. When you listen to men like that it is instructive. You realize that each of us is an individual, an individual who is different from everybody else even if we are members of a group. We can see again in his case the distinction between the conscript and the career soldier.

The career soldier is a professional who has chosen and prepared himself for that sort of a life. He knows that is what he has been trained for and has a sense that he has done his duty. At the same time, together with all this training that he has gone through, there is a sort of feeling of brotherhood within and between the different sections and divisions of the forces. In Algeria, there were men who had been in the Resistance together and who had been through several campaigns in Indochina together and already knew one another. The fact that they had been through the most difficult times of their lives together was extremely important to them.

This was not the case for conscripts. After the war, they found themselves brutally thrown back into civilian life where they were immersed in their own solitude and in their own memories. It is a distinction that is important to grasp.

I would like to draw a comparison with the history of the Americans in Vietnam. They also went through a war that left them with some appalling memories, but they were able to find a form of psychotherapy in films, in writing, in being listened to, in the many documentaries that have been made, that is to say by receiving national recognition. After all, one has only to go to Washington to see a wall on which are inscribed the names of those who died. In France we are still waiting for any such memorial to be put up, a memorial on which the names of those who died in Algeria could be recorded. They have that wall of remembrance and two magnificent statues dedicated to those who fought in Vietnam, so why could there not be a similar monument in the Place de la Concorde? We speak of memorials and remembrance means recognizing and understanding the experience and feelings of others, something that is absolutely vital in my view. Something, also, that is lacking in France, unfortunately.

It should be emphasized that there is another aspect to the situation that is peculiar to France, namely that there exists a sort of silence regarding the war. It is a fundamental problem. The veil seems to be being lifted a bit, but when you look beneath it the problem you often encounter is that the facts have been tampered with or obscured, as regards what happened and who did or did not do what. Without wishing to repeat what has already been said, it seems that some sort of compromise, or rather compromising, agreement has been hatched to protect those who were responsible for this conflict. We have already seen the reaction of one man who was in a position of authority for a long period during the war and who, 35 years later, was astonished to hear that the politicians were responsible for what happened. We now know that those who drew up the policies that were followed bear a heavy burden of responsibility for their consequences. The officer ranks of the armed forces, too, were victims of this sort of attitude.

A subject I would like to return to, as it is something which I lived through myself, is the French departure from Algeria. Those who were present when the French troops left will have lived through some extremely dramatic scenes. My own experiences were marked by the co-relationship between the different wars that were taking place, war between the French and the Algerians, between different sections of the Algerian population, etc. It was really a war that operated on three levels, a triple war, and that was another factor in the complexity and peculiarity of the Algerian War.

My own experiences of the war were quite untypical as I was a doctor and I had the rank of an officer. That allowed me to come and go quite freely, to do my work in the sector, that is to say treating the troops, the people in the area and, in addition, the civilian population. I was based on the Moroccan frontier between Tlemcen-Ain Sefra and a place further south called Sidi-El-Djilali. I was there during three crucial and transitional periods: the ending of hostilities, the ceasefire and then a few days of Algerian independence. Over this period I also had responsibilities associated with my military status and witnessed the terrible events when the ALN broke through on the Moroccan front. The ALN crossed over in force and the situation was exacerbated by the fact that the regiment that had been guarding the sector, the Parachute Regiment, had left the area, so there was a vacuum and, however it came about, the ALN managed to cross French lines. The resistance to the ALN was put up by conscript troops and twenty men were killed. I mention this event because it was during this period, April 1961, that the coup took place.

I also had a legal responsibility to provide medical care. My parents had been teachers in Morocco so I could speak Arabic fairly fluently, something that was of assistance in my dealings with the local population. What I would point out, though, is that the local population had comprised about five thousand people before the war but was only just over eight hundred by the time I left. This shows that, in some areas, the civilian population faced terrible consequences as a result of the War, having to relocate, putting up with poor sanitary conditions and, of course, suffering the physical consequences of war.

After the ceasefire there were two events that had a profound effect upon me and that I shall never forget. The first was the order given by the medical authorities firstly to return to civilian life and secondly to close down all my AMG (Free Medical Care) Centres in and around Tlemcen, where I was based at this period. The OAS had demanded, upon pain of death, that all such centres should close. I was in a position where I could be sure neither of my social security cover nor of my safety, but I disobeyed the orders that had been given. For one thing, I was not prepared to give up on wearing my uniform and red kepi and, for another, I could not give up on my work because I had good reason to believe that I would be directly responsible for an epidemic of tuberculosis in which hundreds of people would die. I still believe that the attitude I took was quite the correct one. Unfortunately, some of my colleagues gave in to the pressure and were responsible for precisely the sort of disasters I have mentioned.

On a human level, I should add that this episode allowed me the opportunity, outside the constraints of the army given that the ceasefire was already in force, to meet and pass my files on to an ALN doctor. This doctor was the only person in a position to take over responsibility for the clinics that were under my supervision and that led to a better understanding between doctors on both sides.

The other episode I should like to mention came when we left Oran. The whole group of doctors were gathered together there and suddenly right in front of us we saw an enormous mass of people. There were hundreds of *pieds-noir* (Algerian-born French) families who had left everything behind and were waiting to find a place on a boat that never seemed to arrive. To reach the gangway from the town of Oran we had to cross a veritable flood of humanity under the protection of the military police despite all the jostling. For that reason, I for one shall never lump the mass of *pied-noir* people together with the OAS.

My final view and last memory of Algeria was of those people shouting in our direction. The other final memory I have is of the death of a friend and colleague, trainee doctor Colin, a father of four, who was killed in an ambush a few months before we left Algeria.

In truth, I found myself leaving the war behind with an extremely unpleasant feeling of frustration, of not having done everything I could have done, a wide-ranging feeling of incomprehension. The only time I felt proud was when some soldiers presented arms to me – and they were ALN soldiers, which is something I find extraordinarily painful.

I would like to see a lot of universities and towns in France follow the example of the conference at Salford and organize conferences and meetings in the same spirit of openness and sincerity.

Notes

1. Translator's note: 'Témoin, Acteur, Historien'.
2. A. Mandouze, *Mémoires d'outre-siècle*, vol. 1, *D'une résistance à l'autre* (Paris: Viviane Hamy, 1998).
3. French equivalent of MI5.

Appendix Algerian War Witnesses – Biographical Details

General Alain Bizard

Volunteering for the 1st Hussar Regiment Alain Bizard took part in the August 1944 Liberation of France and in 1945 attended the French army's officer training academy at Saint Cyr. From 1947 to 1949 he served in Indochina with the 1st Regiment of Chasseurs, returning for a further tour of duty in Indochina in 1950–2. He was then promoted captain and returned to Indochina for a third time in February 1954, in command of a company of the 5th Vietnamese parachute battalion. Captured at Dien Bien Phu on 8 May 1954, he was liberated on 2 September that year and posted to Tunisia, where he commanded the 1st Moroccan tabors on the frontier with Libya. In 1956 he joined the 1st Regiment of Chasseurs Paratroops (1e RCP) in Algeria, with whom he took part in the short-lived operation in the Suez Canal in November that year. In 1960 he left Algeria on secondment to the United States where he graduated from the US Army Command and General Staff College at Fort Leavenworth, Kansas. In a second posting to the United States, commencing in 1962, he took courses at the Armed Forces Staff College at Norfolk, Virginia, and the Special Warfare Center at Fort Bragg, North Carolina. After returning to France he was promoted lieutenant-colonel in 1965, commanding the 13e Régiment de Dragons Parachutistes in 1967. In 1969 he became chief of staff of 4th Division, headquartered at Verdun, and in 1974 he took command of 1st Parachute Brigade. Promoted brigadier-general in 1975, he became Commandant of the military academies of Saint Cyr-Coëtquidan and then commander of 8th Division in 1979. General Bizard's career culminated as a lieutenant-general in command of 3rd Army Corps in 1983.

Colonel Henri Coustaux

Born on 28 February 1915, Henri Coustaux entered the Ecole Polytechnique in 1936 and was commissioned a second lieutenant of artillery in 1938. He saw action in the Battle of France from the Ardennes to Castries with 12th Battalion, 45th Artillery Regiment, being promoted lieutenant on 19 July 1940. After the Armistice he converted from the artillery to the mechanized cavalry and in 1943–4 joined the FFI (Forces Françaises de l'Intérieur), in the 1st Regiment of the Rhône, taking part in the liberation of Lyon. After the Ecole d'Etat-Major in 1944–5 he served from 1945 to 1947 with the 4th Cuirassiers in Occupied Germany. In 1947–9 he was an instructor at the leadership training school at Rouffach-Mutzig in Alsace, before being posted to Indochina until 1951. There he established the Vietnamese leadership training school at Hanoi and Namdinh and commanded a battalion of the 1st Colonial Tank Regiment (1e RCC). His decorations include the Croix de Guerre 1939–45 with one citation and the Croix des Théâtres d'Opérations Extérieures (seven citations). Promoted major in 1951 he served a tour as an instructor at the staff officers' school in Paris and then graduated from the Ecole Supérieure de

Guerre. He served in Algeria from 1956 to 1961, initially as head of the Operations Bureau of the Algiers army corps. On promotion to lieutenant-colonel he assumed command of the 1st Regiment of Chasseurs Paratroops (1e RCP) and was subsequently chief of operations and then deputy chief of staff of the combined-arms staff in Algiers. Promoted colonel, he gained the Croix de Valeur Militaire and was made a Commander of the Légion d'Honneur. Despite not being involved in the failed April 1961 Algiers putsch, he was nonetheless compulsorily retired from the army after it.

Major Paul-Alain Léger

Born on 29 November 1922 in Morocco, where his father was stationed, Paul Léger took part in the student demonstrations against the German occupiers in Paris in 1940. In 1942 he crossed into the unoccupied zone of France, made his way to Algiers and enlisted in the 1st Regiment of Zouaves. He volunteered for parachute training and in December 1943 joined the Free French BCRA (Bureau de Centralisation de Recherches et d'Action) in London. In 1944 he joined the 3rd Regiment of Chasseurs Parachutistes, also known as the 3rd SAS, commanded by the legendary Pierre Château-Jobert. He made combat drops on 17 July 1944 into France, at Cholet, and again into Holland on 7 April 1945. On 1 February 1946 he sailed for Indochina with the 1st Battalion of Parachutists SAS, making combat jumps at Vientiane in Laos, Louang Prabang and Namdinh. Promoted lieutenant in September 1947, he served in French Equatorial Africa in 1948–51 with the Colonial Commandos. Returning to Indochina in 1953–4 he commanded a unit of the GCMA (Groupe de Commandos Mixtes Aéroportés), being promoted captain in January 1954. From 1955 onwards he served in Algeria, initially with the 11e Choc, participating in the Suez and Port Saïd operations of November 1956. In 1957–8 he conceived, organized and directed the GRE (Groupe de Renseignement et d'Exploitation), formed to penetrate the FLN politico-administrative organization (OPA) in Algiers. Using covert agents and enlisting 'turned' former FLN operatives, Léger dislocated the FLN by sowing mistrust among its cadres and prompting widespread fratricide among the militants of Wilaya 4 and then Wilaya 3. He assumed command of the 5th Harka (Moslem) company of the 3rd Parachute Regiment in 1958–9, being decorated an Officer of the Légion d'Honneur and winning 11 citations. In April 1961 he was arrested in Algeria for being implicated in the short-lived putsch against de Gaulle, but was swiftly released and assigned to the French training mission with the Mauritanian army. In October 1964 he was promoted major. Increasingly disillusioned, Paul Léger resigned from the army in 1966 and later published an important volume of memoirs, *Aux carrefours de la guerre* (Plon, 1983). He died on 31 December 1999.

Professor André Mandouze

Born in 1916, André Mandouze graduated from the Ecole Normale Supérieure, having specialized in Augustinian philosophy. He drew his convictions from several Left Catholic movements of his student days, including the Jeunesse Etudiante Chrétienne and Jeunesse Ouvrière Chrétienne. Resistance to Nazism shaped his whole life. While an assistant lecturer at the University of Lyon in 1941, he was an active anti-Nazi and anti-Vichyite in the Second World War and part of the group that produced the clandestine paper *Cahiers du Témoignage Chrétien*, which he went on to edit. Resigning this post, in January 1946 he took up an appointment to teach Latin in the Faculté des Lettres at the University of Algiers. Within the structures of French Algeria he encountered a world contaminated by everything he had fought against from 1940 to 1944. He became strongly anti-colonialist, first denouncing the colonial system in two articles in *L'Esprit* in 1947 and then contacting the Algerian nationalist leaders Messali Hadj and Ferhat Abbas. Using his classrooms and lecture theatres as platforms, he preached an independent Algeria, condemning French colonialism and the use of force to retain control over Algeria. He edited two pro-Moslem periodicals, *Consciences Maghribines* and *Consciences Algériennes*. Mandouze was appalled by the volte-face of the French left-centre Republican Front in 1956. Victorious in the parliamentary elections that January, on a platform to negotiate with the FLN and end the Algerian War, the new government and its prime minister, Guy Mollet, the Socialist Party leader, instead assumed special powers and dispatched conscript troops to Algeria. Mandouze, by now a thorn in the side of the French authorities, was transferred to teach at the University of Strasbourg on 1 April 1956, on the express orders of the Governor-General of Algeria, Robert Lacoste. Mandouze has published two volumes of autobiography: *Mémoires d'Outre-Siècle. D'une Résistance à l'Autre* (Viviane Hamy, 1998) and *A gauche toute, Bon Dieu!* (Viviane Hamy, 2000).

Georges Mattéi

Born in Corsica in 1934, Mattéi lived with his uncle in Burgundy during the Occupation of France. The uncle, a Communist and member of the FTP maquis (Francs-Tireurs et Partisans), was a powerful role model. But it was first-hand experience in Algeria that pushed Mattéi into illegal action to oppose the war. Having fulfilled his conscript service before hostilities erupted, he was in Italy when the French Ministry of Defence ordered him in 1956 to report for reservist duty in Algeria. Initially feeling ambiguous about going on active service, he took part in a demonstration that halted the troop train taking his contingent from Dreux to Marseilles. Assigned to an elite paratroop unit in Kabylie, Mattéi was appalled at the atrocities being committed by French soldiers. His hostility to the Algerian War, racism and colonialism intensified and he became a passionate crusader for a full and honest debate about the conflict, drawing public attention to the issue of torture. In 1957, partly for cathartic reasons, he wrote one of the earliest articles in Jean-Paul Sartre's review *Les Temps Modernes* to expose the systematic use of torture by the army in Algeria. He also took a leading role in the reservists' oppositional organization, the *Mouvement des Rappelés*. Disillusioned with the French Communist Party's failure to offer clear anti-war leadership, Mattéi worked illegally from 1959 as part of Francis Jeanson's pro-FLN network within France. In the 1980s he assisted Jean-Luc Einaudi with research for the latter's book about the massacre of Algerian anti-war protesters by the police in Paris on 17 October 1961, *La Bataille de Paris* (Editions du Seuil, 1991). Drawing on his Algerian war experiences, Mattéi wrote *La Guerre des Gusses* (Balland, 1982; reprinted, Editions de l'Aube, 1995). He died in November 2000.

Dr François Sirkidji

A veteran of the French army medical service in Algeria and founder of the FNACA (Fédération Nationale des Anciens Combattants d'Algérie), François Sirkidji became a leading light in the FNACA in the Grenoble region (*département* of the Isère). He acted as a key intermediary to put some forty Algerian War rank-and-file veterans from that region in contact with Patrick Rotman and Bertrand Tavernier, so that their testimonies could be incorporated into the documentary witness film, *La Guerre sans Nom* (1992).

Index